D0929168

# ON CIVILIZATION, POWER,
# AND KNOWLEDGE

# THE HERITAGE OF SOCIOLOGY

*A Series Edited by* Donald Levine
Morris Janowitz, *Founding Editor*

NORBERT ELIAS

# ON CIVILIZATION, POWER, AND KNOWLEDGE

## Selected Writings

*Edited and with an Introduction by*
STEPHEN MENNELL and
JOHAN GOUDSBLOM

THE UNIVERSITY OF CHICAGO PRESS
*Chicago and London*

Stephen Mennell is professor of sociology at University College, Dublin. Johan Goudsblom is professor of sociology at the University of Amsterdam.

The University of Chicago Press, Chicago 60637
The University of Chicago Press, Ltd., London
© 1998 by The University of Chicago
All rights reserved. Published 1998
Printed in the United States of America
07 06 05 04 03 02 01 00 99 98      5 4 3 2 1

ISBN (cloth): 0-226-20431-6
ISBN (paper): 0-226-20432-4

Library of Congress Cataloging-in-Publication Data

Elias, Norbert.
    Norbert Elias : on civilization, power, and knowledge :
selected writings / edited and with an introduction by
Stephen Mennell and Johan Goudsblom.
        p.      cm. — (The Heritage of sociology)
    Includes bibliographical references (p. ) and index.
    ISBN 0-226-20431-6. — ISBN 0-226-20432-4 (pbk.)
    1. Sociology—Philosophy.    2. Civilization—
Philosophy.    3. Power (Social sciences)    4. Knowledge,
Sociology of.    5. Power (Social sciences)    6. Elias,
Norbert—Influence.    7. Sociology—History—20th cen-
tury.    8. Elias, Norbert.    I. Mennell, Stephen.    II.
Goudsblom, Johan.    III. Title.    IV. Series.
HM26.E43    1998
301'.01—dc21                                        97-20799
                                                                CIP

**riding the storm**

nothing without its order
not the fury of love
to the border of death
nor the desert above

round and round with each other
living     feast without host
to the bother of dying
grinning god's ghost

women lovers of men
unwitting children begotten
tender fruits of bodies
into bodies rotten

into the good earth
pearls of maggot and mould
to the birth of a firefly
turnip and marigold

sky-lark of the owl
bleeding and bled
growls in the dark of the night
world feeding and fed

tear it to pieces    pounce
galaxies into dust
towns into refuse and filth
make them dance as they must

born from a storm of disorder
nomads of time without tiding
in a void without border
riding the storm

Norbert Elias,
"Riding the Storm,"
from *Los der Menschen*

# Contents

# Acknowledgments

The editors would like to acknowledge the help and advice of Eric Dunning, Richard Kilminster, Barbara Mennell, Nico Stehr, Saskia Visser, and the group of postgraduate students at the Jagiellonian University, Kraków, Poland, who were the first to read and try out this selection of readings in an intensive course on Elias in May 1996.

Permission to reprint extracts from Elias's work is acknowledged as follows:

Blackwell Publishers for *The Civilizing Process, The Loneliness of the Dying, Involvement and Detachment, Quest for Excitement, The Society of Individuals,* and *Time: An Essay*

Blackwell Publishers and Random House, Inc., for *The Court Society*

Polity Press and Columbia University Press for *The Germans*

Polity Press and University of California Press for *Mozart: Portrait of a Genius*

Sage Publications for *The Established and the Outsiders* and "The Changing Balance of Power between the Sexes."

# Introduction

Born at the end of the nineteenth century, Norbert Elias (1897–1990) became one of the great sociologists of the twentieth—but that century was itself nearing its close before Elias's work began at last to gain wide recognition. Elias belonged to the generation of intellectual refugees from Nazi Germany. Many of them acquired fame in the universities of America and Britain; probably many more—we can only guess how many—sank into obscurity, never finding a foothold in the English-speaking academic world.[1] Elias's fate was unusual: only when he had passed the normal age of retirement was his early work republished, and only in his seventies, eighties, and early nineties did there appear the many books and articles which form the bulk of his published work.

Elias is best known for his theory of civilizing processes, set out in his magnum opus, *Über den Prozess der Zivilisation*—first published obscurely in 1939—and elaborated in many later writings. *The Civilizing Process* (to use its later English title) is primarily known as a fascinating case study of changing manners among the European upper classes since the Middle Ages. However, it also represents a paradigm of a mode of research, conceptualization, and theorizing which constitutes a radical challenge to many of the fundamental assumptions still prevalent in sociology today. Thus, building further upon the basic insights into the nature of social processes first developed in *The Civilizing Process*, Elias made several major innovative contributions to the study of power and to a truly sociological theory of knowledge.

## Life and Intellectual Context
### The First Twenty-Five Years

Norbert Elias was born in Breslau, Germany, on 22 June 1897, the only child of Hermann and Sophie Elias. His father was a businessman in the textile trade, and the family was comfortably off. Breslau is now—since the frontier changes following World War II—the Polish city of Wrocław, but it was then completely integrated into the German empire. At the distinguished Johannesgymnasium there, Elias received the classical German high school education then favored by the middle classes, ac-

1

quiring a thorough grounding in Latin, Greek, French, mathematics, and science. He was a member of a special group which met with one of the masters to read Kant, and he collected the works of the authors of the German classical era—Schiller, Goethe, Heine, Mörike, Eichendorff, and others. Asked in his old age whether, as a child, he felt more a member of the Jewish community or of the wider German society, Elias replied that the very question reflected events that had unfolded since then.[2] At the time, the issue did not arise. He knew he was both a German and a Jew. He went to the synagogue a few times a year, on the great festival days. (After his childhood he was never a believer in any form of religion.) But the Breslau Jews felt they were German. While they were alert to anti-Semitism, they felt very secure—mistakenly so, as events were to prove.

From an early age, Elias aspired to an academic career. Before he could even begin his university education, however, he served as a soldier in the German army during World War I. In 1915, at the age of eighteen, he enlisted in the Signals Corps, and saw action on both the Eastern and Western fronts. In 1917 he appears to have suffered shell shock, although his recollection of the circumstances was unclear; at any rate, he served out the rest of the war back in Breslau as an army medical orderly, and remembered watching a famous surgeon amputating limbs.[3]

Elias enrolled at Breslau University at the end of the war. His student years were a period of great social and political instability in Germany. The Kaiser had abdicated in the wake of humiliating military defeat, and the Weimar Republic had been established. Most of the officer corps, and a large proportion of the old imperial upper and upper-middle classes held the new republic, its parliamentary institutions, and its socialist leaders in contempt. There were attempts to overthrow the new regime both from the far Left—under the influence of the recent Bolshevik Revolution in Russia—and from the Right. Demobilized officers and men from the army and navy formed fighting bands, the Freikorps; they assassinated political leaders, and killed and intimidated many lesser people among their leftist opponents. One of Elias's own Breslau school friends was among their victims. Even after the eventual suppression of the Freikorps, the stability of the Weimar Republic was further undermined by the galloping inflation of 1922–23, when Elias had to interrupt his studies and take work in industry (as export manager in a local foundry) to support his financially embarrassed parents.

As Elias himself was to remark in retrospect, personal experiences and "the events of [his] time," influenced his thinking at least as much as any book he read.[4] It would be difficult indeed to appreciate the depth of his work without taking into account that he was an eyewitness to the violence and the social, political, and economic turmoil in Germany from the fall of the Kaiser's regime up to and beyond Hitler's accession to power. The theory of civilizing processes, far from being a celebration of the Western way of life, was developed out of Elias's urgent need to understand how the thin veneer of what people had come to think of as "civilization" came to cover and disguise the powerful forces of conflict and violence not far beneath the surface of even such a seemingly stable constitutional state as Germany had appeared to be in Elias's school days under the Kaiser.

As yet, however, Elias was not a sociologist. He registered at Breslau University to read both medicine and philosophy. He completed the first medical degree, the preclinical *Physikum*, but halfway through the first clinical semester he realized he could no longer manage to study both of his subjects, and he dropped medicine in order to concentrate on completing his doctorate under the supervision of the distinguished philosopher Richard Hönigswald (1875–1947). Still, his work in the dissecting room and the knowledge he gained of the biological structure and functioning of the brain remained with him. It did not lead him to reduce mental activity and social behavior to biology. On the contrary, he compared what he knew about the working of the brain with the neo-Kantian image of humans espoused by his philosophy teacher, Hönigswald. There was nothing in the biology of the central nervous system, he found, corresponding to the division taken for granted in philosophy between the "external" world and the "internal" world of "the mind." This notion has been a dominant strand in Western philosophy at least since the Renaissance, running through Descartes to Leibniz's "windowless monads" and culminating in Kant's postulating the innate, unchanging a-priori categories by which every human mind perceives the world outside itself. The connecting thread in this tradition of thought is a concern with how the single, adult individual mind, looking out from inside, is able to have knowledge of the external world. So entrenched is the conception of the mind as "internal" and sharply demarcated from the external world—Elias was later to call this the image of *homo clausus*, the "closed person"—that it is also taken for granted by many sociologists. Elias himself detected it in Talcott Parsons's distinction between "personality" and "social system," but similar *homo clausus* assumptions underlie the work of Max Weber, Karl Popper, and various strands of phenomenology, all of them influential in twentieth-century sociology.[5] It is difficult to resist thinking in terms of *homo clausus*, for it has entered into the very mode of self-experience of people at large in modern societies.

Yet Elias felt dissatisfied with this from an early stage: "The discrepancy between the philosophical, idealist image of man and the anatomical, physiological one unsettled me for many years."[6] Dissecting the musculature of the human face led him to reflect that the communicative signaling of feelings to other humans is a primary peculiarity of the human constitution. The development of emotional communicativeness and of the musculature of the body, including the capacity for smiling and laughing, must have proceeded hand-in-hand, interweaving with each other in a long-term process. Elias gradually came to the view that the *homo clausus* image of the human being was an instance of the philosophical tendency to reduce observable processes over time to something timeless and unchanging—a tendency he was later to label "process-reduction" (*Zustandsreduktion*), detecting it everywhere in the conventional vocabulary of sociology; he came to distrust static expressions like "structure," "boundary," "system," "stratum," and so on, which suggest unchanging conditions rather than the continuous flux of social life.

Most of these ideas were worked out only much later in Elias's career. The immediate consequence even of his initial doubts was a serious rift with Hönigswald over his thesis, entitled *Idee und Individuum: Ein Beitrag zur Philosophie der Geschichte* (Idea and individual: a contribution to the philosophy of history). Elias mounted an assault on Kant's contention that certain categories of thought—Newtonian space, time, causality, and some fundamental moral principles—are not derived from experience but are inherent, eternal, and universal in the human mind. This may look as though Elias were reverting to Locke's empiricism, but he argued—in contradistinction to Locke—that ideas could not be seen as individual products. Intellectual history had to be seen in terms of "chains" of generations, anticipating the emphasis Elias would later place on the need to think of people in the plural, not of the individual in the singular; this argument also faintly anticipated a turn from a philosophical to a sociological formulation of these problems. In terms of the great division in nineteenth-century philosophy, it could perhaps be said that Elias moved from the Kantian into the Hegelian tradition, with its concern with patterns of change in knowledge over time. But that is somewhat misleading, for Elias—perhaps a little soured by his power struggle with Hönigswald—was already moving away from philosophy as a discipline capable of offering solutions to the problems which interested him. When he resumed his studies, as a postdoctoral student in Heidelberg in 1925, it was in sociology, not philosophy.

*Heidelberg and Frankfurt*

Max Weber had died in 1920, but his brother Alfred (1868–1958) occupied a chair of sociology at Heidelberg, and his widow, Marianne, still lived there; between them, they kept alive Weber's memory and intellectual influence. Elias had first learnt of Weber's work from Karl Jaspers in Heidelberg a few years earlier, when he spent a semester away from Breslau. Now he read the work of Weber, and of Marx, Simmel, and other German sociologists, in depth; it was not until very much later, mainly after he had written *The Civilizing Process,* that he seems to have read any of the classics of French, British, or American sociology.

During the Heidelberg years Elias, as a mere Ph.D., was entirely unpaid. Apart from his father's continuing generosity, he relied on earnings from such tasks as teaching German to foreign students; in later years, he used to wonder whether Talcott Parsons may have been one of the American students he taught, though it seems unlikely that neither man would have retained any clear memory of the other.[7] In order to ascend to the first rung of the academic career ladder, it was necessary to write a further thesis, the *Habilitationsschrift,* which qualified one for the rank of *Privatdozent.*[8] Each candidate for *Habilitation* had to be sponsored by a full professor, and Elias was placed on Alfred Weber's list. There were several ahead of him, so quite a few years would have to elapse before he could expect to present his thesis. His proposed subject was on the significance of Florentine society and culture in the transition from prescientific to scientific thinking. Although he had scant Italian, Elias visited Florence, looking up documents on the young Galileo, and on the crucial experimental art of such fifteenth-century artists as Masaccio and Uccello, whose development of perspective and the representation of three dimensions in two he saw as connected with the general question of how people moved from mythical to scientific thinking.[9]

At Heidelberg, Elias became friendly with Karl Mannheim (1893–1947). Although he was only four years older than Elias, Mannheim was already a *Privatdozent.* It was he who introduced Elias into Marianne Weber's salon. In consequence Elias gave his first sociological paper at a meeting on the balcony of Max Weber's house; it was on the sociology of Gothic architecture, and he spoke about differences between French and German society in the Middle Ages and how they were reflected in the structures of cathedrals in the two countries.

Both Alfred Weber and Karl Mannheim influenced Elias, if only because they prompted him to formulate his own position more explicitly in relation to theirs. He strongly resisted being described as a follower of either.[10] Weber was interested in long-term processes of social development and the place of culture within them.[11] He argued that culture could not be reduced to economic relationships or explained in terms of economic interests. It always had to be understood in terms of social behavior, but its pattern of development differed from that of economics, science, and technology. In those, there was progress, whether of a linear or dialectical kind, together with reversals. But in art, religion, and culture in general, there were no progressions and regressions: culture was rather to be seen as the self-realization of this spirit of a people. When, later, Elias developed his own theory of civilizing processes, he departed from this aspect of Alfred Weber's thought; leaving aside the normative issue of "progress," he sought to demonstrate that long-term processes of development with a discernible, although unplanned and unintended, direction of their own may be found in the domain of culture as well as of economics, science, and technology.

During the Heidelberg years, Karl Mannheim was at the peak of his intellectual powers, making path-breaking contributions to the sociology of knowledge in his book *Ideology and Utopia* and such masterful essays as the one on the social origins of conservative thought in Germany.[12] He showed brilliantly how social ideologies could be analyzed and related to the social circumstances of their development. Such an approach may, however, throw into doubt the validity of all human knowledge, and Mannheim found it difficult to define a clear boundary between forms of knowledge which were socially conditioned and "partial" and those which were not. He himself shrank from the full relativistic consequences of his argument. He experimented with several ways of breaking out of relativism. One route was what he called "relationism": if people from different class positions have different partial perspectives on the world, could it perhaps be argued that "truth" is the synthesis of these partial perspectives? Another was an idea which borrowed Alfred Weber's notion of the "socially unattached intelligentsia" and contended that intellectuals, being less closely linked to economic forces, had a less one-sided perspective on social reality than did other classes: they were *potentially* better able to mediate between political ideologies and positions. Elias, in *Reflections on a Life*, professed to find none of Mannheim's proposed routes of escape from relativism very convincing, although his own advocacy of "multiple perspectives" is somewhat similar to Mannheim's relationism.[13] Elias regarded the exposure of the social roots of ideological beliefs as only a beginning, and refused to abandon the quest for increasingly more "reality congruent" knowledge about social life: "For me, criticism of ideology was only a means to an end, a step on the way to a theory of society that would take account of the fact that reality-revealing as well as reality-concealing knowledge can be observed. A doctor's knowledge of the human body, that can heal, is not ideology. Why should one not be in a position to produce non-ideological knowledge of human society?"[14]

That standpoint, which was actually implicit in Mannheim's writings, was to find expression again much later in Elias's discussion of involvement and detachment, in which the problem of "objectivity" in social science is treated as one neither of philosophy, nor of methodology, nor of individual motivation, but as a question of long-term social development in its own right. Elias, later in life, regarded Mannheim as having failed to make a sufficiently radical break with philosophical ways of thinking, especially the Marxist distinction between "consciousness" and "social being," itself a derivative of the tradition which distinguishes between society "outside" and the individual mind "inside." "The dualistic thesis of a being alien to consciousness and consciousness alien to being," wrote Elias, "is a fiction."[15] Although there never seems to have been any hostile break between the two, Elias was later anxious to emphasize the intellectual differences between his views and Mannheim's. Nevertheless, Mannheim and Elias were closely associated for about a decade or more, so it is not surprising that there is a family resemblance between their writings; indeed, the influence may have been in many respects two-way.[16]

Between Karl Mannheim and Alfred Weber there was a latent but strong rivalry, partly intellectual, partly political, perhaps partly simply a matter of older and younger generations. Their animosity burst into the open at the German Sociological Association meeting of 1928 in Zürich, when Mannheim read his paper "Competition as a Cultural Phenomenon."[17] Toennies, Sombart, and—as a junior respondent—Elias praised the paper, but Alfred Weber reacted angrily to a passing reference to himself and liberalism, and to what could be read as a relativizing of the ideal of *Wertfreiheit* (value-freedom) in sociological research, an ideal associated especially with Max Weber.[18] The now-open rift made Elias's position as friend of the one and the *Habilitation* candidate of the other somewhat uncomfortable. So, when the following year Mannheim was called to the chair of sociology at Frankfurt, Elias agreed to go with him as academic assistant. In this post, Elias for the first time received a salary; another advantage was that Mannheim promised him his *Habilitation* after only three years service as assistant, earlier than he could have hoped for with Alfred Weber.

In Frankfurt, Elias chose a new subject for his *Habilitationsschrift*, a study of the royal court of France before the Revolution, of its seemingly bizarre etiquette and the apparently irrational extravagance of the courtiers, and of how these were related both to the changing social balances of power and to the literature, art, and culture of ancien régime France. The thesis was finished, and Elias's *Habilitation* was rushed through early in 1933 immediately after Hitler came to power, but the typescript remained untouched among Elias's papers in exile for more than three decades, the book *Die höfische Gesellschaft* being published only in 1969. A whole half-century passed before *The Court Society* appeared in English.

Frankfurt in the early 1930s offered a rich intellectual milieu. The university's Department of Sociology was housed in rented rooms in the building owned by the independent group of Marxist scholars, the Institut für Sozialforschung, known subsequently as the Frankfurt School. The institute's members then included Max Horkheimer as director, Theodor Adorno, Walter Benjamin, Leo Löwenthal, and Erich Fromm. Although relations between the institute and Mannheim's department seem not to have been very close, they were civil, and Elias was on good terms with Adorno. It has often been noted that there is a certain similarity in the underlying concerns of Elias's *Civilizing Process* and Horkheimer and Adorno's *Dialectic of Enlightenment,*[19] although the fundamental differences in approach—the one thoroughly sociological and rooted in empirical historical evidence, the other an essentially philosophical and normative discourse—are equally striking.[20]

From other disciplines, Elias's circle included the economist Adolf Löwe, the psychoanalyst S. H. Foulkes (later a close friend in London), and Paul Tillich, the philosopher and theologian. Elias's own tasks involved small-group teaching and the supervision of doctoral theses. Students in the department included Gisèle Freund (later a celebrated photographer and sociologist of photography) and Hans Gerth and Kurt Wolff (both subsequently prominent sociologists in America). What might well have become a distinct school of sociology was stifled at the outset. Shortly after the Nazis came to power, Elias's whole circle of students and friends was dispersed all over Europe. He himself lingered in Frankfurt a little longer than most. He remembered going through the institute, to which he still had the keys, removing all traces of left-wing propaganda before the Nazis searched the building. He observed at firsthand their takeover of power in the state and in the university. It was, he noted, both violent and very rationally organized—the two modes were not, and are not, mutually exclusive. Then he himself left for Paris, taking with him what money his father could spare.

Elias himself was never active in a political party (he even claimed never to have voted). Yet, although he did not mention it in *Reflections on a Life,* from his teenage years before the First World War and apparently for many years afterward, he was an active member of a Zionist youth movement called "Blau-Weiss."[21] In terms of the ordinary political spectrum he conceded that he was not right-wing: all his friends were on the Left, and in political arguments his own sympathies were on the Left.[22] But he professed a profound dislike of all political ideologies, which always in his view involved both self-deception and distortion of social reality. They were all instances of fantasy-laden thinking, he argued, and the task of sociology was to unmask myths of all kinds and to help influence and improve society by creating more realistic knowledge about it.[23]

## Exile

Elias's characteristic self-distancing from current political conflicts is seen in an essay he wrote while in exile in Paris, "The Expulsion of the Huguenots from France." The parallel between the fate of the Huguenots in seventeenth-century France and the predicament of the German Jews in the 1930s was quite obvious, but the emotionally distancing device of writing about events of two-and-a-half centuries earlier made it easier to analyze the underlying processes. For all that, in this essay and the more comprehensive theory of established-outsiders relationships it anticipates, Elias cannot completely disguise his powerful sympathy for outsiders of every kind.[24]

In Paris, Elias was soon moving in French intellectual circles and receiving encouragement from the sociologist Celestin Bouglé and the historian of science Alexander Koyré of the Ecole Normale Supérieure—but there was no prospect of academic employment in France. He set up a business with two friends from Frankfurt, making and selling wooden toys, and promptly lost all his money. Although he was to be poor for many years, this, he later recalled, was the only time in his life when he actually went hungry. After nearly two years (1933–35) in Paris, he accepted the invitation of German friends already in England to join them there.

Elias was thirty-eight years old, had published very little, and did not speak English, so his prospects—unlike those of the more senior and much better-known Mannheim—were poor. He received a small grant from a Dutch Jewish charity, and spent his first few years in London completing the two volumes of his magnum opus, *Über den Prozess der Zivilisation*. The origins of the book are not quite clear. As Elias told the story in old age, he was browsing one day in the great Reading Room of the British Museum, came across some successive editions of old manners books, realized their sociological significance, and the whole project began from there. But it is more plausible that the first volume had already been started in Paris. A few copies of that were printed in Breslau in 1937, and the plan was to have the whole book published under the imprint of Akademia Verlag in the Czech capital, Prague. Within a year, however, the Germans invaded Czechoslovakia and closed off that outlet for the book. The second volume, containing Elias's theory of state formation and a concluding "synopsis" which explained how that was related to changes in manners, culture, and typical personality makeup (or "habitus," as Elias called it), was probably written wholly in London. This too was printed in Breslau, but before the work was bound the printer himself fled Germany. Finally, the refugee publishing firm Haus zum Falken, run by Fritz Karger in Basle, Switzerland, agreed to publish both volumes. Elias's father deftly negotiated for the unbound sheets to be shipped from Breslau to Basle, where they were bound and published in 1939 on the eve of the Second World War.

Elias's parents visited him in London in 1938, but refused to accede to his urging that they join him in exile. His father asked what the Nazis could possibly to do him, because he had never broken a law in his life. In 1940 his mother wrote to Elias that his father had died. For a while he continued to receive letters from her, and then she disappeared. Her last letter reached him via the Red Cross from a transit camp for Auschwitz, where she is believed to have been killed in 1941. Even to the end of his life, Elias found it difficult to talk about this without showing his sorrow.

The publication of *Über den Prozess der Zivilisation* was very little noticed, although it was not without its few and scattered admirers even in wartime.[25] Elias was made a senior research fellow at the London School of Economics, which was evacuated to Cambridge for the duration of the war. Then in 1940, like all other "enemy aliens," he was interned for some months at a camp near Liverpool and then on the Isle of Man. Impromptu seminars were organized, and his audience included the teenage Eric Wolf, who after his emigration to the United States was to become celebrated as an anthropologist.[26] After this episode, Elias returned to Cambridge, and around the end of the war worked for British intelligence, screening out unrepentant Nazis among German prisoners of war.

The immediate postwar years were tough ones for Elias. He could find no secure employment but gave occasional lectures in the University of London, and taught adult education courses which, he recalled, had to be good to keep up student enrollments—otherwise he did not receive payment. He went into psychoanalysis, but sometimes was unable to pay for the sessions. During these years he was also involved in psychoanalysis in a professional way, as the only sociologist among the small group of psychoanalysts—notably his old friend S. H. Foulkes—who founded the Group Analytic Society, which now forms one of the major psychoanalytic schools of thought and practice in Britain. Elias's thinking about the ineluctability of interdependence and his rejection of the *homo clausus* conception of the person were further developed in the therapeutic practice of group analysis.[27]

Only in 1954 was Elias offered his first secure university post—at the astoundingly late age of fifty-seven. He joined another refugee scholar, Ilya Neustadt, who had been appointed to head the new Department of Sociology at Leicester. Leicester was a small provincial university, not particularly prestigious, but within a few years Neustadt and Elias had built up one of the largest and most influential sociology departments in the country. In the 1950s and 1960s a very large number of distinguished British sociologists spent time in Leicester either as students or as junior lecturers; thus, to mention no more than two names, both Anthony Giddens and John Goldthorpe were appointed to their first teaching posts by Neustadt and Elias.[28]

## Retirement

Elias formally retired from Leicester in 1962, and then served for two years as Professor of Sociology at the University of Ghana, helping to build a department of sociology there, and also acquiring for himself an impressive collection of West African art. He then returned to Leicester, where he continued to teach part-time, though essentially functioning as (in a phrase President Lyndon Johnson used to describe his own role at the University of Texas) "conversationist in residence." For a time, the Leicester school of sociology had a distinct developmental slant, but this did not long survive Elias's definitive departure from Leicester in the mid-1970s. Neustadt shared many of Elias's views, and provided strong administrative leadership, but himself wrote almost nothing. Elias, on the other hand, was now again writing a great deal—at this time mainly in English—but published very little of it, and his early work in German remained almost totally unknown. He made a strong intellectual impression on many of his students and colleagues, although it would have certainly been greater had there been more evidence in print to justify publicly his own confidence in his distinctive standpoint. In Giddens's works much later, there are clear signs of the influence of Elias's *problématique*, but he was to seek solutions in a much more conventionally philosophical way than Elias, and he seems to have picked up only a garbled, second-hand version of the theory of civilizing processes.[29]

Broadly speaking, British sociology during Elias's Leicester years was antipathetic to his views. The rising sociologists of the postwar generation were reacting against the tradition of British social evolutionism, which had been passed on from Herbert Spencer through L. T. Hobhouse to Morris Ginsberg, who was still teaching at the LSE.[30] They tended to regard any interest in long-term processes of social development as tainted with Victorian notions of "progress," Eurocentric superiority, and "inevitability." Their rejection of developmental perspectives was reinforced by the writings of another key figure at the LSE, the philosopher Karl Popper, who linked the search for an understanding of long-term processes to authoritarian politics, whether of the Left or the Right.[31] And from America came the then-internationally dominant influence of the synchronic functionalism of Talcott Parsons. Elias was later to write of "the retreat of sociologists into the present"—their abandonment of the historical developmental interests of the classic sociologist—as a dominant current in postwar sociology.[32] Elias himself was unabashed in acknowledging the influence of evolutionary theory, although the influence was less directly from Spencer and his heirs than from his reading of current advances in biology, notably the neo-Darwinian synthesis of such British biologists as Sir Julian Huxley and C. H. Waddington, and the implications of the discovery of the structure of DNA by Crick and Watson.[33] He was always most careful, nevertheless, to emphasize the great difference between biological *evolution* and social *development,* avoiding any implication of teleology, "progress," unilinearity, or inevitability, and stressing that social development, unlike biological evolution, can be reversed.[34]

If British sociology was not particularly sympathetic to Elias in the forty years (1935–75) that he lived in the country, he found British society congenial. He took British citizenship in 1952, and read deeply in British history and culture. His first publication in English was on the seemingly obscure topic of the genesis of the profession of naval officer; what initially drew his attention to the navy was that Britain's reliance for attack and defense principally upon sea power rather than an army had had a profound effect on the development of the British state, since a navy is less easily used as an instrument of internal repression.[35] Later he was to write insightfully on the process of "parliamentarization" of politics in the century following the English Civil Wars.[36] In fact, even as early as 1939 he had begun a three-way comparison of the differing tracks of state formation in Germany, France, and Britain,[37] and the comparison was deepened in the essays from the 1960s to the 1980s which make up *The Germans.*[38] The influence of his British sojourn is particularly clear in the work on the sociology of sport which he began with Eric Dunning in the 1960s.[39] Elias asked what kind of society must we live in today for people to enjoy so much the excitement and tensions engendered by physical contests where no blood flows and the contestants do no serious harm to each other. But he also asked what it was about British society that explained why so many of the sports now popular around the world had originated, or been formalized, in the British Isles. For a good many years, Elias was to be best known in Britain as a sociologist of sport.

Another product of the Leicester years was *The Established and the Outsiders*, which Elias wrote with his graduate student John L. Scotson.[40] Though, outwardly, it was merely a study of a small community on the outskirts of the city, Elias used the book for a major theoretical elaboration of his sociology, emphasizing the importance of the dimension of power in social relations (see chapter 13 below). In the late 1960s he wrote a whole book on the changing balance of power between the sexes, which was unfortunately lost when Elias left every existing draft in a pile in his room at the University of Leicester, whence they were removed to an incinerator by an overzealous cleaner. Elias later reconstructed from memory the part of the book which dealt with marriage in ancient Rome, and it is included in this volume (chapter 11); this, however, is no more than a fragment, dealing only with the upper classes in remote antiquity. The anecdote about the book's loss tells us something about Elias's working habits. He was very careful in his writing, but careless in keeping his writings in order. His typescripts, copiously amended in his difficult handwriting, were often worked over for many years and left lying in drawers, sometimes for decades.

Recognition finally came to Elias in his early seventies, after *Über den Prozess der Zivilisation* was reissued and *Die höfische Gesellschaft* was published for the first time in 1969. English translations were, however, long in coming, and the acclaim he first received, especially in Germany and the Netherlands, drew him back to the Continent. He lived for some years at the Zentrum für Interdisziplinäre Forschung at Bielefeld in Germany, and then settled permanently in Amsterdam, where a whole research school of younger social scientists came to flourish under his influence.[41] Elias gradually resumed writing mainly in German, though all the essays on sport and nearly all the work on knowledge and the sciences continued to be written in English.

In his last years, Elias received many honors in Germany, the Netherlands, France, and Italy. To the end, however, he was markedly less known among English-speaking sociologists. He visited the United States in 1978, when the first volume of *The Civilizing Process* was published by Urizen Books, with Richard Sennett hosting a conference in his honor in New York. Successful though that was in itself, there was no follow-up, and Elias never became much recognized among American sociologists for anything but that single volume in isolation. Champions such as Alan Sica and later Thomas Scheff were isolated voices.[42] When Elias returned briefly to teach at the University of Indiana, Bloomington, in 1979, it was as a guest in Germanic studies. That, at least, was typical: wherever Elias's influence made itself felt, it was never confined narrowly to sociologists. Meanwhile, in Britain, the Theory Group of the

British Sociological Association held a successful conference on his work in Oxford in 1980, but it was not until right at the end of his life that he was invited by the full BSA to give a public lecture, and then he happened not to be well enough to travel. Writing to the very last, Elias died at his home in Amsterdam, aged 93, on 1 August 1990.

## The Theory of Civilizing Processes
### *History and Format of Elias's Magnum Opus*

In the latter half of the twentieth century, historians and social scientists have tended to steer clear of an issue which preoccupied their nineteenth-century precursors: the question of how what may loosely be called human "psychological" makeup changes in the course of long-term social development. Nineteenth-century social evolutionists tended to discuss these matters in the framework of a unilinear sequence of stages, from "savagery" through "barbarism" to "civilization." Members of industrial societies like themselves, they thought, were the product of "progress," and had reached a state of being "civilized," with the clear implication of being better and superior. At the close of the second millennium, Western people at large are much more hesitant in using such language. The loss of European world hegemony, coupled with the many traumas of twentieth-century history—mass wars, totalitarianism, and genocide (especially when they occurred in Europe)—have undermined confidence in progress, let alone any sense of superiority.

Writing in the 1930s, when the murderous nature of the Nazi regime was already evident, and with firsthand experience of the slaughter on the Western Front and the extreme social disorder of the Weimar period, Elias began *The Civilizing Process* with a forty-page discussion of how, since the middle of the eighteenth century, the concept of civilization (and, especially in Germany, the related concept of "culture") had become loaded with a wide range of evaluative connotations expressing the West's sense of superiority (see chapter 3).[43] He noted that it was derived from *civilité*, the word courtiers had used since the sixteenth century to describe their own polished manners and courtly modes of behavior, and originally to distinguish them from the more rough and ready *courtoisie* of their medieval forebears. But, by the nineteenth century, the ways in which people in the West used the *word* "civilization" showed that they had already largely forgotten the civilizing *process:* it was for them completed and taken for granted. At this stage, confident of the superiority of their own, now apparently inherent and eternal standards, they wished only to "civilize" others: the lower classes of their own countries and, especially, the natives of lands now being colonized by European powers. This led Elias to attempt to reconstruct, from the evidence of manners books written for actual and aspirant upper-class people in Europe since the Middle Ages, the process through which standards of what constituted courtesy, civility, and civilization had changed over the centuries. As he stated with great emphasis, he wished to examine the *facts* to which these increasingly value-laden concepts had originally referred. And he wished to show that the changes in the direction of more-civilized behavior and feeling were connected with broader processes of social development.

Summarized most briefly, the argument in *The Civilizing Process* focuses on related long-term changes in *behavior, power,* and *habitus.* After the discussion on the sociogenesis of the concepts civilization and culture, the bulk of the first volume is devoted to an extensive empirical inquiry into "civilization as a specific transformation of human behavior"—more popularly known nowadays as the celebrated history of manners. The second volume opens with a thoroughgoing treatise on "feudalization and state formation," analyzing long-term changes in the structure of power which formed the background for the changes in manners described in the first volume. Then, finally, the insights gained in the previous parts are summed up in a synopsis, called "towards a theory of civilizing processes," showing how the changes in behavior and power are reflected in changes in personality structure or habitus.

The basic idea underlying the whole book is that there is a link between the long-term structural development of societies and changes in people's social behavior and habitus. By "habitus," Elias said he meant almost exactly what is captured by the everyday expression "second nature."[44] It refers to those levels of our personality makeup which are not inherent or innate but are very deeply habituated in us by learning through social experience from birth onward—so deeply habituated, in fact, that they feel "natural" or inherent even to ourselves. It seems that our individual habitus guides our behavior; but, then, habitus itself is formed and continues to be molded in social situations, marked by specific power differentials, and those situations, in turn, are embedded in larger social structures which change over time.

These are very grand and general observations; what Elias did in *The Civilizing Process* was to develop them by examining very concrete and vivid historical data. Thus, in order to trace the long-term changes in conduct and mentality, he consulted European manners books from the late Middle Ages to the Victorian period, and quoted striking passages about changing habits of eating, washing, spitting, blowing one's nose, urinating, and defecating. He focused particularly on the most basic, "natural" or "animalic" of human functions because these are things human beings cannot biologically avoid doing no matter what society, culture, or age they live in. Moreover, infants are born in the same emotional condition everywhere, so that the lifetime point of departure is always the same. Therefore if a significant change occurs in the way these functions are handled, it may be seen directly. In the European case, many of these matters came to be hidden behind the scenes of social life and, increasingly invested with feelings of shame, also hidden behind the scenes of mental life—as constraints which one generation had painfully to learn became so deeply habituated in later generations that they were repressed into the unconscious. Something similar happened to the states' means of violence; confined literally and metaphorically to barracks, they continued to exert a steady but largely unnoticed "civilizing" pressure on citizens.

It would be well-nigh impossible to understand the course of civilizing processes in Western Europe over the past four or five centuries without relating them to processes of state formation. Elias's theory of state formation implicitly begins from Max Weber's definition of the state as an organization which successfully upholds a claim to binding rule making over a territory by virtue of commanding a monopoly of the legitimate use of violence, but he by-passes the problematic term "legitimacy" by linking a rising level of internal security and calculability in everyday life directly to the formation of habitus.[45] He is more interested than Weber in the process through which a monopoly of the means of violence (and taxation) is established and extended. After discussing the early European Middle Ages, during which centrifugal forces were dominant in the process of feudalization, resulting in the extreme fragmentation of territory and of effective rule, Elias outlines the long-term processes at work afterward, when centripetal forces, fluctuating and with regressions, regained the upper hand—much earlier in the territories that were to become England and France than in those that were to become Germany and Italy.[46] The earlier stages of state formation involved a series of "elimination contests" between numerous rival territorial magnates, a violent competition with a compelling sequential dynamic through which successively larger territorial units emerged with more-effective central monopoly apparatuses (see chapter 8). The contests were less the result of the aggressiveness of individual magnates than the cause: more pacific rulers simply would not survive, given the structure of the contests and of their interdependence with each other. "It is not aggression which triggers conflicts," remarked Elias aphoristically, "but conflicts which trigger aggression."[47] The other side of the process, however, needs equally to be stressed: the internal pacification of larger and larger territories by the more and more effective monopoly apparatuses.

State formation was only one process interweaving with others to enmesh individuals in increasingly complex webs of interdependence. Internal pacification of territory facilitated trade, which fostered the growth of towns and division of labor and generated taxes which supported larger administrative and military organizations, which in turn facilitated the internal pacification of larger territories, and so on—a cumulative process experienced as a compelling force by people caught up in it and contributing to it. Furthermore, according to Elias, the slowly rising standards of habitual self-restraint engendered in people in turn reinforced the upward spiral—being necessary, for example, to the formation of gradually more effective and calculable administration. In his view it was futile to seek single causal factor explanations; rather he sought to trace how various causal strands interwove over time to produce an overall process with increasing momentum.

## Civilizing Processes on Different Levels

*The Civilizing Process* deals mostly with developments in Western Europe, although there are a few excursuses on other times and places. At several points, however, Elias reminds his readers that conditions in early medieval Europe in no way represented a "beginning" of the human civilizing process. In his later writings, he made this idea more explicit, and he came to distinguish among civilizing processes on three levels:

*The individual level.* Infants and children have to acquire through learning the adult standards of behavior and feeling prevalent in their society; to speak of this as a civilizing process is more or less to use another term for "socialization," a process that has a typical structure and sequence. Researchers from Freud and Piaget onward have debated the details of the sequence of childhood development, but few would now question that there is a sequence.

*The level of particular societies.* The second level is more controversial. Where did these standards come from? As Elias never tired of emphasizing, no human society has ever lacked such standards of behavior and feeling; in that sense there is no zero point in the civilizing of behavior, and it is quite wrong to describe any past society as "uncivilized."[48] Yet the standards prevalent in any society have not always been the same. Central to Elias's argument is the contention that it is possible to identify long-term civilizing processes in the shaping of standards of behavior and feeling over many generations within particular cultures.

That these standards change is not disputed; what generates controversy is the proposition that the changes take the form of structured processes of change with a discernible—though unplanned—direction over time. *The level of humanity as a whole.* This third level brings us back to the sorts of questions posed by the social evolutionists of the Victorian era. Particularly in his later works, Elias himself became increasingly preoccupied with very long-term processes in the development of human society as a whole. No civilizing process in any particular human group, it must be remembered, represents an absolute beginning. It never proceeds *in vacuo,* without reference to other—earlier or contemporary—civilizing processes undergone by other human groups. Just as every individual lifetime civilizing process is a part of a longer-term development in a particular society, so also are civilizing processes in every society parts of still longer-term civilizing processes which encompass humanity as a whole. In this even longer-term perspective, humanity has undergone a collective learning process in which it has acquired such distinctively human skills as speech; the use of fire; the making of tools and weapons from wood, stone, and metals; and the vast and still-growing stock of knowledge.

Elias's book on time and timing (see chapter 14) brings out particularly clearly the link between social and personality changes arising from the necessity of coordinating more and more complicated sequences of activities, and implies (if it does not explicitly state) that this link should hold in all cultures.[49] In the original book *The Civilizing Process,* however, the focus is mainly on developments in Western Europe, and the conclusions refer primarily to the problem of how changes in the structure of society have affected individual habitus. Among the trends Elias discusses in this context are the processes of "psychologization," rationalization, and the advance of thresholds of shame and embarrassment.

The concept of "psychologization" is linked to the idea that as webs of interdependence spread, more people become involved in more complex and more impenetrable relationships. Less abstractly: more people are forced more often to pay more attention to more people, in more varying circumstances. This produces pressures toward greater consideration of the consequences of one's own actions for other people on whom one is in one way or another dependent. Moreover, if the power ratios become more even, this gives an extra impulse toward an increase in "mutual identification." This idea, while not new to Elias—it was expressed very clearly by Alexis de Tocqueville—has a very direct bearing on matters of violence and cruelty.[50] As Elias noted in *The Germans,* conscience formation has changed in the course of the twentieth century: "The feeling of responsibility which people have for each other is certainly minimal, looked at in absolute terms, but compared with before it has increased."[51]

"Rationalization," Elias stresses, has no absolute beginning in human history. There was no point at which human beings suddenly began to possess "reason" and a "conscience." Nor was there a stage when they were completely "irrational." It is equally misleading to think of rationality as some kind of property of individual minds in isolation from each other: "There is no such thing as 'reason,' only at most 'rationalization.'"[52] The term "rationalization" refers to changes in the way people habitually orient themselves in the world in which they live, and these changes are directly related to the way they are bonded with each other. In other words, the forms of behavior we call rationality are produced within a social figuration in which short-term impulses are subordinated to longer-term projects: "The complementary concepts of 'rationality' and 'irrationality' refer to the relative parts played by short-term affects and long-term conceptual models of observable reality in individual behaviour. The greater the importance of the latter in the delicate balance between affective and reality-oriented commands, the more 'rational' is behaviour."[53] Elias contends that "'rational understanding' is not the motor of the 'civilizing' of . . . behaviour."[54] Rationalization is an aspect of civilizing processes, not, as Weber would make it, the principal propellant of long-term social development.

Elias's remarks about the "advance of thresholds of shame and embarrassment" go to the heart of his theory. Shame and embarrassment are personal emotions, deeply affecting the individual's state of mind; at the same time they are socially induced emotions par excellence. If a person feels that he or she has been observed committing an offense against good manners, that is reason for shame; seeing someone else commit a similar offense is a cause for embarrassment. As the written and unwritten rules of etiquette became more encompassing and subtler, the range of occasions for transgressing those rules and, therefore, for shame and embarrassment increased. Erving Goffman described with great acumen how people in contemporary society experience and cope with embarrassment and shame; Elias's theory provides a framework for explaining the *sociogenesis* of such situations.

## Civilizing and Decivilizing Pressures

As the section on shame and embarrassment—or repugnance—clearly shows, it would be a serious misreading of the theory of civilizing processes to see it as a model of progress, let alone *inevitable* progress. On the contrary, the internal pacification of territory was highly contingent and precarious. Violence continues to play a part even in the most internally pacified society, even though—like defecation, urination, nakedness, and the rest—it may over time come to be increasingly hidden behind the scenes of social life. It may be "confined to barracks," but it is still there: "The armour of civilized conduct would crumble very rapidly if, through a change in society, the degree of insecurity that existed earlier were to break in upon us again, and if danger became as incalculable as once it was. Corresponding fears would burst the limits set to them today."[55]

There is a certain asymmetry between civilizing and decivilizing processes: the former can only be relatively long-term, while the latter can become dominant very quickly. In this respect civilization and decivilization may be regarded in the same light as processes of integration and disintegration in general: growth and development generally take more time than death and decay. It is also likely that both civilizing and decivilizing tendencies, or pressures, are *always* present. The civilizing processes go on continuously: even if there are no noticeable changes in behavior, people continue to struggle to solve the problems posed to them in their lives by decivilizing pressures—whether those pressures make themselves felt as an inner temptation to let things go or as the threat of violence from others. The question is always which forces gain the upper hand, in the short term or the long term.[56]

The balance between civilizing and decivilizing pressures involves the interplay between external constraints (*Fremdzwänge*, constraints by external circumstances, mainly pressures exerted *by other people*) and self-constraints (*Selbstzwänge*) in the control of behavior in the average person. Elias argues that in Europe over the past few centuries, a shift has taken place strengthening the part played by self-constraints (see "The Social Constraint towards Self-Constraint," chapter 1 below). However, as Elias frequently stresses, the European civilizing process has not simply veered in the direction of *more* self-control, but has involved complex changes in the pattern of controls. In particular, he speaks of controls becoming "more even," "more automatic," and "more all-round," as well as of a movement toward "diminishing contrasts and increasing varieties." By "more even" and "more automatic" self-constraints, Elias is referring to changes in the social standards concerning temperament. The relative volatility of medieval people has often been noted by historians; at a later stage, people whose moods fluctuated so rapidly would come to be regarded as having a psychological problem. People in general came gradually to be expected to show less-extreme oscillations of mood, and the controls over emotional expression became more reliable or calculable. "More all-round" refers to a decline in the differences between various spheres of life, such as contrasts between what is allowed in public and in private, between conduct in relation to one category of people as against another, or between "normal" behavior and that permissible on special occasions, like carnivals, which are seen as exceptions to the rules.

Finally, the phrase "diminishing contrasts, increasing varieties" (see chapter 2) points to the observation that with reduced inequalities between social groups certain extreme forms of behavior, such as those freely expressing complete contempt or humiliation, are no longer allowed, while a far wider range of forms of conduct has become possible and permissible in an increasing variety of highly differentiated social settings.

These distinctions shed interesting light on the question of whether the rise of what is called the "permissive society" in the latter part of the twentieth century represents a reversal of the main trend of the European civilizing process traced by Elias. He himself preferred to speak of recent "informalizing processes," and interpreted them as involving a "highly controlled decontrolling of emotional controls."[57] While it is clear that at an outward, behavioral level certain trends have been reversed—tolerance regarding the naked body, for example, now seems closer to pre-Victorian than Victorian standards—nevertheless, at a deeper level informalization processes in general seem to represent an unequivocal continuation of the historic trends toward diminishing contrasts, increasing varieties, and more "all-roundedness." Because they involve a less tyrannical form of conscience formation and more conscious deliberation, it is easy to overlook how far the new, more liberal standards presuppose an extremely reliable capacity for controlling one's impulses and a high level of mutual identification. They do not, in general, appear to involve a switch backward in the balance from self-constraint toward external constraints.

The balance may, however, be tipped back if the level of danger that people face in their everyday lives increases and becomes less calculable. The operation of self-constraints will not remain the same if changes take place in the patterning of external constraints—especially the behavior of other people. People's calculations of power ratios and the external constraints with which they have to reckon always play a part in the steering of conduct, and if those calculations suddenly or gradually yield different outcomes, behavior will change. The pattern of people's fears responds to changes in the dangers they face.

During the times of social crisis—military defeats, political revolutions, rampant inflation, soaring unemployment, separately or, as happened in Germany after the First World War, in rapid sequence—fears rise because control of social events has declined. Rising fears make it still more difficult to control events. That renders people still more susceptible to wish fantasies about means of alleviating the situation. A vicious circle or "double-bind process" is set up, as happened in Germany after 1918, fostering the rise of the Nazis and the appeal of racial beliefs—one instance of the more general category of "fantasy-laden" beliefs. The Weimar Republic plainly provided fertile soil for such beliefs, as Elias shows in his discussion of the decline of the state's monopoly of violence in that period (see chapter 9). The grim paradox is that it was the return to a highly effective state monopolization of the means of violence under Hitler, together with the renewed dangers and fears provided by the Second World War, that permitted the mass killings to be so effectively organized.[58] As Elias noted, in this, as in other aspects, "National Socialism revealed, perhaps in an especially blatant form, what are common conditions of contemporary societies, tendencies of acting and thinking which can also be found elsewhere."[59]

## The Centrality of Power
### *The Game Models*

As the discussion of the interconnectedness of civilization and state formation clearly shows, power is an essential dimension of the theory of the civilizing process—and of Elias's sociology in general. Some of the most explicit statements about the centrality of power are to be found, perhaps unexpectedly, in the chapter entitled "Game Models" from *What Is Sociology?* (chapter 7 below). The game models are designed to show what the subject matter of sociology is: that is, the manifold groupings formed by human beings who are *interdependent* in a variety of ways. In order to understand the feelings, thoughts, and actions of any group of people, we have always to consider the many social needs by which these people are bonded to each other and to other people—needs which range from sheer physical security and material well-being to intellectual orientation and emotional satisfaction, and which the people themselves often do not even consciously experience as "social." In most cases the dependencies, while being reciprocal, are unequal: usually one party in a social relationship tends, at least in certain respects, to be more dependent than the other party. The result is an uneven power balance: party *A* is more powerful than party *B*, and that directly affects the way both parties act and feel toward each other.

These elementary observations have profound and far-reaching implications. The game models turn out to be an ingenious device for bringing out the pervasive effects of both interdependence and power, not only at the directly observable level of two individuals engaged in interaction but also at the far more complex level of multilayered organizations such as national states. Starting out with an extremely simple example and then enlarging the perspective step by step, Elias shows how an approach aimed at discovering the structure of interdependence and power can illuminate persistent sociological problems and help reveal some basic principles about social processes.

The models are presented as "didactic" devices. They do not constitute a theory or a neat conceptual scheme, but are rather (to use a phrase of Harold Garfinkel's) "aids to a sluggish imagination." The sequence of models begins with one representing a "primal contest" of unregulated and murderous conflict between two human groups; this was designed as a limiting case to remind us that Talcott Parsons too readily defined "structuredness" in social life as deriving essentially from shared norms and values. While indeed it is difficult to conceive of a group totally lacking in norms and values, relationships *between* groups may be. The figuration of the primal contest represents a limiting case of completely unplanned interdependence.

The subsequent models then represent games—which do have some rules—in which the number of players and the extent of structural complexity increase and power differentials within contests decrease. The models demonstrate the not-altogether-commonplace insight that the more relatively equal become the power ratios among large numbers of people and groups (a process Elias called "functional democratization"), the more likely is it that the outcome will be something that no single person or group has planned or anticipated. Elias considerably broadens the idea of the "unanticipated consequences of purposive social action," which Robert Merton traced back to (*inter alia*) Adam Smith's "hidden hand" and Hegel's "cunning of reason."[60] Yesterday's unintended social consequences are today's unintended social conditions of intended human actions.[61] There thus arise structured processes, ones which, although no one has planned or intended them, have a discernible structure and direction of their own. These are then experienced as compelling processes by the people who are caught up in them—forces which seem external to and beyond the control of humans, and yet ultimately consist only of constraints exerted by people on each other. Examples of such long-term processes are the division of labor, the increase in human population, the emergence of a "world system" of economic relations, the "scientification" of human knowledge—and civilizing processes.

### The Monopoly Mechanism

As noted above, the changes in manners documented in Volume 1 of *The Civilizing Process* were part of a thorough transformation of the power structure in medieval and early modern Europe. One way in which this transformation became manifest was what Elias called "the taming of the warriors": an upper stratum of warlords who, in the early Middle Ages, ruled over their own territories almost unrestrained by any outside authority, and were gradually transformed into a courtly aristocracy, subject to the never-ceasing constraints of life at a royal court.

In order to account for this shift in the balance of power, Elias had to go into greater historical detail. His interest was not restricted to specific historical events as such, however; he wished to disclose the general pattern of the processes that eventually led to the rise of states ruled by one central government. He noted first of all that, after the fall of the Roman Empire in Western Europe, centrifugal forces prevailed for a long time. Even if Charlemagne managed to unite a huge empire during his lifetime, his successors lacked the means to keep it together. For many centuries, centripetal forces were too weak to sustain a stable central power over a large territory for any considerable period.

But then, gradually, a process of social differentiation and integration among increasingly larger groups became dominant. Chains of interdependence grew longer, allowing for greater concentrations of power. Under these changing circumstances, the *monopoly mechanism* could take effect—the same mechanism which economists had observed in the capitalist market system, and which Karl Mannheim had noted in the field of intellectual competition. This mechanism was seen by Elias as operating in the area of military struggle and political domination. He identified it as a major mechanism in the process of state formation—long before "state formation" was put on the agenda of historical sociology by Perry Anderson and Charles Tilly and others.[62]

As chapter 8 in this volume shows, Elias distinguished several stages in the development of the monopoly of organized violence and taxation. After its initial formation, this dual monopoly tended at first to be controlled by a single individual or family. In the course of time, however, in a succession of either major upheavals or more gradual reforms, control would shift to broader social strata.

France, Britain, and Germany represent three variations upon this general theme. Developments in France hold center stage in *The Civilizing Process,* but comparative references to Britain and Germany are frequent. In *The Germans* Elias examined a case of a state's weakening monopoly over organized force: the Weimar period, preceding the Nazis' accession to government power (see chapter 9).

The way in which the exercise of physical violence is organized, and especially the degree to which it is submitted to a central controlling agency, permeate all social relations to an extent that is not always realized. One way of testing and illustrating this insight is to look at the development of sport and other leisure pastimes. Thus, in a study of alleged antecedents of modern sport in antiquity, Elias noted that the game contests in ancient Greece and Rome were marked by a relatively high incidence of physical violence, which was, at the time, considered normal and did not appear to give rise to feelings of abhorrence or moral indignation (see chapter 10). Elias found these facts to be completely in accord with his theory of civilizing processes: "According to it, one expects that state formation and conscience formation, the level of socially permitted physical violence and the threshold of repugnance against using it or witnessing it, differ in specific ways at different stages in the development of societies" (p. 167 below).

## Established and Outsiders Relations

Elias's personal biography and his sociological theory came nowhere nearer convergence than in his propositions about established-outsiders relationships. He first presented the distinction as such in the report on an empirical study, carried out with John L. Scotson, a school teacher who was also a graduate student of sociology at Leicester. *The Established and the Outsiders,* published in 1965, would seem at first sight to belong to the genre of mainly descriptive community studies. It portrayed the strained relationships between two neighboring zones in "Winston Parva"—the fictitious name given to a working-class area on the outskirts of an industrial city in England. However, the authors claimed to have written more than just a report of empirical findings; they stressed the "paradigmatic character" of their work. Winston Parva in their view represented "a model indicating how helplessly people may be trapped in a conflict situation by specific developments." Their aim was to explore and explain the nature of this social trap.

There can be no doubt that, while Scotson collected the field data, it was Elias who did the conceptual and theoretical work.[63] The facts of the case were straightforward and yet puzzling. The two zones of Winston Parva known as the Village and the Estate were quite similar according to most conventional "objective" measures used by sociologists, such as occupation, education, and type of housing. At the same time, there were clear social barriers and marked differences in status between the zones. The Village was generally associated with higher, the Estate with lower, social status. The question was why this should be so; the key to the solution, according to Elias, was power: "As elsewhere people allowed themselves to be ranked lower than others because they could not prevent it. They had not enough power."[64]

The inquiry, then, was directed at the question of what resources of power were more readily available to the Villagers than to the residents of the Estate. The first step in the theoretical analysis was to regard the situation in Winston Parva as representing a stage in a process which occurs again and again in human society, a process in which two formerly independent groups become interdependent.[65] Seen in this light, Winston Parva was, in the real social world, an example of the imaginary case of the "primal contest" that Elias was to introduce later as a preliminary game model in *What Is Sociology?* (see chapter 7 below). The Village had been built in the last two decades of the nineteenth century; many people who lived there at the time of the investigation were descendants of the first generation of residents. The Estate was built in the 1930s, and most of its current residents had not settled there before the 1940s. These facts about Winston Parva's past had a direct bearing on its present: the history of the neighborhood was part of its structure.[66] It provided the Villagers with resources of power that the Estate residents lacked—social cohesion and a sense of superiority.

In the Village, a network of "old families" had developed, enabling its members to occupy strategic positions in local associations as well as in informal channels of communication. Throughout this network, there was a continuous exchange of gossip, which served as a source of information, amusement, and approval and disapproval (see chapter 13). Incidents of "unruly behavior" in the Estate were eagerly recounted to reinforce the impression that, whereas the Villagers excelled in good manners and decency, people in the Estate were incapable of ordering their own lives. People from the Estate, being outsiders to the gossip network, found it practically impossible to escape the stigmatizing effect of this stereotype.

In the first edition of *The Established and the Outsiders* the more general implications of the model were mentioned only in passing. Elias later added a long introduction in which he spelled out its theoretical relevance. The model enabled him to use insights from Karl Marx, Max Weber, and Sigmund Freud, and at the same time—to use a favorite phrase of Elias himself in lectures and conversation—to "go beyond" each of these authors. From Marx he borrowed the insight into the fundamental importance of power differentials in society; but he rejected the exclusive attention to the means of production as a source of power. He drew on Weber for an appreciation of the "multidimensional" character of social hierarchies, but he avoided the tradition mistakenly derived from Weber which regarded those hierarchies as if they consisted of three separate "dimensions" to be called class, status, and power. Elias turned to Freud for his insight into the importance of self-esteem and the role of fantasies in determining the sense of self; he found, however, that Freud focused too much on the individual as a self-contained unit (a *homo clausus*), and neglected the fundamental fact that "a person's we-image and we-ideal form as much part of that person's self-image and self-ideal as the image and ideal of him- or herself as the unique person to which he or she refers as 'I.'"[67]

Elias combined his critical readings of Marx, Weber, and Freud in drawing up his model of established-outsiders relationships. Established and outsiders were for him what Herbert Blumer called sensitizing concepts, pointing to the complexities of inequality actually observed within the flux of social relationships. Elias later spelled out how the model could be applied to a whole range of social inequalities—between ethnic groups, colonized and colonizing, children and adults, gays and straights, men and women, and so on.[68] He also pointed at promising connections with other conceptual and theoretical schemes. Thus, by indicating *group charisma* as a characteristic of establishments, and *group disgrace* as a characteristic of outsiders, he worked toward a synthesis of ideas from Weber and Freud, and by showing the close association between group disgrace and anomie, he made a link with the theoretical tradition of Emile Durkheim. He also indicated relations between the established-outsiders model and his own theory of the civilizing process, and in several of his later writings he applied the model to examine the monopolization of the means of orientation by religious and scientific establishments.[69]

## Knowledge and the Sciences
### Knowledge as a Source of Power

In his zeal to disclose the economic basis of power and to unmask religion and philosophy as mere ideology, Karl Marx had relegated all ideas, and by implication all knowledge, to the sphere of "superstructure." Elias regarded this as a grave and fatal error. In one of his later essays he asked his readers to imagine a "knowledgeless" group—that is, a group to which no knowledge has been transmitted from previous generations: "The idea of such a group evidently is an unrealizable thought experiment, but it demonstrates quite clearly that human groups, which certainly cannot survive without food or protection from physical violence, also cannot survive without knowledge.[70] Given the vital necessity of knowledge as a means of orientation for human beings, and given also its inherently social nature, the sociology of knowledge has to be an integral part of sociology. It has to address the development of knowledge as a long-term intra- and intergenerational process as well as the tendencies of specific groups to monopolize access to particular kinds of knowledge.

For any child growing up, the acquisition of knowledge begins with information about the child's own social world. Later in life, gossip continues to be a major source of orientation (see chapter 13). As Elias remarks, gossip always has two poles: those who gossip and those about whom they gossip.[71]

Such bipolarity is, according to Elias, characteristic of all forms of knowledge: both the knowing subject and the object known play a part. The balance between the "subjective" and the "objective" elements may, however, vary considerably. Observations about this unstable bipolar relationship form the opening gambit of one of Elias's earliest essays on the sociology of knowledge, "Problems of Involvement and Detachment" (see chapter 12). But the essay, which was later expanded into a book, is not merely concerned with the old problem of objectivity in the social sciences. Rather, it represents the first elaboration of Elias's theory of the long-term development of human knowledge and the rise of the sciences in the context of the history of humanity as a whole.

Elias's characteristic trick is to turn what have traditionally been regarded as philosophical problems into sociological questions susceptible to theoretical-empirical investigation. Beginning from Max Weber's discussion of *Wertfreiheit,* Elias immediately undermines the idea of a static polarity between objective and subjective points of view. It is rather a continuum, and he chooses the terms "involvement" and "detachment" because they do not refer to two mutually exclusive, absolute states but rather to marginal poles between which people's thoughts and actions are normally steered—through impulses and controls exerted both by themselves and by others.

Adult behavior in any society normally lies on a scale between two extremes. If it regularly goes too far in either direction, ordered social life becomes impossible. But different societies vary a good deal in their modes of thinking and feeling: "The way in which individual members of a group experience whatever affects their senses, the meaning which it has for them, depends on the standard forms of dealing with, and of thinking and speaking about, these phenomena which have gradually evolved in their society" (p. 218 below). For example, the distinction between living and inanimate objects—now taken entirely for granted by people in modern societies—took the "combined conceptual labour of many generations" to become firmly established. People can have dreams about humans being turned into trees—a fantasy represented for example in the Greek myth of Daphne—but how, at first, could they know that what happened in dreams could not happen in reality? "Magic-mythical" thinking, argues Elias, is the *primary* mode of human experience, and the boundary between fantasy and reality only gradually becomes firmer: "For small children everywhere, the difference between fantasy and reality is blurred. They learn the distinction between fantasy and reality, like other items of knowledge, in accordance with the standard reached in their society."[72] How firmly the line is drawn between dreams and reality depends on public standards within a particular human group, and these tend in industrial societies to be comparatively very firm.

Structuralist theorists like Claude Lévi-Strauss have investigated myth in the hope of discovering universal patterns of the human mind; when one adopts "the view from afar," all human beings and all societies have characteristics in common.[73] But, as one shortens the focal length of the investigative lens, it is also apparent that there have been profound differences between the knowledge, thought, and feelings of different societies, and that standards have changed and developed in the course of long-term social processes. That is not at all to say that magic-mythical thinking ceases to exist in industrial-scientific societies. Rather, as people grow up, it becomes a more or less submerged layer of the personality structure: Freud (and Jung) discovered it there and called it the "unconscious."

The controls on magic-mythical thinking have become particularly tight in science. The scientification of knowledge, as a developmental process, involves an advance in social standards of self-constraint similar to that which plays a central part in the civilizing process—the same pressures toward greater foresight and rationalization are involved. All science, Elias contends, involves a "detour via detachment"—a taking into account of longer chains of causes and consequences, and a striving for higher levels of synthesis.

Elias sees a clear connection between, on the one hand, a relatively high prevailing level of danger and low level of control which people have over the forces which affect their lives and, on the other hand, the extent to which their modes of knowledge are emotionally involved and fantasy laden. The stock of human knowledge grew demonstrably more slowly in the earlier stages of human society—the paleolithic period endured for ninety per cent of the time between the appearance of *Homo sapiens* and the present day—and this was related to the dangers people faced:

> Wholly dependent on phenomena whose course they could neither foresee nor influence to any considerable extent, they lived in extreme insecurity, and, being most vulnerable and insecure, they could not help feeling

strongly about every occurrence they thought might affect their lives; they were too deeply involved to look at natural phenomena, like distant observers, calmly. Thus, on the one hand, they had little chance of controlling their own strong feelings in relation to nature and of forming more detached concepts of natural events as long as they had little control over them; and they had, on the other hand, little chance of extending their control over non-human surroundings as long as they could not gain greater mastery over their own strong feelings in relation to them and increase their control over themselves. (P. 222 below)

If it was so difficult for earlier humans to escape the "double bind" of fears and dangers to achieve more detached knowledge of, and somewhat greater control over, the impersonal forces of nature, how much greater were the difficulties involved in understanding and to some extent mastering social forces (meaning the forces exerted by people on one another)—especially as those social forces became increasingly more complex.[74] This is one reason why—as Auguste Comte perceived in the nineteenth century—the development of the social sciences came later than that of the biological sciences, and much later than the physico-chemical ones. Elias spoke of a "triad of basic controls," comprising: (a) control over extrahuman forces ("nature"), (b) control over interpersonal or social forces, and (c) control over intrapersonal forces, meaning people's control over themselves as individuals (social-psychological controls).[75] The three forms of control are interdependent, though they do not grow in a simple, linear way. For example, advances in control over natural dangers ("technological" advances) are likely to bring with them changes in social relations (such as longer chains of interdependence, and resulting "integration conflicts"), which then become more difficult to control, leading to a further increase in people's involvement, and often passionate partisanship, which makes it even more difficult to achieve more detached and less fantasy-laden forms of knowledge.

Too often, the history of the sciences is seen in purely intellectual terms. But, Elias reminds us, it is people "in the round" who are involved in the search for knowledge, and their fears and emotions and fantasies are involved in this as much as in other areas of their lives. Elias (like Freud before him) illustrated the point by referring to the Copernican and Darwinian revolutions. Both the heliocentric model of the solar system and the evolutionary theory of speciation not only ran counter to millennia of common sense but also posed an emotional challenge to humans' elementary self-love. Speaking of the triumph of the Copernican view, Elias pointed out that it was no coincidence that it happened at the time of the Reformation, when the church's long monopoly over the means of orientation in Europe was breaking up. Nor was it by chance that Galileo was persecuted when the Counter-Reformation was attempting to reassert that monopoly. Here there is an obvious connection with Elias's discussion of the "monopoly mechanism" in state formation processes. Indeed these are not, on closer observation, two entirely separate monopolies; for the church's power rested upon its *armed* monopoly of the official interpretation of the world. Another link with the theory of civilizing processes is the part played in the rise of science by the formation of scientific societies, relatively autonomous from both state and church and exercising increasingly strict social control over what could be regarded as acceptable scientific practice and knowledge; Elias makes a further connection with his wider thinking when he refers to disciplinary communities as "scientific establishments."[76]

Galileo's experiments rolling balls down inclined planes represented a breakthrough in empirical observation and theorizing. Until about that time, it had *not* been obvious that the same general principles would apply *universally*. Thereafter, as Robert Merton, among others, pointed out, a religiously motivated interest in discovering the universal laws of God's creation was one of the driving forces among early scientists.[77] The acceptance of the ideal of the universal "covering law" as the goal of all scientific knowledge was, however, to have deleterious consequences, especially for the biological and social sciences. Elias uses his "continuum of models" (pp. 234ff below) to argue that only for understanding the loosely integrated congeries investigated by classical physics is the model of the timeless, reversible, and law-like connections appropriate.[78] Related concepts such as "independent variables," directly derived from the classical physics model, are treacherous when employed in the biological or social sciences. Influenced by his medical training, and especially by his studies in embryology, Elias always emphasized that theories in the biological sciences typically had to be framed in four dimensions—three of space, plus *time*—and processes of biological development (whether of a single organism or of a species) were generally not reversible. Theories in the social sciences, he wrote, were still more complicated. They had to be framed in *five* dimensions: the three of space, plus time and conscious *experience*. Elias regarded *The Civilizing Process* as a paradigmatic instance of just such a developmental theory in five dimensions. Unlike biological evolution, however, processes of social development may in certain circumstances be reversed.

In Elias's view, a theory of knowledge should deal equally with the development of both the most mundane (or "practical") and the most sophisticated (or "theoretical") means of orientation used by human beings. Hitherto, neither sociological nor philosophical theories of knowledge had attained this degree of inclusiveness. The model of the involvement-detachment continuum was intended to "steer the ship between the Scylla of philosophical absolutism and the Charybdis of sociological relativism."[79] Sociological theories of knowledge, from Marx through Mannheim to modern ethnomethodological and similar approaches, have paid most attention to knowledge near the more involved pole of the involvement-detachment continuum. The tradition of philosophical epistemology, on the other hand, concentrates on knowledge toward the more detached pole. The one tradition has emphasized how knowledge of reality may be distorted, the other how undistorted knowledge of reality may be attained.

Underlying both philosophical absolutism and sociological relativism, says Elias, is a shared assumption. This shared assumption and the dichotomy it implies between truth and falsehood, or between science and ideology, reduces everything that people know to two diametrically opposite states: *either* absolute dependence of knowledge on the situation of the groups where it is used or produced *or* absolute independence from it.[80] Elias rejects this shared assumption. Most scientific knowledge, he points out, has the character of "a structured flux"—a continuous adding and filtering of new insights—and, at the same time, modern ideologies have absorbed a good deal of factual sociological and economic knowledge, compared with the ideologies of earlier ages. There are no zero points of involvement and detachment—forms of knowledge have to be located along the continuum. Elias's account of the growth of scientific knowledge is broadly consistent with that given in Thomas S. Kuhn's influential *The Structure of Scientific Revolutions*, although he rejected the impression of discontinuity raised by Kuhn, for he sensed that Kuhn too was facing the abyss of relativism.[81] To a certain extent Elias's account is also consonant with more recent linguistically and culturally orientated theories such as those influenced by Michel Foucault and Bruno Latour, in that Elias emphasizes that knowledge is used for practical purposes within specific groups of people; what saved him from the pit of relativism into which such perspectives normally fall was that his was always a developmental approach: in the long term, the stock of human knowledge had grown, attained higher levels of synthesis, and could be seen to have made possible more complex forms of control over the forces of nature and society. Animism, for instance, may function perfectly well as a means of orientation at certain stages of social development, but it does not make it possible to send humans to the moon; whether sending men to the moon is a good thing and represents "progress" is beside the point—all that matters is that knowledge at a higher level of synthesis is necessary for it.

## The Critique of Homo Clausus

Elias was consistently critical of the central tradition of Western philosophy, and of the hold which it continued to have (thanks to the power of philosophers as an established group within universities) over sociologists' modes of thinking. A basic motif has run through Western philosophy since Plato, becoming more strongly emphasized since the Renaissance in classical philosophy from Descartes through Locke and Hume to Kant, and onward to Husserl and Popper. It has stamped an almost indelible mark on sociological theorizing from Weber through Parsons to the many contemporary writers influenced in one way or another by phenomenology. It is the conception of the person (in the singular) as the "subject" of knowledge, a single thinking mind inside a sealed container from which each one looks out and struggles to fish for knowledge of the "objects" outside in the "external world." Among those objects are other minds, equally locked inside their own sealed containers, and one of the most difficult questions epistemologists (and sociologists influenced by them) pose for themselves is of how one thinking subject inside its own container can ever know anything of what is being thought and what is known by those objects—those other subjects—thinking away inside their own containers in turn.

Elias labels this conception the *homo clausus,* the "We-less I" devoid of we-images shared with fellow humans (see chapter 15).[82] The counterpart to this conception of the isolated ego is the implicit notion of the "knowledgeless group," devoid of symbols and concepts handed down from previous generations. To all this, Elias counterposes his own conceptual starting point of *homines aperti* ("open people"), bonded together in various ways and degrees.

In his discussion of *homo clausus* Elias enters into some detail about the varying manifestations of this static duality between subject and object. It is always associated with a doubt that the world outside, "external reality," really exists or can be known at all. It was already to be seen in Plato's celebrated image of the prisoners in a cave, watching the shadows cast on the wall by the fire behind them. In Descartes the perception of the individual as a thinking ego isolated in his own head is captured in the famous proposition *Cogito, ergo sum;* Descartes rescues him by resort to the argument that if there is no firm evidence of an external reality, the only certainty that seems to remain is the internal reality of the individual person pondering these perplexities.

It was Kant, however, in relation to whose philosophy Elias first formulated his own position. Elias explains his objections to Kantianism along the following lines. Kant delved into his own consciousness and there discovered that concepts like substance, space, time, and cause could not possibly be based on his experience. Therefore he concluded that they must come from a frame of mind set a priori in his own brain. In other words, the form of objects as he perceived them reflected not the properties of the objects in themselves (the *Ding an sich*), but the natural or innate mental properties of the subject. Having discovered this innate frame of mind in himself, Kant very cautiously said that we may conclude that other subjects also have this a-priori frame of mind, although we can *never* be certain of that. Here he was very consistent, because once one has the idea that a frame of mind given by nature determines one's thinking, so that one can never be sure that objects really correspond to one's thinking, then one can never be sure of the existence of other subjects either—because other subjects are also then phenomena which may possibly be distorted by the pre-given structure of one's own reason.

Elias argues that this trap has continued to ensnare most philosophical epistemology since Kant. Philosophers no longer speak of a pre-given "reason," but they use "logic" or "language" in an equivalent way to denote a pre-given unchanging and eternal form behind the changing contents of knowledge with equivalent results. There is no secure foundation for knowledge, for only the thinking mind is structured; the objects of human thinking seem to stand separated from the knowing subject on a structureless swamp. Elias uses the general label "nominalism" for this assumption, which is manifested in various forms: rationalist philosophy, which starts from the assumption that the person's "ratio" is ordered, if nothing else; the linguistic variant, seen in Wittgenstein, with his idea of language games in which our thinking is caught; the deductionist variant, which starts from the assumption that all human thought has to follow pre-existing laws of "logic." This conception of one, unchanging logic of rationality, Elias remarks, gives the impression that, by means of it, the theory of relativity could as easily have been discovered by Albertus Magnus as by Albert Einstein, and he uses the successive world records in athletics for the men's 5,000 metres, since Paavo Nurmi won it in the 1920s, as an analogy for how scientific knowledge actually grows—by successive small advances over currently existing knowledge, stimulated by the pressures of social competition.[83]

There is an obvious escape route from the impasse in which transcendental philosophers have been stuck for centuries.

> That way, however, is closed to them. They cannot use it without losing their identity. They are like people enclosed in a room from which they try

to escape. They try to unlock the windows, but the windows resist. They climb up the chimney, but the chimney is blocked. Yet the door is not locked; it is open all the time. If only they knew it, they could easily leave the room. But they cannot open the door, because to do so would disagree with the rules of the game which they as philosophers have set themselves. They cannot open the door, because that would not be philosophical.[84] So what is this door of the philosophers' self-made prison? The escape is to recognize that no person's knowledge has its beginning in him- or herself. Each of us, with all our reflections, perceptions, intuitions, and experiences, stands on the shoulders of others. In order to understand the pattern of all these intellectual activities and traits as they are today, one has to retrace the long intergenerational process in the course of which they *have become* what they are. Kant, it must be remembered, like everyone else, argued with a language he had learned socially. He asked, "Where does my concept of 'cause' come from?" He was right that it did not come from his own experience: he had not learned it by himself. But he *had* learned it from his teachers. The concept of cause was there in his society. Several generations earlier it had not been. It had gone through a long process of development in society, the intergenerational transmission of symbols slowly adding to the stock of knowledge and of the categories available for use in thinking by people in society.

The crux of *homo clausus,* then, is not just that it is a *single* isolated mind, but that it is also a single, isolated *adult* mind. Once that is recognized and abandoned, the central problem of the theory of knowledge is no more problematic than how from birth onward children learn and use the symbolically transmitted fund of knowledge of all kinds, and themselves become adult minds and personalities.

What does a sociology not based on *homo clausus* look like? The alternative image of *homines aperti* is of course precisely what underlies *The Civilizing Process,* tracing as it does changes in personality structure hand-in-hand with changes in the structure of human relations in societies as parts of an overall process. *The Civilizing Process* also contains an explanation for the strength of the *homo clausus* image, why it seems so self-evidently valid to people at large. The increasing social constraint toward self-restraint, a central element in civilizing processes, does indeed strengthen each person's feeling of being a *homo clausus.* Elias does not dispute that this sense of the self inside its container looking out is very real as a mode of self-experience in modern societies. What he does question is whether it is universal and inevitable, found equally in all societies, wherever and whenever. It is no accident that this mode of self-experience became much more accentuated in Europe from the Renaissance. For it was precisely then that a major spurt of the European civilizing process occurred. And it was precisely then that Descartes gave definitive expression to the philosophers' *homo clausus;* his thought captured just this mode of self-experience. The sealed container in which we sense ourselves is clamped with the iron bands of the self-controls forged in a long-term civilizing process. It would require a further stage in that same process before the firm hold on our self-perception of the *homo clausus* image of individuals as "thinking statues" (see chapter 15) could be loosened and a more realistic view of the social nature of human knowledge become possible.

## Figurational Sociology

Two key concepts in Elias's sociology are *interdependence* and *process.* He always insisted on making the crucial distinction between interdependence and "interaction." Interactionist approaches to sociology— whether in the traditions of symbolic interactionism, of Erving Goffman, of phenomenology and ethnomethodology, or indeed of Talcott Parsons—begin implicitly or explicitly from two *homines clausi,* two isolated adult individuals, acting and reacting to each other's actions. Such theories typically then attempt, uncertainly and unsuccessfully, to build upward and outward from the dyad to interaction between larger and larger groups of people and then, still more vaguely, to larger-scale organizations, institutions, and societies.

But this is a misleading way to start thinking about society. Humans are interdependent with other humans from their moment of birth. Every human infant is highly dependent on adult humans, but they in turn are dependent on the infant, if only because they love and value it. Throughout life, we depend on others for things we need, want, or value; and others are dependent on us for things *they* need. This simple fact means that power ratios are a feature of *all* human relationships.[85] Because people are usually not equally dependent on each other, the power ratios between them are usually unequal. And power ratios change over time—not just at random, but in structured *processes.* For instance, the power ratio between children and the adults on whom they are at first overwhelmingly dependent changes in a characteristic way over their lifetimes, and by the time the parents have reached old age the power ratio has usually tilted over in the opposite direction, in favor of their offspring. Similarly, the power ratios between social classes or between states change in the course of continual power struggles—in ways of which it is unlikely that they are completely devoid of structure, even if those structures are not always clearly understood.

As a generic term to denote the protean variety of social formations—

large and small, from the most durable to the most ephemeral—of interdependent individuals Elias adopted the word *figuration*. Among his reasons for selecting this particular expression was that its more open and more dynamic connotations made it a suitable alternative to "system"—the central concept in Parsons's once-dominant sociological theory. Elias explained what he meant by figurations through an analogy with dances:

> One should think of a mazurka, a minuet, a polonaise, a tango, or rock 'n'roll. The image of the mobile figurations of interdependent people on a dance floor perhaps makes it easier to imagine states, cities, families, and also capitalist, communist, and feudal systems as figurations. By using this concept, we can eliminate the antithesis, resting finally on different values and ideals, immanent today in the use of the words "individual" and "society." One can certainly speak of a dance in general, but no-one will imagine a dance as a structure outside the individual or as a mere abstraction. The same dance figurations can certainly be danced by different people; but without a plurality of reciprocally orientated and dependent individuals, there is no dance. Like every other social figuration, a dance figuration is relatively independent of the specific individuals forming it here and now, but not of individuals as such. It would be absurd to say that dances are mental constructions abstracted from observations of individuals considered separately. The same applies to all other figurations. Just as small dance figurations change—becoming now slower, now quicker—so too, gradually or more suddenly, do the large figurations we call societies.[86]

Elias argued that there was a need for new means of speaking and thinking, which would actually simplify the work of sociologists: "The complexity of many modern sociological theories is due not to the complexity of the field of investigation which they seek to elucidate, but to the kind of concepts employed. These may be concepts which either have proved their worth in other (usually physical) sciences, or are treated as self-evident in everyday usage, but which are not at all appropriate to the investigation of specifically social functional nexuses."[87]

At the heart of Elias's critique of sociological categories and conceptualization is his notion of "process reduction," by which he means the pervasive tendency to reduce processes conceptually to states.[88] It is seen as much in everyday language as in the specialized discourses of the sciences: "We say, 'The wind is blowing,' as if the wind were actually a thing at rest which, at a given point in time, begins to move and blow. We speak as if the wind were separate from its blowing, as if a wind could exist which did not blow."[89] This tendency is very widespread in the languages Benjamin Lee Whorf called "Standard Average European,"

38 Introduction

which most commonly assimilate the experience of change and process
through sentences made up of a noun or substantive, apparently referring to a thing at rest, and a verb to indicate that it then moves or
changes.[90] This tendency was already hardening in antiquity, and was
reinforced by Aristotelian logicians and grammarians. The grammatical
pressure makes it difficult to escape this mode of thinking, whether in
everyday speech or in the sciences.

In sociology, the pressure toward process reduction is seen in taken-
for-granted concepts such as the "actor" as distinct from his or her activity, or "structures" as distinct from "processes," or "objects" as
distinct from relationships. This is a special handicap when studying figurations of interdependent people. We too often speak and think as if the
objects of our thought—including people—were both static and unin-
volved in relationships. Concepts of this kind appear to refer to separate,
motionless objects, but on closer scrutiny they actually refer to people in
the plural, who are now or were in the past constantly in movement and
constantly relating to other people. Above all, at the very center of problems of sociological thinking, the concepts of the "individual" and of
"society" have this same quality of seeming to refer to static and isolated
objects.

> Consequently we always feel impelled to make quite senseless conceptual
> distinctions, like "the individual and society," which makes it seem that
> "the individual" and "society" were two separate things, like tables and
> chairs or pots and pans. One can find oneself caught up in long discussions
> of the nature of the relationship between these two apparently separate
> objects. Yet on another level of awareness one may know perfectly well
> that societies are composed of individuals, and that individuals can only
> possess specifically human characteristics such as their abilities to speak,
> think, and live, in and through their relationships with other people—"in
> society."[91]

This is why Elias, in his own writing, always tried to use process concepts
and ways of thinking. When he wrote about civilization, he meant civil*ization,* though the pressure of convention incessantly tends to reduce
the process to a fixed state in everyday speech. Sometimes his struggle to
avoid process reduction leads him to use awkward-sounding neologisms
like "courtization," "scientification," and "sportization." This can be
off-putting and inelegant in English, but, even so, it is part of Elias's serious purpose.

Elias's approach came to be known as figurational sociology, though
he was not keen on the term; for one thing, even the word *figuration* can
be subject to process-reducing pressures and come to be used in as static

a way as *system* once was. Elias came to prefer to call himself a process sociologist. Whatever it is called, we can finally identify four interrelated principles underlying his work:

1. Sociology is about people in the plural—human beings who are interdependent with each other in a variety of ways, and whose lives evolve in and are significantly shaped by the social figurations they form together.
2. These figurations are continually in flux, undergoing changes of many kinds—some rapid and ephemeral, others slower but perhaps more lasting.
3. The long-term developments taking place in human figurations have been and continue to be largely unplanned and unforeseen.
4. The development of human knowledge takes place within human figurations, and is one important aspect of their overall development.[92]

These principles are deceptively simple, and most sociologists would be prepared to agree with them, but they are more difficult to practice consistently in sociological research and writing.

Elias always denied that he wished to form a distinct school in sociology. For he was at once both less and more ambitious than the charge suggests. Less, because he had no wish to lay down a fixed set of doctrines of the type, often based on some philosophical stance, which underlie most theoretical "perspectives" in sociology. He wanted, rather, to encourage people to pursue through further research some of the problems of humans' life together to which he drew attention; in this modest ambition of initiating a research tradition he had some belated success. On the other hand, he also had a far greater ambition. He believed he had diagnosed many of the faults which beset the social sciences throughout his long lifetime, and he wanted his insights to find acceptance by social scientists in general. The excerpts from his writings presented in this volume are therefore designed not to stake out yet another "approach" in sociology, but to show the interest and value of Elias's ideas to the discipline as a whole.

## A Note on the Selections

The selections from Elias's work are being republished here with only minor changes and corrections, which we have made silently. Where the text is not complete, the omission of passages is marked with an ellipsis. Elias's original section numbering, where he employs it, has been retained. We have omitted some of Elias's notes, mainly where they were of a purely bibliographical character, and where necessary we have renumbered the notes that we retained.

# Notes

1. See H. S. Hughes, *The Sea-Change: The Migration of Social Thought, 1930–1965* (New York: Harper & Row, 1975).
2. Elias, *Reflections on a Life* (Oxford: Polity Press, 1994), pp. 10–11.
3. Ibid., pp. 26–27.
4. From a personal letter quoted in Johan Goudsblom, "Responses to Norbert Elias's Work in England, Germany, the Netherlands and France," Peter R. Gleichmann, Johan Goudsblom, and Hermann Korte, eds., *Human Figurations: Essays for / Aufsätze für Norbert Elias* (Amsterdam: Stichting Amsterdams Sociologisch Tijdschrift 1977), pp. 37–98.
5. Talcott Parsons, *Social Systems and the Evolution of Action Theory* (New York: Free Press, 1977), p. 164, and many other places throughout Parsons's work. Elias criticized Parsons on this score in his introduction to the second edition of *The Civilizing Process* (written in 1969), pp. 185–88. (All references to *The Civilizing Process* are to the one-volume edition [Oxford: Basil Blackwell, 1994].)
6. Elias, *Reflections*, p. 88.
7. Norbert Elias, in personal conversation with Stephen Mennell, 1987. See also Parsons, *Social Systems*, pp. 23–25.
8. See Max Weber's account of the German academic profession, in "Science as Vocation," in Hans Gerth and C. Wright Mills, eds., *From Max Weber* (New York: Oxford University Press, 1946), pp. 12–56.
9. Elias (*Reflections*, p. 98) traced his inspiration for this topic to the work of Leonardo Olschki (*Geschichte der neusprachlichen wissenschaftlichen Literatur*. Bd. 1: *Die Literatur der Technik und der angewandten Wissenschaften vom Mittelalter bis zur Renaissance* [Heidelberg: Carl Winter, 1918]; Bd. 2: *Bildung und Wissenschaft in Zeitalter der Renaissance in Italien* [Florenz: L. S. Olschkis Verlag, 1922]; Bd. 3: *Galilei und seine Zeit* [Halle: M. Niemeyer, 1924].) Olschki also became a refugee from Hitler, but his fate was to become one of those who fell into complete obscurity.
10. Elias, *Reflections*, p. 88.
11. Alfred Weber, *Kulturgeschichte als Kultursoziologie* (Leiden: Sijthoff, 1935).
12. Karl Mannheim, *Ideology and Utopia,* trans. Louis Wirth and Edward Shils (London: Routledge & Kegan Paul, 1936; the original, substantially different German version was published in 1929); "Conservative Thought" (first published in German in 1927), in Mannheim, *Essays on Sociology and Social Psychology* (London: Routledge & Kegan Paul, 1953), pp. 74–164.
13. Elias, *What Is Sociology?* (New York: Columbia University Press, 1978), pp. 122–28.
14. Elias, *Reflections*, p. 109.
15. Ibid., p. 106.
16. Richard Kilminster has argued that there are signs of Elias's influence in Mannheim's work as well as vice versa, although it is a difficult case to prove, because Elias published almost nothing during the years of his closest association with Mannheim. For his part, Mannheim included Elias's unpublished *Habilitationsschrift* in bibliographical notes, but never referred to Elias's work in his own writings. On the intellectual connections between Elias and Mannheim overall, see Kilminster, "Norbert Elias and Karl Mannheim: Closeness and Distance," *Theory, Culture and Society* 10, no. 3 (1993): 81–114.
17. "Die Bedeutung der Konkurrenz im Gebiete des Geistigen," published in English translation as "Competition as a Cultural Phenomenon," in Karl Mannheim, *Essays on the Sociology of Knowledge,* trans. Paul Kecskemeti (London: Routledge & Kegan Paul, 1952), pp. 191–229.

18. Elias's contribution to the discussion on Karl Mannheim's essay "Die Bedeutung der Konkurrenz im Gebiete des Geistigen," in *Verhandlungen des 6. Deutschen Soziologentages vom 17.–19.9.1928 in Zürich*, Tübingen, s.110–11. (Substantial excerpts of Elias's remarks have been published in English translation in Volker Meja and Nico Stehr, eds., *Knowledge and Politics: The Sociology of Knowledge Dispute* [London: Routledge, 1990].)

19. Max Horkheimer and Theodor W. Adorno, *Dialectic of Enlightenment*, trans. John Cumming (London: New Left Review Editions, 1974; originally published in German in 1947).

20. Artur Bogner, "Elias and the Frankfurt School," *Theory, Culture and Society*, 4, nos. 2–3 (1987): 249–85.

21. See Jörg Hackeschmidt, "Norbert Elias—Zionist and 'Bündisch' Activist," in *Figurations: Newsletter of the Norbert Elias Foundation*, no. 3 (June 1995): 4–5, and his book *Von Kurt Blumenfeld zu Norbert Elias oder Die Erfindung einer jüdischen Nation* (Hamburg: Europäische Verlaganstalt, 1997).

22. Elias, *Reflections*, p. 43, and his book *Von Kurt Blumenfeld zu Norbert Elias oder Die Erfindung einer jüdischen Nation* (Hamburg: Europäische Verlaganstalt, 1997).

23. See Elias, *What Is Sociology?*, esp. chap. 2, "The Sociologist as a Destroyer of Myths."

24. Norbert Elias and John L. Scotson, *The Established and the Outsiders*, 2d ed. (London: Sage, 1994; 1st ed. published by Frank Cass [London, 1965]). Only very much later, in *The Germans*, and most explicitly in *Reflections* (pp. 121–30), did Elias write directly about the Jews as an outsider group.

25. See Johan Goudsblom, "Responses to Norbert Elias's Work in Germany, England, the Netherlands and France," in Gleichmann, Goudsblom, and Korte, eds., *Human Figurations*, pp. 37–97. Some early responses to Elias's work came to light subsequently and are not mentioned in the 1977 article. These include a review of *The Civilizing Process* by the French sociologist Raymond Aron and extensive references to it by the historians Charles and Mary Beard, Arnold Toynbee, and Ernst H. Gombrich. See Johan Goudsblom, "Aufnahme und Kritik der Arbeiten von Norbert Elias: kurze Ergänzung der Rezeptionsgeschichte," in Peter Gleichmann, Johan Goudsblom, and Hermann Korte, eds., *Macht und Zivilisation: Materialien zu Norbert Elias' Zivilisationstheorie* (Frankfurt: Suhrkamp, 1984), 2:305–11. See also below, n. 42.

26. Eric R. Wolf, "Encounter with Norbert Elias," in Gleichmann, Goudsblom and Korte, eds., *Human Figurations*, pp. 28–35.

27. See Elias, "Sociology and Psychiatry," in S. H. Foulkes and G. Stewart Prince, eds., *Psychiatry in a Changing Society* (London: Tavistock Publications, 1969), pp. 117–44.

28. See Richard Brown, "Norbert Elias in Leicester: Some Recollections," *Theory, Culture and Society*, 4, nos. 2–3 (1987): 533–39. The importance of the Leicester department in the development of British sociology is emphasized by John Eldridge in "Sociology in Britain: A Going Concern," in Christopher G. A. Bryant and Henk A. Becker, eds., *What Has Sociology Achieved?* (London: Macmillan, 1990), pp. 157–78. See also below, n. 63.

29. See Eric Dunning's critique of Giddens in "Comments on Elias's 'Scenes from the Life of a Knight,'" *Theory, Culture and Society*, 4, nos. 2–3 (1987): 366–71; and Richard Kilminster, "Structuration Theory as a World-View," in C. G. A. Bryant and David Jary, eds., *Giddens's Theory of Structuration: A Critical Appreciation* (London: Routledge, 1991), pp. 25–55.

30. See the earlier volume in the Heritage of Sociology series, Phillip Abrams, ed., *The Origins of British Sociology, 1834–1914* (Chicago: University of Chicago Press, 1968).

31. K. R. Popper, *The Open Society and Its Enemies*, 2 vols. (London: Routledge &

Kegan Paul, 1945), and *The Poverty of Historicism* (London: Routledge & Kegan Paul, 1957). See Elias, "Das Credo eines Metaphysikers: Kommentare zu Poppers *Logik der Forschung,*" *Zeitschrift für Soziologie,* 14, no. 2 (1985): 93–114. Cf. Eric Dunning, "In Defence of Developmental Sociology: A Critique of Popper's *Poverty of Historicism,* with Special Reference to the Theory of Auguste Comte,*" Amsterdams Sociologisch Tijdschrift* 4, no. 3 (1977): 327–49.

32. Elias, "The Retreat of Sociologists into the Present," *Theory, Culture and Society* 4, nos. 2–3 (1987): 223–47. Late in his career, in *Societies: Evolutionary and Comparative Perspectives,* and *The System of Modern Societies* (Englewood Cliffs, NJ: Prentice-Hall, 1966 and 1971), Parsons himself resuscitated a version of social evolutionism, although arguably he still adhered to the view that "a theory of the processes of change of social systems as systems . . . logically presupposes a theory of social structure" (*The Social System* [Glencoe, IL: Free Press, 1951]), p. 480.

33. Among the books Elias referred to in his own writings were Julian Huxley, *The Uniqueness of Man* (London: Chatto & Windus, 1941), C. H. Waddington, *The Strategy of the Genes* (London: Allen & Unwin, 1957), and James B. Watson, *The Double Helix* (New York: Athenaeum, 1968). Modern biological evolutionism has more recently found an eloquent advocate in Richard Dawkins, among whose books *The Blind Watchmaker* (London: Longman, 1986) would be notably consonant with Elias's views were it not for the startling fact that Dawkins allows for the sciences only of living and of nonliving matter.

34. Elias, "Reflections on the Great Evolution," in *Involvement and Detachment* (Oxford: Blackwell, 1987), pp. 121–78; and *What Is Sociology?* chap. 6, "The Problem of the Inevitability of Social Development," pp. 158–74.

35. Elias, "Studies in the Genesis of the Naval Profession," *British Journal of Sociology* 1, no. 4 (1950): 291–309.

36. Elias, Introduction to Elias and Dunning, *Quest for Excitement* (Oxford: Blackwell, 1986), pp. 26–40.

37. Elias, "Excursus on Some Differences in the Paths of Development of England, France and Germany," pp. 339–44, in *The Civilizing Process* (Oxford: Blackwell, 1994).

38. Elias, *The Germans: Power Struggles and the Development of Habitus in the Nineteenth and Twentieth Centuries* (Oxford: Polity Press, 1996).

39. Elias and Dunning, *Quest.*

40. N. Elias and J. L. Scotson, *The Established and the Outsiders* (London: Frank Cass, 1965; 2d ed. with additional material, London: Sage, 1994.) See also n. 63 below.

41. See Willem Kranendonk, ed., *Society as Process: A Bibliography of Figurational Sociology in the Netherlands* (Amsterdam: Publicatiereeks Sociologisch Instituut, 1990).

42. Alan Sica, "Sociogenesis versus Psychogenesis: The Unique Sociology of Norbert Elias," *Mid-American Review of Sociology* 9, no. 1 (1984): 49–78; Thomas J. Scheff, *Bloody Revenge: Emotions, Nationalism and War* (Boulder, CO: Westview Press, 1994). Many years earlier, the great American historians Charles and Mary Beard had been among the scattered few readers of the original German edition of *Über den Prozess der Zivilisation.* Their book *The American Spirit* (New York, Macmillan 1942), the fourth and final volume of their work *The Rise of American Civilization,* contains an extensive discussion of Elias's ideas; see esp. p. 58. A sign of growing recognition of Elias in American sociology is the section devoted to his figurational sociology in the fourth edition of George Ritzer, *Modern Sociological Theory* (New York: McGraw-Hill, 1996), pp. 375–89.

43. See John Rundell and Stephen Mennell, eds., *Civilization and Culture: Classical and Critical Readings* (London: Routledge, forthcoming 1998).

44. See p. 287 below. "Habitus" was used in the original German text of *The Civilizing Process,* but translated into English as "personality makeup"; in recent years, it has been used as a technical term by Pierre Bourdieu, who has paid tribute to Elias's general intellectual influence, although he probably adopted the concept quite independently of Elias. See also p. 54 below.

45. Max Weber, *Economy and Society,* 2 vols. (Berkeley: University of California Press, 1978; original German ed., 1922).

46. Elias, *Civilizing Process,* pp. 273–334.

47. Norbert Elias, *The Germans* (Oxford: Polity Press, 1996), p. 461n. Elias makes this statement, "somewhat bluntly" as he admits, "as a deliberate challenge to Konrad Lorenz and other researchers who attribute to humans an instinct of aggression analogous to the sexual drive."

48. It is still quite common for the word "civilization" to be used only in connection with societies which, after the adoption of agriculture, developed cities. Elias, on the contrary, used it also in relation to pre-agrarian human groups such as hunter-gatherer and pastoral tribal societies. See also Johan Goudsblom, *Fire and Civilization* (London: Penguin Books, 1992), pp. 3–6.

49. Elias, *Time: An Essay* (Oxford: Blackwell, 1992).

50. Tocqueville cites Mme. de Sévigné's jocular comments on people being broken on the wheel after the tax riots in Rennes in 1675 as an instance of the lack of feeling of members of one social class for the sufferings of members of another, and speaks of the subsequent "softening of manners as social conditions become more equal" (*Democracy in America* [New York: Schocken, 1961], Pt. 2, Bk. 3, Chap. 1). Quoted in John Stone and Stephen Mennell, eds., *Alexis de Tocqueville on Democracy, Revolution and Society.* (Chicago: University of Chicago Press, 1980), pp. 102–6.

51. Elias, *The Germans,* p. 26.

52. Elias, *Civilizing Process,* p. 480.

53. Elias, *Court Society,* p. 92.

54. Elias, *Civilizing Process,* p. 95.

55. Ibid., p. 253n.

56. Stephen Mennell, "Decivilizing Processes: Theoretical Significance and Some Lines for Research," *International Sociology* 5, no. 2 (1990): 205–23.

57. For a summary of the debate on this issue, in which the work of Cas Wouters is particularly important, see Stephen Mennell, *Norbert Elias: An Introduction* (Oxford: Blackwell, 1992), pp. 241–46. Elias responded to the debate in one of his last essays, "Changes in European Standards of Behaviour in the Twentieth Century," in *The Germans,* pp. 23–43.

58. It has been suggested that it was during the Weimar period, rather than under the Nazi regime, that decivilizing forces were most clearly dominant. See Jonathan Fletcher, "Towards a Theory of Decivilizing Processes," *Amsterdams Sociologisch Tijdschrift* 22, no. 2 (1995): 283–96.

59. Elias, *The Germans,* p. 303. The idea that "rationalization," precisely in Elias's sense, played its part in facilitating the organization of the mass killings is a key point made by Zygmunt Bauman in his *Modernity and the Holocaust* (Oxford: Polity Press, 1989).

60. Robert K. Merton, "The Unanticipated Consequences of Purposive Social Action," *American Sociological Review* 1, no. 6 (1936): 894–904. For a fuller comparison of Merton's and Elias's views of unintended consequences, see Stephen Mennell, "'Individual' Action and Its 'Social' Consequences in the Work of Elias," in Gleichmann, Gouldsblom, and Korte, eds., *Human Figurations,* pp. 99–109.

61. Johan Goudsblom, *Sociology in the Balance* (Oxford: Blackwell 1977), p. 149.

62. In *The Formation of National States in Western Europe* (Princeton, Princeton University Press, 1975), Tilly used the terms "state building" and "state making" with more overtly voluntaristic connotations than "state formation"—his preferred term in *Coercion, Capital and European States,* AD *990–1990* Cambridge, MA: Basil Blackwell, 1990). In their first publications on state formation, neither Tilly nor Perry Anderson referred to Elias.

63. In 1975, Scotson wrote a brief introduction to sociology (*Introducing Society: A Basic Introduction to Sociology* [London: Routledge & Kegan Paul, 1975]). In that text he did not mention Elias—a sad but typical reflection of the low esteem in which his work was held by British sociologists at the time. He was not considered to have made any significant theoretical contributions—not even by one of his closest collaborators.

64. Elias and Scotson, *The Established and the Outsiders* (1965), p. 40.

65. Ibid., p. 17.

66. Ibid., p. 21.

67. Ibid., p. xliii.

68. See the introduction to the 1974 Dutch translation, finally published in English in the 1994, second edition of *The Established and the Outsiders,* pp. xv–lii.

69. See, e.g., Elias and Scotson, *The Established and the Outsiders,* pp. 122, 152 ff.

70. Elias, "The Retreat of Sociologists into the Present," *Theory, Culture and Society* 4 (1987): 230.

71. Elias and Scotson, *The Established and the Outsiders,* p. 101.

72. Elias, "The Fisherman in the Maelstrom," in *Involvement and Detachment* (Oxford: Blackwell, 1987), p. 56.

73. See, e.g., Claude Lévi-Strauss, *Structural Anthropology,* trans. Claire Jacobson and Brooke Grundfest Schoepf (New York: Basic Books, 1963); *The Savage Mind* (London: Weidenfeld & Nicolson, 1968).

74. "Double bind" was a favorite expression of Elias's in his late works; it is not clear whether he directly borrowed it from Gregory Bateson.

75. Elias, *What Is Sociology?* (New York: Columbia University Press, 1978), pp. 156–67.

76. Elias, "Scientific Establishments," in N. Elias, R. Whitley, and H. G. Martins, eds., *Scientific Establishments and Hierarchies* (Dordrecht: Reidel, 1982), pp. 1–69.

77. R. K. Merton, *Science, Technology and Society in Seventeenth-Century England* (New York: Humanities Press, [1938] 1978).

78. The classical model is now outdated even as a representation of the kind of connections investigated by modern physicists; Elias was well aware of the changes which have stemmed from modern cosmology and field theory. See "Reflections on the Great Evolution: Two Fragments," in *Involvement and Detachment,* pp. 119–78.

79. Elias, "Sociology of Knowledge: New Perspectives," *Sociology* 5, no. 2 (1971): 149–68, and 5, no. 3 (1971): 355–70, at p. 258.

80. Ibid., p. 364.

81. Thomas S. Kuhn, *The Structure of Scientific Revolutions* (Chicago: University of Chicago Press, 1962); cf. Elias, "Theory of Science and History of Science: Comments on a Recent Discussion," *Economy and Society* 1, no. 2 (1972): 117–33.

82. Elias, *The Society of Individuals* (Oxford: Blackwell, 1991), p. 200.

83. Elias, "Sociology of Knowledge," p. 365; "Zur Grundlegung einer Theorie sozialer Prozese," *Zeitschrift für Soziologie* 6, no. 2 (1977): 127–49.

84. Elias, "Scientific Establishments," p. 15.

85. Elias often used "power balance" or "balance of power" as alternatives to "power ratio." It has been found, however, that the word "balance" is often misunderstood as imply-

ing equal interdependence; but Elias, on the contrary, meant to indicate labile, generally unequal tension balances, tilting one way and then the other. "Ratio" is a less-ambiguous word.
86. Elias, *The Civilizing Process*, p. 214.
87. Elias, *What Is Sociology?* p. 111.
88. The German word is *Zustandreduktion*—literally "state reduction." After prolonged discussion between Stephen Mennell and Elias, it was translated as "process reduction," because it is not states which are reduced, but processes that are reduced to
states.
89. Elias, *What Is Sociology?* p. 112.
90. Benjamin Lee Whorf, *Language, Thought and Reality* (Cambridge, MA: MIT
Press, 1956).
91. Elias, *What Is Sociology?* p. 113.
92. For further details, see Goudsblom, *Sociology in the Balance*, pp. 6–8.

# I

CIVILIZATION

# 1

# The Social Constraint towards Self-Constraint

The observer of the civilizing process finds himself confronted by a whole tangle of problems. To mention a few of the most important at the outset, there is, first of all, the most general question . . . . The civilizing process is a change of human conduct and sentiment in a quite specific direction. But, obviously, individual people did not at some past time intend this change, this "civilization", and gradually realize it by conscious, "rational", purposive measures. Clearly, "civilization" is not, any more than rationalization, a product of human "ratio" or the result of calculated long-term planning. How would it be conceivable that gradual "rationalization" could be founded on pre-existing "rational" behaviour and planning over centuries? Could one really imagine that the civilizing process had been set in motion by people with that long-term perspective, that specific mastery of all short-term affects, considering that this type of long-term perspective and self-mastery already presuppose a long civilizing process?

In fact, nothing in history indicates that this change was brought about "rationally", through any purposive education of individual people or groups. It happened by and large unplanned; but it did not happen, nevertheless, without a specific type of order. It has been shown in detail above how constraints through others from a variety of angles are converted into self-restraints, how the more animalic human activities are progressively thrust behind the scenes of men's communal social life and invested with feelings of shame, how the regulation of the whole instinctual and affective life by steady self-control becomes more and more stable, more even and more all-embracing. All this certainly does not spring from a rational idea conceived centuries ago by individual people and then implanted in one generation after another as the purpose of action and the desired state, until it was fully realized in the "centuries of progress". And yet, though not planned and intended, this transformation is not merely a sequence of unstructured and chaotic changes.

From *The Civilizing Process* (one-vol. ed., 1994), pp. 443–56

What poses itself here with regard to the civilizing process is nothing other than the general problem of historical change. Taken as a whole this change is not "rationally" planned; but neither is it a random coming and going of orderless patterns. How is this possible? How does it happen at all that formations arise in the human world that no single human being has intended, and which yet are anything but cloud formations without stability or structure?

The present study, and particularly those parts of it devoted to the problems of social dynamics, attempts to provide an answer to these questions. It is simple enough: plans and actions, the emotional and rational impulses of individual people, constantly interweave in a friendly or hostile way. *This basic tissue resulting from many single plans and actions of men can give rise to changes and patterns that no individual person has planned or created. From this interdependence of people arises an order sui generis, an order more compelling and stronger than the will and reason of the individual people composing it.*[1] It is this order of interweaving human impulses and strivings, this social order, which determines the course of historical change; it underlies the civilizing process.

This order is neither "rational"—if by "rational" we mean that it has resulted intentionally from the purposive deliberation of individual people; nor "irrational"—if by "irrational" we mean that it has arisen in an incomprehensible way. It has occasionally been identified with the order of "Nature"; it was interpreted by Hegel and some others as a kind of supra-individual "Spirit", and his concept of a "cunning of reason" shows how much he too was preoccupied by the fact that all the planning and actions of people give rise to many things that no one actually intended. But the mental habits which tend to bind us to opposites such as "rational" and "irrational", or "spirit" and "nature", prove inadequate here. In this respect, too, reality is not constructed quite as the conceptual apparatus of a particular standard would have us believe, whatever valuable services it may have performed in its time as a compass to guide us through an unknown world. *The immanent regularities of social figurations are identical neither with regularities of the "mind", of individual reasoning, nor with regularities of what we call "nature", even though functionally all these different dimensions of reality are indissolubly linked to each other.* On its own, however, this general statement about the relative autonomy of social figurations is of little help in their understanding; it remains empty and ambiguous, unless the actual dynamics of social interweaving are directly illustrated by reference to specific and empirically demonstrable changes. Precisely this was one of the tasks to which Part One of this volume was devoted. It was attempted there to show what kind of interweaving, of mutual dependence between people, sets in motion, for example, processes of feudalization. It was shown how the compulsion of competitive situations drove a number of feudal lords into conflict, how the circle of competitors was slowly narrowed, and how this led to the monopoly of one and finally—in conjunction with other mechanisms of integration such as processes of increasing capital formation and functional differentiation—to the formation of an absolutist state. This whole reorganization of human relationships went hand in hand with corresponding changes in men's manners, in their personality structure, the provisional result of which is our form of "civilized" conduct and sentiment. The connection between these specific changes in the structure of human relations and the corresponding changes in the structure of the personality will be discussed again shortly. But consideration of these mechanisms of integration is also relevant in a more general way to an understanding of the civilizing process. Only if we see the compelling force with which a particular social structure, a particular form of social intertwining, veers through its tensions to a specific change and so to other forms of intertwining,[2] can we understand how those changes arise in human mentality, in the patterning of the malleable psychological apparatus, which can be observed over and again in human history from earliest times to the present. And only then, therefore, can we understand that the psychological change involved by civilization is subject to a quite specific order and direction, although it was not planned by individual people or produced by "reasonable", purposive measures. Civilization is not "reasonable"; not "rational",[3] any more than it is "irrational". It is set in motion blindly, and kept in motion by the autonomous dynamics of a web of relationships, by specific changes in the way people are bound to live together. But it is by no means impossible that we can make out of it something more "reasonable", something that functions better in terms of our needs and purposes. For it is precisely in conjunction with the civilizing process that the blind dynamics of men intertwining in their deeds and aims gradually leads towards greater scope for planned intervention into both the social and individual structures—intervention based on a growing knowledge of the unplanned dynamics of these structures.

But which specific changes in the way people are bonded to each other mould their personality in a "civilizing" manner? The most general answer to this question too, an answer based on what was said earlier about the changes in Western society, is very simple. From the earliest period of the history of the Occident to the present, social functions have become more and more differentiated under the pressure of competition. The more differentiated they become, the larger grows the number of functions and thus of people on whom the individual constantly depends in all his actions, from the simplest and most commonplace to the more complex and uncommon. As more and more people must attune their conduct to that of others, the web of actions must be organized more and more strictly and accurately, if each individual action is to fulfil its social function. The individual is compelled to regulate his conduct in an increasingly differentiated, more even and more stable manner. That this involves not only a conscious regulation has already been stressed. Precisely this is characteristic of the psychological changes in the course of civilization: the more complex and stable control of conduct is increasingly instilled in the individual from his earliest years as an automatism, a self-compulsion that he cannot resist even if he consciously wishes to. The web of actions grows so complex and extensive, the effort required to behave "correctly" within it becomes so great, that beside the individual's conscious self-control an automatic, blindly functioning apparatus of self-control is firmly established. This seeks to prevent offences to socially acceptable behaviour by a wall of deep-rooted fears, but, just because it operates blindly and by habit, it frequently indirectly produces such collisions with social reality. But whether consciously or unconsciously, the direction of this transformation of conduct in the form of an increasingly differentiated regulation of impulses is determined by the direction of the process of social differentiation, by the progressive division of functions and the growth of the interdependency chains into which, directly or indirectly, every impulse, every move of an individual becomes integrated.

A simple way of picturing the difference between the integration of the individual within a complex society and within a less complex one is to think of their different road systems. These are in a sense spatial functions of a social integration which, in its totality, cannot be expressed merely in terms of concepts derived from the four-dimensional continuum. One should think of the country roads of a simple warrior society with a barter economy, uneven, unmetalled, exposed to damage from wind and rain. With few exceptions, there is very little traffic; the main danger which man here represents for other men is an attack by soldiers or thieves. When people look around them, scanning the trees and hills or the road itself, they do so primarily because they must always be prepared for armed attack, and only secondarily because they have to avoid collision. Life on the main roads of this society demands a constant readiness to fight, and free play of the emotions in defence of one's life or possessions from physical attack. Traffic on the main roads of a big city in the complex society of our time demands a quite different moulding of the psychological apparatus. Here the danger of physical attack is minimal. Cars are rushing in all directions; pedestrians and cyclists are trying to thread their way through the *mêlée* of cars; policemen stand at the main crossroads to regulate the traffic with varying success. But this external control is founded on the assumption that every individual is himself regulating his behaviour with the utmost exactitude in accordance with the necessities of this network. The chief danger that people here represent for others results from someone in this bustle losing his self-control. A constant and highly differentiated regulation of one's own behaviour is needed for the individual to steer his way through traffic. If the strain of such constant self-control becomes too much for an individual, this is enough to put himself and others in mortal danger.

This is, of course, only an image. The tissue of chains of action into which each individual acts within this complex society is woven is far more intricate, and the self-control to which he is accustomed from infancy far more deeply rooted, than this example shows. But at least it gives an impression of how the great formative pressure on the make-up of "civilized" man, his constant and differentiated self-constraint, is connected to the growing differentiation and stabilizing of social functions and the growing multiplicity and variety of activities that continuously have to be attuned to each other.

The pattern of self-constraints, the template by which drives are moulded, certainly varies widely according to the function and position of the individual within this network, and there are even today in different sectors of the Western world variations of intensity and stability in the apparatus of self-constraint that seem at face value very large. At this point a multitude of particular questions are raised, and the sociogenetic method may give access to their answers. But when compared to the psychological make-up of people in less complex societies, these differences and degrees within more complex societies become less significant, and the main line of transformation, which is the primary concern of this study, emerges very clearly: as the social fabric grows more intricate, the sociogenetic apparatus of individual self-control also becomes more differentiated, more all-round and more stable.

But the advancing differentiation of social functions is only the first, most general of the social transformations which we observe in enquiring into the change in psychological make-up known as "civilization". Hand in hand with this advancing division of functions goes a total reorganization of the social fabric. It was shown in detail earlier why, when the division of functions is low, the central organs of societies of a certain size are relatively unstable and liable to disintegration. It has been shown how, through specific figurational pressures, centrifugal tendencies, the mechanisms of feudalization, are slowly neutralized and how, step by step, a more stable central organization, a firmer monopolization of physical force, are established. The peculiar stability of the apparatus of mental self-restraint which emerges as a decisive trait built into the habits of every "civilized" human being stands in the closest relationship to the monopolization of physical force and the growing stability of the central organs of society. Only with the formation of this kind of relatively stable monopolies do societies acquire those characteristics as a result of which the individuals forming them get attuned, from infancy, to a highly regulated and differentiated pattern of self-restraint; only in conjunction with these monopolies does this kind of self-restraint require a higher degree of automaticity, does it become, as it were, "second nature".

When a monopoly of force is formed, pacified social spaces are created which are normally free from acts of violence. The pressures acting on individual people within them are of a different kind than previously. Forms of non-physical violence that had always existed, but had hitherto always been mingled or fused with physical force, are now separated from the latter; they persist in a changed form internally within the more pacified societies. They are most visible so far as the standard thinking of our time is concerned as types of economic violence. In reality, however, there is a whole set of means whose monopolization can enable men as groups or as individuals to enforce their will upon others. The monopolization of the means of production, of "economic" means, is only one of those which stand out in fuller relief when the means of physical violence become monopolized, when, in other words, in a more pacified state society the free use of physical force by those who are physically stronger is no longer possible.

In general, the direction in which the behaviour and the affective make-up of people change when the structure of human relationships is transformed in the manner described, is as follows: societies without a stable monopoly of force are always societies in which the division of functions is relatively slight and the chains of action binding individuals together are comparatively short. Conversely, societies with more stable monopolies of force, always first embodied in a large princely or royal court, are societies in which the division of functions is more or less advanced, in which the chains of action binding individuals together are longer and the functional dependencies between people greater. Here the individual is largely protected from sudden attack, the irruption of physical violence into his life. But at the same time he is himself forced to suppress in himself any passionate impulse urging him to attack another physically. And the other forms of compulsion which now prevail in the pacified social spaces pattern the individual's conduct and affective impulses in the same direction. The closer the web of interdependence becomes in which the individual is enmeshed with the advancing division of functions, the larger the social spaces over which this network extends and which become integrated into functional or institutional units—the more threatened is the social existence of the individual who gives way to spontaneous impulses and emotions, the greater is the social advantage of those able to moderate their affects, and the more strongly is each individual constrained from an early age to take account of the effects of his own or other people's actions on a whole series of links in the social chain. The moderation of spontaneous emotions, the tempering of affects, the extension of mental space beyond the moment into the past and future, the habit of connecting events in terms of chains of cause and effect—all these are different aspects of the same transformation of conduct which necessarily takes place with the monopolization of physical violence, and the lengthening of the chains of social action and interdependence. It is a "civilizing" change of behaviour.

The transformation of the nobility from a class of knights into a class of courtiers is an example of this. In the earlier sphere, where violence is an unavoidable and everyday event, and where the individual's chains of dependence are relatively short, because he largely subsists directly from the produce of his own land, a strong and continuous moderation of drives and affects is neither necessary, possible nor useful. The life of the warriors themselves, but also that of all others living in a society with a warrior upper class, is threatened continually and directly by acts of physical violence; thus, measured against life in more pacified zones, it oscillates between extremes. Compared to this other society, it permits the warrior extraordinary freedom in living out his feelings and passions; it allows savage joys, the uninhibited satisfaction of pleasure from women, or of hatred in destroying and tormenting anything hostile. But at the same time it threatens the warrior, if he is defeated, with an extraordinary degree of exposure to the violence and the passions of others, and with such radical subjugation, such extreme forms of physical torment as are later, when physical torture, imprisonment and the radical humiliation of individuals has become the monopoly of a central authority, hardly to be found in normal life. With this monopolization, the physical threat to the individual is slowly depersonalized. It no longer depends quite so directly on momentary affects; it is gradually subjected to increasingly strict rules and laws; and finally, within certain limits and with certain fluctuations, the physical threat when laws are infringed is itself made less severe.

The greater spontaneity of drives and the higher measure of physical threat that are encountered wherever strong and stable central monopolies have not yet formed are, as can be seen, complementary. In this social structure the victorious have a greater possibility of giving free rein to their drives and affects, but greater too is the direct threat to one man from the affects of another, and more omnipresent the possibility of subjugation and boundless humiliation if one falls into the power of another. This applies not only to the relationship of warrior to warrior, for whom in the course of monetarization and the narrowing of free competition an affect-moderating code of conduct is already slowly forming; within society at large the lesser measure of restraint impinging upon seigneurs initially stands in sharper contrast than later to the confined existence of their female counterparts and to the radical exposure to their whims of dependents, defeated, and bondsmen.

To the structure of this society with its extreme polarization, its continuous uncertainties, corresponds the structure of the individuals who form it and of their conduct. Just as in the relations between man and man danger arises more abruptly, the possibility of victory or liberation more suddenly and incalculably before the individual, so he is also thrown more frequently and directly between pleasure and pain. The social function of the free warrior is indeed scarcely so constructed that dangers are long foreseeable, that the effects of particular actions can be considered three or four links ahead, even though his function is slowly developing in this direction throughout the Middle Ages with the increasing centralization of armies. But for the time being it is the immediate present that provides the impulse. As the momentary situation changes, so do affective expressions; if it brings pleasure this is savoured to the full, without calculation or thought of the possible consequences in the future. If it brings danger, imprisonment, defeat, these too must be suffered more desolately. And the incurable unrest, the perpetual proximity of danger, the whole atmosphere of this unpredictable and insecure life, in which there are at most small and transient islands of more protected existence, often engender, even without external cause, sudden switches from the most exuberant pleasure to the deepest despondency and remorse. The personality, if we may put it thus, is incomparably more ready and accustomed to leap with undiminishing intensity from one extreme to the other, and slight impressions, uncontrollable associations are often enough to induce these immense fluctuations.[4]

As the structure of human relations changes, as monopoly organizations of physical force develop and the individual is held no longer in the sway of constant feuds and wars but rather in the more permanent compulsions of peaceful functions based on the acquisition of money or prestige, affect-expressions too slowly gravitate towards a middle line. The fluctuations in behaviour and affects do not disappear, but are moderated. The peaks and abysses are smaller, the changes less abrupt.

We can see what is changing more clearly from its obverse. Through the formation of monopolies of force, the threat which one man represents for another is subject to stricter control and becomes more calculable. Everyday life is freer of sudden reversals of fortune. Physical violence is confined to barracks; and from this store-house it breaks out only in extreme cases, in times of war or social upheaval, into individual life. As the monopoly of certain specialist groups it is normally excluded from the life of others; and these specialists, the whole monopoly organization of force, now stand guard only in the margin of social life as a control on individual conduct.

Even in this form as a control organization, however, physical violence and the threat emanating from it have a determining influence on individuals in society, whether they know it or not. It is, however, no longer a perpetual insecurity that it brings into the life of the individual, but a peculiar form of security. It no longer throws him, in the swaying fortunes of battle, as the physical victor or vanquished, between mighty outbursts of pleasure and terror; a continuous, uniform pressure is exerted on individual life by the physical violence stored behind the scenes of everyday life, a pressure totally familiar and hardly perceived, conduct and drive economy having been adjusted from earliest youth to this social structure. It is in fact the whole social mould, the code of conduct, which changes; and accordingly with it changes, as has been said before, not only this or that specific form of conduct but its whole pattern, the whole structure of the way individuals steer themselves. The monopoly organization of physical violence does not usually constrain the individual by a direct threat. A strongly predictable compulsion or pressure mediated in a variety of ways in constantly exerted on the individual. This operates to a considerable extent through the medium of his own reflection. It is normally only potentially present in society, as an agency of control; the actual compulsion is one that the individual exerts on himself either as a result of his knowledge of the possible consequences of his moves in the game in intertwining activities, or as a result of corresponding gestures of adults which have helped to pattern his own behaviour as a child. The monopolization of physical violence, the concentration of arms and armed men under one authority, makes the use of violence more or less calculable, and forces unarmed men in the pacified social spaces to restrain their own violence through foresight or reflection; in other words it imposes on people a greater or lesser degree of self-control.

This is not to say that every form of self-control was entirely lacking in medieval warrior society or in other societies without a complex and stable monopoly of physical violence. The agency of individual self-control, the super-ego, the conscience or whatever we call it, is instilled, imposed and maintained in such warrior societies only in direct relation to acts of physical violence; its form matches this life in its greater contrasts and more abrupt transitions. Compared to the self-control agency in more pacified societies, it is diffuse, unstable, only a slight barrier to violent emotional outbursts. The fears securing socially "correct" conduct are not yet banished to remotely the same extent from the individual's consciousness into his so-called "inner life". As the decisive danger does not come from failure or relaxation of self-control, but from direct external physical threat, habitual fear predominantly takes the form of fear of external powers. And as this fear is less stable, the control apparatus too is less encompassing, more one-sided or partial. In such a society extreme self-control in enduring pain may be instilled; but this is complemented by what, measured by a different standard, appears as an extreme form of freewheeling of affects in torturing others. Similarly, in certain sectors of medieval society we found extreme forms of asceticism, self-restraint and renunciation, contrasting to a no less extreme indulgence of pleasure in others, and frequently enough we encounter sudden switches from one attitude to the other in the life of an individual person. The restraint the individual here imposes on himself, the struggle against his own flesh, is no less intense and one-sided, no less radical and passionate than its counterpart, the fight against others and the maximum enjoyment of pleasures.

What is established with the monopolization of physical violence in the pacified social spaces is a different type of self-control or self-constraint. It is a more dispassionate self-control. The controlling agency forming itself as part of the individual's personality structure corresponds to the controlling agency forming itself in society at large. The one like the other tends to impose a highly differentiated regulation upon all passionate impulses, upon men's conduct all around. Both— each to a large extent mediated by the other—exert a constant, even pressure to inhibit affective outbursts. They damp down extreme fluctuations in behaviour and emotions. As the monopolization of physical force reduces the fear and terror one man must have for another, but at the same time reduces the possibility of causing others terror, fear or torment, and therefore certain possibilities of pleasurable emotional release, the constant self-control to which the individual is now increasingly accustomed seeks to reduce the contrasts and sudden switches in conduct, and the affective charge of all self-expression. The pressures operating upon the individual now tend to produce a transformation of the whole drive and affect economy in the direction of a more continuous, stable and even regulation of drives and affects in all areas of conduct, in all sectors of his life.

And it is in exactly the same direction that the unarmed compulsions operate, the constraints without direct physical violence to which the individual is now exposed in the pacified spaces, and of which economic restraints are an instance. They too are less affect-charged, more moderate, stable and less erratic than the constraints exerted by one person on another in a monopoly-free warrior society. And they, too, embodied in the entire spectrum of functions open to the individual in society, induce incessant hindsight and foresight transcending the moment and corresponding to the longer and more complex chains in which each act is now automatically enmeshed. They require the individual incessantly to overcome his momentary affective impulses in keeping with the longer-term effects of his behaviour. Relative to the other standard, they instil a more even self-control encompassing his whole conduct like a tight ring, and a more steady regulation of his drives according to the social norms. Moreover, as always, it is not only the adult functions themselves which immediately produce this tempering of drives and affects; partly automatically, partly quite consciously through their own conduct and habits, adults induce corresponding behaviour-patterns in children. From earliest youth the individual is trained in the constant restraint and foresight that he needs for adult functions. This self-restraint is ingrained so deeply from an early age that, like a kind of relay-station of social standards, an automatic self-supervision of his drives, a more differentiated and more stable "super-ego" develops in him, and a part of the forgotten drive impulses and affect inclinations is no longer directly within reach of the level of consciousness at all.

Earlier, in warrior society, the individual could use physical violence if he was strong and powerful enough; he could openly indulge his inclinations in many directions that have subsequently been closed by social prohibitions. But he paid for this greater opportunity of direct pleasure with a greater chance of direct and open fear. Medieval conceptions of hell give us an idea of how strong this fear between man and man was. Both joy and pain were discharged more openly and freely. But the individual was their prisoner; he was hurled back and forth by his own feelings as by forces of nature. He had less control of his passions; he was more controlled by them.

Later, as the conveyor belts running through his existence grow longer and more complex, the individual learns to control himself more steadily; he is now less a prisoner of his passions than before. But as he is now more tightly bound by his functional dependence on the activities of an ever-larger number of people, he is much more restricted in his conduct, in his chances of directly satisfying his drives and passions. Life becomes in a sense less dangerous, but also less emotional or pleasurable, at least as far as the direct release of pleasure is concerned. And for what is lacking in everyday life a substitute is created in dreams, in books and pictures. So, on their way to becoming courtiers, the nobility read novels of chivalry; the bourgeois now contemplate violence and erotic passion in films. Physical clashes, wars and feuds diminish, and anything recalling them, even the cutting up of dead animals and the use of the knife at table, is banished from view or at least subjected to more and more precise social rules. But at the same time the battlefield is, in a sense, moved within. Part of the tensions and passions that were earlier directly released in the struggle of man and man must now be worked out within the human being. The more peaceful constraints exerted on him by his relations to others are mirrored within him; an individualized pattern of near-automatic habits is established and consolidated within him, a specific "super-ego", which endeavours to control, transform or suppress his affects in keeping with the social structure. But the drives, the passionate affects, that can no longer directly manifest themselves in the relationships *between* people, often struggle no less violently *within* the individual against this supervising part of himself. And this semi-automatic struggle of the person with himself does not always find a happy resolution; not always does the self-transformation required by life in this society lead to a new balance between drive-satisfaction and drive-control. Often enough it is subject to major or minor disturbances, revolts of one part of the person against the other, or a permanent atrophy, which makes the performance of social functions even more difficult, or impossible. The vertical oscillations, if we may so describe them, the leaps from fear to joy, pleasure to remorse are reduced, while the horizontal fissure running right through the whole person, the tension between "super-ego" and "unconscious"—the wishes and desires that cannot be remembered—increases.

Here too the basic characteristics of these patterns of intertwining, if one pursues not merely their static structures but their sociogenesis, prove to be relatively simple. Through the interdependence of larger groups of people and the exclusion of physical violence from them, a social apparatus is established in which the constraints between people are lastingly transformed into self-constraints. These self-constraints, a function of the perpetual hindsight and foresight instilled in the individual from childhood in accordance with his integration in extensive chains of action, have partly the form of conscious self-control and partly that of automatic habit. They tend towards a more even moderation, a more continuous restraint, a more exact control of drives and affects in accordance with the more differentiated pattern of social interweaving. But depending on the inner pressure, on the condition of society and the position of the individual within it, these constraints also produce peculiar tensions and disturbances in the conduct and drive economy of the individual. In some cases they lead to perpetual restlessness and dissatisfaction, precisely because the person affected can only gratify a part of his inclinations and impulses in modified form, for example in fantasy, in looking-on and overhearing, in daydreams or dreams. And sometimes the habituation to affect-inhibition goes so far—constant feelings of boredom or solitude are examples of this—that the individual is no longer capable of any form of fearless expression of the modified affects, or of direct gratification of the repressed drives. Particular branches of drives are as it were anaesthetized in such cases by the specific structure of the social framework in which the child grows up. Under the pressure of the dangers that their expression incurs in the child's social space, they become surrounded with automatic fears to such an extent that they can remain deaf and unresponsive throughout a whole lifetime. In other cases certain branches of drives may be so diverted by the heavy conflicts which the rough-hewn, affective and passionate nature of the small human being unavoidably encounters on its way to being moulded into a "civilized" being, that their energies can find only an unwanted release through bypasses, in compulsive actions and other symptoms of disturbance. In other cases again, these energies are so transformed that they flow into uncontrollable and eccentric attachments and repulsions, in predilections for this or that peculiar hobby-horse. And in all these cases a permanent, apparently groundless inner unrest shows how many drive energies are dammed up in a form that permits no real satisfaction.

Until now the individual civilizing process, like the social, runs its course by and large blindly. Under the cover of what adults think and plan, the relationship that forms between them and the young has functions and effects in the latter's personalities which they do not intend and of which they scarcely know. Unplanned in that sense are those results of social patterning of individuals to which one habitually refers as "abnormal"; psychological abnormalities which do not result from social patterning but are caused by unalterable hereditary traits need not be considered here. But the psychological make-up which keeps within the social norm and is subjectively more satisfying comes about in an equally unplanned way. It is the same social mould from which emerge both more favourably and more unfavourably structured human beings, the "well-adjusted" as well as the "mal-adjusted", within a very broad spectrum of varieties. The automatically reproduced anxieties which, in the course of each individual civilizing process and in connection with the conflicts that form an integral part of this process, attach themselves to specific drives and affect impulses sometimes lead to a permanent and total paralysis of these impulses, and sometimes only to a moderate regulation with enough scope for their full satisfaction. Under present conditions it is from the point of view of the individuals concerned more a question of their good or bad fortune than that of anybody's planning whether it is the one or the other. In either case it is the web of social relations in which the individual lives during his most impressionable phase, during childhood and youth, which imprints itself upon his unfolding personality where it has its counterpart in the relationship between his controlling agencies, super-ego and ego, and his libidinal impulses. The resulting balance between controlling agencies and drives on a variety of levels determines how an individual person steers himself in his relations with others; it determines that which we call, according to taste, habits, complexes or personality structure. However, there is no end to the intertwining, for although the self-steering of a person, malleable during early childhood, solidifies and hardens as he grows up, it never ceases entirely to be affected by his changing relations with others throughout his life. The learning of self-controls, call them "reason" or "conscience", "ego" or "super-ego", and the consequent curbing of more animalic impulses and affects, in short the civilizing of the human young, is never a process entirely without pain; it always leaves scars. If the person is lucky—and as no one, no parent, no doctor, and no counsellor, is at present able to steer this process in a child according to a clear knowledge of what is best for its future, it is still largely a question of luck—the wounds of the civilizing conflicts incurred during childhood heal; the scars left by them are not too deep. But in less favourable cases the conflicts inherent in the civilizing of young humans—conflicts with others and conflicts within themselves—remain unsolved, or, more precisely, though perhaps buried for a while, open up once more in situations reminiscent of those of childhood; the suffering, transformed into an adult form, repeats itself again and again, and the unsolved conflicts of a person's childhood never cease to disturb his adult relationships. In that way, the interpersonal conflicts of early youth which have patterned the personality structure continue to perturb or even destroy the interpersonal relationships of the grown-up. The resulting tensions may take the form either of contradictions between different self-control automatisms, sunken memory traces of former dependencies and needs, or of recurrent struggles between the controlling agencies and the libidinal impulses. In the more fortunate cases, on the other hand, the contradictions between different sections and layers of the controlling agencies, especially of the super-ego structure, are slowly reconciled; the most disruptive conflicts between that structure and the libidinal impulses are slowly contained. They not only disappear from waking consciousness, but are so thoroughly assimilated that, without too heavy a cost in subjective satisfaction, they no longer intrude unintentionally in later interpersonal relationships. In one case the conscious and unconscious self-control always remains diffuse in places and open to the breakthrough of socially unproductive forms of drive energy; in the other this self-control, which even today in juvenile phases is often more like a confusion of overlapping ice-floes than a smooth and firm sheet of ice, slowly becomes more unified and stable in positive correspondence to the structure of society. But as this structure, precisely in our times, is highly mutable, it demands a flexibility of habits and conduct which in most cases has to be paid for by a loss of stability.

Theoretically, therefore, it is not difficult to say in what lies the difference between an individual civilizing process that is considered successful and one that is considered unsuccessful. In the former, after all the pains and conflicts of this process, patterns of conduct well adapted to the framework of adult social functions are finally formed, an adequately functioning set of habits and at the same time—which does not necessarily go hand-in-hand with it—a positive pleasure balance. In the other, either the socially necessary self-control is repeatedly purchased, at a heavy cost in personal satisfaction, by a major effort to overcome opposed libidinal energies, or the control of these energies, renunciation of their satisfaction, is not achieved at all; and often enough no positive pleasure balance of any kind is finally possible, because the social commands and prohibitions are represented not only by other people but also by the stricken self, since one part of it forbids and punishes what the other desires.

In reality the result of the individual civilizing process is clearly unfavourable or favourable only in relatively few cases at each end of the scale. The majority of civilized people live midway between these two extremes. Socially positive and negative features, personally gratifying and frustrating tendencies, mingle in them in varying proportions.

The social moulding of individuals in accordance with the structure of the civilizing process of what we now call the West is particularly difficult. In order to be reasonably successful it requires with the structure of Western society a particularly high differentiation, an especially intensive and stable regulation of drives and affects, of all the more elementary human impulses. It therefore generally takes up more time, particularly in the middle and upper classes, than the social moulding of individuals in less complex societies. Resistance to adaptation to the prevailing standards of civilization, the effort which this adaptation, this profound transformation of the whole personality, costs the individual,

is always very considerable. And later, therefore, than in less complex
societies the individual in the Western world attains with his adult social
function the psychological make-up of an adult, the emergence of which
by and large marks the conclusion of the individual civilizing process.

But even if in the more differentiated societies of the West the modelling of the individual self-steering apparatus is particularly extensive
and intense, processes tending in the same direction, social and individual civilizing processes, most certainly do not occur only there. They are
to be found wherever, under competitive pressures, the division of functions makes large numbers of people dependent on one another, wherever a monopolization of physical force permits and imposes a
co-operation less charged with emotion, wherever functions are established that demand constant hindsight and foresight in interpreting the
actions and intentions of others. What determines the nature and degree
of such civilizing spurts is always the extent of interdependencies, the
level of the division of functions, and within it, the structure of these
functions themselves.

## Notes

1. There is today a widespread notion that the forms of social life and particular social
institutions are to be explained primarily by the purpose they have for the people who are
thus bound together. This idea makes it appear as if people, understanding the usefulness
of these institutions, once took a common decision to live together in this way and no other.
But his notion is a fiction and if only for that reason not a very good instrument of research.

The consent given by the individual to live with others in a particular form, the justification on grounds of particular purposes for the fact that he lives for example within a
state, or is bound to others as a citizen, official, worker, or farmer and not as a knight, priest
or bondsman, or as a cattle-rearing nomad—this consent and this justification are something retrospective. In this matter the individual has little choice. He is born into an order
with institutions of a particular kind; he is conditioned more or less successfully to con-
form to it. And even if he should find this order and its institutions neither good nor useful,
he could not simply withdraw his assent and jump out of the existing order. He may try to
escape it as an adventurer, a tramp, an artist or writer, he may finally flee to a lonely island—even as a refugee from this order he is its product. To disapprove and flee it is no less
a sign of conditioning by it than to praise and justify it.

One of the tasks still remaining to be done is to explain convincingly the compulsion
whereby certain forms of communal life, for example our own, come into being, are preserved and changed. But access to an understanding of their genesis is blocked if we think of
them as having come about in the same way as the works and deeds of individual people: by
the setting of particular goals or even by rational thought and planning. The idea that from
the early Middle Ages Western men worked in a common exertion and with a clear goal and
a rational plan, towards the order of social life and the institutions in which we live today,
scarcely answers the facts. How this really happened can be learned only through a study of
the historical evolution of these social forms by accurately documented empirical enquiries.
Such a study of a particular segment, the aspect of state organization, has been attempted

above. But this has also given rise to some insight of broader significance, for example a certain understanding of the nature of socio-historical processes. We can see how little is really achieved by explaining institutions such as the "state" in terms of rational goals. The goals, plans and actions of individual people constantly intertwine with those of others. But this intertwining of the actions and plans of many people, which, moreover, goes on continuously from generation to generation, is itself not planned. It cannot be understood in terms of the plans and purposeful intentions of individuals, nor in terms which, though not directly purposive, are modelled on teleological modes of thinking. We are here concerned with processes, compulsions and regularities of a relatively autonomous kind. Thus, for example, a situation where many people set themselves the same goal, wanting the same piece of land, the same market or the same social position, gives rise to something that none of them intended or planned, a specifically social datum: a competitive relationship with its peculiar regularities as discussed earlier. Thus it is not from a common plan of many people, but as something unplanned, emerging from the convergence and collision of the plans of many people, that an increasing division of functions comes into being, and the same applies to the integration of larger and larger areas in the form of states, and to many other socio-historical processes.

And only an awareness of the relative autonomy of the intertwining of individual plans and actions, of the way the individual is bound by his social life with others, permits a better understanding of the very fact of individuality itself. The coexistence of people, the intertwining of their intentions and plans, the bonds they place on each other, all these, far from destroying individuality, provide the medium in which it can develop. They set the individual limits, but at the same time give him greater or lesser scope. The social fabric in this sense forms the substratum from which and into which the individual constantly spins and weaves his purposes. But this fabric and the actual course of its historical change as a whole, is intended and planned by no-one.

For further details on this cf. N. Elias, *What Is Sociology?*, trans. Stephen Mennell and Grace Morrissey (London, 1978).

2. For a discussion of the problem of the social process, cf. *Social Problems and Social Processes: Selected Papers from the Proceedings of the American Sociological Society* (1932), ed. E. S. Bogardus (Chicago, 1933).

For a criticism of the earlier biologistic notion of social processes, cf. W. F. Ogburn, *Social Change* (London, 1923), pp. 56f.:

The publication of the *Origin of Species*, setting forth a theory of evolution of species in terms of natural selection, heredity and variation, created a deep impression on the anthropologists and sociologists. The conception of evolution was so profound that the changes in society were seen as a manifestation of evolution and there was an attempt to seek the causes of these social changes in terms of variation and selection. . . . Preliminary to the search for causes, however, attempts were made to establish the development of particular social institutions in successive stages, an evolutionary series, a particular stage necessarily preceding another. The search for laws led to many hypotheses regarding factors such as geographical location, climate, migration, group conflict, racial ability, the evolution of mental ability, and such principles as variation, natural selection, and survival of the fit. A half-century or more of investigations on such theories has yielded some results, but the achievements have not been up to the high hopes entertained shortly after the publication of Darwin's theory of natural selection.

The inevitable series of stages in the development of social institutions has not only not been proven but has been disproven. . . .

For more recent tendencies in the discussion of the problem of historical change, cf. A. Goldenweiser, "Social Evolution", in *Encyclopedia of Social Sciences* (New York, 1935), vol. 5, pp. 656ff. (with comprehensive bibliography). The article concludes with the reflection:

> Since the World War students of the social sciences without aiming at the logical orderliness of evolutionary schemes have renewed their search for relatively stable tendencies and regularities in history and society. On the other hand, the growing discrepancy between ideals and the workings of history is guiding the sciences of society into more and more pragmatic channels. If there is a social evolution, whatever it may be, it is no longer accepted as a process to be contemplated but as a task to be achieved by deliberate and concerted human effort.

This study of the civilizing process differs from these pragmatic efforts in that, suspending all wishes and demands concerning what ought to be, it tries to establish what was and is, and to explain in which way, and why, it became as it was and is. It seemed more appropriate to make the therapy depend on the diagnosis rather than the diagnosis on the therapy.
Cf. F. J. Teggart, *Theory of History* (New Haven, 1925), p. 148: ". . . the investigation of how things have come to be as they are . . .".
3. Cf. E. C. Parsons, *Fear and Conventionality* (New York, London, 1914). The divergent view, e.g. in W. G. Sumner, *Folkways* (Boston, 1907), p. 419: "It is never correct to regard any one of the taboos as an arbitrary invention or burden laid on society by tradition without necessity . . . they have been sifted for centuries by experience, and those which we have received and accepted are such as experience has proved to be expedient."
4. See the fine account by J. Huizinga, *The Waning of the Middle Ages* (London, 1924), ch. 1.
What was said above also applies, for example, to societies with a related structure in the present-day Orient and, to various degrees depending on the nature and extent of integration, to so-called "primitive" societies.
The extent to which children in our society—however imbued with characteristics of our relatively advanced civilization—still show glimpses of the other standard with its simpler and more straightforward affects and its proneness to sudden changes of mood, is shown, for example, by the following description of what children like in films (*Daily Telegraph*, 12 February, 1937): "Children, especially young children, like aggression. . . . They favour action, action and more action. They are not averse from the shedding of blood, but it must be dark blood. Virtue triumphant is cheered to the echo; villainy is booed with a fine enthusiasm. When scenes of one alternate with scenes of the other, as in sequences of pursuit, the transition from the cheer to the boo is timed to a split second."
Also closely connected to the different force of their emotional utterances, their extreme reaction in both directions, fear and joy, revulsion and affection, is the specific structure of taboos in simpler societies. [I]n the medieval West not only the manifestations of drives and affects in the form of pleasure but also the prohibitions, the tendencies to self-torment and asceticism were stronger, more intense and therefore more rigorous than at later stages of the civilizing process.
Cf. also R. H. Lowie, "Food Etiquette", in *Are we civilised?* (London, 1929), p. 48: ". . . the savage rules of etiquette are not only strict, but formidable. Nevertheless, to us their table manners are shocking."

# 2

# Diminishing Contrasts, Increasing Varieties

The civilizing process moves along in a long sequence of spurts and counter-spurts. Again and again a rising outsider stratum or a rising survival unit as a whole, a tribe or a nation state, attains the functions and characteristics of an establishment in relation to other outsider strata or survival units which, on their part, are pressing from below, from their position as oppressed outsiders, against the current establishment. And again and again, as the grouping of people which has risen and has established itself is followed by a still broader and more populous grouping attempting to emancipate itself, to free itself from oppression, one finds that the latter, if successful, is forced in turn into the position of an established oppressor. The time may well come when the former oppressed groups, freed from oppression, do not become oppressors in turn; but it is not yet in sight.

There are, of course, many unsolved problems raised by this vista. In the present context it may be enough to draw attention to the fact that by and large the lower strata, the oppressed and poorer outsider groups at a given stage of development, tend to follow their drives and affects more directly and spontaneously, that their conduct is less strictly regulated than that of the respective upper strata. The compulsions operating upon the lower strata are predominantly of a direct, physical kind, the threat of physical pain or annihilation by the sword, poverty or hunger. That type of pressure, however, does not induce a stable transformation of constraints through others, or "alien" constraints, into "self"-restraints. A medieval peasant who goes without meat because he is too poor, because beef is reserved for the lord's table, i.e. solely under physical constraint, will give way to his desire for meat whenever he can do so without external danger, unlike the founders of religious orders from the upper strata who deny themselves the enjoyment of meat in consideration of the after-life and the sense of their own sinfulness. A totally destitute person who works for others under constant threat of hunger or in penal servitude, will stop working once the threat of external force ceases, unlike the wealthy merchant who goes on and on working for himself although he probably has enough to live on without this work.

From *The Civilizing Process* (1994), pp. 460–65

He is compelled to do it not by simple need but by the pressure of the competition for power and prestige, because his profession, his elevated status, provide the meaning and justification of his life; and for him constant self-constraint has made work such a habit that the balance of his personality is upset if he is no longer able to work.

It is one of the peculiarities of Western society that in the course of its development this contrast between the situation and code of conduct of the upper and lower strata decreases considerably. Lower-class characteristics are spreading to all classes. The fact that Western society as a whole has gradually become a society where every able person is expected to earn his living through a highly regulated type of work is a symptom of this: earlier, work was an attribute of the lower classes. And at the same time, what used to be distinguishing features of the upper classes are likewise spreading to society at large. The conversion of "alien" social constraints into self-restraints, into a more or less habitual and automatic individual self-regulation of drives and affects—possibly only for people normally protected from external, physical threat by the sword or starvation—is taking place in the West increasingly among the broad masses, too.

Seen at close quarters, where only a small segment of this movement is visible, the differences in social personality structure between the upper and lower classes in the Western world today may still seem considerable. But if the whole sweep of the movement over centuries is perceived, one can see that the sharp contrasts between the behaviour of different social groups—like the contrasts and sudden switches within the behaviour of individuals—are steadily diminishing. The moulding of drives and affects, the forms of conduct, the whole psychological make-up of the lower classes in the more civilized societies, with their growing importance in the entire network of functions, is increasingly approaching that of other groups, beginning with the middle classes. This is the case even though a part of the self-constraints and taboos among the latter, which arise from the urge to "distinguish themselves", the desire for enhanced prestige, may initially be lacking in the former, and even though the type of social dependence of the former does not yet necessitate or permit the same degree of affect-control and steadier foresight as in the upper classes of the same period.

This reduction in the contrasts within society as within individuals, this peculiar commingling of patterns of conduct deriving from initially very different social levels, is highly characteristic of Western society. It is one of the most important peculiarities of the "civilizing process". But this movement of society and civilization certainly does not follow a straight line. Within the overall movement there are repeatedly greater or lesser counter-movements in which the contrasts in society and the fluctuations in the behaviour of individuals, their affective outbreaks, increase again.

What is happening under our eyes, what we generally call the "spread of civilization" in the narrower sense, that is, the spread of our institutions and standards of conduct beyond the West, constitutes, as we have said, the last wave so far within a movement that first took place for several centuries within the West, and whose trend and characteristic patterns, including science, technology and other manifestations of a specific type of self-restraint, established themselves here long before the concept of "civilization" existed. From Western society—as a kind of upper class—Western "civilized" patterns of conduct are today spreading over wide areas outside the West, whether through the settlement of Occidentals or through the assimilation of the upper strata of other nations, as models of conduct earlier spread within the West itself from this or that upper stratum, from certain courtly or commercial centres. The course taken by all these expansions is only slightly determined by the plans or desires of those whose patterns of conduct were taken over. The classes supplying the models are even today not simply the free creators or originators of the expansion. This spread of the same patterns of conduct from the "white mother-countries or fatherlands" follows the incorporation of the other areas into the network of political and economic interdependencies, into the sphere of elimination struggles between and within the nations of the West. It is not "technology" which is the cause of this change of behaviour; what we call "technology" is itself only *one* of the symbols, one of the last manifestations of that constant foresight imposed by the formation of longer and longer chains of actions and the competition between those bound together by them. "Civilized" forms of conduct spread to these other areas because and to the extent that in them, through their incorporation into the network whose centre the West still constitutes, the structure of their societies and of human relationships in general is likewise changing. Technology, education—both these are facets of the same overall development. In the areas into which the West has expanded, the social functions with which the individual must comply are increasingly changing in such a way as to induce the same constant foresight and affect-control as in the West itself. Here, too, the transformation of the whole of social existence is the basic condition of the civilization of conduct. For this reason we find in the relation of the West to other parts of the world the beginnings of the reduction in contrasts which is peculiar to every major wave of the civilizing movement.

This recurrent fusion of patterns of conduct of the functionally upper classes with those of the rising classes is not without significance regarding the curiously ambivalent attitude of the upper classes in this process. The habituation to foresight, and the stricter control of behaviour and the affects to which the upper classes are inclined through their situation and functions, are important instruments of their dominance, as in the case of European colonialism, for example. They serve as marks of distinction and prestige. For just this reason such a society regards offences against the prevailing pattern of drive and affect control, any "letting go" by their members, with greater or lesser disapproval. This disapproval increases when the social power and size of the lower, rising group increase, and concomitantly, the competition for the same opportunities between the upper and lower groups becomes more intense. The effort and foresight which it costs to maintain the position of the upper class is expressed in the internal commerce of its members with each other by the degree of reciprocal supervision they practise on one another, by the severe stigmatization and penalties they impose upon those members who breach the common distinguishing code. The fear arising from the situation of the whole group, from their struggle to preserve their cherished and threatened position, acts directly as a force maintaining the code of conduct, the cultivation of the super-ego in its members. It is converted into individual anxiety, the individual's fear of personal degradation or merely loss of prestige in his own society. And it is this fear of loss of prestige in the eyes of others, instilled as self-compulsion, whether in the form of shame or sense of honour, which assures the habitual reproduction of distinctive conduct, and the strict drive-control underlying it, in individual people.

But while on the one hand these upper classes—and in some respects, as noted above, the Western nations as a whole have an upper-class function—are thus driven to maintain at all costs their special conduct and drive-control as marks of distinction, on the other their situation, together with the structure of the general movement carrying them along, forces them in the long run to reduce more and more these differences in standards of behaviour. The expansion of Western civilization shows this double tendency clearly enough. This civilization is the characteristic conferring distinction and superiority on Occidentals. But at the same time the Western people, under the pressure of their own competitive struggle, bring about in large areas of the world a change in human relationships and functions in line with their own standards. They make large parts of the world dependent on them and at the same time, in keeping with a regularity of functional differentiation that has been observed over and again, become themselves dependent on them. On the one hand they build, through institutions and by the strict regulation of their own behaviour, a wall between themselves and the groups they colonize and whom they consider their inferiors. On the other, with their social forms, they also spread their own style of conduct and institutions in these places. Largely without deliberate intent, they work in a direction which sooner or later leads to a reduction in the differences both of social power and of conduct between colonists and colonized. Even in our day the contrasts are becoming perceptibly less. According to the form of colonization and the position of an area in the large network of differentiated functions, and not least to the region's own history and structure, processes of commingling are beginning to take place in specific areas outside the West similar to those sketched earlier on the example of courtly and bourgeois conduct in different countries within the West itself. In colonial regions too, according to the position and social strength of the various groups, Western standards are spreading downwards and occasionally even upwards from below, if we may adhere to this spatial image, and fusing to form new unique entities, new varieties of civilized conduct. *The contrasts in conduct between the upper and lower groups are reduced with the spread of civilization; the varieties or nuances of civilized conduct are increased.* This incipient transformation of Oriental or African people in the direction of Western standards represents the last wave of the continuing civilizing movement that we are able to observe. But as this wave rises, signs of new and further waves in the same direction can already be seen forming in it; for until now the groups approaching the Western upper class in colonial areas as the lower, rising class are primarily the upper classes within those nations.

One step further back in history one can observe in the West itself a similar movement: the assimilation of the lower urban and agrarian classes to the standards of civilized conduct, the growing habituation of these groups to foresight, to a more even curbing and more strict control of the affects, and a higher measure of individual self-constraint in their case too. Here too, according to the structure of the history of each country, very diverse varieties of affect-formation emerge within the framework of civilized conduct. In the conduct of workers in England, for example, one can still see traces of the manners of the landed gentry and of merchants within a large trade network, in France the airs of courtiers and a bourgeoisie brought to power by revolution. In the workers too, we find a stricter regulation of conduct, a type of courtesy more informed by tradition in colonial nations which have for a long period had the function of an upper class within a large interdependent network, and less polished control of the affects in nations that achieved colonial expansion late or not at all, because strong monopolies of force and taxation, a centralization of national power—preconditions for any lasting colonial expansion—developed later in them than in their competitors.

Further back, in the seventeenth, eighteenth and nineteenth centuries—earlier or later according to the structure of each nation—we find the same pattern in a still smaller circle: the interpenetration of the standards of conduct of the nobility and the bourgeoisie. In accordance with the power-relationship, the product of interpenetration is dominated first by models derived from the situation of the upper class, then by the pattern of conduct of the lower, rising classes, until finally an amalgam emerges, a new style of unique character. Here, too, the same dualism in the position of the upper class is visible that can be observed today in the vanguard of "civilization". The courtly nobility, the vanguard of "*civilité*", is gradually compelled to exercise a strict restraint of the affects and an exact moulding of conduct through its increasing integration in a network of interdependencies, represented here by the pincer formed of monarchy and bourgeoisie in which the nobility is trapped. For the courtly nobility, too, the self-restraint imposed on them by their function and situation serves at the same time as a prestige value, a means of distinguishing themselves from the lower groups harrying them, and they do everything within their power to prevent these differences from being effaced. Only the initiated member should know the secrets of good conduct; only within good society should this be learned. Gratian deliberately wrote his treatise on "savoir-vivre", the famous "Hand Oracle", in an obscure style, a courtly princess once explained,[1] so that this knowledge could not be bought by anyone for a few pence; and Courtin does not forget, in the introduction to his treatise on "Civilité", to stress that his manuscript was really written for the private use of a few friends, and that even printed it is intended only for people of good society. But even here the ambivalence of the situation is revealed. Owing to the peculiar form of interdependence in which they lived, the courtly aristocracy could not prevent—indeed, through their contacts with rich bourgeois strata whom they needed for one reason or another, they assisted—the spreading of their manners, their customs, their tastes and their language to other classes. First of all in the seventeenth century, these manners passed to small leading groups of the bourgeoisie—the "Excursus on the Modelling of Speech at Court" gives a vivid example[2]—and then, in the eighteenth century, to broader bourgeois strata; the mass of *civilité*-books that appeared at that time shows this clearly. Here too the force of the current of interweaving as a whole, the tensions and competition leading within it to ever-greater complexity and competition leading within it to ever-greater complexity and functional differentiation, to the individual's dependence on an ever-larger number of others, to the rise of broader and broader classes, proved stronger than the barricade the nobility had been seeking to build around themselves.

It is at small functional centres that the foresight, more complex self-discipline, more stable super-ego formation enforced by growing inter-dependence, first becomes noticeable. Then more and more functional circles within the West change in the same direction. Finally, in conjunction with pre-existing forms of civilization, the same transformation of social functions and thus of conduct and the whole personality begins to take place in countries outside Europe. This is the picture which emerges if we attempt to survey the course followed up to now by the Western civilizing movement in social space as a whole.

## Notes

1. Introduction to the French translation of Gratian's "Hand Oracle" written by Amelot de la Houssaie, Paris, 1684. *Oraculo Manuale* published in 1647, went through about twenty different editions during the seventeenth and eighteenth centuries in France alone under the title *L'Homme de Cour*. It is in a sense the first handbook of courtly psychology, as Machiavelli's book on the prince was the first classical handbook of courtly-absolutist politics. Machiavelli, however, seems to speak more from the point of view of the prince than does Gratian. He justifies more or less the "reason of state" of emergent absolutism. Gratian, the Spanish Jesuit, despises reason of state from the bottom of his heart. He elucidates the rules of the great courtly game for himself and others as something with which one has to comply because there is no alternative.

It is not without significance, however, that despite this difference, the conduct recommended by both Machiavelli and Gratian appears to middle-class people as more or less "immoral", although similar modes of conduct and sentiment are certainly not lacking in the bourgeois world. In this condemnation of courtly psychology and courtly conduct by the non-courtly bourgeoisie is expressed the specific difference of the whole social moulding of the two classes. Social rules are built into the personality of non-courtly bourgeois strata in a different way than in the courtly class. In the former the super-ego is far more rigid and in many respects stricter than in the latter. The belligerent side of everyday life certainly does not disappear in practice from the bourgeois world, but it is banished far more than in the courtly class from what a writer or any person may *express,* and even from consciousness itself.

In courtly-aristocratic circles "thou shalt" is very often no more an expression of expediency, dictated by the practical necessities of social life. Even adults in these circles always remain aware that these are rules that they must obey because they live with other people. In middle-class strata the corresponding rules are often rooted far more deeply in the individual during childhood, not as practical rules for the expedient conduct of life, but as semi-automatic promptings of conscience. For this reason the "thou shalt" and the "thou shalt not" of the super-ego is far more constantly and deeply involved in the observation and understanding of reality. To give at least one example from the innumerable ones that might be quoted here, Gratian says in his precept "Know thoroughly the character of those with whom you deal" (No. 273): "Expect practically nothing good of those who have some natural bodily defect; for they are accustomed to avenge themselves on Nature. . . ." One of the middle-class English books of manners of the seventeenth century, that likewise had wide circulation and had their origin in the well-known rules of George Washington, *Youth's Behaviour* by Francis Hawkins (1646), gives pride of place to "thou shalt not" and so gives behaviour and observation in the same case a different, moral twist (No. 31): "Scorne not any for the infirmityes of nature, which by no art can be amended, nor do thou delight to put them in minde of them, since it very oft procures envye and promotes malice even to revenge."

In a word, we find in Gratian, and after him in La Rochefoucauld and La Bruyère in the form of general maxims, all the modes of behaviour which we encounter, for example in Saint-Simon, in the practice of court life itself. Again and again we find injunctions on the necessity to hold back the affects (No. 287): "Never act while passion lasts. Otherwise you will spoil everything." Or (No. 273): "The man prejudiced by passion always speaks a language different from what things are; passion, not reason, speaks in him." We find the advice to adopt a "psychological attitude", a permanent observation of character (No. 273): "Know thoroughly the character of those with whom you deal." Or the result of such knowledge, the observation (No. 201): "All those who appear mad are mad, and so are half of those who do not appear mad." The necessity of self-observation (No. 225): "Know your dominant fault." The necessity for half-truths (No. 210): "Know how to play with truth." The insight that real truth lies in the truthfulness and substantiality of the whole existence of a person, not in his particular words (No. 175): "The substantial man. It is only Truth that can give a true reputation; and only the substance which can be turned to profit." The necessity for farsightedness (No. 151): "Think today of tomorrow, and of a long time beyond." Moderation in all things (No. 82): "The sage has compressed all wisdom into this precept: Nothing to Excess." The specifically courtly-aristocratic form of perfection, the temperate polishing of a moderated and transformed animalic nature all around, the levity, charm, the new beauty of the animal-made man (No. 127): "Le JE-NE-SAIS-QUOI. Without it all beauty is dead, all grace is graceless . . . the other perfections are ornaments of Nature, the 'Je-ne-sais-quoi' is that of perfection. It is noticeable even in the manner of reasoning. . . ." Or, from a different aspect, the man without affectation (No. 123): "The man without affectation. The more perfections there are the less there is affectation. The most eminent qualities lose their price if we discover affectation in them, because we attribute them rather to an artificial constraint than to a person's true character." War between man and man is inevitable; conduct it decently (No. 165): "Make good war. To conquest villainously is not to conquer but to be conquered. Anything that smells of treason infects one's good name." Over and again in these precepts recurs the argument based on regard for other people, on the necessity to preserve a good reputation, in a word, an argument based on *this-worldly,* social necessities. Religion plays a small part in them. God appears only in the margin and at the end as something outside this human circle. All good things, too, come to a man from other people (No. 111): "Make friends. To have friends is a second being . . . all the good things we have in life depend on others."

It is this justification of rules and precepts not by an eternal moral law but by "external" necessities, consideration of other people, which above all causes these maxims and the whole courtly code of conduct to appear "amoral" or at least "painfully realistic" to the bourgeois observer. Betrayal, for example, the bourgeois world feels, should be forbidden not for practical reasons, concern for one's "good reputation" with other people, but by an inner voice, conscience, in a word, by morality. The same change in the structure of commands and prohibitions that was seen earlier in the study of eating habits, washing and other elementary functions, reappears here. Rules of conduct which in courtly aristocratic circles are observed even by adults largely from consideration and fear of other people, are imprinted on the individual in the bourgeois world rather as a self-constraint. In adults they are no longer reproduced and preserved by direct fear of other people, but by an "inner" voice, a fear automatically reproduced by their own super-ego, in short by a moral commandment that needs no justification.

2. Cf. *The Civilizing Process* (1994), p. 88–93.

# 3

# The Development of the Concept of *Civilité*

1. The decisive antithesis expressing the self-image of the West during the Middle Ages is that between Christianity and paganism or, more exactly, between correct, Roman-Latin Christianity, on the one hand, and paganism and heresy, including Greek and Eastern Christianity, on the other.[1]

In the name of the Cross, and later in that of civilization, Western society wages, during the Middle Ages, its wars of colonization and expansion. And for all its secularization, the watchword "civilization" always retains an echo of Latin Christendom and the knightly-feudal crusade. The memory that chivalry and the Roman-Latin faith bear witness to a particular stage of Western society, a stage which all the major Western peoples have passed through, has certainly not disappeared.

The concept of *civilité* acquired its meaning for Western society at a time when chivalrous society and the unity of the Catholic Church were disintegrating. It is the incarnation of a society which, as a specific stage in the formation of Western manners or "civilization", was no less important than the feudal society before it. The concept of *civilité*, too, is an expansion and symbol of a social formation embracing the most diverse nationalities, in which, as in the Church, a common language is spoken, first Italian and then increasingly French. These languages take over the function earlier performed by Latin. They manifest the unity of Europe, and at the same time the new social formation which forms its backbone, court society. The situation, the self-image, and the characteristics of this society find expression in the concept of *civilité*.

2. The concept of *civilité* received the specific stamp and function under discussion here in the second quarter of the sixteenth century. Its individual starting point can be exactly determined. It owes the specific meaning adopted by society to a short treatise by Erasmus of Rotterdam, *De civilitate morum puerilium* (On civility in children), which appeared in 1530. This work clearly treated a theme that was ripe for discussion. It immediately achieved an enormous circulation, going through edition after edition. Even within Erasmus's lifetime—that is, in the first six

From *The Civilizing Process* (1994), pp. 42–47

years after its publication—it was reprinted more than thirty times.[2] In all, more than 130 editions may be counted, 13 of them as late as the eighteenth century. The multitude of translations, imitations and sequels is almost without limit. Two years after the publication of the treatise the first English translation appeared. In 1534 it was published in catechism form, and at this time it was already being introduced as a schoolbook for the education of boys. German and Czech translations followed. In 1537, 1559, 1569 and 1613 it appeared in French, newly translated each time.

As early as the sixteenth century a particular French type face was given the name *civilité*, after a French work by Mathurin Cordier which combined doctrines from Erasmus's treatise with those of another humanist, Johannes Sulpicius. And a whole genre of books, directly or indirectly influenced by Erasmus's treatise, appeared under the title *Civilité* or *Civilité puérile;* these were printed up to the end of the eighteenth century in this *civilité* type.[3]

3. Here, as so often in the history of words, and as was to happen later in the evolution of the concept *civilité* into *civilisation*, an individual was the instigator. By this treatise, Erasmus gave new sharpness and impetus to the long-established and commonplace word *civilitas*. Wittingly or not, he obviously expressed in it something that met a social need of the time. The concept *civilitas* was henceforth fixed in the consciousness of people with the special sense it received from his treatise. And corresponding words were developed in the various popular languages: the French *civilité*, the English "civility", the Italian *civiltà*, and the German *Zivilität*, which, admittedly, was never so widely adopted as the corresponding words in the other great cultures.

The more or less sudden emergence of words within languages nearly always points to changes in the lives of people themselves, particularly when the new concepts are destined to become as central and long-lived as these.

Erasmus himself may not have attributed any particular importance to his short treatise *De civilitate morum puerilium* within his total *oeuvre*. He says in the introduction that the art of forming young people involves various disciplines, but that the *civilitas morum* is only one of them, and he does not deny that it is *crassissima philosophiae pars* (the grossest part of philosophy). This treatise has its special importance less as an individual phenomenon or work than as a symptom of change, an embodiment of social processes. Above all, it is the resonance, the elevation of the title word to a central expression of the self-interpretation of European society, which draws our attention to this treatise.

4. What is the treatise about? Its theme must explain to us for what

purpose and in what sense the new concept was needed. It must contain indications of the social changes and processes which made the word fashionable.

Erasmus's book is about something very simple: the behaviour of people in society—above all, but not solely, "outward bodily propriety". It is dedicated to a noble boy, a prince's son, and written for the instruction of boys. It contains simple thoughts delivered with great seriousness, yet at the same time with much mockery and irony, in clear, polished language and with enviable precision. It can be said that none of its successors ever equalled this treatise in force, clarity, and personal character. Looking more closely, one perceives beyond it a world and a pattern of life which in many respects, to be sure, are close to our own, yet in others still quite remote; the treatise points to attitudes that we have lost, that some among us would perhaps call "barbaric" or "uncivilized". It speaks of many things that have in the meantime become unspeakable, and of many others that are now taken for granted.[4]

Erasmus speaks, for example, of the way people look. Though his comments are meant as instruction, they also bear witness to the direct and lively observation of people of which he was capable. "Sint oculi placidi, verecundi, compositi", he says, "non torvi, quod est truculentiae . . . non vagi ac volubiles, quod est insaniae, non limi quod est suspiciosorum et insidias molentium. . . ." This can only with difficulty be translated without an appreciable alteration of tone: a wide-eyed look is a sign of stupidity, staring a sign of inertia; the looks of those prone to anger are too sharp; too lively and eloquent those of the immodest; if your look shows a calm mind and a respectful amiability, that is best. Not by chance do the ancients say: the seat of the soul is in the eyes. "Animi sedem esse in oculis."

Bodily carriage, gestures, dress, facial expressions—this "outward" behaviour with which the treatise concerns itself is the expression of the inner, the whole man. Erasmus knows this and on occasion states it explicitly: "Although this outward bodily propriety proceeds from a well-composed mind, nevertheless we sometimes find that, for want of instruction, such grace is lacking in excellent and learned men".

There should be no snot on the nostrils, he says somewhat later. A peasant wipes his nose on his cap and coat, a sausage maker on his arm and elbow. It does not show much more propriety to use one's hand and then wipe it on one's clothing. It is more decent to take up the snot in a cloth, preferably while turning away. If when blowing the nose with two fingers something falls to the ground, it must be immediately trodden away with the foot. The same applies to spittle.

With the same infinite care and matter-of-factness with which these

things are said—the mere mention of which shocks the "civilized" man
of a later stage with different affective moulding—we are told how one
ought to sit or greet. Gestures are described that have become strange to
us, e.g., standing on one leg. And we might reflect that many of the
bizarre movements of walkers and dancers that we see in medieval paint-
ing or statues not only represent the "manner" of the painter or sculptor
but also preserve actual gestures and movements that have grown
strange to us, embodiments of a different mental and emotional structure.

The more one immerses oneself in the little treatise, the clearer becomes this picture of a society with modes of behaviour in some respects
related to ours, and in many ways remote. We see people seated at table:
"A dextris sit poculum, et cultellus escarius rite purgatus, ad laevam pa-
nis", says Erasmus. The goblet and the well-cleaned knife on the right,
on the left the bread. That is how the table is laid. Most people carry a
knife, hence the precept to keep it clean. Forks scarcely exist, or at most
for taking meat from the dish. Knives and spoons are very often used
communally. There is not always a special implement for everyone: if
you are offered something liquid, says Erasmus, taste it and return the
spoon after you have wiped it.

When dishes of meat are brought in, usually everyone cuts himself a
piece, takes it in his hand, and puts it on his plate if there are plates, otherwise on a thick slice of bread. The expression *quadra* used by Erasmus
can clearly mean either a metal plate or a slice of bread.

"Quidam ubi vix bene considerint mox manus in epulas conjiciunt".
Some put their hands into the dishes when they are scarcely seated, says
Erasmus. Wolves or gluttons do that. Do not be the first to take from a
dish that is brought in. Leave dipping your fingers into the broth to the
peasants. Do not poke around in the dish but take the first piece that presents itself. And just as it shows a want of forbearance to search the
whole dish with one's hand—"in omnes patinae plagas manum mit-
tere"—neither is it very polite to turn the dish round so that a better piece
comes to you. What you cannot take with your hands, take on your
*quadra*. If someone passes you a piece of cake or pastry with a spoon, either take it with your *quadra* or take the spoon offered to you, put the
food on the *quadra,* and return the spoon.

As has been mentioned, plates too are uncommon. Paintings of table
scenes from this or earlier times always offer the same spectacle, unfamiliar to us, that is indicated by Erasmus's treatise. The table is sometimes covered with rich cloths, sometimes not, but always there is little
on it: drinking vessels, saltcellar, knives, spoons, that is all. Sometimes
we see the slices of bread, the *quadrae,* that in French are called *tranchoir*

or *tailloir*. Everyone, from the king and queen to the peasant and his wife, eats with the hands. In the upper class there are more refined forms of this. One ought to wash one's hands before a meal, says Erasmus. But there is as yet no soap for this purpose. Usually the guest holds out his hands, and a page pours water over them. The water is sometimes slightly scented with chamomile or rosemary.[5] In good society one does not put both hands into the dish. It is more refined to use only three fingers of the hand. This is one of the marks of distinction between the upper and lower classes.

The fingers become greasy. "Digitos unctos vel ore praelingere vel ad tunicam extergere . . . incivile est", says Erasmus. It is not polite to lick them or wipe them on one's coat. Often you offer others your glass, or all drink from a communal tankard. Erasmus admonishes: "Wipe your mouth beforehand". You may want to offer someone you like some of the meat you are eating. "Refrain from that", says Erasmus, "it is not very decorous to offer something half-eaten to another". And he says further: "To dip bread you have bitten into the sauce is to behave like a peasant, and it shows little elegance to remove chewed food from the mouth and put it back on the *quadra*. If you cannot swallow a piece of food, turn round discreetly and throw it somewhere."

Then he says again: "It is good if conversation interrupts the meal from time to time. Some people eat and drink without stopping, not because they are hungry or thirsty, but because they can control their movements in no other way. They have to scratch their heads, poke their teeth, gesticulate with their hands, or play with a knife, or they can't help coughing, snorting, and spitting. All this really comes from a rustic embarrassment and looks like a form of madness."

But it is also necessary, and possible, for Erasmus to say: Do not expose without necessity "the parts to which Nature has attached modesty". Some prescribe, he says, that boys should "retain the wind by compressing the belly". But you can contract an illness that way. And in another place: "Reprimere sonitum, quem natura fert, ineptorum est, qui plus tribuunt civilitati, quam saluti" (Fools who value civility more than health repress natural sounds). Do not be afraid of vomiting if you must, "for it is not vomiting but holding the vomit in your throat that is foul".

5. With great care Erasmus marks out in his treatise the whole range of human conduct, the chief situations of social and convivial life. He speaks with the same matter-of-factness of the most elementary as of the subtlest questions of human intercourse. In the first chapter he treats "the seemly and unseemly condition of the whole body", in the second "bodily culture", in the third "manners at holy places", in the fourth

banquets, in the fifth meetings, in the sixth amusements, and in the seventh the bedchamber. This is the range of questions in the discussion of which Erasmus gave new impetus to the concept of *civilitas*.

Not always is our consciousness able to recall this other stage of our own history without hesitation. The unconcerned frankness with which Erasmus and his time could discuss all areas of human conduct is lost to us. Much of what he says oversteps our threshold of delicacy.

But precisely this is one of the problems to be considered here. In tracing the transformation of the concepts by which different societies have tried to express themselves, in following back the concept of civilization to its ancestor *civilité*, one finds oneself suddenly on the track of the civilizing process itself, of the actual change in behaviour that took place in the West. That it is embarrassing for us to speak or even hear of much that Erasmus discusses is one of the symptoms of this civilizing process. The greater or lesser discomfort we feel towards people who discuss or mention their bodily functions more openly, who conceal and restrain these functions less than we do, is one of the dominant feelings expressed in the judgment "barbaric" or "uncivilized". Such, then, is the nature of "barbarism and its discontents" or, in more precise and less evaluative terms, the discontent with the different structure of affects, the different standard of repugnance which is still to be found today in many societies which we term "uncivilized", the standard of repugnance which preceded our own and is its precondition. The question arises as to how and why Western society actually moved from one standard to the other, how it was "civilized". In considering this process of civilization, we cannot avoid arousing feelings of discomfort and embarrassment. It is valuable to be aware of them. It is necessary, at least while considering this process, to attempt to suspend all the feelings of embarrassment and superiority, all the value judgments and criticism associated with the concepts "civilization" or "uncivilized". Our kind of behaviour has grown out of that which we call uncivilized. But these concepts grasp the actual change too statically and coarsely. In reality, our terms "civilized" and "uncivilized" do not constitute an antithesis of the kind that exists between "good" and "bad", but represent stages in a development which, moreover, is still continuing. It might well happen that our stage of civilization, our behaviour, will arouse in our descendants feelings of embarrassment similar to those we sometimes feel concerning the behaviour of our ancestors. Social behaviour and the expression of emotions passed from a form and a standard which was not a beginning, which could not in any absolute and undifferentiated sense be designated "uncivilized", to our own, which we denote by the word "civilized". And to understand the latter we must go back in time to that from which it emerged. The "civilization" which we are accustomed to regard as a possession that comes to us apparently ready-made, without our asking how we actually came to possess it, is a process or part of a process in which we are ourselves involved. Every particular characteristic that we attribute to it—machinery, scientific discovery, forms of state, or whatever else—bears witness to a particular structure of human relations, to a particular social structure, and to the corresponding forms of behaviour. The question remains whether the change in behaviour, in the social process of the "civilization" of man, can be understood, at least in isolated phases and in its elementary features, with any degree of precision.

## Notes

1. S. R. Wallach, *Das abendländische Gemeinschaftsbewußtsein im Mittelalter* (Leipzig and Berlin, 1928); *Beiträge zur Kulturgeschichte des Mittelalters und der Renaissance,* ed. W. Goetz, vol. 34, pp. 25–29. Here "Latins" refers to Latin Christianity, i.e., the West in general.

2. The *Bibliotheca Erasmiana* (Ghent, 1893) records 130 editions or, more precisely, 131, including the text of 1526 which unfortunately was unavailable to me, so that I am unaware how far it coincides with subsequent editions.

After the *Colloquies,* the *Moriae encomium,* the *Adagia,* and *De duplici copia verborum ac rerum commentarii, De Civilitate* achieved the highest number of editions of Erasmus's own writings. (For a table of numbers of editions of all works by Erasmus, cf. Mangan, *Life, Character and Influence of Desiderius Erasmus of Rotterdam* [London, 1927], vol. 2, pp. 396ff.) If account is taken of the long series of writings more or less closely related to Erasmus's civility-book, and so of the wide radius of its success, its significance as compared to his other writings must doubtless be estimated still more highly. An idea of the direct impact of his books is given by noting which of them were translated from scholarly language into popular languages. There is as yet no comprehensive analysis of this. According to M. Mann, *Erasme et les débuts de la réforme française* (Paris, 1934), p. 181, the most surprising thing—as far as France is concerned—is "the preponderance of the books of instruction or piety over those of entertainment or satire. The *Praise of Folly,* the *Colloquies . . .* have scarcely any place in this list. . . . It was the *Adages,* the *Preparation for Death* and the *Civility in Boys* that attracted translators and that the public demanded". A similar success analysis for German and Dutch regions would probably yield somewhat different results. It may be supposed that the satirical writings had a somewhat greater success there. . . .

The success of the Latin edition of *De civilitate* was certainly considerable. Kirchhoff (in *Leipziger Sortimentshändler im 16 Jahrhundert;* quoted in W. H. Woodward, *Desiderius Erasmus* [Cambridge, 1904], p. 156, n. 3) ascertains that in the three years 1547, 1551, and 1558 no less than 654 copies of *De civilitate* were in stock, and that no other book by Erasmus was listed in such numbers.

3. Compare the notice on the writings on civility by A. Bonneau in his edition of the *Civilité puérile . . . .*

4. Despite its success in his own time, this work has received relatively little attention in the Erasmus literature of more recent times. In view of the book's theme, this is only too

understandable. This theme—manners, etiquette, codes of conduct—however informative on the moulding of people and their relations, is perhaps of only limited interest for historians of ideas. What Ehrismann says of a *Hofzucht* (Court discipline) in his *Geschichte der deutschen Literatur bis zum Ausgang des Mittelalters,* vol. 6 , pt. 2, p. 330, is typical of a scholarly evaluation frequently encountered in this field: "A book of instruction for youths of noble birth. Not raised to the level of a teaching on virtue".

In France, however, books of courtesy from a particular period—the seventeenth century—have received increasing attention for some time, stimulated no doubt by the work of D. Parodie . . . and above all by the comprehensive study by M. Magendie, *La politesse mondaine* (Paris, 1925). Similarly, the study by B. Groethuysen, *Origines de l'esprit bourgeois en France* (Paris, 1927), also takes literary products of a more or less average kind as a starting point in tracing a certain line in the changes in people and the modification of the social standard (cf., e.g., pp. 45 ff.). . . .

5. Reprinted in part in A. Franklin, *La vie privée d'autrefois: les repas,* (Paris, 1889), pp. 164, 166, which has numerous other quotations on this subject.

# 4

# The Changing Functions of Etiquette

3. It is always of some significance which aspect of living is given a special accent by being allocated a room or rooms at the centre of a house. This is especially true of the *ancien régime* where the upper class, above all the king, did not rent rooms already built and limited in size by rational calculation, but where needs, particularly that for prestige, determined expenditure and thus the shape of a building.

In this sense it is not without interest to note that the middle room on the first floor, from the windows of which one could overlook the whole approach in a straight line, the Marble Court, the Cour Royal, and in the distance the *avant-cour,* was the king's bedroom. Of course, this arrangement first expressed no more than a custom commonly found in the country seats of great lords. They, too, liked to use the middle room on the first floor as the bedroom. The use of this arrangement in the Château may therefore be taken as an expression of how much the king felt himself to be the lord of the house in it; but, as was said earlier, these functions—of king and lord of the house—merged in the case of Louis XIV to an extent which is at first almost unimaginable to us. The magnitude of his rule was reflected in his domestic functions. The king was, as it were, lord of the house throughout the land, and lord of the land even in his most seemingly private chambers. The form taken by the royal bedroom—and not only the *bed*room—is directly influenced by this. This room was, as is known, the theatre of a peculiar ritual hardly less solemn than a state ceremony. It reveals vividly how indissolubly the ruler's character as lord of the house merged with his function as king.

The ceremonies in Louis XIV's bedchamber are mentioned often enough. But it is not enough in this context to regard them as a curiosity, a dusty exhibit in an historical museum which surprises the onlooker only by its bizarreness. Our intention here is to bring them alive step by step so that we can understand through them the structure and functioning of the court figuration of which they are a segment, and so understand the characters and attitudes of the people who form this figuration and are formed by it.

From *The Court Society,* pp. 82–93 (footnotes with bibliographical references are omitted)

As an example of the structure and the elaboration of court life we shall therefore now describe in detail, step by step, one of the ceremonies that took place in the king's bedchamber and which put into proper perspective both his significance in the narrower sense, and this type of rule in the broader sense, just as one would today describe a work-process at a factory or legal procedures in an office, or the royal ritual of a simple tribe; this ceremony is the *levée*, the getting up of the king.

4. Usually at eight o'clock, at any rate at a time decided by himself, the king is woken each morning by his first valet, who sleeps at the foot of the royal bed. The doors are opened by pages.[1] One of them has already notified the Lord Chamberlain[2] and the first Gentleman of the Bedchamber, a second the court kitchen concerning the breakfast; a third stands in the doorway and admits only those lords who have the right to enter.

This right was very exactly graded. There were six different groups of people who were allowed to enter in turn. This was spoken of as the various *entrées*. First came the *Entrée familière*. Taking part were above all the illegitimate sons and grandchildren of the king (*Enfants de France*), princes and princesses of the blood, the first physician, the first surgeon, the first valet and page.

Then came the *Grande entrée,* consisting of the *grands officiers de la chambre et de la garderobe*[3] and the noble lords to whom the king had granted this honour. Then followed the *Première entrée* for the king's readers, the intendants for entertainment and festivities and others. After that came the *Entrée de la chambre* which included all the other *officiers de la chambre* together with the *grand-aumonier,* the ministers and secretaries of state, the *conseillers d'Etat,* the officers of the bodyguard, the Marshal of France and others. Admittance to the fifth *entrée* depended to a certain extent on the goodwill of the first Gentleman of the Bedchamber and, of course, on the king's favour. To this *entrée* belonged gentlemen and ladies of nobility who stood in such favour that the Gentleman of the Bedchamber admitted them; they thus had the advantage of approaching the king before all others. Finally there was a sixth form of entry, and this was the most sought-after of all. On this occasion, one did not enter through the main door of the bedroom but through a back door; this *entrée* was open to the sons of the king including illegitimate ones, together with their families and sons-in-law; and also, for example, to the powerful *surintendant des bâtiments.* To belong to this group was an expression of high favour; for the people included could enter the royal cabinets at any time when the king was not holding council or had begun a special task with his ministers, and they could remain in the room until the king went to mass and even when he was ill.

We can see that everything was very exactly regulated. The first two groups were admitted while the king was still in bed. The king wore a small wig; he never showed himself without a wig even when lying in bed. When he had got up and the Lord Chamberlain, with the first Gentleman of the Bedchamber, had laid out his robe, the next group was called, the *Première entrée*. When the king had put on his shoes he called the *officiers de la chambre* and the doors were opened for the next *entrée*. The king took his robe. The *maître de la garderobe* pulled his nightshirt by the right sleeve, the first servant of the wardrobe by the left; his dayshirt was brought by the Lord Chamberlain or one of the king's sons who happened to be present. The first valet held the right sleeve, the first servant of the wardrobe the left. Thus the king put on his shirt. Then he rose from his armchair and the *maître de la garderobe* helped him to fasten his shoes, buckled his dagger at his side, put on his coat, etc., etc. Once the king had finished dressing he prayed briefly while the first almoner, or in his absence another cleric, quietly said a prayer. Meanwhile the whole court was waiting in the great gallery on the garden side, that is, behind the king's bedroom, that ran the whole width of the middle part of the Château on the first floor.[4] Such was the *levée* of the king.

What is most striking in this is the minute exactitude of organization. But this was not, as we can see, rational organization in the modern sense, however precisely predetermined each part of it was, but a type of organization by which each act received a prestige-character symbolizing the distribution of power at the time. What are thought of usually, if not always, as secondary functions within the present social structure were often primary functions there. The king used his most private acts to establish differences of rank and to distribute distinctions, favours or proofs of displeasure. This already indicates that etiquette had a major symbolic function in the structure of this society and its form of government. It is necessary to proceed to other areas of court life to make this function visible, and to see its different roles for the king and for the nobility.

5. The attitude that was visible earlier in connection with the hierarchy of houses emerges still more clearly here. Now that it is seen operating in conjunction with the determining factor in this state-society, the king, at least the outlines of the social compulsions that brought about such an attitude begin to stand out. For the king to take off his nightshirt and put on his dayshirt was doubtless a necessary procedure; but in the social context it was at once invested with a different meaning. The king turned it into a privilege distinguishing those present from others. The Lord Chamberlain had the right to assist; it was precisely ordained that he should cede this right to a prince and to no one else; and it was exactly

the same with the right to be present at the *entrées*. This presence had
none of the practical purposes that we first tend to suppose. But each act
in the ceremony had an exactly graded prestige-value that was imparted
to those present, and this prestige-value became to an extent self-
evident. It became, like the size of the courtyard or the ornamentation of
a noble's house, a *prestige-fetish*. It served as an indicator of the position
of an individual within the balance of power between the courtiers, a
balance controlled by the king and very precarious. The direct use-value
of all these actions was more or less incidental. What gave them their
gravity was solely the importance they conferred on those present within
court society, the power, rank and dignity they expressed.

The fetish character of every act in the etiquette was clearly developed
at the time of Louis XIV. But the connection with certain primary functions was still preserved. He was strong enough to intervene at any time
to prevent a complete freewheeling of etiquette, the total submergence of
the primary by the secondary functions.[5]

Later, however, this connection was loosened and the nature of acts of
etiquette as prestige-fetishes emerged quite nakedly. Now the motive
force that gave life to etiquette, reproducing it over and over again in this
society, becomes particularly clear. Once the hierarchy of special rights
within the etiquette was established, it was maintained solely by the
competition between the people enmeshed in it, each being understandably anxious to preserve any privilege, however trivial, and the power it
conferred. So the mechanism perpetuated its own ghostly existence like
an economy uncoupled from its purpose of providing the means of life.
At the time of Louis XVI and Marie-Antoinette people lived under
broadly the same etiquette as under Louis XIV. All those involved, from
the king and queen to the nobles of various grades, had long borne it only
against their will. We have enough testimonies to the extent to which, as
it became detached from primary functions, it lost all dignity. Nevertheless it survived uncurtailed up to the Revolution. For to give it up would
have meant—from the king down to his valet—to forfeit privilege, to
lose power and prestige. How idle its functioning finally was, how the
secondary power and prestige-functions in which the people were enmeshed finally overwhelmed the primary ones, is clearly shown by the
following example:

The queen's *levée* took a similar course to that of the king. The maid
of honour had the right to pass the queen her chemise. The lady in waiting helped her put on her petticoat and dress. But if a princess of the royal
family happened to be present, she had the right to put the chemise on the
queen. On one occasion the queen had just been completely undressed
by her ladies. Her chambermaid was holding the chemise and had just

presented it to the maid of honour when the Duchess of Orléans came in. The maid of honour gave it back to the chambermaid who was about to pass it to the duchess when the higher-ranking Countess of Provence entered. The chemise now made its way back to the chambermaid, and the queen finally received it from the hands of the countess. She had had to stand the whole time in a state of nature, watching the ladies complimenting each other with her chemise. Certainly, Louis XIV would never have tolerated such subordination of the main purpose of etiquette. Nevertheless, the social and psychological structure that finally produced this freewheeling was already visible in his reign.

6. This structure merits closer investigation; for it illustrates peculiarities of the compulsions that interdependent people exert on each other within a figuration of a kind to be found in many other societies. Etiquette and ceremony increasingly became, as the above examples showed, a ghostly *perpetuum mobile* that continued to operate regardless of any direct use-value, being impelled, as by an inexhaustible motor, by the competition for status and power of the people enmeshed in it—a competition both between themselves and with the mass of those excluded—and by their need for a clearly graded scale of prestige. In the last analysis this compelling struggle for ever-threatened power and prestige was the dominant factor that condemned all those involved to enact these burdensome ceremonies. No single person within the figuration was able to initiate a reform of the tradition. Every slightest attempt to reform, to change the precarious structure of tensions, inevitably entailed an upheaval, a reduction or even abolition of the rights of certain individuals and families. To jeopardize such privileges was, to the ruling class of this society, a kind of taboo. The attempt would be opposed by broad sections of the privileged who feared, perhaps not without justification, that the whole system of rule that gave them privilege would be threatened or would collapse if the slightest detail of the traditional order were altered. So everything remained as it was.

Undoubtedly the ceremonial was a burden to all concerned. 'One went only unwillingly to Court, and complained aloud when one had to', the Countess Genlis records in the late eighteenth century. But one went. The daughters of Louis XV had to attend the *couchée*, when the king took off his boots. They would quickly put on large, gold-embroidered crinolines over their indoor gowns, tie the prescribed long court train round their waists, hide the rest under a big taffeta coat and set off with their ladies in waiting, chamberlains and lackeys with torches, running to be in time, through the corridors of the Château to the king, to return in a wild chase a quarter of an hour later. Etiquette was borne unwillingly, but it could not be breached from within, not only because the king demanded its preservation, but because the social existence of the people enmeshed in it was itself bound to it. When Marie-Antoinette began to tamper with the traditional rules of etiquette, it was the high nobility themselves who protested, as was only too understandable; but if it had hitherto been the prerogative of a duchess to be seated in the presence of the queen, it was deeply mortifying to duchesses to see others of lower rank likewise seated. And when the old Duc de Richelieu said to the king at the end of the *ancien régime:* 'Under Louis XIV one kept silent, under Louis XV one dared to whisper, under you one talks quite loudly', it was not because he approved of this development but because he disapproved of it. The bursting of their chains would have meant, for the court nobles, the disintegration of their status as an aristocracy. Of course, one could have said: 'I shall have no more part of this ceremony', and isolated nobles perhaps did so. But this also meant forfeiting privileges, losing power, and declining relative to others. In short, it meant humiliation and, to an extent, self-immolation, unless the person concerned possessed other assurances of his value and pride, of his selfhood and identity, in his own eyes or in those of other people.

Within the court mechanism, one person's desire for status kept others vigilant. And once a stable balance of privileges had emerged, no one could break out without laying hands on these privileges, the basis of his whole personal and social existence.

The people thus enmeshed held each other fast in this situation, however grudgingly they bore it. Pressure from those of lower rank or the less privileged forced the more favoured to maintain their advantages, and conversely the pressure from above compelled those on whom it weighed to escape it by emulation, forcing them too into the competition for status. Someone who had the right to attend the first *entrée* or to pass the king his shirt, looked down on and would not give way to someone who was only admitted to the third. The prince would not give way to the duke, the duke to the marquis, and all together as *noblesse* would and could not yield to those who were not nobles and had to pay taxes. One attitude fostered the other, and through pressure and counter-pressure the social mechanism achieved a certain equilibrium. It was in etiquette, visible to all, that this equilibrium was expressed. It signified for everyone yoked into it an assurance of his carefully graded social existence, though only a fragile assurance. For given the tensions by which this social system was both riddled and maintained, every link within it was incessantly exposed to attack by lower or almost equal-ranking competitors who, whether by performing services, through the king's favour or merely by clever tactics, sought to bring about shifts in etiquette and so in the order of rank.

A shift in the hierarchy that was not reflected in a change of etiquette could not occur. Conversely, the slightest change in people's position in etiquette meant a change in the order of rank at court and within court society. And for this reason each individual was hypersensitive to the slightest change in the mechanism, stood watch over the existing order, attentive to its finest nuances, unless he happened to be trying to change it to his own advantage. In this way, therefore, the court mechanism revolved in perpetual motion, fed by the need for prestige and the tensions which, once they were there, it endlessly renewed by its competitive process.

7. Louis XIV had certainly not created the mechanism of ceremonial. But thanks to certain opportunities open to his social function he had used, consolidated and extended it; and he did so from a standpoint that was significantly different from that of the nobility enmeshed in it. A concrete example of the way ceremonial functioned in his hands, supplementing the general description of a particular ceremony, may clarify its importance to the king.

Saint-Simon, in connection with a conflict over rank, had resigned from military service. He informed the king that for reasons of health he regretfully could no longer serve. Louis XIV was not pleased. Saint-Simon found out in confidence that on receiving the news, he had said: 'One more who is abandoning us'.

Shortly afterwards Saint-Simon went back for the first time to the king's *couchée*. It was the custom at this event for a priest to hold a special chandelier, although the room was brightly lit. Each time, the king designated someone present to whom the priest had to give the chandelier. This was a mark of distinction. The procedure to be followed was exactly prescribed. 'One took off one's glove', Saint-Simon writes, 'stepped forward, held the chandelier for a few moments while the king was lying down, and then returned it to the first valet.' Saint-Simon was understandably surprised when, that evening, despite his resignation from the army, the king appointed him to hold the chandelier.

'The king did so', he comments, 'because he was vexed with me and did not want to show it. But that was the only thing I received from him for three years. In this time he used every opportunity to show me his disfavour. He did not speak to me, looked at me as if accidentally, never said a word to me about my resignation from the army.'

Louis XIV's attitude on this occasion is very revealing: etiquette here is not a ghostly perpetual motion machine controlled by no one; from the king's standpoint, it serves a clear purpose. He does not merely adhere to the traditional order of rank. Etiquette everywhere allows latitude that he uses as he thinks fit to determine even in small ways the reputations of people at court. He uses the psychological structure corresponding to the hierarchical-aristocratic social structure. He uses the competition for prestige to vary, by the exact degree of favour shown to them, the rank and standing of people at court, to suit his purposes as ruler, shifting the balance of tensions within the society as his need dictates. Etiquette is not yet petrified; in the king's hands it is a highly flexible instrument of power.

In the earlier discussion of the court attitude to living space it clearly emerged with what care and deliberation, with what special calculations of prestige the shape and decoration of rooms were differentiated. The scene at the king's *couchée* described by Saint-Simon shows analogous behaviour in a different context. It also shows somewhat more clearly the function of this careful differentiation of all outward aspects of court society: the king is vexed but he does not fly into a rage, he does not discharge his anger directly in an affective outburst. He controls himself and expresses his relationship to Saint-Simon in a carefully measured attitude which reproduces the exact nuance that he thinks it desirable to express in this case. The minor distinction, combined with the slighting of Saint-Simon at other times, constitutes the graduated response to the latter's conduct. And this measured calculation of one's position in relation to others, this characteristic restraint of the affects, is typical of the attitude of the king and of court people in general.

8.  What produces this attitude? Let us begin by attempting to find out what function the measured calculation of attitudes, the observation of nuances in the relationships of person to person, had for the bulk of court people.

They were all more or less dependent on the king. The smallest nuance in his behaviour towards them was therefore important to them; it was the visible indicator of their relation to him and their position within court society. But this dependence indirectly shaped the behaviour of court people towards each other.

Their rank within court society was, of course, determined first of all by that of their house, their official title. At the same time, however, permeating and modifying the official hierarchy, an actual order of rank which was far more finely shaded, uninstitutionalized and unstable established itself within court society. A courtier's position in this depended on the favour he enjoyed with the king, his power and importance within the field of court tensions. There was, for example, an institutional hierarchy among dukes, based primarily on the ancientness of their houses. This order was legally enshrined. But at the same time the duke of a younger house might currently enjoy higher esteem, through his relations to the king or his mistress or any other powerful group, than one from an older house. The real position of a person in the network of court society was always governed by both factors, official rank and actual power position, but the latter finally had greater influence on behaviour towards him. The position a person held in the court hierarchy was therefore extremely unstable. The actual esteem he had achieved forced him to aspire to improve his official rank. Any such improvement necessarily meant a demotion of others, so that such aspirations unleashed the only kind of conflict—apart from warlike deeds in the king's service—which was still open to the court nobility, the struggle for position within the court hierarchy.

One of the most interesting of these struggles was the one waged by the Duke of Luxembourg against the sixteen dukes and peers of France who were of older rank. Saint-Simon begins his account of this struggle with the following words that graphically illustrate the two sides of the court hierarchy just mentioned, and the way they interacted: 'M. de Luxembourg, proud of his successes and the applause of the *monde* at his triumphs, believed himself strong enough to move from the eighteenth rank of ancientness that he held among his peers to the second, immediately behind M. d'Uzès'.

9. The actual order of rank within court society constantly fluctuated. The balance within this society was, as we have said, very precarious. Now small, almost imperceptible tremors, now large-scale convulsions incessantly changed the positions of people and the distance between them. To keep abreast of these upheavals was vitally important to court people. For it was dangerous to be discourteous to a person whose stock was rising. It was no less dangerous to be unduly amiable to a person who was sinking in the hierarchy, was close to disfavour; or one should only do so if it served a particular purpose. A constant, precisely calculated adjustment of behaviour towards everyone at court was therefore indispensable. The behaviour one courtier judged appropriate to another at a given time was for this order, as for observers, an exact indicator of how high he currently stood in social opinion. And as an individual's stock was identical to his social existence, the nuances of behaviour by which people reciprocally expressed their opinion on it took on extraordinary importance.

This whole bustle of activity had a certain resemblance to a stock exchange. In it, too, a society actually present formed changing assessment of value. But at a stock exchange what is at stake is the value of commercial houses in the opinion of investors; at court it was the value of the people present in each other's opinion. And while at the former even the slightest fluctuation can be expressed in figures, in the latter a person's value was expressed primarily in the nuances of social intercourse. The gradations of domestic ornamentation appropriate to the rank of a house's owner which, according to the *Encyclopédie,* could only be learned by frequenting good society, are crude—as is the division into estates itself—compared to the delicate shades of behaviour that were needed to express the actual order of rank at court at any time.

From such contexts one gains understanding of the specific type of rationality that formed in court circles. Like every type of rationality, this evolves in conjunction with particular constraints enforcing control of the affects. A social figuration within which an extensive transformation of external into internal compulsions takes place is a permanent condition for the production of forms of behaviour the distinctive feature of which we denote by the concept of 'rationality'. The complementary concepts of 'rationality' and 'irrationality' refer to the relative parts played by short-term affects and long-term conceptual models of observable reality in individual behaviour. The greater the importance of the latter in the unstable balance between affective and reality-orientated directives, the more 'rational' behaviour is—provided the control of the affective directives does not go too far. For pressure from and saturation by the affects is itself an integral component of human reality.

But the type of reality-orientated conceptual model involved in the control of human behaviour varies with the structure of social reality itself. Accordingly, the 'rationality' of court people is different from that of the professional bourgeoisie. On closer investigation it could be shown that the former is one of the early stages and pre-conditions of the latter. Common to both is a preponderance of longer-term reality-orientated considerations over momentary affects in the fluctuating balance of tensions controlling behaviour in particular social fields and situations. But in the bourgeois type of 'rational' behaviour-control, the calculation of financial gains and losses plays a primary role, while in the court aristocratic type the calculation is of gains and losses of prestige, finance and prestige respectively being the means to power in these societies. As we saw, in court circles a gain in prestige was sometimes bought with a financial loss. What appeared 'rational' and 'realistic' by court standards was thus 'irrational' and 'unrealistic' by bourgeois ones. Common to both was control of behaviour with a view to gaining power *as it was understood at the time, that is, in accordance with the figuration of people existing then.*

It must be enough to indicate the problem. It shows how inadequate is a simple, absolute conceptual antithesis between two poles that leaves no room for a clear formulation of the many evolutionary constellations lying between the fictitious absolutes 'rational' and 'irrational'. Clearly, to do justice to the facts, far more refined and subtle concepts are needed; but they are not available.

Court 'rationality', if we may call it so, derived its specific character neither, like scientific rationality, from the endeavour to know and control extra-human natural phenomena, nor, like bourgeois rationality, from the calculated planning of strategy in the competition for economic power; it arose, as we saw, from the calculated planning of strategy in face of the possible gain or loss of status in the incessant competition for this kind of power.

Competitive struggles for prestige and status can be observed in many social formations; it may be that they are to be found in all societies. What is observed in court society has in this sense a paradigmatic value. It points to a social figuration that draws the individuals forming it into an especially intense and specialized competition for the power associated with status and prestige.

In face of such phenomena the attempt is often made to make do with explanations from individual psychology, for example by attributing an unusually strong 'urge to dominate' to the people concerned. But explanations of this type are, in their whole approach, inadequate here. The assumption underlying them, that in this society many individuals happened to come together who were endowed by nature with an especially strong desire to dominate, or with any other individual qualities that can explain the special nature of court competition for prestige, is one of the many attempts to explain something unexplained by something inexplicable.

We stand on firmer ground if, instead of a large number of separate individuals, we take the figuration formed by them as our starting point. Viewed from this standpoint, it is not difficult to understand the measured attitudes, the calculated gestures, the ever-present nuances of speech, in short the specific form of rationality that became second nature to the members of this society, that they exercised with effortless elegance and which, indeed, like the specific control of affects which its exercise demanded, was an indispensable instrument in the continuous competition for status and prestige.

## Notes

1. Saint-Simon describes this somewhat differently: he says that the doctor and, while she lived, the king's wet-nurse first came in to rub him down.

2. The office of *grand chambellan* or lord chamberlain was one of the great court offices. Its occupant had supervision over all officers of the king's chamber.

3. All these court offices were purchasable; admittedly, the king's permission was needed and also, in the reign of Louis XIV, they were reserved exclusively for the nobility.

4. Analogous structures such as a very large terrace were very often found in the country seats of higher nobles. It is interesting to see how building custom was used here for the

purposes of court etiquette. The gallery or terrace, . . . otherwise perhaps a place of relaxed conviviality, here also served as an antechamber for the court nobility; and its special size was used to assemble the whole court.

5. The reconstruction of such a ceremony at close quarters makes it easier, as we can see, to understand the meaning of this social phenomenon in the wider context of the power structure. In the ceremony at least three functional levels are fused into an indivisible functional complex; use-function, prestige-function and power or state function. The polarity postulated by Max Weber of instrumental rationality and value-rationality turns out not to be very applicable to such phenomena.

# 5

# Mozart: The Artist in the Human Being

Mozart is among the artists whose works have passed the ever-renewed test of generations especially convincingly. This is not true without reservations. Many of the compositions of his childhood and youth are now forgotten or arouse little response. The great curve of his social existence—the prodigy pampered by the high society of Europe, the more difficult fame of his industrious twenties and early thirties, the loss of popularity, especially in Vienna, the growing indigence and the isolation of his last years, then the very uneven rise of his fame after his death—all that is well enough known and does not need to be discussed in detail here. What is surprising, perhaps, is that Mozart survived his dangerous phase as a child prodigy without his talent being destroyed.

One not infrequently comes across the idea that the maturing of a talent of 'genius' is an autonomous, 'inner' process that takes place more or less in isolation from the human fate of the individual concerned. This idea is bound up with the other common notion that the creation of great works of art is independent of the social existence of their creator, of his or her development and experience as a human being among others. In keeping with this, biographers of Mozart often assume that the understanding of Mozart the artist, and thus of his art, can be divorced from the understanding of Mozart the man. This separation is artificial, deceptive and unnecessary. Although the present state of knowledge does not allow us to lay bare the connections between the social existence and the works of an artist as if with a scalpel, it is possible to probe them in some depth.[1]

At the present stage of civilisation the transfiguration of the mysterious element in genius may satisfy a deeply-felt need. At the same time, it is one of many forms of the deification of 'great' people, the other side of which is contempt for ordinary people. By elevating the former above the human measure, one depresses the latter below it. Our understanding of an artist's achievement and the joy taken in his or her works is not diminished but is reinforced and deepened if we attempt to grasp the connection between the works and the artist's fate in the society of his or her fellows. The special gift or, as it was called in Mozart's day, the 'ge-

From *Mozart: Portrait of a Genius*, pp. 50–63

nius' a person *has* rather than *is,* is itself one of the elements determining his or her social fate, and is to that extent a social fact, just like the simple gifts of people without genius.

In Mozart's case—unlike that of Beethoven, for example—the relation of the 'man' to the 'artist' has been especially confusing for many scholars, because the picture of him that emerges from letters, reports and other evidence assorts ill with the preconceived ideal of a genius. Mozart was a simple man, not particularly impressive if one met him in the street, sometimes childish and in private conversation far from sparing in the use of metaphors relating to excreta. From an early age he had a strong need of love, which manifested itself in the short years of his manhood both in the physical urge and in the constant desire for the affection of his wife and his public. The question is how someone equipped with all the animal needs of an ordinary human being could produce music which seemed to those who heard it devoid of all animality. Such music is characterised by terms such as 'deep', 'sensitive', 'sublime' or 'mysterious'—it seems to be part of a world different from that of ordinary experience, in which the mere collection of less sublime aspects of human beings has a debasing effect.

The reason why this Romantic dichotomy has survived so tenaciously is clear. It is a reflection of the ever-renewed conflict between civilised people and their animality, which has never been properly resolved in all the stages of development up to now. The idealising image of the genius is enlisted as an ally of the forces that individuals marshal on behalf of their spirituality against their bodily self. The battlefield is displaced. The resulting division, whereby the mystery attributed to a genius on one hand and his or her ordinary humanity on the other are consigned to separate pigeon-holes, expresses an inhumanity deeply rooted in the European intellectual tradition. This is an unsolved problem of civilisation.

Every spurt of civilisation, no matter where or on what level of human development it takes place, represents an attempt by human beings in their dealings with each other to pacify the untamed animal impulses which are a part of their natural endowment by means of socially generated counter-impulses, or to sublimate and transform them culturally. This enables people to live with each other and with themselves without being constantly exposed to the uncontrollable pressure of their animalic impulses—their own and those of others. If people remained, as they grew up, the same impulsive creatures they were as children, their chances of survival would be extremely slight. They would be without learned means of orientation in their search for food, they would be helplessly susceptible to each momentary urge, and would thus be a permanent burden and a danger to themselves and others.

But the social canons and methods by which people build up drive-controls in their communal life are not brought into being deliberately; they evolve over long periods, blindly and without plan. Irregularities and contradictions in those controls, huge fluctuations in their severity or leniency, are therefore among the recurrent structural features of the civilising process. We encounter whole groups of people, or just individual people, who develop extreme forms of regulation of their animal impulses, who are inclined to wall up their impulses and to combat, with an immense expenditure of energy, people who do not do likewise. We also come across people who do the opposite, forming a very loose structure of drive-controls and impatiently trying to satisfy momentary impulses. Something of the former type's civilising over-reaction is still detectable in a canon of thought whose exponents are ready to divide humanity into two abstract categories, denoted by labels such as 'nature' and 'culture' or 'body' and 'mind', without the least attempt to investigate the connection between the phenomena to which these concepts refer. The same applies to the tendency to draw a sharp dividing line between artist and human being, genius and 'ordinary person'. It applies to the tendency to treat art as something floating in mid-air, outside and independent of the social lives of people.

Undoubtedly, there are characteristics of the human arts, particularly music, which encourage such an attitude. To begin with, there are processes of sublimation through which human fantasies, converted into musical creations, can be divested of their animality without necessarily forfeiting their elementary dynamic, their impetus and strength, or the anticipated sweetness of fulfilment. Many of Mozart's works bear witness to an extraordinary transforming power of this kind.

A second feature of music, and of art in general—particularly in the complex, highly specialised form it takes in more developed societies—contributes to this tendency for it to be seen in isolation from its human context. Its resonance is clearly not confined to contemporary members of the society to which its creator belongs. It is one of the most significant characteristics of the human products we call 'works of art' that they are relatively autonomous in relation to their producer and their producer's society. Often enough, a work of art is only perceived as a masterpiece when it begins to strike a chord in people coming after the producer's generation. What qualities of a work, and what structural features of the social existence and the society of its creator, cause the creator to be regarded as 'great' by later generations—sometimes despite a lack of resonance among his or her contemporaries? This is an open question which is still often disguised as an eternal mystery today.

However, the relative autonomy of the work of art and the complex of problems associated with it do not relieve us of the obligation to investigate the connection between the experience and the fate of the creative artist in his or her society, that is, between this society itself and the works produced by the artist.

*       *

The relevance of this problem to our theme is greater than it might appear at first glance. The problem is not confined to music, or even to art. Clarification of the connections between an artist's experience and his or her work is also important for an understanding of ourselves as human beings. It makes the truism that people make music and enjoy listening to it, and do so at all stages of human development from the simplest to the most complex, seem somewhat less obvious and familiar. It replaces this idea by the larger question as to the special nature of those beings who have all the structural features of highly developed animals and are at the same time able to create, and respond to, magical forms, musical enchantments such as Mozart's *Don Giovanni* or his last three symphonies. Despite its sociological significance, the problem of the human capacity for sublimation has been somewhat neglected, as compared with the capacity for repression. In the present context, even if we cannot solve it, we are inevitably confronted by this question.

In talking about Mozart we find ourselves all too readily using terms like 'innate genius' or 'inborn ability to compose'; but these are thoughtless expressions. If we say that a feature of a person is inborn, we imply that it is genetically determined, biologically inherited in the same way as hair or eye colour. But it is simply impossible for a person to have a natural, genetically rooted propensity for anything as artificial as Mozart's music. Even before his twentieth birthday Mozart had written a large number of pieces in the special style that was fashionable at European courts at that time. With the facility that made him famous as a prodigy among his contemporaries, he composed exactly the kind of music that had emerged in his society, and only there, as a result of a peculiar development—that is to say, sonatas, serenades, symphonies, masses, etc. His ability to manipulate the complex musical instruments of his time—Mozart's father describes how effortlessly he learned to play the organ at the age of seven[2]—cannot have been given him by nature any more than his mastery of these musical forms.

That Mozart's imagination expressed itself in sound patterns with a spontaneity and energy reminiscent of a natural force is beyond doubt.

But if a force of nature was at work here, it was certainly a much less specific force than the one that manifested itself in the particular idiom of his prolific inventions. Mozart's extraordinary facility in composing and playing music conforming to the social music canon of his time can be explained only as an expression of a sublimating transformation of natural energies, not as an expression of natural or inborn energies per se. If a biological predisposition played a part in his special talent, it can only have been a highly general, unspecified predisposition, for which we do not at present have even an adequate term.

It is conceivable, for example, that biological differences are involved in differing capacities for sublimation. In that sense one could imagine that Mozart possessed to an unusually high degree an innate, constitutional capacity to come to terms with the difficulties in early childhood that everyone has to contend with, through sublimation in the form of musical fantasies. But even that is a risky assumption. The reasons why particular mechanisms like projection, repression, identification or sublimation are preferred in the development of a particular personality are hardly known. No one will seriously doubt that even as a young child Mozart displayed a particularly strong ability to transform instinctual energies by sublimation. Nothing is taken away from Mozart's greatness or importance, or the joy communicated by his works, if that is said. On the contrary, here is a bridge over the fatal abyss that opens if one tries to separate Mozart the artist from the man.

However, to understand this unity, we need to go a few steps further. There cannot be many steps, as the question of sublimation is relatively unexplored.

Among the factors which clearly influence the process of sublimation are the extent and direction of sublimation in the parents of a child, or in other adults with whom the child has close contact in early life. Later, too, models of sublimation, such as suitable teachers, can exert a decisive influence through their personalities. Furthermore, one often has the impression that a person's position in the chain of generations has a special influence on the likelihood of sublimation; in other words, sublimation is easier for people in the second or third generation.

Mozart's father was a man with a pronounced pedagogic tendency. He was a gifted musician of the middle rank, and not unknown among his contemporaries as the author of a violin tutor. An ambitious, intelligent craftsman's son with a broad education, he had achieved a certain success as deputy conductor at the Salzburg court, but not enough to satisfy his aspirations. His whole desire for fulfilment in his social existence was thus focused on his children, above all his son. For him his son's musical education eclipsed all other tasks, including his own profession.

Not enough is known about Mozart's relationship to his mother; but this situation with a musician father seeking fulfilment for an urgent, unsatisfied yearning through his son is a not unfavourable constellation for a resolution of early childhood conflicts through sublimation. Thus Leopold Mozart greeted his son's first attempts at composition with tears in his eyes. A strong bond of love formed between him and his son, who was rewarded for each musical achievement with a big prize in terms of affection. This undoubtedly favoured the child's development in the direction desired by his father. More will be said later about these connections.

*      *

It may be useful to explore in somewhat more detail the peculiar ability of Mozart's that we have in mind when we call him a 'genius'. To be sure, it would be better to avoid this Romantic concept. What it means is not difficult to define. It means that Mozart could do something that the great majority of people are unable to do, which is beyond their powers of imagination: Mozart could give free rein to his fantasies. They poured out in a flood of sound-patterns which, when heard by other people, stimulated their feelings in the most diverse ways. The decisive factor in this was that while his imagination expressed itself in combinations of forms that stayed within the framework of the social canon of music which he had assimilated, these forms went far beyond the combinations previously known and the feelings they conveyed. It is this ability to produce innovations in the field of sound which convey a potential or actual message to others, produce a resonance in them, that we attempt to pin down with concepts such as 'creativity' as applied to music and, *mutatis mutandis,* to art in general.

In using such terms one is frequently unaware that most people are capable of producing innovative fantasies. Many dreams are of this kind. 'I've just dreamed something extraordinary', people sometimes say. 'It's as if someone quite different from me was dreaming', so a young girl expressed it, 'I have no idea how I get such ideas.' The point at issue here has nothing to do with dream contents. The pioneering work done by Freud and some of his pupils in this area is untouched by it. Here we are concerned with the creative side of dream-work. New and often quite incomprehensible connections are revealed in dreams.[3]

But the innovative fantasies of dreaming people, and even daydreams, differ in a specific way from the fantasies that become a work of art. They are usually chaotic, or at least disordered and confused and, although often of burning interest to the dreamer, of little or no interest to other people. The peculiarity of innovatory fantasies in the form of works of art is that they are fantasies kindled by material which is accessible to many people. In a word, they are de-privatised fantasies. That sounds simple, but the whole difficulty of artistic creation shows itself when someone tries to cross this bridge—the bridge of de-privatisation. It could also be called the bridge of sublimation. To take such a step people must be able to subordinate the power of fantasy expressed in their personal night-dreams or daydreams to the intrinsic regularities of the material, so that their products are cleansed of all purely I-related residues. In other words, in addition to their I-relevance, they must give their fantasies you-, he-, she-, we- and they-relevance. It is to meet this requirement that the fantasies are subordinated to a material, whether of words, colours, stone, sounds or whatever else.

In addition, the influx of fantasies into a material without loss of spontaneity, dynamism or innovatory force requires capabilities that go beyond mere fantasising in a given material. It needs a thorough familiarity with the intrinsic regularities of the material, a comprehensive training in handling them and an extensive knowledge of their properties. This training, the acquisition of this knowledge, brings certain dangers with it. It can impair the strength and spontaneity of the fantasies; in other words, it can infringe *their* intrinsic dynamics. Instead of developing them further by applying them to the material, one can completely paralyse them. For the transforming, de-animalising, civilising of the elemental fantasy-stream by the knowledge-stream and, if all goes well, the final merging of the two as the material is manipulated are, in part, the resolution of a conflict. The acquired knowledge, which includes acquired thinking or, in the reified language of tradition, 'reason', or, in Freudian terms, the 'ego', opposes the more animalic energy-impulses when they try to take control of the skeletal muscles and thus of action. That these libidinal impulses also flow through the chambers of memory in their effort to control human action, kindling the fire of dream fantasies in them—that in the work of the artist they are purified by a stream of knowledge until they finally merge with it—therefore represents a reconciliation between originally antagonistic tendencies of the personality.

And there is something else. The creation of a work of art, the manipulation of the material concerned, is an open-ended process; the artist is advancing along a path that he or she has never trodden before and, in the case of the great master, that no one has trodden before. Art creators experiment. They test their fantasies on the material, on the material of their fantasy, which is constantly taking new shape. At every moment they have the possibility of going either here or there. They can go off the rails, and say to themselves as they step back: 'That doesn't work, doesn't sound right, doesn't look right. That's facile, trivial, falls apart, doesn't link up into a taut, integrated structure.' It is therefore not only the internal dynamics of the fantasy-stream nor only the knowledge stream that is involved in the production of an art-work, but also a controlling element of the personality, the producer's artistic conscience, a voice that says: 'This is how it should be; like this it looks right, sounds right, feels right, and not like that.' If production moves along known paths, this individual conscience speaks with the voice of the social canon of art. But if artists develop the familiar canon further, as Mozart did in his later years, they must rely on their own artistic conscience. As they immerse themselves in their material they must take quick decisions as to whether the direction their spontaneous fantasy is taking them as they work on the material matches its immanent dynamics or not.

On this level, too, therefore, there is a reconciliation and fusion of two originally conflicting currents or tendencies within the artist—at least in societies where the production of art-works is a highly specialised and complex activity. These societies demand of their adult members a very extensive differentiation of the id, ego and super-ego functions. If the libidinal fantasy-stream flows relatively unchecked by knowledge and conscience into a material, artistic forms can appear dislocated and disconnected, as is seen, for example, in drawings by schizophrenics. Unsuitable elements, which only mean something to the creator, may be juxtaposed. The intrinsic regularities of the material, by means of which the artist's feelings and vision can be communicated to others, are clumsily used or violated, so that they are unable to perform their socialising function.

The pinnacle of artistic creation is achieved when the spontaneity and inventiveness of the fantasy-stream are so fused with knowledge of the regularities of the material and the judgement of the artist's conscience that the innovative fantasies emerge as if by themselves in a way that matches the demands of both material and conscience. This is one of the most socially fruitful types of sublimation process.[4]

\* \*

Mozart is a representative of this type in its most clear-cut form. In his case the spontaneity of the fantasy-stream was largely unbroken by being converted into music. Often enough musical inventions flowed from him as dreams emanate from a sleeping person. Some reports suggest that while he was in the company of other people he would sometimes be secretly listening to a piece of music that was taking shape within him. He would then hastily excuse himself, the reports say; after a while he would come back in good spirits. He had just, as we say, 'composed' one of his works.

The fact that at such times a work composed itself, so to speak, by it-self was the result not only of the intimate fusion of his fantasy-stream with his craftsman's knowledge of the timbre and range of the instru-ments of his time or the traditional forms of music. It also sprang from the union of both, knowledge and fantasy, with his highly developed and extremely sensitive artistic conscience. What we feel to be the perfection of many of his works is due equally to his rich imagination, his compre-hensive knowledge of the musical material and the spontaneity of his musical conscience. However great the innovations of his musical fan-tasy, he never struck a wrong note. He knew with somnambulistic cer-tainty which sound-figures—within the framework of the social canon in which he worked—conformed to the immanent dynamics of the mu-sic he wrote, and which he had to reject.

The inspiration comes. Sometimes it unrolls by itself like the dreams of a sleeper, leaving its trace more or less completely on the recorder we call 'memory', so that the artist can inspect his own ideas like a spectator viewing the work of another. He can check them as if from a distance, elaborate and correct them or, if his artistic conscience falters, make them worse. Unlike dream ideas, those of the artist are attuned both to the material and to society. They are a specific form of communication, intended to elicit applause, resonance of a positive or negative kind, to arouse joy or anger, clapping or booing, love or hate.

This simultaneous attunement both to the material and to society, the connection between which may not be apparent at first sight, is far from accidental. Each of the materials characteristic of a particular artistic field has its own inexhaustible regularities and a corresponding resis-tance to the will of the creator. If a work of art is to come into being the personal fantasy-stream must be so transformed that it can be repre-sented in one of these materials. The art producer—no matter now spon-taneous the fusion of fantasy and material may be—has constantly to resolve the tensions that arise between them. Only then can fantasy take on form, become an integral part of a work and thereby become com-municable, able to produce a response in others, if not necessarily in the contemporaries of the artist.

This also means, however, that no artist is ever a wholly effortless cre-ator of works of art, not even Mozart. The extremely high degree of fu-sion between his fantasy-stream and the immanent dynamics of his material, the astonishing ease with which long sequences of sound-figures came into his consciousness, their inventiveness blending as if of its own accord with the immanent ordering of their sequential structure, by no means always dispensed Mozart from the task of working the ma-terial over under the eye of his conscience. All the same, he is said to have remarked once, late in his life, that it was easier for him to compose than not to do so.[5]

This is a revealing statement, and there is good reason to believe it authentic. At first sight it may sound like the utterance of a favourite of the gods. Only on looking more closely do we find that we have before us a very painful admission by a tormented man.[6]

Perhaps this brief discussion of the personality structures that were at work in a person as astonishing as Mozart, and not only in him, may do something to make the familiar way of talking about Mozart the man and Mozart the artist as if they were two different people seem less plausible. Once, Mozart the man was idealised to make him fit in with the preconceived idea of a genius. Now there is sometimes a tendency to treat Mozart the artist as a kind of superman and Mozart the man with slight contempt. That is not a judgement that he deserves. It rests not least on the idea mentioned earlier that his musical ability was an inherited gift of nature, with no connection to the rest of his personality. It may help to correct such ideas by recalling the extensive musical knowledge and highly developed conscience that were bound up inseparably with his musical creation. Many standard comments on Mozart that we meet in this context, assertions such as 'Mozart simply did not understand himself', reinforce the idea that artistic conscience is one of the inborn functions of a person, and therefore of Mozart. But conscience, whatever its specific form, is innate to no one. At most the potential for forming a conscience is a natural human endowment. This potential is activated and shaped into a specific structure through a person's life with others. The individual conscience is society-specific. This is seen in Mozart's artistic conscience, its attunement to a music as peculiar as that of court society.

## Notes

1. One of the peculiarities of the literature on Mozart is the fact that even a writer who sets out like St. George to slay the dragon of the idealising cult of genius and to make the treasure available, pure and unfalsified, to mankind, turns out to be at bottom another worshipper of idols. Seldom has the idea of man who develops into a great artist entirely from 'within', independently of his human fate, been elaborated on a higher level of reflection by a Mozart biographer than by Wolfgang Hildesheimer; and he does so, it seems to me, because of the same misunderstanding of 'human greatness' that he attacks in other biographies. The following quotation will serve as a brief example (Hildesheimer, *Mozart* [London: Dent, 1983], p. 48): 'Surely, Mozart's development as a musician cannot be reduced to his increasing facility. Rather, like every great artist, he develops by gradually sounding the depths of his potential world, and conquering it, according to an inner law. This is especially true of Mozart, in that all his experience found its way exclusively into his work, not into the development of his personality, or into a maturation process, or verbally

expressed wisdom, or a world view.' Poor Mozart! His music can mature without Mozart the man undergoing any process of maturation. A personality only reveals its development by uttering words of wisdom, by elaborating a comprehensive philosophical world view as well as operas and fantasies. One wonders if this is not a little narrow-minded. What harsh, intellectual inhumanity, what lack of empathy and compassion for a non-intellectual person speaks from these words!

2. Letter of 11 June 1763.

3. The libido stream flows through the cells of our memories and manipulates the stored forms and events like a practised theatre director, driving them forth in new scenes. Who writes the scenarios of our dreams? A half-automatic part of ourselves, director and actor at once, it transforms the material of our memories, makes something new from it, links it up in scenes we have never experienced.

4. To refer to this transformation of libidinal forces as a 'defense mechanism' is to indicate only one of its functions. In psychoanalytical terminology one might say that through sublimation the three agencies that Freud describes as separate—ego, id and super-ego—are reconciled.

5. Letter of September 1791 to da Ponte (its authenticity has been questioned): Hildesheimer, [*Mozart*], p. 193.

6. Mozart, in his unsatisfied desire for love, suffered much and dealt with his suffering by creating works which were sometimes graceful and playful, and sometimes deeply moving. That he failed to achieve the desired success with them was due not least to his extremely strict conscience. Mozart felt his gift, of which he was very conscious, as an obligation, and he refused to betray it even when this would have made his life easier. Of course, that was not entirely his decision. It was partly an unconscious compulsion, but it was *also* a decision. And because he unhesitatingly followed his conscience beyond the point where he jeopardised the response and thus forfeited the love and applause of the public that he also needed, because of this he deserves—as a man who was an artist— the admiration and gratitude of posterity.

# 6

# The Loneliness of the Dying

Closely bound up, in our day, with the greatest possible exclusion of death and dying from social life, and with the screening-off of dying people from others, from children in particular, is a peculiar embarrassment felt by the living in the presence of dying people. They often do not know what to say. The range of words available for use in this situation is relatively narrow. Feelings of embarrassment hold words back. For the dying this can be a bitter experience. While still alive, they are already deserted. But even here, the problem that dying and death poses for those left behind does not exist in isolation. The reticence and lack of spontaneity in expressing feelings of sympathy in the critical situations of other people is not limited to the presence of someone who is dying or in mourning. At our stage of civilization it manifests itself on many occasions that demand the expression of strong emotional participation without loss of self-control. It is similar with situations of love and tenderness.

In all such cases it is especially the younger generations that, more than in earlier centuries, are forced back on their own resources, their own individual powers of invention, in seeking the right words for their feelings. Social tradition provides individual people with fewer stereotyped expressions or standardized forms of behaviour that might make it easier to meet the emotional demands of such situations. Conventional phrases and rituals are, of course, still in use, but more people than earlier feel uneasy using them, because they seem shallow and worn-out. The ritual formulae of the old society, which made it easier to cope with critical life-situations such as this, sound stale and insincere to many young people; new rituals reflecting the current standard of feeling and behaviour, which might make it easier to cope with the recurrent crises in life, do not yet exist.

It would give a false picture to suggest that the stage-specific problems in the relation of the healthy to the dying, the living to the dead, are an isolated datum. What emerges here is a part-problem, an aspect of the general problem of civilization at its present stage.

From *The Loneliness of the Dying*, pp. 23–29

In this case, too, the peculiarity of the present situation may be better seen by reference to an example of the same problem from the past. In late October 1758 the Margravine of Bayreuth, the sister of King Frederick II of Prussia, lay dying. The King was not able to travel to see her, but sent in haste his own physician Cothenius, in case he could still help. He also sent verses and the following letter, dated 20 October 1758:

> Most tenderly-beloved Sister,
> Receive kindly the verses I am sending you. My heart is so filled with you, your danger and my gratitude, that your image constantly rules my soul and governs all my thoughts, waking or dreaming, writing prose or poetry. Would that Heaven might grant the wishes of your recovery that I daily send there! Cothenius is on his way; I shall worship him if he can preserve the person who in all the world is closest to my heart, whom I esteem and honour and for whom I remain, until the moment when I too return my body to the elements, most tenderly-beloved sister, your loyal and devoted brother and friend,
> Frederick.

The king wrote this valedictory letter to his sister not in French, but in German, which he did seldom. We can imagine that this letter brought solace to the dying woman and eased her departure from the living—if she was still able to read it.

The German language is not particularly rich in finely shaded expressions for non-sexual emotional attachments between people—non-sexual, whatever their origin may be. Words corresponding to the English 'affection' and 'affectionate' are lacking. *Zuneigung* and *zugetan*, suggesting the idea of 'inclination', do not quite convey the temperate warmth of the English term, and are less commonly used. Frederick's 'most tenderly-beloved sister' is, no doubt, a very exact expression of his feeling. Would it be used today? His attachment to his sister was probably the strongest bond to a woman or to any person in his life. We can assume that the feelings verbalized in this letter are sincere. The affection between brother and sister was reciprocal. He clearly understood that an assurance of his undiminished affection would bring comfort to the dying woman. But the expression of these feelings is clearly made easier for him by his implicit trust in certain linguistic conventions of his society which he allows to guide his pen. The modern reader, with a sharp ear for the clichés of the past, may experience 'your image' that 'constantly rules my soul' as conventional, and 'would that Heaven might grant the wishes' as theatrically Baroque, particularly in the mouth of a monarch not noted for piety. Frederick does indeed use conventional terms to express his feelings. But he is able to use them in such a way that the sincerity of his feelings is apparent, and we may suppose that the recipient of the letter felt this sincerity. The structure of communications was such that those to whom they were addressed could distinguish between sincere and insincere uses of the courtly phrases, while our ears no longer discern these nuances of civility.

This sharply illuminates the present situation. The brief spurt of informalization[1] still in progress makes us especially mistrustful of the ready-made rituals and 'flowery' phrases of earlier generations. Many socially prescribed formulae have the aura of past systems of rule about them; they can no longer be used mechanically like the *om mani padme* around the prayer-wheels of Buddhist monks. But at the same time the change accompanying the present stage of civilization produces in many people an unwillingness and often an incapacity to express strong emotions, either in public or in private life. They can only be ventilated, so it seems, in political and social conflict. In the seventeenth century men could weep in public; today this has become difficult and infrequent. Only women are still able, still socially allowed, to do so—for how much longer?

In the presence of dying people—and of mourners—we therefore see with particular clarity a dilemma characteristic of the present stage of the civilizing process. A shift towards informality has caused a whole series of traditional patterns of behaviour in the great crisis-situations of human life, including the use of ritual phrases, to become suspect and embarrassing for many people. The task of finding the right word and the right gesture therefore falls back on the individual. The concern to avoid socially prescribed rituals and phrases increases the demands on the individual's powers of invention and expression. This task, however, is often beyond people at the current stage of civilization. The way people live together, which is fundamental to this stage, demands and produces a relatively high degree of reserve in expressing strong, spontaneous affects. Often they are able only under exceptional pressure to overcome the barrier blocking actions resulting from strong feelings, and their verbalization. Thus, unembarrassed discourse with or to dying people, which they especially need, becomes difficult. It is only the institutionalized routines of hospitals that give a social framework to the situation of dying. These, however, are mostly devoid of feeling and contribute much to the isolation of the dying.

Religious death rituals can arouse in believers the feeling that people are personally concerned about them, which is doubtless their real function. Apart from these, dying is at present a largely unformed situation, a blank area on the social map. The secular rituals have been largely emptied of feeling and meaning; traditional secular forms of expression lack the power to convince. Taboos prohibit any excessive show of strong feelings, although they may be present. And the traditional aura of mystery surrounding death, with the remnants of magical gestures—opening the windows, stopping the clocks—makes death less amenable to treatment as a human, social problem that people have to solve with and for each other. At present those close to the dying often lack the ability to give them support and comfort by proof of their affection and tenderness. They find it difficult to press dying people's hands or to caress them, to give them a feeling of undiminished protection and belonging. Civilization's overgrown taboo on the expression of strong, spontaneous feelings ties their tongues and hands. And living people may half unconsciously feel death to be something contagious and threatening; they involuntarily draw back from the dying. But, as with every parting of people who are intimate, a gesture of undiminished affection is, for the one taking final leave, perhaps the greatest help, apart from the relief of physical pain, that those left behind can give.

## Note

1. Cf. Cas Wouters, 'Informalisation and the civilising process', in *Human Figurations: Essays for Norbert Elias,* ed. Peter R. Gleichmann, Johan Goudsblom and Hermann Korte (Amsterdam, 1977), pp. 437–53.

# II

POWER

# 7

# Game Models

Given the present state of sociological thinking, one of the persistent problems of sociology is on what grounds sociologists can claim that they have a field of their own distinct from that of biologists, psychologists, historians and other groups of specialists. For the subject matter of sociology is 'society', and societies are after all nothing but composite units of which individual human beings form the component parts. Is it not therefore necessary for sociologists to rely in the first instance on the findings of all those other disciplines which, like human biology, psychology or history, study individual human beings—the constituent parts of societies as such—and then to see whether they as sociologists have anything to add to the findings of these other disciplines? Would it not, moreover, be best and most obvious for sociologists first to study individual people singly, and then to see whether they can distil from a great mass of such individual studies any generalizations which can be presented as properties of 'societies'?

Quite a number of sociologists do in fact proceed in this manner. They investigate the behaviour, views and experience of individual people and process their results statistically. By means of inquiries of this type, focused on the 'component parts' of societies, they endeavour to bring to light the characteristics of the 'composite units', of the societies themselves. And as some of their findings do in fact indicate social connections and regularities beyond the reach of other disciplines concerned with the study of human being singly, these sociological findings are often implicitly treated as the solution to the problem of whether or not sociology can claim some kind of autonomy in relation to these other individual-centred social sciences. It is an answer which relies on scientific practice, on success or claimed success in solving empirical problems, rather than on a clear theoretical answer as to why it should be possible for sociologists, by studying the behaviour or experience of individual people, to carve out a special field of inquiry for themselves which is not already covered by other disciplines which also study individual people.

It is quite understandable that many people have believed in the past,

From *What Is Sociology?* pp. 71–99

and may still believe today, that all things social can and should be explained in terms of the psychological or perhaps even physical characteristics of people. The classical tradition of the physical sciences has been immensely influential. According to that tradition, the way to investigate a composite unit is to dissect it into its component parts, then to study the properties of the component parts in isolation, and finally to explain the distinguishing properties of the composite unit in terms of its component parts. Thus, the properties of molecules may be explained in terms of the properties of atoms, and these in turn in terms of their component particles. But does this method hold good for all fields of investigation? The difficulty is that the tradition of scientific atomism (as we may call it for short) lives on in theory, while scientific practice in many fields has run in a different direction. As has been shown elsewhere in greater detail,[1] the more closely integrated are the components of a composite unit, or in other words the higher the degree of their functional interdependence, the less possible it is to explain the properties of the latter only in terms of the former. It becomes more necessary not just to explore a composite unit in terms of its component parts, but also to explore the way in which these individual components are bonded to each other so as to form a composite unit. The study of the configuration of the unit parts, or in other words the structure of the composite unit, becomes a study in its own right. This is the reason why sociology cannot be reduced to psychology, biology, or physics: its field of study—the figurations of interdependent human beings—cannot be explained if one studies human beings singly.[2] In many cases the opposite procedure is advisable—one can understand many aspects of the behaviour or actions of individual people only if one sets out from the study of the pattern of their interdependence, the structure of their societies, in short from the figurations they form with each other.

Some people tend to shrink from this insight. They confuse it with a metaphysical assumption of long standing which is often summed up in the saying 'the whole is more than the sum of its parts'. Using the term 'whole' or 'wholeness' creates a mystery in order to solve a mystery. This aberration must be mentioned because many people appear to believe that one can only be one or the other—either an atomist or a holist. Few controversies are as unattractive as that in which two groups of antagonists run around in circles, each defending its own speculative and untestable thesis by attacking another that is equally speculative and untestable on the grounds that no third alternative is possible. In the case of atomism and holism, it most certainly is.

How exactly does it come about that people, because of their interdependence and the way their actions and experience intermesh, form a type of figuration, a kind of order which is relatively autonomous from the type of order encountered if, like biologists or psychologists, one investigates individual people either as representatives of their species or as isolated persons?

This question does present difficulties. Answering it is made easier if, as a kind of mental experiment, the way in which human aims and actions intertwine is demonstrated by means of a series of models. In this way, the inherently complex processes of interweaving are temporarily isolated in close focus, and thereby made more easily understandable. The models shortly to be described are, with the exception of the first, models of contests which (in the simpler forms at least) resemble real games like chess, bridge, football or tennis. They represent contests played out—more or less—according to rules. The first model, which we shall call the 'Primal Contest', is however a theoretically highly significant exception; it represents a real and deadly contest between two groups, and is not at all like a game. Both the Primal Contest and the game models are useful as an exercise in sociological imagination, which customary forms of thought tend to block. All the models are based on two or more people measuring their strength against each other. This is the basic situation encountered wherever people enter into or find themselves in relations with one another. The awareness of it, however, is often suppressed when people reflect on human relationships. There is no need to say why this is so. Every reader may think out the reasons for himself without much difficulty; he can look upon the task as a kind of game contest between himself and the author. In fact, challenges such as this are just what is under discussion here. They form a normal part of all human relationships. Smaller or larger trials of strength recur again and again: am I stronger?—are you stronger? After a while people may arrive at a certain balance of power, which according to social and personal circumstances may be stable or unstable.

For many people, the term 'power' has a rather unpleasant flavour. The reason is that during the whole development of human societies, power ratios have usually been extremely unequal; people or groups of people with relatively great power chances used to exercise those power chances to the full, often very brutally and unscrupulously for their own purposes. The offensive connotations which consequently cling to the concept 'power' may prevent people distinguishing between the factual data to which the concept of power refers and their evaluation of these data. So it is useful to concentrate here on the former. Balances of power are not only to be found in the great arena of relations between states, where they are often spectacular and attract most attention. They form an integral element of all human relationships. This is the way the following models should be read. It must also be borne in mind that power balances, like human relationships in general, are bi-polar at least, and usually multi-polar. The models may help towards a better understanding of such power balances, not as extraordinary but as everyday occurrences. From the day of its birth, a baby has power over its parents, not just the parents over the baby. At least, the baby has power over them as long as they attach any kind of value to it. If not, it loses its power. The parents may abandon the baby if it cries too much. They may starve it and, deliberately or not, cause it to die, if it has no function for them. Equally bi-polar is the balance of power between a slave and his master. The master has power over his slave, but the slave also has power over his master, in proportion to his function for his master—his master's dependence in him. In relationships between parents and infants, master and slave, power chances are distributed very unevenly. But whether the power differentials are large or small, balances of power are always present whenever there is functional interdependence between people. In this respect, simply to use the word 'power' is likely to mislead. We say that a person possesses great power, as if power were a thing he carried about in his pocket. This use of the word is a relic of magico-mythical ideas. Power is not an amulet possessed by one person and not by another; it is a structural characteristic of human relationships—of *all* human relationships.

The models demonstrate the relational character of power in a simplified form. In order to use the models of game contests to bring a series of power figurations into close focus, the concept of 'power ratios' is replaced here by the term 'relative strength of the players'. Even this phrase can be misunderstood as an absolute. However, it is obvious that a player's playing 'strength' varies in relation to his opponent's. The same goes for power, and for many other concepts in our language. The game models help to show how much clearer sociological problems become, and how much easier it is to deal with them, if one reorganizes them in terms of balances rather than reifying terms. Concepts of balance are far more adequate for what can actually be observed in investigating the nexus of functions which interdependent human beings have for each other than are concepts modelled on stationary objects.

Rule-governed human relationships cannot be understood if there is a tacit assumption that norms or rules are universally present from the outset as an unvarying property of human relationships. This assumption bars the way to asking and observing how and in what circumstances contests which are played out without rules transform themselves into relationships, *with* set rules. Wars and other kinds of human relationships with few or no rules are proof enough that this is not merely a hypothetical problem. Sociological theories which make it appear that norms are the mainspring of social relationships cannot account for the possibility of human relationships without norms and regulations; they give a distorted view of human societies. This is why the game models are prefaced by the Primal Contest, a model which shows a relationship between two groups totally unregulated by norms. According to a strong sociological tradition, norms are identified with structure. The Primal Contest may serve as a reminder that it is perfectly possible for relationships between people to be structured even though they are played without rules. Even a situation that appears to be the height of disorder to the people involved in it forms part of a social order. There is no reason why historical 'disorders'—wars, revolutions, rebellions, massacres and power struggles of every kind—cannot be explained. To do that is in fact one of the tasks of sociology. It would be impossible to explain normless conflicts if they had no structure and, in that sense, no order. The distinction between 'order' and 'disorder', so significant for the people involved, is sociologically speaking without significance. *Among men, as in nature, no absolute chaos is possible.*

So, if the word 'society' is used here as a technical term for a specific level of integration, and if relationships at this level are seen as constituting an order of a particular kind, the word 'order' is not being used in the sense in which it is used when people speak of 'law and order' or, in adjectival form, of an 'orderly' as opposed to a 'disorderly' person. One is talking about an order in the same sense that one talks of a natural order, in which decay and destruction as structured processes have their place alongside growth and synthesis, death and disintegration alongside birth and integration. For the people involved, these manifestations seem, with good cause, to be contradictory and irreconcilable. As objects of *study,* they are indivisible and of equal importance. Therefore it would be misleading to explain the process of social interweaving only in terms of models which refer to human relationships regulated by fixed norms. The Primal Contest may serve as a reminder of what it is that becomes socially regulated.

## Primal Contest: Model of a Contest without Rules

Two small tribal groups, A and B, get in each other's way when hunting for food in a great tract of wild forest. Both are hungry. For reasons not apparent to either, it has for some time been getting more and more difficult for them to find enough to eat. Game has become scarcer, roots and wild fruit harder to find, and the rivalry and enmity between the two groups has grown consequently fiercer. Group A consists of big, powerfully-built men and women, with few young people or children. Group B, their opponents, are smaller, less powerfully-built, quicker on their feet and, on average, considerably younger.

So the two groups get in each other's way. They are caught up in a long drawn-out struggle with each other. The smaller people of Group B creep at night into the other's camp, kill one or two of them in the dark, and vanish swiftly when the dead men's fellows, slower and more heavily built, try to pursue them. The men of Group A have their revenge some time later. They kill women and children of Group B while the men are out hunting.

Here, as in other similar cases, a fairly enduring antagonism reveals itself as a form of functional interdependence. The two groups are rivals for shrinking food resources. They are dependent upon each other: as in a game of chess (which was originally a war game), each move of one group determines each move of the other and *vice versa*. The internal arrangements in each group are determined to a greater or lesser extent by what each group thinks the other might do next. Fierce antagonists, in other words, perform a function for each other, because the interdependence of human beings due to their hostility is no less a functional relationship than that due to their position as friends, allies and specialists bonded to each other through the division of labour. Their function for each other is in the last resort based on the compulsion they exert over each other by reason of their interdependence. It is not possible to explain the actions, plans and aims of either of the two groups if they are conceptualized as the freely chosen decisions, plans and aims of each group considered on its own, independently of the other group. They can be explained only if one takes into account the compelling forces the groups exert upon each other by reason of their interdependence, their bilateral function for each other as enemies.

The concept of 'function', as it has been used in some sociological and anthropological literature, especially by 'structural-functionalist' theorists, is not only based on an inadequate analysis of the subject matter to which it relates, but also contains an inappropriate value judgement which, moreover, is made explicit in neither interpretation nor use. The inappropriateness of the evaluation is due to the fact that they tend—unintentionally—to use the terms for those tasks performed by one part of the society which are 'good' for the 'whole', because they contribute to the preservation and integrity of the existing social system. Human activities which either fail or appear to fail to do that are therefore branded as 'dysfunctional'. It is plain that at this point social beliefs have become mixed up in scientific theory. For this reason alone it is useful to look more carefully into the implications of the model of the two warring tribal groups. As enemies they perform a function for each other of which one must be aware if one is to understand the actions and plans of either of the two tribal groups. Here, as can be seen, the term 'function' is not used as an expression for a task performed by a section within a harmonious 'whole'. The model indicates that, like the concept of power, the concept of function must be understood as a concept of *relationship*. We can only speak of social functions when referring to inter-dependencies which constrain people to a greater or lesser extent. This element of coercion can be clearly seen in the function performed by each tribal group as the enemy of the other. The difficulty in using the concept of function as a quality of a single social unit is simply that it leaves out the reciprocity, the bi-polarity or multi-polarity of all functions. It is im-possible to understand the function A performs for B without taking into account the function B performs for A. That is what is meant when it is said that the concept of function is a concept of relationship.

To put it at its simplest, one could say: when one person (or a group of persons) lacks something which another person or group has the power to withhold, the latter has a function for the former. Thus men have a function for women and women for men, parents for children and chil-dren for parents. Enemies have a function for each other, because once they have become interdependent they have the power to withhold from each other such elementary requirements as that of preserving their physical and social integrity, and ultimately survival.

To understand the concept of 'function' in this way demonstrates its connection with power within human relationships. People or groups which have functions for each other exercise constraint over each other. Their potential for withholding from each other what they require is usually uneven, which means that the constraining power of one side is greater than that of the other. Changes in the structure of societies, in the overall nexus of functional interdependencies, may induce one group to question another group's power of constraint, their 'potential for with-holding'. In that case, these changes initiate trials of strength, which can erupt suddenly in the form of acute and even violent power struggles, or they may smoulder for long periods of time as a standing conflict inher-ent in the structure of a society during a certain phase of its development. Today, built-in tensions and conflicts of this kind are characteristic of the interdependent functions of workers and entrepreneurs, as of those be-tween groups of states. In previous periods, they were characteristic of the triangular relationship between kings, nobles and citizens, or be-tween segments of a tribe.[3] They are no less characteristic of the func-tional interdependencies between husbands and wives or parents and children. At the root of these trials of strength are usually problems such as these: Whose potential for withholding what the other requires is greater? Who, accordingly, is more or less dependent on the other? Who, therefore, has to submit or adapt himself more to the other's demands? In more general terms, who has the higher power ratio, and can therefore steer the activities of the other side to a greater extent than they can steer his own activities—can put more pressure on them than they can put on him? If the overall structure of societies changes, the question may become whether one side can defunctionalize the other, destroy the whole set of social positions on which the other side's power rests, or physically destroy its opponents altogether.[4]

The Primal Contest represents as it were a borderline case. Here, one side aims at depriving the other not only of their social functions but of their very lives. In studying men's changing interdependencies and the interweaving of their aims and activities, one cannot lose sight of the interdependence of violent antagonists represented by the Primal Contest model. Only if one is aware of this last resort relationship between humans—interdependence through an all-out struggle for survival—is it possible to see the basic nature of the problems mentioned before: how have people been able—and how are they able—to regulate some of their interdependencies in such a way that they need not resort to this ultimate way out of tensions and conflicts? At the same time, this model of a contest without rules can serve as a reminder that all relationships between men, all their functional interdependencies, are processes. Today these concepts are often used in a manner which suggests that they refer to a stationary condition, in which any change is quite accidental. Terms like 'interweaving' point to the processual nature of such relationships.

Returning to the example of the course of the struggle between two tribes, it shows clearly the immanent dynamics of a conflict relationship. In such a life-or-death conflict, each side is constantly both planning its next foray and living always on the alert in anticipation of the other side's next move. Since they have no common norms as a means of orientation, each side relies for its orientation entirely on its idea of the power resources of the other side in relation to its own—on its idea of their respective strength, cunning, weapons, food supply and food reserves. These power resources and relative strength, which in this case mean above all physical force and the planning of strategies for physical survival and annihilation, are constantly being tested in raids and skirmishes. Each side tries to weaken the other by any means. Here one is indeed confronted with a continuous interweaving, move upon move, in which every single person is totally involved. In this case, as can be seen, groups are no longer represented in terms of concepts such as norms, rules, ideal-types and so on, which make it appear that they are constituted exclusively through intellectual processes; the interweaving concerns human beings in the round. The models have to be read as representations of human beings bonded to each other in time and space. Among the problems implied by the Primal Contest model are the following: Will the group of older, taller, more muscular but slower people succeed in enticing the nimbler, smaller, less experienced but more agile people away from their camp and kill some of their women and children? Will the latter group succeed in goading the first with abuse until they become furious and pursue the second group, stumble into their traps and get killed? Will they weaken and destroy each other to the point where both are beyond recovery? That is why even this case of the interdependence between violent enemies locked in a life-and-death struggle is a *process* of interweaving. The sequence of moves on either side can only be understood and explained in terms of the immanent dynamics of their interdependence. If the sequence of actions of either side were studied in isolation, it would appear without rhyme or reason. The functional interdependence of the moves of the two sides is no less great in this case than in the case of rule-governed conflict or cooperation. Even though the interweaving of the two sides in the sequence of time is a process without norms, it is nevertheless a process with a clear structure which can be analysed and explained.

## Game Models: Models of Interweaving Processes with Norms

Like the opening model of a contest without rules, the models of game contests with rules are simplifying intellectual experiments. With their help it is possible to bring out more graphically the processual character of relationships between interdependent people. At the same time, they show how the web of human relations changes when the distribution of power changes. One of the ways in which simplification has been brought about is by substituting a series of assumptions about players' relative strength in the game for differences in relative power potentials of interdependent people or groups in their relations with each other. The models are arranged in such a way as to bring out more clearly the transformation which the web of human interrelations undergoes when power differentials decrease.

### Two-Person Games

(1a) Imagine a game played by two people in which one player is very much superior to the other, A being a very strong player, B a very weak one. In this case, A has a very high measure of control over B. To a certain extent A can force B to make particular moves. In other words, A has 'power' over B. This term means no more and no less than that A can control B's moves to a very great extent. But this 'capacity to compel' is not unlimited; player B, relatively weak though he is, has a degree of power over A. For just as B, in making each move, has to take his bearings from A's preceding moves, so must A take his bearings from B's preceding moves. B may not be as strong as A, but he must have some strength—if it were zero, there would be no game. In other words, in any game the participants always have control *over each other*. When speaking of the 'power' A has over B, the concept does not refer to an absolute, but to a *power ratio*—the difference (in A's favour) between A's and B's strength in the game. This difference—the uneven balance between the two players' strengths in the game—determines to what extent player A's moves can shape player B's moves, or *vice versa*. According to the assumptions of model (1a), the differential between the players' strengths in the game (their power ratio) in A's favour is very great. Correspondingly great is A's ability to force a particular move (a particular 'behaviour' or 'action') on his opponent.[5]

However, A's greater strength in the game does not only give him a high degree of control over his opponent B. It also gives him, *in addition,* a high degree of control over the game as such. Though his control of the game is not absolute, he can determine its course (the game process) and therefore also the result of the game, to a very great extent. In interpreting this model, it is important to make this conceptual distinction between two kinds of control which result from one player's greatly superior strength: on the one hand, the control he can exert over his opponent, and, on the other hand, the control it gives him over the course of the game as such. That is not to say that because it is possible to make this distinction between control over the player and control over the game, one can think and speak as if the player and the game exist independent of each other.

(1b)  Imagine that the differential between A's strength and B's strength in the game diminishes. It does not matter whether this comes about by B's strength increasing or by A's decreasing. A's chances of controlling B's moves by means of his own—that is, his power over B—diminishes proportionately; B's chances of controlling A increase correspondingly. The same is true of A's ability to determine the game process and result. The more the differential between A's and B's strength decreases, the less power will either player have to force a particular tactic on the other. Both players will have correspondingly less chance to control the changing figuration of the game; and the less dependent will be the changing figuration of the game on the aims and plans for the course of the game which each player has formed by himself. The stronger, conversely, becomes the dependence of each of the two players' overall plans and of each of their moves on the changing figuration of the game—on the game process. The more the game comes to resemble a social process, the less it comes to resemble the implementation of an individual plan. In other words, to the extent that the inequality in the strengths of the two players diminishes, there will result from the interweaving of moves of two individual people a game process *which neither of them has planned*.

## Multi-person Games at One Level

(2a) Imagine a game in which player A is playing simultaneously against several other players, B, C, D and so on, under the following conditions: A is far superior in strength to any single one of his opponents, and he is playing against each one separately. In this case the figuration of the players is not very different from that in model 1a. Players B, C, D and so on are not playing jointly but separately, and the only connection between them therefore is the fact that each individual is playing privately against the same equally superior opponent, A. It is therefore basically a series of games for two people, each game having its own balance of power and developing in its own way. The courses taken by the games are not directly interdependent. In each of these games A is overwhelmingly the more powerful; he has a very high degree of control both over his opponent and over the course of the game itself. In each of these games the distribution of power is unequivocally unequal, inelastic and stable. Perhaps one ought to add that the position might alter to A's disadvantage if the number of independent games he is playing should increase. It is possible that his superiority in strength over the independent players, B, C, D and the rest, might gradually suffer as a result of an increase in the number of opponents, all independent of each other. There is a limit to the span of active relationships independent one from another which one person can pursue simultaneously—in separate compartments, so to speak.

(2b) Imagine a game in which player A plays simultaneously against several weaker opponents, not separately but against all of them together. Thus he plays a single game against a group of opponents, each one of whom taken by himself is weaker than A.

This model allows for various constellations in the balance of power. The simplest is that in which players B, C, D and their colleagues form a group directed against A, and are undisturbed by tensions among themselves. Even in this case there is more doubt than in (2a) about the distribution of power between A and the opposing group, and about the possibility of one side or the other controlling the course of the game. Undoubtedly the unequivocal formation of a group by many weaker players represents a lessening of A's superiority. Compared with (1a) there is much less certainty about the control and planning of the game and therefore less certainty in predicting its outcome. If groups formed by weaker players do not have strong inner tensions, that is a power factor to their advantage. Conversely, if groups formed by weaker players do have strong inner tensions, that is a power factor to the advantage of their opponent. The greater the tensions, the greater the chances of A to control the moves of B, C, D and their allies, as well as the general course of the game.

In contrast with models of type (1) and the transitional model (2a) in which the games in question are for two people, or, to put it differently, bi-polar groups, (2b) is an example of a multi-polar game or a game for several people. It can be regarded as a transitional model to (2c).

(2c) Imagine that A's strength decreases in a multi-polar game compared with that of his opponents, B, C, D and others. A's chances to control the moves of his opponents, and to control the course of the game as such, change in the same direction as in (1b), provided that the group of opponents is fairly united.

(2d) Imagine a game in which two groups, B, C, D, E, . . . and U, V, W, X, . . . play against each other according to rules which give both sides equal chances of winning, and with each side having approximately the same strength. In this case neither side is able to exercise a decisive influence over the other in the flurry of move and countermove. The game process in this case cannot be controlled by either of the two groups on its own. The intertwining of moves made alternately by each player and group of players builds up to form a certain kind of order, which can be defined and explained. But, in order to do so, an observer needs to distance himself from the positions taken by both sides, as they appear when considered alone. The order in question is a specific kind of order, an ordered network or figuration, within which no action by either side can be regarded as the action of that one side alone. It must rather be interpreted as continuing the interweaving process and forming a part of the future interweaving of actions made by both sides.

*Multi-person Games on Several Levels*

Imagine a game for many people in which the number of participants is constantly growing. This increases the pressure on the players to change their grouping and organization. An individual player will have to wait

longer and longer for his turn to move. It will become more and more difficult for a player to put together a mental picture of the course of the
game and its figuration. Lacking such a picture, he may become disori-
entated. He finds a fairly clear picture of the course of the game and of its
general figuration, which changes constantly as the game proceeds, so
that he may plan his next move accordingly. The figuration of interdependent players and of the game which they play together is the framework for each individual's moves. He must be in a position to picture this
figuration so that he may decide which move will give him the best
chance of winning or of defending himself against his opponents' attacks. But there is a limit to the span of the web of interdependence
within which an individual player can orientate himself suitably and
plan his personal strategy over a series of moves. If the number of interdependent players grows, the figuration, development and direction of
the game will become more and more opaque to the individual player.
However strong he may be, he will become less and less able to control
them. From the point of view of the individual player, therefore, an intertwining network of more and more players functions increasingly as
though it had a life of its own. Here too the game is nothing more than a
game played by many individuals. But as the number of players grows
the individual player not only finds the game increasingly opaque and
uncontrollable, but he also gradually becomes *aware* of his inability to
understand and control it. Both the figuration of the game and the individual player's picture of it—the way in which he perceives the course of
the game—change together in a specific direction. They change in functional interdependence, as two inseparable dimensions of the same
process. They can be considered separately, but not as *being* separate.

As the number of players grows, it becomes harder for each individual—and therefore for all the players—to make suitable or correct
moves, judged from his own position in the totality of the game. The
game will become increasingly disorganized; its functioning will deteriorate. As functioning deteriorates,[6] a growing pressure is exerted on the
group of players to reorganize themselves. There are several possibilities
open; three will be mentioned here, though it is possible to examine only
one of them at length.

An increase in the number of players can cause the group of players to
disintegrate, splintering into a number of smaller groups. Their relationship to each other can take two possible forms. The splinter groups can
either move further apart and then continue to play the game quite independently of every other group. Or they can make up a new figuration of
interdependent groups, each playing more or less autonomously, though
all remain rivals for certain chances, equally sought after by all groups.

A third possibility is that the group of players—in certain circumstances which cannot be entered into here—remains integrated, turning, however, into a highly complex figuration; a two-tier group can develop out of the one-tier group.

### (3a) *Two-Tier Games Model: Oligarchic Type*

Pressure exerted on the individual players by an increase in the number of players can cause a change within a group of players. From a group in which every individual plays together on the same level it may turn into a 'two-level' or 'two-tier' group of players. All players remain interdependent, but they no longer all play directly with each other. This function is taken over by the special functionaries who coordinate the game—representatives, delegates, leaders, governments, royal courts, monopolistic élites and so forth. Together they form a second, smaller group, a second-tier group as one might say. These are the people who play directly with and against each other, but they are nevertheless bound in one way or another to the mass of players who now make up the first storey. Also, there can be no second level without a first level; the people on the second level have no function except with regard to those on the first level. Both levels are dependent on each other and possess different reciprocal power chances corresponding to the degree of their dependence on each other. But the distribution of power between the people of the first and second levels can vary enormously. The power differential between the players of the first and second tier can be very great—in the latter's favour—and it can become smaller and smaller.

Let us take the first case. The power differential between first and second tier is very large. Only the players of the second tier participate directly and actively in the game. They have a monopoly over access to the game: every player in the second level finds himself in a circle of activity, such as can already be observed in single-level games. There is a small number of players, so every player is in a position to picture the figuration of players and game; he can plan his strategy in accordance with this picture and intervene directly with each move in the perpetually moving figuration of the game. In addition he can influence this figuration to a greater or lesser extent, depending on his own position within the group, and he can follow the consequences of his moves for the progress of the game. He can observe other players' countermoves, and how the interweaving of his own moves with those of others is expressed through the constantly changing figuration of the game. He may imagine that the course of the game, as he sees it unfold before him, is more or less transparent to him. Members of pre-industrial oligarchic élites—for example courtiers, men like the Duc de Saint-Simon, memoir-writer in the time of Louis XIV—usually felt that they had a precise knowledge of the unwritten rules governing the game at the hub of the state society.

The illusion that the game is essentially transparent is never completely justified in reality; and two-tier figurations—not to mention three-, four- and five-tier figurations, which are left out here for the sake of simplicity—are far too complicated constructions for their structure and direction of development to be clarified without thorough scientific investigation. But such investigations only begin to be possible at a stage of development where people are able at the same time to be aware of their lack of knowledge. This enables them to recognize the relative opacity of the game to which their moves relate, and the possibility of amending their lack of knowledge by means of systematic research. This is only marginally possible within the framework of dynastic aristocratic societies, which correspond to an oligarchic two-tier model. The game played by the group on the upper level will be viewed by the players not as a game process but as an accumulation of actions of individuals. The explanatory value of this 'view of the game' is the more limited because no individual player in a two-tier game, however great his strength, has anything like the same ability as player A in model (1a) to control the other players or, more important, to determine the game process. Even in a game with no more than two tiers, the figuration of game and players already possesses a degree of complexity which prevents any one individual from using his superiority to guide the game in the direction of his own goals and wishes. He makes his moves both *out of* the network and *into* the network of interdependent players, where there are alliances and enmities, cooperation and rivalry at different levels. At least three, if not four, different balances of power may be distinguished in a two-tier game. They interlock like cogwheels, and so people who are enemies on one level may be allies on another. First there is the power balance within the small group at the upper level, secondly the power balance between players at the first level and players at the second, thirdly the power balance between the groups at the lower level and, if one wishes to go even further, one might add the power balance *within* each of these lower-level groups. Models with three, four, five and more levels would have power balances which were correspondingly more interwoven. In fact they would be better, more suitable models for the majority of contemporary state-societies.[7] We will limit ourselves here to two-tier games models.

In a two-tier game of the older, oligarchic kind, the balances of power in favour of the upper tier is very disproportionate, inelastic and stable. The smaller circle of players on the upper level is very superior in strength to the larger circle on the lower level. Nevertheless, the interdependence of the two circles imposes limitations on every player, even on those at the upper level. Even a player on the upper level in a position of very great strength has less scope for controlling the course of the game than, for example, player A in model (2b). Also, it is remarkable how much slighter are his scope for control and his chances of controlling the game than those of player A in model (1a). There is a good reason for stressing this difference again: in historical descriptions—which are often concerned only with the small circle of players on the higher levels of a multi-level society—the actions of the players in question are quite often explained as if they were the moves of player A in model (1a). But in reality the three or four interdependent balances of power in a two-tier oligarchic model make possible many constellations which considerably limit the chances for control of even the stronger layer on the upper level. If the overall balance of such a game allows for the possibility that all players on both levels may unite and play together against the strongest player, A, then A's chance of using strategy to force them to make the moves which seem desirable to him are extremely slight, and their chance of using strategy to force him to make the moves they have chosen is very good. On the other hand if there are rival groups of players on the upper level, which are fairly equal in strength and balance each other out, without one or other of them holding the key to decisive victory, then an individual player A, on the higher level but standing outside any of the groupings, will have a good chance of guiding the rival groups and thereby the course of the game, as long as he does it with the greatest caution and the greatest understanding of the characteristics of these complex figurations. In this case his strength rests on the insight and skill with which he can seize the chances offered by the constellation of power weightings, and make them the basis of his strategy. In the absence of A, the groups on the lower levels will be strengthened by rivalry between groups on the upper level.

(3b) *Game Models on Two Levels: Simplified, Increasingly Democratic Type*

Imagine a two-level model in which the strength of the lower-level players is growing slowly but steadily in relation to the strength of the upper-level players. If power differentials between the two groups diminish, reducing their inequality, then the balance of power will become more flexible and elastic. It will be more likely to fluctuate, in one direction or the other.

A, the strongest player on the upper level, may still be superior to the other upper-level players. When the lower-level players become more powerful, moves made by A during the game will fall under the sway of a far more complicated figuration than that influencing A in the previous model (3a). There too the grouping of the players who form the lower tier has no mean bearing on the course of the game. But it still has comparatively little manifest power, and as good as no direct sway on the grouping of the upper level. Usually the lower-level players exercise only latent and indirect influence, one reason for which is that they lack organization. Among the manifest signs of their latent strength are the neverending vigilance of the upper-level players and the closely-woven net of precautions serving to keep them under control, and which is often tightened when their potential strength increases. In any case the dependencies which bind the upper-level players to those of the lower level constrain the former much less noticeably. Their superiority is still so vast that they are often inclined to the conviction that they are absolutely free of the low-level players and can conduct themselves in whatever way they like. They feel themselves to be constrained and confined only by their interdependence with their fellow-players on the same level, and by the balance of power existing between them.

If power differentials between the two levels decrease, the dependencies which bind the upper to the lower level will become stronger—and since they are stronger, all the participants will become more aware of them. They will become more noticeable. If power differentials diminish further, the functions of upper-level players change and in the end the players themselves change. As long as power differentials are great, it will appear to people on the upper level as if the whole game and the lower-level players in particular are there for their benefit. As power balances shift, this state of affairs changes. Increasingly it appears to all participants as though the upper-level players are there for the benefit of the lower-level players. The former gradually become more openly and unambiguously functionaries, spokesmen or representatives of one or other of the lower-level groups. In model (3a) the game within the small upper-level circle is clearly the centre of the whole two-tier game, and the lower-level players appear on the whole to be peripheral figures, mere statistics. But in model (3b), as the influence of the lower-level players over the game grows, the game becomes increasingly complex for all players on the upper level. Each one's strategy, in his relations with the lower-level groups he represents, becomes as important an aspect of the game as his strategy in relation to the other upper-level players. Every individual player is now constrained and confined to a much greater degree, kept in check by the number of simultaneous interdependent games he must play with players or groups of players who are becoming less and less socially inferior. The overall figuration of these interwoven games becomes visibly differentiated and often cannot be clearly surveyed even by the most gifted player, so that it becomes more and more difficult for a player to decide entirely on his own which will be the most suitable next move.

Upper-level players—party oligarchs, for example—are increasingly able to be effective in their special positions only if they become members of more or less organized groups. Groups of players from *both* levels may indeed still band together to form a kind of figuration which enables an individual to maintain a balance between interdependent but rival groups. In this way he reaches a position which gives him greater power chances than any other individual in the figuration. But under conditions which bring about a decrease in power differentials—a general diffusion of power chances among players and groups of players—if a figuration makes unusually great power chances accessible to a single player or small group of players, it will be extremely unstable, in accordance with this latent power structure. Such a figuration will usually only emerge in times of crisis and can only with considerable difficulty be maintained for a longer period. Even a player presently in a position of particular strength will now be far more answerable to players on the lower level, whose position has become stronger, than was a player in a similarly strong position under the conditions prevailing in model (3a). The game puts a constant strain on a player in this position, a much greater strain than on a similarly placed player under the conditions of model (3a). Under conditions like those in model (3a), a player and his group in such a position may in fact appear to control and guide the whole game themselves. As the distribution of power weightings becomes less unequal and more diffuse, it also becomes plainer how little the game can be controlled and guided from any single player's or group's position. Indeed, the opposite is the case. It becomes clear how much the course of the game—which is the product of the interweaving moves of a large number of players, between whom there is a diminished and diminishing power differential—determines in its turn the structure of the moves of every single player.

The conception players have of their game will change accordingly—that is their 'ideas', the means of speech and thought by which they attempt to assimilate and master their experience of the game. Instead of players believing that the game takes its shape from the individual moves of individual people, there is a slowly growing tendency for impersonal concepts to be developed to master their experience of the game. These impersonal concepts take into account the relative autonomy of the game process from the intentions of individual players. A long and laborious process is involved, working out communicable means of thought which will correspond to the character of the game as something not immediately controllable, even by the players themselves. Metaphors are used which oscillate constantly between the idea that the course of the game can be reduced to the actions of individual players and the other idea that it is of a supra-personal nature. Because the game cannot be controlled by the players, it is easily perceived as a king of superhuman' entity. For a long time it is especially difficult for players to comprehend that their inability to control the game derives from their mutual dependence and positioning as players, and from the tensions and conflicts inherent in this intertwining network.

## Commentary

1. Whatever their theoretical content, these models of interweaving are not theoretical in the customary sense of the word. They are *didactic models*. Their primary purpose here is to facilitate a reorientation of our powers of imagination and conceptualization in order to understand the nature of the tasks confronting sociology. People say that the task of sociology is to investigate society. But it is not made at all clear what we are to understand by 'society'. In many ways sociology seems to be a science in search of a subject. This is partly because the verbal materials and conceptual tools our language puts at our disposal for defining and investigating this subject are not flexible enough. Any attempt to develop them further so that they correspond to the peculiarity of this subject matter will cause difficulties in communication. These didactic models are a means of overcoming such difficulties. By using the image of people playing a game as a metaphor for people forming societies together, it is easier to rethink the static ideas which are associated with most of the current concepts used in this context. They must be transformed into the far more versatile concepts which are needed if we are to improve our mental equipment for tackling the problems of sociology. One only needs to compare the imaginative possibilities of such static concepts as the individual and society or ego and system with the imaginative possibilities opened up by the metaphoric use of various images of games and players; the comparison will help us to understand that these models have served to unleash our powers of imagination.

2. At the same time the models serve to make certain problems about social life more accessible to scientific reflection. These problems actually play a central part in all human relationships, but are too often ignored in theorizing about them. The most important of them is the *problem of power*. In part its neglect can be traced back to the simple fact that the social phenomena to which this concept refers are extremely complex. To simplify the problem, a single form—perhaps the military

or the economic form—of the many possible sources of power which can be accessible to people is often taken as *the* source of power, to which all forms of the exercise of power may be traced. But this simply conceals the problem. The difficulties encountered in reflecting on problems of power stem from the polymorphous nature of sources of power. To explore the problems raised here either at length or exclusively is not the purpose of these models. The task here is not to solve the problem of power but simply to bring it in out of the cold and make it easily accessible as one of the central problems of sociological effort. The necessity for doing this is connected with the obvious difficulty of examining questions of power without becoming emotionally involved. Another person's power is to be feared: he can compel us to do a particular thing whether we want to or not. Power is suspect: people use their power to exploit others for their own ends. Power seems unethical: everyone ought to be in a position to make all his own decisions. And the mist of fear and suspicion which clings to this concept is understandably transferred to its use in a scientific theory. One may say that someone 'has' power and leave it at that, although such usage, which implies that power is a thing, leads down a blind alley. A more adequate solution to problems of power depends on power being understood unequivocally as a structural characteristic of a relationship, all-pervading and, as a structural characteristic, neither good nor bad. It may be both. We depend on others; others depend on us. In so far as we are more dependent on others than they are on us, more reliant on others than they are on us, they have power over us, whether we have become dependent on them by their use of naked force or by our need to be loved, our need for money, healing, status, a career, or simply for excitement. Be that as it may, in direct relationships between two people, A's relationship to B is also always B's relationship to A. In such relationships A's dependence on B is always connected with B's dependence on A, except in marginal situations. But it is possible for one to be very much slighter than the other. It may be the case that B's power over A, his chance of controlling and guiding A's course of action, is greater than A's power over B. This balance of power is weighted in B's favour. The models in the first series illustrate some of the simplest types of balance of power in direct relationships between two people, and the corresponding outcomes of the relationships. At the same time they may also help to correct our habit of using the concept of relationship as a static concept, and to remind us that all relationships—like human games—are processes.

But relationships, and the conditions of dependence involved in them, may comprise not just two but many people. Take a figuration formed by many interdependent people in which all positions are endowed with approximately equal power chances. A is not more powerful than B, nor B more powerful that C, nor C more powerful than D and so on, and *vice versa*. Being interdependent with so many people will very probably often compel individual people to act in a way they would not act except under compulsion. In this case one is inclined to personify or reify interdependence. The mythology dictated by linguistic usage urges us to believe that there must be 'someone' who 'has power'. So, because we feel the pressure of 'power', we always invent a person who exercises it, or a kind of superhuman entity like 'nature' or 'society' in which we say power resides. In thought, we hold them responsible for the constraints to which we feel ourselves subject. There are certain practical and theoretical disadvantages in our not at the moment being able to distinguish clearly between the constraints which *every possible interdependence* between people exerts over those people—even in a figuration where all positions are equally endowed with power chances—and the constraints which stem from the variation in power chances between different social positions. But we cannot now go into the range of problems glimpsed here. It must suffice to say that the potential people we are born would never develop into the actual people we become if we were never subjected to any of the constraints of interdependence. But that is most certainly not to say that present forms of interdependence exercise the kind of constraint which is conducive to optimal realization of human potentials.

3. In model (1a) the structure of the game is largely determined by the intentions and actions of *one* person. The course of the game can be explained in terms of the plans and goals of one individual. Thus model (1a) probably corresponds best with the ideas of a large number of people about how social events can be explained. At the same time it is reminiscent of a well-known theoretical model of society, which starts with the interaction of two individuals who were independent of each other to begin with. Expressed differently, it starts with the interaction of 'ego' and 'alter'. But the model has not been properly thought through. The relationship is still fundamentally seen as a state, not a process. The problems raised by this view of the nature of human interdependencies and power balances, together with all related problems, are still beyond the horizons of so-called action theories. At most they take into account the fact that intentional interactions have unintended consequences. But they conceal a circumstance which is central to sociological theory and practice, namely that unintentional human interdependencies lie at the root of every intentional interaction. The Primal Contest model perhaps expresses this most directly. It is not possible to construct an adequate sociological model without taking into consideration that there are

types of interdependence which impel ego and alter to fight and kill each other.

As a model for certain relationships, model (1a) is certainly of use. There are cases to which it can be applied, and it would be a mistake to disregard it. The relationship between player A and player B may be similar to that between a specialist and a non-specialist, a slave-owner and a slave, or a famous painter and a patron. As a model of societies, however, model (1a) is at best of marginal use.

By contrast, model (2c), and model (3b) even more, offer a certain amount of help towards understanding what we mentioned as the basic experience of the nascent science of sociology—the experience that out of the intertwining of many people's actions there may emerge social consequences which no one has planned. Both these game models indicate the conditions under which players may slowly begin to encounter a problem: that a game process, which comes about entirely as a result of the interweaving of the individual moves of many players, takes a course *which none of the individual players has planned, determined or anticipated*. On the contrary, the unplanned course of the game repeatedly influences the moves of each individual player. So these models help to shed some light on one of the main problems facing sociology, insufficient understanding of which constantly leads to misunderstandings about the subject matter and problems of sociology.

There is a constant discussion about what the subject matter of sociology actually is. If the answer is 'society', as is often claimed, then many will think of it as an aggregation of individual people. The question one encounters most often runs like this: Can anything be said about society which could not be found out from studying individual people, for example, from physiological or individual psychological analyses? Model (2c) and, in particular, model (3b) show us in which direction we must seek the answers to such questions. These models point to the possibility that the course of a game played by 30, 300 or 3000 players cannot be controlled and guided by any of those players. As the gap between the power potentials of the players decreases, this becomes the more probable. Here the game process gains relative autonomy from the plans and intentions of any of the individual players who create and maintain the game by their actions. This can be expressed negatively by saying that the course of the game is not in the power of any one player. The other side of the coin is that the course of the game itself has power over the behaviour and thought of the individual players. For their actions and ideas cannot be explained and understood if they are considered on their own; they need to be understood and explained within the framework of the game. The model shows how people's interdependence as players exerts constraint over each of the individuals bonded together in this way; the constraint stems from the particular nature of their relatedness and interdependence as players. In this instance, too, power is the structural characteristic of a relationship. On first meeting models of type (3b), it may seem puzzling that we can no longer point to any one individual or even any single group of individuals who exercise unilateral power over all the others. After a while it becomes easier to understand that as power differentials lessen between interdependent individuals and groups there is a diminishing possibility that any participants, whether on their own or as groups, will be able to influence the overall course of the game. But chances to control the game may increase again as people become more and more distanced from their own intertwining network, and gain more insight into the structure and dynamics of the game. The relative autonomy of sociology in relation to disciplines like physiology and psychology, which concern themselves with individual people, is ultimately based on the relative autonomy in relation to individual actions, or the structural processes which result from the interdependence and interweaving of the actions of many people. This autonomy always exists, but people become especially sharply conscious of it at times when society is becoming increasingly differentiated, and chains of interdependence are lengthening. The increasing number of individuals forming these chains are bound together across increasing distances by the specialization of their functions. Given the conditions of this figuration, it is especially noticeable that the processes of interweaving are self-regulating, and relatively autonomous in relation to the people who form the web. In sum, we are dealing with a level of integration which, in relation to lower levels of integration like individual human organisms, evinces specific characteristics, forms of organization which are quite inaccessible to comprehension and scientific investigation if we attempt to explain them solely by reducing them to their individual components (individual people, individual organisms) as in psychological or biological forms of explanation.

Game models are an excellent way of representing the distinctiveness of the forms of organization which are met with on the level of integration represented by human societies. Our heritage of speech and thought puts a certain pressure on us to interpret all nexuses of events as unilinear chains of cause and effect. Two explanations of unilinear chains are closely related. The older is in terms of the actions of a personal Creator. Gradually during the course of human history, this explanation has been joined by the unilinear chain explanation in terms of an impersonal cause. When complex patterns of interweaving are encountered, it is usual to try to explain even these in terms of the same categories of cause and effect and the same picture of unilinear sequences. Only, in this case, people usually imagine that all that is necessary is to make a big bundle of short, unilinear, connecting chains of this sort. Instead of explaining whatever needs to be explained in terms of a cause or a Creator, they explain it by means of five, ten or even a hundred 'factors', 'variables' or whatever the term may be. But just try to apply this type of explanation to a player's twelfth move in a two-person game on one level, where both players are equally strong. We are inclined to interpret this move in terms of the character of the person who made it. Perhaps it might be explained psychologically as a manifestation of his great intelligence or, more physiologically, in terms of his overtiredness. Any of these explanations might be justifiable but none of them is sufficient. For the twelfth move in such a game can no longer be adequately explained in terms of short, unilinear causal sequences. Nor can an explanation be based on the individual character of one or the other player. This move can only be interpreted in the light of the way the preceding moves of both players have intertwined, and of the specific figuration which has resulted from this intertwining. Any attempt to ascribe this intertwining to one or the other player alone, or even to a mere accumulation of both as originator or cause, is doomed to inadequacy. Only the progressive interweaving of moves during the game process, and its result—the figuration of the game prior to the twelfth move—can be of service in explaining the twelfth move. The player uses this figuration to orientate himself before making his move. Yet this process of interweaving and the current state or figuration of the game, by which the individual player orientates himself, exhibit an order of their own. That order is a phenomenon with structures, connections and regularities of distinctive kinds, none of which exists above and beyond individuals, but is rather the result of the continual combination and interweaving of individuals. All we say about 'societies' or 'social facts' refers to this order which, as we have said, includes specific types of 'disorder' resembling those in the Primal Contest model, as well as constantly recurring types of disintegrative or unravelling processes.

When we consider this, it becomes obvious that many of the customary conceptual structures, which force themselves on our attempts to think about such facts, do not correspond to the particular level of integration to which they refer. Among them, for example, are much-used turns of phrase like 'man and his environment' or his 'social background'. Consider game models. It would not occur to anyone to describe the game process in which a player cooperates with and against others, as his 'environment', 'surroundings' or 'background'. The contrast which is repeatedly drawn between 'individual' and 'society' makes it seem as though individuals could in some sense exist independent of society, and *vice versa*. This seems highly questionable in the light of models showing processes of interweaving. And it is a scientific superstition that in order to investigate them scientifically one must necessarily dissect processes of interweaving into their component parts. Sociologists often no longer do this, although a number of them seem to have guilty consciences about their omission.

Sociologists, especially when they are working empirically, often use a theoretical framework and conceptual tools which are mostly quite well suited to the distinctive character of the particular kind of order produced by human interweaving, and to the character of societies and changing figurations made up of interdependent people. But there is perhaps still a need for them to work out clearly what they are doing, to become fully aware of it, and so to justify it. Consider for example Durkheim's explanation of certain regularities in suicide rates for various groups of people. He bases it on specific differences between the interweaving-structures they belong to. Statistics play an essential part; but their function is that of indicators, pointing to specific variations in the way people are caught up in a network of relationships. Whether one is trying to study the relationships between kings and parliaments in medieval Europe[8] or whether one is investigating the relationship between 'the established and the outsiders'[9] or the strategy of a charismatic leader or of an absolute ruler in the inner circles of his court, one is always dealing with interweaving of the kind illustrated here with the help of a few models.

# Notes

1. See N. Elias, 'Problems of involvement and detachment', *British Journal of Sociology*, vol. 7, no. 3, 1956, pp. 226–52.

2. What we call 'figuration' with reference to the constituent parts is identical with what we call 'structure' with reference to the composite unit. If we speak of the structure of societies and of the figuration or pattern of bonding of the individuals who form these societies, we are in fact speaking of the same thing as seen from different angles.

3. E. E. Evans-Pritchard's well-known analysis of the function of feuds between Nuer lineage groups is an instructive example of the teleological use of the concept of function. It is debased into a concept of the purpose served in conserving an existing social system. 'The function of the feud, viewed in this way, is therefore to maintain the structural equilibrium between opposed tribal segments which are, nevertheless, politically fused in relation to larger units.' (E. E. Evans-Pritchard, *The Nuer,* Oxford, 1940, ch. 3, p. 159.) It might be more appropriate to say that during the period of the inquiry the functions which the segmentary groups possessed for each other as allies and fellow-tribesmen outweighed their function as rivals to each other.

4. A detailed examination of functions and power in relations between specialized

groups is to be found in N. Elias, *The Court Society,* Oxford, 1983, ch. 2 and 4.

5. There is no need to emphasize the critical reflection on action and interaction theories, which pay little if any attention to the structure of pressures which one person's or one group's 'action' exercises upon that of others.

6. The concept of 'impaired functioning' in the context of observable social processes is not to be confused with Merton's concept of 'dysfunction', which is useless for sociological research. The Mertonian concept is based on a predetermined set of values; it refers to an ideal image of harmoniously functioning static societies—an image which does not correspond to anything observable in real life.

7. Many societies which have not yet developed into states nevertheless operate on more than two levels. Even in a federation of tribes as simply and loosely integrated as that of the old Iroquois, the federal procedure when an individual wanted to put a proposal to the federation was as follows (the source is a contemporary account by the Rev. Asher Wright, quoted in Edmund Wilson, *Apologies to the Iroquois,* London, 1960, p. 1974):

> A measure must first gain the assent of the proposer's family, then his clan, next of the four related clans in his end of the council house, then of his nation, and then in due course of order the business would be brought up before the representatives of the Confederacy. In the reverse order the measures of the general council were sent down to the people for their approval. It was a standing rule that all action should be unanimous. Hence the discussions, without any known exception, were always continued till all opposition was reasoned down, or the proposed measure abandoned.

8. H. J. Königsberger, '*Dominium regale* or *dominium et regale?:* Monarchies and Parliaments in Early Modern Europe', in *Human Figurations: Essays for Norbert Elias,* ed. P. Gleichmann, J. Goudsblom and H. Korte, Amsterdam, 1977.

9. N. Elias and J. Scotson, *The Established and the Outsiders,* London, 1965.

# 8

# On the Monopoly Mechanism

1. The society of what we call the modern age is characterized, above all in the West, by a certain level of monopolization. Free use of military weapons is denied the individual and reserved to a central authority of whatever kind,[1] and likewise the taxation of the property or income of individuals is concentrated in the hands of a central social authority. The financial means thus flowing into this central authority maintain its monopoly of military force, while this in turn maintains the monopoly of taxation. Neither has in any sense precedence over the other; they are two sides of the same monopoly. If one disappears the other automatically follows, though the monopoly rule may sometimes be shaken more strongly on one side than on the other.

Forerunners of such monopoly control of taxes and the army over relatively large territories have previously existed in societies with a less advanced division of functions, mainly as a result of military conquest. It takes a far advanced social division of functions before an enduring, specialized apparatus for administrating the monopoly can emerge. And only when this complex apparatus has evolved does the control over army and taxation take on its full monopoly character. Only then is the military and fiscal monopoly firmly established. From now on social conflicts are not concerned with removing monopoly rule but only with the question of who are to control it, from whom they are to be recruited and how the burdens and benefits of the monopoly are to be distributed. It is only with the emergence of this continuing monopoly of the central authority and this specialized apparatus for ruling that dominions take on the character of "states".

Within them a number of other monopolies crystallize around those already mentioned. But these two are and remain the key monopolies. If they decay, so do all the rest, and with them the "state".

2. The question at issue is how and why this monopoly structure arises.

In the society of the ninth, tenth and eleventh centuries it definitely does not yet exist. From the eleventh century—in the territory of the for-

From *The Civilizing Process* (1994), pp. 345–55

mer western Frankish empire—we see it slowly crystallizing. At first each warrior who controls a piece of land exerts all the functions of rule; these are then gradually monopolized by a central ruler whose power is administered by specialists. Whenever he pleases, he wages wars to gain new land or defend his own. Land-acquisition and the governmental functions going with its possession are, like its military defence, left to "private initiative", to use the language of a later age. And since, with the increasing population of the area, hunger for land is extremely keen, competition for it throughout the country is rife. In this competition both military and economic means are used, in contrast to that of the nineteenth century, for example, which, given the state monopoly of physical violence, is waged solely by economic means.

A reminder of the competitive struggles and the monopolization taking place directly under our own eyes is not without value for an understanding of monopoly mechanisms in earlier stages of society. In addition, consideration of the old in conjunction with the new helps us to see this social development as a whole. The later part of the movement presupposes the earlier, and the centre of both is the accumulation of the most important means of production of the time, or at least control over it, in fewer and fewer hands—earlier the accumulation of land, later that of money.

The mechanism of monopoly formation has already been briefly discussed: if, *in a major social unit*—so the mechanism may be roughly summarized—*a large number of the smaller social units which, through their interdependence, constitute the larger one, are of roughly equal social power and are thus able to compete freely—unhampered by pre-existing monopolies—for the means to social power, i.e., primarily the means of subsistence and production, the probability is high that some will be victorious and others vanquished, and that gradually, as a result, fewer and fewer will control more and more opportunities, and more and more units will be eliminated from the competition, becoming directly or indirectly dependent on an ever-decreasing number.* The human figuration caught up in this movement will therefore, unless countervailing measures are taken, approach a state in which all opportunities are controlled by a single authority: a system with open opportunities has become a system with closed opportunities.

The general pattern followed by this sequence is very simple: in a social area there are a certain number of people and a certain number of opportunities which are scarce or insufficient in relation to the needs of the people. If we assume that to begin with each of the people in this area fights one other for the available opportunities, the probability that they will maintain this state of equilibrium indefinitely and that no partner will triumph in any of these pairs is extremely small, if this is indeed a free competition uninfluenced by any monopoly power; and the probability that sooner or later individual contestants will overcome their opponents is extremely high. But if some of the contenders are victorious, their opportunities multiply; those of the vanquished decrease. Greater opportunities accumulate in the hands of one group of the original rivals, the others being eliminated from direct competition with them. Assuming that each of the victors now struggles with the others, the process is repeated: once again one group is victorious and gains control of the power chances of the vanquished; a still smaller number of people control a still greater number of power chances; a still greater number of people are eliminated from the free competition; and the process is repeated until finally, in the extreme case, one individual controls all power chances and all the others are dependent on him.

In historical reality it is certainly not always individual people who become embroiled in this mechanism; frequently it is large associations of people, for example territories or states. The course of events in reality is usually far more complicated than in this schematic pattern, and full of variations. It often happens, for example, that a number of weaker parties combine to bring down an individual who has accumulated too many possibilities and grown too strong. Should they succeed and take over the possibilities of this party, or some of them, they then fight among themselves for predominance. The effect, the shift in power balances, is always the same. In this way, too, an ever-increasing number of power chances tend to accumulate in the hands of an ever-diminishing number of people through a series of elimination contests.

The course and pace of this shift in favour of the few at the expense of the many depend to a large extent on the relation between the supply and demand of opportunities. If we assume that the level of demand and the number of opportunities remain unchanged overall in the course of the movement, the demand for opportunities will increase with the shift in the power relations; the number of the dependents and the degree of their dependence will increase and change in kind. If relatively independent social functions are increasingly replaced by dependent ones in society—for example, free knights by courtly knights and finally courtiers, or relatively independent merchants by dependent merchants and employees—the moulding of affects, the structure of drives and consciousness, in short the whole social personality structure and the social attitudes of people are necessarily changed at the same time. And this applies no less to those who are approaching a monopoly position than to those who have lost the possibility of competing and have fallen into direct or indirect dependence.

3. For this process should in no way be understood merely as one whereby fewer and fewer people become "free" and more and more "unfree", although in some phases it appears to answer this description. If the movement is viewed as a whole, we can recognize without difficulty that—at least in highly differentiated societies—dependence undergoes a peculiar qualitative change at a certain stage of the process. The more people are made dependent by the monopoly mechanism, the greater becomes the power of the dependent, not only individually but also collectively, in relation to the one or more monopolists. This happens not only because of the small number of those approaching the monopoly position, but because of their own dependence on ever more dependents in preserving and exploiting the power potential they have monopolized. Whether it is a question of land, soldiers or money in any form, the more that is accumulated by an individual, the less easily can it be supervised by this individual, and the more surely he becomes by his very monopoly dependent on increasing numbers of others, the more he becomes dependent on his dependents. Such changes in power and dependence relationships often take centuries to become perceptible, and centuries more to find expression in lasting institutions. Particular structural properties of society may place endless obstacles in the way of the process, yet its mechanism and trend are unmistakable. The more comprehensive the monopolized power potential, the larger the web of functionaries administering it and the greater the division of labour among them; in short, the more people on whose work or function the monopoly is in any way dependent, the more strongly does this whole field controlled by the monopolist assert its own weight and its own inner regularities. The monopoly ruler can acknowledge this and impose on himself the restraints that his function as the central ruler of so mighty a formation demands; or he can indulge himself and give his own inclinations precedence over all others. In the latter case the complex social apparatus which has developed along with this private accumulation of power chances will sooner or later lapse into disorder and make its resistance, its autonomous structure, all the more strongly felt. In other words, the more comprehensive a monopoly position becomes and the more highly developed its division of labour, the more clearly and certainly does it move towards a point at which its one or more monopoly rulers become the central functionaries of an apparatus composed of differentiated functions, more powerful than others, perhaps, but scarcely less dependent and fettered. This change may come about almost imperceptibly by small steps and struggles, or through the whole groups of dependents asserting their social power over the monopoly rulers by force; in one

way or another the power first won through the accumulation of chances in private struggles tends, from a point marked by an optimal size of possessions, to slip away from the monopoly rulers into the hands of the dependents as a whole, or, to begin with, to groups of dependents, such as the monopoly administration. The privately owned monopoly in the hands of a single individual or family comes under the control of broader social strata, and transforms itself as the central organ of a state into a public monopoly.

The development of what we today call a "national economy" is an illustrative example of this process. The national economy develops from the "private economy" of feudal ruling houses. More precisely, there is at first no distinction between what are later opposed as "public" and "private" income and expenditure. The income of the central rulers derives primarily from their personal family or domanial possessions; expenses for the ruler's court, hunts, clothes or presents are met from this income in exactly the same way as the cost of the relatively small administration, paid soldiers if any, or the building of castles. Then, as more and more land comes together in the hands of one ruling house the management of income and expenditure, the administration and defence of his property become increasingly difficult for the individual to supervise. But even when the direct possessions of the ruling house, its domanial estate, are no longer by any means the most important source of the ruler's income, even when, with the increasing commercialization of society, duties from the whole country flow into the "chambers" of the central ruler and when, with the monopoly of force, the monopoly of land has become at the same time one of duties or taxes, even then the central ruler at first continues to control this revenue as if it were the personal income of this household. He can still decide how much of it should be spent on castles, presents, his kitchen and the court, and how much on keeping the troops and paying the administration. The distribution of the income from the monopolized resources is his prerogative. On closer examination, however, we find that the monopolist's freedom of decision is restricted more and more by the immense human web that his property has gradually become. His dependence on his administrative staff increases and, with it, the influence of the latter; the fixed costs of the monopoly apparatus constantly rise; and at the end of this development the absolute ruler with his apparently unrestricted power is, to an extraordinary degree, governed by and functionally dependent on the society he rules. His absolute sovereignty is not simply a consequence of his monopoly control of opportunities, but the function of a particular structural peculiarity of society in this phase, of which more will be said later. But however that may be, even the budget of French absolutism still contains no distinction between the "private" and "public" expenditure of the king.

How the transformation into a public monopoly finally finds expression in the budget is well enough known. The wielder of central power, whatever title he may bear, is allocated a sum in the budget like any other functionary; from it the central ruler, king or president, meets the expenses of his household or court; expenditure necessary for the governmental organization of the country is strictly separated from that used by individuals for personal ends. Private monopoly rule has become public monopoly rule, even when in the hands of an individual as the functionary of society.

The same picture emerges if we trace the formation of the governmental apparatus as a whole. It grows out of what might be called the "private" court and domanial administration of the kings or princes. Practically all the organs of state government result from the differentiation of the functions of the royal household, sometimes with the assimilation of organs of autonomous local administration. When this governmental apparatus has finally become the public affair of the state, the household of the central ruler is at most one organ among others and finally hardly even that.

This is one of the most pronounced examples of the way in which private property becomes a public function, and the monopoly of an individual—won in contests of elimination and accumulation over several generations—is finally socialized.

It would take us too far afield to show here what is actually meant by saying that the "private" power of individuals over monopolized resources becomes "public", or "state", or "collective" power. As was said earlier, all these expressions have their full meaning only when applied to societies with extensive division of functions; only in such societies are the activities and functions of each individual directly or indirectly dependent on those of many others, and only here is the weight of these many intertwined actions and interests so great that even the few with monopoly control over immense possibilities cannot escape its pressure.

Social processes involving the monopoly mechanism are to be found in many societies, even those with relatively low division of functions and integration. There, too, every monopoly tends, from a certain degree of accumulation onwards, to escape the control of any single individual and to pass into that of entire social groups, frequently starting with the former government functionaries, the first servants of the monopolists. The process of feudalization is one example of this. It was shown earlier how, in the course of this process, control over relatively large territorial possessions and military power slips away from the monopoly ruler in successive waves, first to his former functionaries or their heirs, then to the warrior class as a whole with its own internal hierarchy. In societies with a lower degree of interdependence between social functions, this shift away from private monopoly control leads either to a kind of "anarchy", a more or less complete decay of the monopoly, or to its appropriation by an oligarchy instead of an individual dynasty. Later, such shifts in favour of the many lead not to a disintegration of the monopoly, but only to a different form of control over it. Only in the course of a growing social interdependence of all functions does it become possible to wrest monopolies from arbitrary exploitation by a few without causing them to disintegrate. Wherever the division of functions is both high and increasing, the few who, in successive waves, claim monopoly power sooner or later find themselves in difficulty, at a disadvantage in face of the many, through their need of their services and thus their functional dependence on them. The human web as a whole, with its increasing division of functions, has an inherent tendency that opposes increasingly strongly every private monopolization of resources. The tendency of monopolies, e.g. the monopoly of force or taxation, to turn from "private" into "public" or "state" monopolies, is nothing other than a function of social interdependence. A human web with high and increasing division of functions is impelled by its own collective weight towards a state of equilibrium where the distribution of the advantages and revenues from monopolized opportunities in favour of a few becomes impossible. If it seems self-evident to us today that certain monopolies, above all the key monopoly of government, are "public", held by the state, although this was by no means the case earlier, this marks a step in the same direction. It is entirely possible that obstructions may again and again be placed in the path of such a process by the particular conditions of a society; a particular example of such obstructions was shown earlier in the development of the old Germano-Roman Empire. And wherever a social web exceeds a certain size optimal for that particular monopoly formation, similar breakdowns will occur. But the impulsion of such a human web towards a quite definite structure, in which monopolies are administered to the advantage of the whole figuration, remains perceptible, no matter what factors may repeatedly intrude as countervailing mechanisms to arrest the process in recurrent situations of conflict.

Considered in general terms, therefore, the process of monopoly formation has a very clear structure. In it, free competition has a precisely definable place and a positive function: it is a struggle among many for resources not yet monopolized by any individual or small group. Each social monopoly is preceded by this kind of free elimination contest; each such contest tends towards monopoly.

As against this phase of free competition, monopoly formation means on the one hand the closure of direct access to certain resources for increasing numbers of people, and on the other a progressive centralization of the control of these resources. By this centralization, such resources are placed outside the direct competition of the many; in the extreme case they are controlled by a single social entity. The latter, the monopolist, is never in a position to use the profit from his monopoly for himself alone, particularly in a society with a high division of functions. If he has enough social power, he may at first claim the overwhelming part of the monopoly profit for himself, and reward services with the minimum needed for life. But he is obliged, just because he depends on the services and functions of others, to allocate to others a large part of the resources he controls—and an increasingly large part, the larger his accumulated possessions become, and the greater his dependence on others. A new struggle over the allocation of these resources therefore arises among those who depend on them. But whereas in the preceding phase the competition was "free", that is, its outcome depended solely on who proved stronger or weaker at a given time, it now depends on the function or purpose for which the monopolist needs the individual to supervise his dominion. Free competition has been replaced by one that is controlled, or at any rate controllable, from a central position by human agents; and the qualities that promise success in this restricted competition, the selection it operates, the human types it produces, differ in the extreme from those in the preceding phase of free competition.

The difference between the situation of the free feudal nobility and that of the courtly nobility is an example of this. In the former, the social power of the individual house, a function of both its economic and military capacity and of the physical strength and skill of the individual, determines the allocation of resources; and in this free competition the direct use of force is indispensable. In the latter, the allocation of resources is finally determined by the man whose house or whose predecessors have emerged victoriously from the struggle by violence, so that he now possesses the monopoly of force. Owing to this monopoly, the direct use of force is now largely excluded from the competition among the nobility for the opportunities the prince has to allocate. The means of struggle have been refined or sublimated. The restraint of the affects imposed on the individual by his dependence on the monopoly ruler has increased. And individuals now waver between resistance to the compulsion to which they are subjected, hatred of their dependence and unfreedom, nostalgia for free knightly rivalry, on the one hand, and pride in the self-control they have acquired, or delight in the new possibilities of pleasure that its acquisition opens, on the other. In brief, this is a new spurt in the civilizing process.

The next step is the seizure of the monopolies of physical force and taxation, with all the other governmental monopolies based on them, by the bourgeoisie. The latter is at this stage a class which, in its totality, controls certain economic opportunities in the manner of an organized monopoly. But these opportunities are still so evenly spread among its members that relatively large numbers of them can compete freely. What this class is struggling with the princes for, and what it finally attains, is not the destruction of monopoly rule. The bourgeoisie do not aspire to re-allocate these monopolies of taxation and military and police power to their own individual members; their members do not want to become landowners each controlling his own military means and his own income from taxes. The existence of a monopoly for raising taxes and exerting physical violence is the basis of their own social existence; it is the precondition for the restriction to economic, non-violent means, of the free competition in which they are engaged with each other for certain economic opportunities.

What they are striving for in the struggle for monopoly rule, and what they finally attain is not, as noted before, a division of the existing monopolies but a different distribution of their burdens and benefits. That control of these monopolies now depends on a whole class instead of an absolute prince is a step in the direction just described; it is a step on that road which leads the opportunities given by this monopoly to be allocated less and less according to the personal favour and interests of individuals, and increasingly according to a more impersonal and precise plan in the interests of many interdependent associates, and finally in the interests of an entire interdependent human figuration.

In other words, through centralization and monopolization, opportunities that previously had to be won by individuals through military or economic force, can now become amenable to planning. From a certain point of development on, the struggle for monopolies no longer aims at their destruction; it is a struggle for control of their yields, for the plan according to which their burdens and benefits are to be divided up, in a word, for the keys to distribution. Distribution itself, the task of the monopoly ruler and administration, changes in this struggle from a relatively private to a public function. Its dependence on all the other functions of the interdependent human network emerges more and more clearly in organizational form. In this entire structure the central functionaries are, like everyone else, dependent. Permanent institutions to control them are formed by a greater or lesser portion of the people dependent on this monopoly apparatus; and control of the monopoly, the filling of its key positions, is itself no longer decided by the vicissitudes of "free" competition, but by regularly recurring elimination contests without force of arms, which are regulated by the monopoly apparatus, and thus by "unfree" competition. In other words, what we are accustomed to call a "democratic regime" is formed. This kind of regime is not—as the mere view of certain economic monopoly processes of our time might make it appear—incompatible with monopolies as such and dependent for its existence on the freest possible competition. On the contrary it presupposes highly organized monopolies, and it can only come into being or survive under certain conditions, in a very specific social structure at a very advanced stage of monopoly formation.

Two main phases can thus be distinguished in the dynamics of a monopoly mechanism, as far as we are at present able to judge. First, the phase of free competition or elimination contests, with a tendency for resources to be accumulated in fewer and fewer and finally in one pair of hands, the phase of monopoly formation; secondly, the phase in which control over the centralized and monopolized resources tends to pass from the hands of an individual to those of ever greater numbers, and finally to become a function of the interdependent human web as a whole, the phase in which a relatively "private" monopoly becomes a "public" one.

Signs of this second phase are not lacking even in societies with a relatively low division of functions. But, clearly, it can only attain its full development in societies with a very high and rising division of functions.

The overall movement can be reduced to a very simple formula. Its starting point is a situation where a whole class controls unorganized monopoly opportunities and where, accordingly, the distribution of these opportunities among the members of this class is decided by free competition and open force; it is then driven towards a situation where the control of monopoly opportunities and those dependent on them by one class, is centrally organized and secured by institutions; and where the distribution of the yields of monopoly follows a plan that is not exclusively governed by the interests of single individuals or single groups, but is oriented on the overall network of interdependencies binding all participating groups and individuals to each other and on its optimal functioning. For in the long run the subordination of the quest for the optimal functioning of the overall network of interdependencies to the optimization of sectional interests invariably defeats its own end.

So much for the general mechanism of competition and monopoly formation. This schematic generalization takes on its full significance only in conjunction with concrete facts; by them it must prove its worth.

When we talk of "free competition" and "monopoly formation" we usually have present-day facts in mind; we think first of all of a "free competition" for "economic" advantages waged by people or groups within a given framework of rules through the exertion of economic power, and in the course of which some gradually increase their control of economic advantages while destroying, subjecting or restricting the economic existence of others.

But these economic struggles of our day do not only lead before our eyes to a constant restriction of the scope for really "monopoly-free" competition and to the slow formation of monopolistic structures. As has already been indicated, they actually presuppose the secure existence of certain very advanced monopolies. Without the monopoly organization of physical violence and taxation, limited at present to national boundaries, the restriction of this struggle for "economic" advantages to the exertion of "economic" power, and the maintenance of its basic rules, would be impossible over any length of time even within individual states. In other words, the economic struggles and monopolies of modern times occupy a particular position within a larger historical context. And only in relation to this wider context do our general remarks on the mechanism of competition and monopoly take on their full meaning. Only if we bear in mind the sociogenesis of these firmly established "state" monopoly institutions—which during a phase of large-scale expansion and differentiation, no doubt open the "economic sphere" to unrestricted individual competition, and thus to new private monopoly formations—only then can we distinguish more clearly amidst the multitude of particular historical facts the interplay of social mechanisms, the ordered structure of such monopoly formations.

## Note

1. On the importance of the monopoly of physical force in the building of "states", cf. above all Max Weber, *Economy and Society* (New York, 1968).

# 9

## The Decay of the State Monopoly of Violence in the Weimar Republic

### 1

The decrease in the power-ratio of the older Wilhelmine establishment after the defeat of 1918 did not have the same significance for its noble and middle-class strata. The nobles, whose claim to power and pre-eminence had been legitimized primarily through military successes, and who, as mostly agrarian strata, had already forfeited power through increasing industrialization, lost their privileged position in the state apparatus with the military defeat and the abdication of the Kaiser. There was, however, one exception, and that was that their dominant position in the German armed forces at first remained unshaken. The loss of their privileges, which had been buttressed, for example in Prussia by the Upper House of the Diet and a three-tiered suffrage system, meant a gain for the upper middle classes. The topmost middle-class groups, until then a second-grade elite, saw themselves transported at a stroke to the position of upper strata. What the middle classes of France had achieved through revolutions—liberation from the privileges and political supremacy of the aristocracy—fell of its own accord into the laps of the middle classes of Germany after the First World War, with the uprising of the workers and soldiers and the disappearance of the throne. But this gain was counterbalanced by the simultaneous increase in power achieved by the organized working class through the disintegration of the absolutist regime and the transition to an authentic parliamentary republic, that is, one dependent on majority voting.

Had the industrial working class been organizationally unified, then their party could possibly have won a long-term position of supremacy within the framework of a constitution granting the party with the majority of votes the right to govern. But as an unintended consequence of the Russian Revolution and the coming to power of the Communist

From *The Germans,* pp. 214–23

Party in Russia, the organized working class in Europe split into two camps which feuded bitterly with each other: the camp of those who sought a way of organizing society which would serve the interests of the workers without violence; and those who sought to achieve this in the end by the use of violence, following the Russian example.

This splitting of the working class and their sympathizers in the middle-class intelligentsia into a nationalist and a Russophile group had far-reaching consequences. One of them is as clear as daylight: organizational unity was for the industrial working class a more important determinant of their power-ratio than it was for middle-class groups. The split into two antagonistic camps therefore had as one unplanned consequence a considerable reduction in the power-potential of the workers. But that was not the only one.

I do not need to go into the question here of whether the unsuccessful and oppressive tsarist regime would have crumbled after its defeat in the First World War even without the use of extra-state violence. In any case, the example of the violent revolution in Russia had an extraordinarily long-lasting, widespread impact, both as model and as nightmare. The fact that in Russia the use of extra-state violence had proved to be an effective means of ousting a ruling group from control over the centralized state monopolies of force and taxation, and in enabling the leaders of the violent groups to take over these monopolies, had such strong and long-lasting effects on the relationship between extra-state and state use of force in other countries that this type of violence, under the name of revolution—as already remarked, either as model or as nightmare—became one of the dominant action models of our century.

Far more even than the nineteenth century stood in the shadow of the French Revolution, the twentieth century has stood in the shadow of the Russian Revolution. One reason for this difference is that belief in the ideals of the French Revolution was not linked to a belief in the necessity of using violence—revolution—for the realization of these ideals. Nor did it possess any firm theoretical base in a canon of authoritative books. The extraordinarily far-reaching effect of the Russian Revolution acquired its specific character, however, precisely because in this case it was both linked to a belief in the necessity of violence and based on a theory set out in books. Certainly the starting point was the class stratification of industrial (and also of predominantly agrarian) countries, with their often firmly institutionalized and unequal distribution of power. But over and above that, there was a small number of books of intellectually high calibre which served to standardize and spread the belief. And in them, in the works of Marx and Engels, realization of the ideals of greater equality and humanity was intimately linked, even theoretically, with the use of extra-state violence. In the French Revolution, the use of violence was by and large spontaneous and unplanned. After the Russian Revolution, it became an integral part of the plans of weaker outsider groups. Moreover, the leaders, who had come to power in Russia through the use of extra-state violence, and their successors, who were now masters of a mighty empire, supported the spreading of their ideals to sympathetic groups in other countries.

And this is where the peculiar dialectical dynamics of the use of violence come into play. The Russophile movements outside Russia which, following this model, sought to realize their ideals in the last instance through extra-state violence, and which relied primarily on sectors of the working class and smaller groups of the middle-class intelligentsia, set themselves against other groups which for their part planned to counter the danger of violence posed by the former with the help of their own extra-state violence. In order to prevent the violent conquest of the state monopolies by the other side, they themselves prepared to conquer these monopolies.

That was the problem. Up to the present, there has been relatively little understanding of how the use of violence by a particular group against another gives rise with a high degree of probability to the use of violence by the other group against the former, as soon as there is the slightest chance to do so. The violence of the second group then in many cases triggers off increased violence from the first group. If such a process, a double-bind process, is once set in motion, then it is exceedingly difficult to halt; it often gains a momentum of its own. It gains a self-perpetuating and very often escalating power over the people, the opposing groups which constitute it, and becomes a trap forcing each of the participating sides, out of fear of the violence of the other side, to fight each other with violence.

Since the Russian Revolution, many countries in the world, perhaps all countries, have found themselves caught up in the vicious circle of such a mechanism. The fact that the use of extra-state violence has proved its value in the struggle against the state's violence has triggered off violent double-bind processes across the world. One of the first countries in which this spread became evident was Germany. Compared with Russia, it had reached a considerably higher level of industrialization, urbanization, national education and all other relevant aspects of a modernization process. Correspondingly, the German industrial working class was organized and politically educated to a far greater extent than the Russian. This meant that in middle-class circles the fear was even greater that, after the Russian Revolution with its violent expropriation of private property and with its very close connection with the military defeat of the tsarist regime, a revolution would also follow in Germany after the defeat of its imperial regime, with a programmatic change of power and property relations. The indubitable growth in power that the German workers had won, partly in the course of the war itself and partly in the wake of the defeat, reinforced this fear.

## 2

The splitting of the German workers' organizations in the wake of the Russian Revolution into a camp advocating non-violent reform and another advocating violent revolution corresponded to a parallel development on the middle-class side. Here, too, there were groups who fixed their objectives within the framework of the existing state monopoly of force and organized their business with each other through the game-rules which this monopoly safeguarded, and others who advocated the use of extra-state violence especially in the fight against the workers' organizations and the state which gave these organizations legitimacy. But whereas the pro-violence (thus anti-state) and anti-violence (thus pro-state) workers' organizations feuded furiously with each other, between the analogous middle-class organizations there was an open or tacit agreement. Not only defence associations, secret associations and other violent groups, but also wide sections of the middle class who were not prepared personally to use violence in internal struggles were inclined to be hostile towards the republic. As a result, the latter did not hesitate to support the former in every possible way. After 1918 the high value placed on physical force among sectors of the German middle class which had already been encountered in the Wilhelmine era was accordingly strengthened; but now it acquired a new character and tone.

In the Kaiser's Germany, the resort to violence in internal conflicts, such as in the case of a strike, was an affair of state and therefore used for the most part without much thought; it appeared to be a self-evident and legitimate use of the state monopoly of violence. But just as the use of physical violence in the course of the Russian Revolution was in large measure a conscious and deliberate form of the exercise of violence, theoretically supported by Marx's high valuation of revolution, so now, in the middle-class camp as well, the threat and use of violence became consciously manipulated, thought-out weapons in the power struggle between class organizations. Double-bind processes in the course of which the threat of violence by communist groups provoked and reinforced similar threats from 'fascist' groups, and vice versa, were from now on, as has been said, permanent part-aspects of the development of many countries in Europe and elsewhere. The extent to which the state monopoly of force could be broken in particular cases depended on the strength and stability of the central state power, in particular on the efficiency of the monopoly of force itself and on the closely connected security and stability of a state-society's economic development.

It was characteristic of Germany's situation at the end of the 1914–18 war that the new ruling authorities had control only to a quite limited extent over the military and police forces, which are necessary for maintaining the monopoly of physical violence and, with it, domestic peace. The German state in the Weimar period was to that extent a rudimentary state. It was this which gave the violent movements and organizations on the side of both the middle class and the working class their chance.

The capacity of the government, in other words, to employ the executive organs of the violence-monopoly, the armed forces and the police, in support of parliamentary and government decisions was very limited. In relation to the republican central government which represented a kind of alliance between the moderate middle class and the moderate working class, the army, still led by the nobility, possessed an independence and a power-potential of its own that its predecessor in the Kaiser's Germany did not have.[1] As is similarly the case in many developing countries of our own times—for example, in some Latin American republics—the top military command in the Weimar Republic followed their own political goals, too. In the power-play of that period, they represented a semi-independent focal point of power. As a result, the national government could at best rely on the police forces of particular provinces (*Länder*) to maintain the peace and to track down and punish the perpetrators of violent acts. By and large, the Prussian police were at its disposal for such tasks, but those of other provinces, such as Bavaria, were not.

Of considerable importance for the struggle between the violent middle-class and workers' organizations, too, was the fact that, on the one hand, the social democratic representatives of workers in the government, men like Ebert, Scheidemann and Noske, wanted strongly to reform the still quasi-autocratic imperial regime into a parliamentary regime unhindered by any privileges whatsoever, but, on the other hand, they simultaneously renounced the use of physical violence for achieving workers' interests with great resolve and an astonishingly strong emotional aversion. They were therefore hardly less hostile towards that part of the working class that was orientated towards the Russian example, towards a violent revolution, than were the middle-class associations and organizations.

That was one of the reasons leading to an alliance—a marriage of convenience—between the people's representatives and the high command of the army (and even with individual *Freikorps*). The alliance contributed, together with the workers' strike, to the failure of the first attempt on the middle-class side to topple the government, the Kapp putsch.[2] At the same time, however, it showed the high dependency of the Weimar government on the semi-autonomous army and with it the essential weakness of the regime. Together with the Social Democratic Party and the trades unions, the officer corps was one of the nuclei of organization which had remained more or less intact despite the incipient disintegration that followed the defeat. These two groups, represented by Ebert and Groener, formed a kind of alliance in the desperate situation and confusion after 1918. What united them was a very realistic awareness of the danger threatening the country of violent attempted *coups d'état* of every colour, whether from the side of middle-class/military circles or by groups of communist workers. It was predictable that all such attempts would bring allied intervention in their train.

3

From the very beginning, therefore, the state structure of the first German republic had two faces. On the one hand, the struggle of class interests and class ideals was carried on in the form of a party struggle on the parliamentary stage, relatively non-violently, according to parliamentary rules and in the full searchlight of the public gaze. On the other hand, this struggle was also fought out by defence associations and secret societies using physical violence in a conspiratorial twilight. In these murky and violent battles, however, the balance of power was far more unevenly distributed than in the parliamentary party struggles. In the parliamentary context, the representatives of workers' organizations concerned with securing non-violent reform now had access to power-chances through the potential or actual take-over of government and other state positions which had previously been closed to them. In the struggle of the violent gangs, on the other hand, the middle-class organizations won the upper hand early on, after the communist-orientated ones had relatively quickly been subdued. They attempted to destroy the republican state and social structure from within by undermining that state monopoly of violence and by making the people associated with it uneasy through acts of terror of the most diverse types. In this way, they wanted to bring the hated system to the point of collapse. And in the end, aided by economic crisis, they succeeded, when the legitimate state power was taken over by the man who had distinguished himself in the competitive struggle with other paramilitary organizations by the particularly hard and systematic use of non-legal, extra-state means of violence.

I have the impression that this undermining of the German state from within through acts of terror, through the systematic use of violence, has still not as yet been accorded the historiographical significance which it actually deserves. That has obscured insight into the paradigmatic meaning which this threat, and, in the end, the near paralysis of the state monopoly of violence in the Weimar period, have for the understanding of similar processes elsewhere and of the function of state monopolies of violence in human societies in general. It has become customary to examine economic developments largely in isolation from political developments. These, for their part, are generally understood in terms of the development of legal institutions. The difficulty is to show convincingly that the development of the organization of violence, with its integration and disintegration spurts, is no less structured than, for example, the organization of the social production of goods.

I must deny myself the chance of showing here in detail the direction and the transformations of this extra-parliamentary power struggle which was played out between 1918 and 1933 in the half-light of an illegality which the state either tolerated or could no longer prevent and which was also connected with the parliamentary power struggles. It must be enough to establish that a continuous line of development in a subculture and in circles of people led from the terror acts of the guerrillas in the first years of the republic to the brawling at public meetings and street fighting of the early 1930s. My own experiences in this period have certainly contributed to sharpening my understanding of the problematic of the state monopoly of violence and how it is related to collective changes in behaviour, whether in a more civilizing or a more barbarizing direction. It is probably difficult for the crescendo of extra-state acts of violence which prepared the way for Hitler's takeover to reach the ears of the younger generations of our times. But perhaps a brief reference to a personal experience I remember may help.

In 1932, I attended a meeting in the Frankfurt *Gewerkschaftshaus* (Trade Union Headquarters) about a student's scholarship. During a pause in the conversation, I asked, 'What preparations have you made to defend yourselves in the *Gewerkschaftshaus* in the case of an armed attack?' I remember the silence which followed this question. Then began a rather stormy debate which made it clear to me that I had brought out into the open a thought which had for some time lurked in the back of the minds of several of those present. But they had not trusted themselves to express openly in words the possibilities which it raised, because they posed too great a contradiction to the tenor of the life to which they were accustomed, because it was too terrible to look the fact squarely in the eye that their accustomed way of life was now coming to an end. Besides, there were even one or two voices which declared such events to be utterly impossible. The conviction of the speakers that a kind of historical providence would always ensure the victory of what they regarded as 'reason' over forces of darkness was unshakeable.[3]

The question arose as to what one could do. It was obvious that, in the intensifying battles of the violent right- and left-wing extra-state associations, the right were in the process of gaining the upper hand. I wanted to know why that was the case. I still remember most vividly the picture which emerged then and from further questioning. It points to some of the structural characteristics of Hitler's victory which could easily be overlooked.

Republican defence associations, such as the social democratic orientated 'Black-Red-Gold' Ex-Servicemen's Association (*Reichsbanner Schwarz-Rot-Gold*), lacked three things which were essential for victory or even for simply enduring these violent extra-parliamentary power struggles between fighting organizations with 'proletarian' and 'bourgeois' goals.

1. Such organizations were expensive. The money at the disposal of the defence associations of the organized workers for buying weapons, uniforms and other equipment was minimal in comparison with the money available to the other side. Only to a limited extent could they afford to offer their members fully paid posts, or to pay for loss of earnings or transport costs. And they were, on the whole, dependent on the voluntary participation of people who, after work or on their days off, put on their uniforms to take part in exercises, street demonstrations, guard the halls where speakers were appearing, and to take part in the ensuing, often rather dangerous, brawls. The opposing associations, especially Hitler's storm-troopers, had a far higher percentage of full-time mercenaries. They could afford to bring in unemployed people, drill them and ideologically indoctrinate them.

2. Furthermore, the fighting associations of the organized working class suffered from a dearth of officers. The overwhelming majority of German officers were on the other side. The sharp division that had existed in the Wilhelmine empire between officers and other ranks thus affected the efficiency of these extra-state fighting organizations after the war. The 'proletarian' defence associations quite simply lacked a militarily educated leadership and organizers.

3. Finally, there was no adherence to a military tradition in their circles, no predisposition for warlike activities, which was almost a matter of course on the other side.

No wonder, therefore, that the workers' associations in these violent extra-parliamentary power struggles often came off second best, and that their propagandists, not least in election meetings, often had a hard time. No wonder, either, that wide sections of the population, tired of violence and commotion, gave their votes to the leader of the evidently stronger battalions.

It is thus much more than a literary metaphor when, looking back on the Weimar period, one speaks of an increasing 'paralysis' of the state monopoly of violence, or of an increasing 'undermining' of the German state from within. The destruction of the parliamentary-republican regime was one of the political goals of wide sections of the German middle class as early as the immediate post-war years. The other was military rearmament as a step on the path to recovering Germany's position as a great power. But in the early days after the war, this was hardly anything more than wishful thinking. Such goals were unrealistic to start with because, after the signing of the peace treaty, extra-parliamentary defence associations could no longer appear in the open. In the early 1920s, the victorious powers, the Allies, kept watch with undiminished attentiveness to see that Germany's military potential did not exceed the limits imposed by the Treaty of Versailles. This was one of the major reasons why the terrorist acts of violence of those years, through which the perpetrators were already hoping to wear down and if possible bring about the collapse of the parliamentary republic, took a rather different form from those in the late 1920s and early 1930s.

Especially in this early phase, they were far more conspiratorial in character than at the time of the Great Depression and afterwards. In the later period, the Allies' fear of German militarism was being slowly pushed into the background by their fear of Russian militarism. A strengthening of anti-Russian and anti-communist forces in Germany was therefore not in the least displeasing for many Western statesmen. It thus came about that the bourgeois-orientated paramilitary defence associations, which had already been pursuing their foreign policy/national goals and their domestic policy/social goals using the same violent means, gradually emerged from the conspiratorial twilight. They could now show themselves relatively openly in public and, through public threats and acts of violence, contribute to bringing about those very chaotic circumstances which they laid at the door of the parliamentary republic as a sign of its weakness and unfitness. The struggles on the parliamentary and extra-parliamentary levels which had taken place alongside each other in the early days of the republic now affected each other more and more closely, and in the end fused together when parliament legalized the organizations which supported extra-parliamentary violence.

The economic crisis from 1929 onwards most certainly did not affect Germany alone. But in Germany at that time, the economic crisis stood in a double-bind relationship with a political crisis bordering on civil war. Both aspects of the crisis mutually reinforced each other. The economic crisis, deepened by the political crisis, fanned the flames of the violent political clashes, and vice versa. In the end, the republic of the Weimar period foundered on the structural weakness of its monopoly of violence and the purposeful exploitation of this weakness by middle-class organizations which, because of the lack of a parliamentary tradition, felt that the parliamentary-republican regime discriminated against them and therefore sought to destroy it.

## Notes

1. In his *A History of the Weimar Republic* (trans. I. F. D. Morrow and L. Marie Sieveking, London, Methuen, 1936, p. 105), Arthur Rosenberg argues that:

> True revolutionaries would, above all, have faced the danger that threatened from the army. The National Assembly might have declared in the manner of the [French Revolutionary] Convention that the Republic was in danger. It might have called all Socialists and Republicans to arms to save their country. A general armament of the people would have rendered the Free Corps harmless, would have nipped in the bud any danger of individual *coups,* would have secured the eastern frontier against the Poles, and might even possibly have strengthened the position of Germany in face of the Entente at the peace negotiations.

Rosenberg is referring to the models of the French and English Revolutions. He sees the regularities of revolutionary processes exclusively as sequences of intra-state events. He accordingly fails to recognize the foreign political situation of the young German republic. It is extremely unlikely that the Allies would have simply accepted such a *levée en masse* of the German population, arms at the ready. Such a mass uprising—even if the national army would have stood for it, even if the weapons had been available—would have been possible only with overt or covert revolutionary slogans. The Russian revolutionary movement was already getting badly on the nerves of the Western Allies. A similar movement in Germany would have been the signal for them to invade.

2. The *Reichswehr* gave its support at this point not from sympathy with the parliamentary republic, but because it considered this first attempt to overthrow the government and the subsequent proclamation of a dictatorship to be premature. Its policy was to bide its time. However much its hopes and wishes resembled those of the rebels, the older and more experienced leaders of the officer corps saw clearly that the time had not come for rearmament, not for doing away with the multi-party state in favour of a regime with the strength and popularity to undertake rearmament. This hesitation on the part of the *Reichswehr* was partly responsible for the fact that it was not until 1933 that a party dictatorship arose, and that this came about by means of the formal parliamentary path, bringing with it, among other things, the dissolution of the existing parties and trade unions.

3. The following quotation usefully illustrates how much this belief contributed to the failure of its opponents, especially the intellectuals among them, to recognize the political potential of the Hitler movement. As early as 1924, Emil Julius Gumbel had written in his book *Verschwörer:*

> National Socialism can only be understood instinctively. It contradicts even the most primitive standards of rationality. It is a passion, created from economic necessity and

the bitterness of the soul that it leads to. It has nothing to do with realistic forms of politics. Its entire rationale comes from romanticism. . . . [The] idea of a racially pure state cannot possibly be put into practice, of course, and the demands for this are naturally merely mouthings, but they find support among the youth. . . . Such ideas lead naturally to a direct way of realizing them: attacks against Jewish people on the street, destruction of newspapers and so on, since this level corresponds to the lowest, most violent instincts. . . . (pp. 177f)

These remarks make clear why the pattern of thought nowadays known as 'rationalism', with the related concept of human reason as a natural endowment—which formed in close relationship with the wave of pacification in developing absolutist states and later within nation-states which furthered internal pacification—makes it difficult for its exponents to incorporate into their picture of humanity the control or non-control of violence in dealing with conflict between humans as a universal problem of social life. In line with the level of civilization expressed in concepts such as 'intellect', 'reason' or 'rationality', their upholders do not yet reflect upon the civilizing conditions of their respective concepts. They therefore do not know that a high degree and peculiar form of pacification are among the conditions for the movement they call 'rationalism', and thus also for their concepts of 'reason' of 'understanding'. The use of violence as a social fact is then quite simply relegated to the realm of the irrational, if not the anti-rational, and thus remains in principle incomprehensible.

# 10

# The Genesis of Sport in Antiquity

## 1

Many types of sports which today are played in a more or less identical manner all over the world originated in England.[1] They spread from there to other countries mainly in the second half of the nineteenth and first half of the twentieth centuries. Football, in the form which became known in England as 'Association Football' or, by a popular abbreviation, as 'soccer', was one of them. Horse-racing, wrestling, boxing, tennis, fox-hunting, rowing, croquet and athletics were others. But none of the others was quite as widely and, in many cases, quite as rapidly adopted and absorbed by other countries as their own as the soccer type of football. Nor did they enjoy quite as much popularity.[2]

The English term 'sport', too, was widely adopted by other countries as a generic term for this specific type of pastimes. That 'sports', the specific type of English pastimes which spread to many other countries mainly between 1850 and 1950, had certain distinguishing characteristics in common which justified their designation as such, namely as 'sports', has probably been noted more in other countries than in England itself. A German commentator wrote in 1936:

> As is well known, England was the cradle and the loving 'mother' of sport
> . . . It appears that English technical terms referring to this field might become the common possession of all nations in the same way as Italian technical terms in the field of music. It is probably rare that a piece of culture has migrated with so few changes from one country to another.[3]

That 'sport'—the social datum as well as the word—was initially a stranger in other countries can be shown from many examples. The timing of a process of diffusion and adoption is always a significant datum in the context of a sociological diagnosis. Thus in Germany in 1810, an aristocratic writer who knew England was still able to say, '"Sport" is as untranslatable as "gentleman".'[4] In 1844 another German author

Published as "The Genesis of Sport as a Sociological Problem" in *Quest for Excitement*, pp. 126–49 wrote with regard to the term 'sports', 'We have no word for this and are almost forced to introduce it into our language.'[5] The diffusion of the English term 'sport' as an expression which German people could understand as a matter of course continued to be slow up to the 1850s. It gradually gained momentum in conjunction with the increase of sports activities themselves. Finally, in the twentieth century, 'Sport' became fully established as a German word.

In France, the *Larousse du XIXième Siècle* characterized the term 'sport' thus: 'Sport—sportt—English word formed from the old French "desport", pleasure, diversion . . .' It complained about the importation of such terms 'which obviously corrupt our language but we have no customs barriers in order to prohibit their importation at the frontier.'[6] Other imports from England to France, factual as well as verbal, were 'turf', 'jockey', 'steeplechase', 'match', 'sweepstake' and 'le boxe'. Already under Louis XVIII horse-racing and betting became more regularized in France in accordance with English models. The fashion disappeared during the revolution but was revived with the reestablishment of a more or less aristocratic upper class. A jockey club was founded in Paris in 1833. In fact, the aristocratic or 'Society' type of pastimes, which dominated the meaning of the term 'sport' in England itself in the first half of the nineteenth century, spread to other countries and was adopted there by corresponding social elites before the more popular types such as football developed the characteristics of a 'sport', were perceived as such in England itself and spread in that form to other countries, as a pastime of middle- and working-class groups. In Germany as in France, some English terms which belonged to the language of the upper-class type of sport were taken up as early as the eighteenth century. From about 1744 on, an older term '*baxen*' appeared in the more literate form of '*boxen*'. It is as significant for our understanding of the development of European societies as it is for that of sport itself that the first types of English sports which were taken up by other countries were horse-racing, boxing, fox-hunting, and similar pastimes, and that the diffusion of ball games such as football and tennis and of 'sport' generally in the more contemporary sense began only in the second part of the nineteenth century.

The transformation of a polymorphous English folk game into Association Football or 'soccer' had the character of a fairly long development in the direction of greater regulation and uniformity. It culminated in the codification of the game more or less on a national level in 1863. The first German football club playing according to English rules was founded, characteristically enough in Hanover, in 1878. In the Netherlands, the first football club was founded in 1879/80, in Italy about 1890. Football federations were founded in Switzerland in 1895, in Germany in 1900, and in Portugal in 1906, indicating the increase in the number of clubs in each country. In the Netherlands alone, 25 different football clubs with more than ten members each existed as early as 1900/01. By 1910/11, the number of clubs had risen to 134. From 1908 onwards, football became—with interruptions—a regular part of the Olympic Games.

As the game spread to other countries, the term 'football' itself, often suitably transformed and, in most, though not all cases, associated with the 'soccer' type of English football, entered other languages. In France it retained its original form. In Germany it was transformed without great difficulty into '*Fussball*'. In Spain it became '*futbol*' with characteristic derivatives such as '*futbolero*' and '*futbolista*'. In Portugal it became '*futebol*', in Holland '*voetbal*'. In the United States, too, the term 'football' was for a time connected with the soccer type of game, but there the term changed its meaning in accordance with the changing fortunes of the game itself. The dominant American style of playing football gradually changed from the soccer type. Some of the leading American universities, so it seems, diverged from its rules, at first influenced by a Canadian variant of the English rival of soccer, 'rugby' football or 'rugger', which they then developed further in their own way. But the term 'football' remained attached to the different style of playing the game which evolved gradually and finally became standardized in the States while the Association type of the game became known there purely and simply as 'soccer' in contrast to the continued use of '*futbol*' and '*futebol*' for this form of the game in the Latin-American states.

One could give many other examples of this diffusion from England and the absorption by other countries of sport and the terms associated with it. As a first approach, these few may be enough to indicate the problem.

## 2

What accounts for the fact that, mainly in the nineteenth and twentieth centuries, an English type of pastimes called 'sport' set the pattern for a world-wide leisure movement? Pastimes of this type evidently corresponded to specific leisure needs which made themselves felt in many countries during that period. Why did they emerge in England first? What characteristics in the development and structure of English society account for the development there of leisure activities with the specific characteristics which we designate as 'sport'? What are these characteristics? And what distinguished pastimes which came to possess them from earlier pastimes?

164

At first glance, one may well feel that this array of questions is based on wrong assumptions. Surely, contemporary societies are not the first and not the only ones whose members have enjoyed sport? Did not people play football in England and in other European countries in the Middle Ages? Did not the courtiers of Louis XIV have their tennis courts and enjoy their *'jeu de paume'*? And above all the ancient Greeks, the great pioneers of 'athletics' and other 'sports', did they not, like ourselves, organize local and inter-state game-contests on a magnificent scale? Is not the revival of the Olympic Games in our own times a sufficient reminder of the fact that 'sport' is nothing new?

It is difficult to clarify the question whether the type of game-contests which developed in England under the name 'sport' during the eighteenth and nineteenth centuries and which spread from there to other countries was something relatively new or whether it was a revival of something old which had unaccountably lapsed, without looking briefly into the question of whether in fact the game-contests of ancient Greece had the characteristics of what we now regard as 'sport'. The term 'sport' is at present often used rather loosely to cover game-contests of many kinds. Like the term 'industry', it is used both in a wider and a narrower sense. In the wider sense, it refers, like the term 'industry', to specific activities of pre-state tribal societies and pre-industrial state-societies as well as to corresponding activities of industrial nation-states. If one uses the term 'industry' in this wider sense, one is at present nevertheless well aware of its narrower and more precise meaning, of the fact that the 'industrialization process' of the nineteenth and twentieth centuries is something rather new and that the specific types of production and work which have developed in recent times under the name 'industry' have certain unique structures that can be determined sociologically with considerable precision and clearly distinguished from other types of production. If one speaks of 'sport', however, one still uses the term indiscriminately both in a wider sense in which it refers to the game-contests and physical exercises of all societies and in a narrower sense in which it refers to the specific type of game-contests which, like the term itself, originated in England and spread from there to other societies. This process—one might call it the 'sportization' of game-contests if that did not sound rather unattractive—points to a problem which is fairly clear: can one discover in the recent development of the structure and organization of those leisure activities which we call 'sport' trends which are as unique as those in the structure and organization of work which we refer to when we speak of a process of industrialization?

This is an open question. One can easily misread it. Given the prevailing evaluation of work as something of much higher value than leisure activities of all kinds, it can easily suggest that any transformation, whether of leisure activities in general or of game-contests in particular, which has taken place in the last 200 years or so must have been the 'effect' of which industrialization was the 'cause'. The implicit expectation of causal connections of this type closes the issue before it has been properly opened. One may, for instance, consider the possibility that both industrialization and the transformation of specific leisure occupations into sports are interdependent part-trends within an overall transformation of state societies in recent times. But only if one ceases to treat changes in social spheres which rate higher in the value scale of one's society as 'causes', and changes in lower ranking spheres as 'effects', can one hope to clarify the problem which one encounters here. And the clarification of the problem itself—that of the genesis of sport—is the main task of this essay. In this as in other cases, it is easier to find solutions if one is quite clear what the problem is.

## 3

The following excerpt from the article on athletics in a recent edition of the *Encyclopaedia Britannica* can probably be regarded as a reasonable summary of the conventional views on this problem:

> The earliest historical records of athletics are of the Grecian Olympic Games (*c.* 800 BC) . . . terminated by order of the Emperor Theodosius in AD 394. The history of athletics between the fall of Rome in the fifth century and the nineteenth century is quite sketchy. Religious festivals in the Middle Ages were often accompanied by crude ball games between rival towns or guilds. These were the forerunners of the great spectator sports of the twentieth century: soccer, baseball, tennis, football, etc. The coming of the Industrial Revolution in the mid-eighteenth century and the later introduction of sports as a regular extra-curricular activity in public schools by Thomas Arnold (*c.* 1830) provided a spur which led to the great development of sport during the Victorian age of England. Capping the athletic revival of the nineteenth century was the restoration of the Olympic Games at Athens in 1896. As the twentieth century dawned, interest in all competitive sports reached a peak and despite two world wars and numerous minor hostilities, this interest continues to grow.

This summary, as one can see, states a number of reasonably well-documented facts. It occasionally hints at an explanation such as the spur supposedly given to sport through the initiative of Dr. Arnold. But it is hardly designed to open the eyes of a reader to the many unsolved problems buried under the smooth surface of the narrative. How, for instance, is it to be explained that the religious festivals of Middle Ages were accompanied by games which were 'crude' while the religious festivals in antiquity at Olympia and elsewhere were apparently less crude and thus more akin to those of the nineteenth and twentieth centuries? And how is it to be determined that these are less crude? How can one determine, with a reasonable degree of precision, variations in 'crudeness', in civilizing standards in the performance of games? And how can one explain them? How can one explain the 'great development of sport', the 'athletic revival of the nineteenth century'? If one remembers the tournaments of the Middle Ages or the innumerable folk-games of that age—unsuppressed and, in fact, unsuppressable even if the authorities disapproved of them, as the recurrent edicts against playing football in England and other European countries indicate—one can hardly say that there was not a very lively interest in game-contests as such. Was the difference between the game-contests that people enjoyed prior to the eighteenth century and those which they enjoyed in the age of the 'industrial revolution' simply a question of a higher or lower degree of 'crudeness'? Was it due to the fact that the latter were less savage, that they were more 'civilized'? And is that one of the distinguishing characteristics of 'sport'? But in that case, is it justified to speak of a 'revival'? Is the sports movement of the nineteenth and twentieth centuries another 'Renaissance', an unexplained 'rebirth' of something which existed in antiquity, perished in the Middle Ages and, for unknown reasons, was simply reborn in our time? Were the game-contests of antiquity less 'crude' and less savage? Were they, like ours, relatively restrained and representative of a comparatively high sensitivity against playfully inflicting serious injuries on others for the delight of spectators? Or is the tendency to present the modern sports movement as the revival of a similar movement in antiquity one of those benevolent ideological legends innocently used as a means for strengthening the unity of a movement that is full of tensions and conflicting tendencies and for heightening its glamour and prestige? In that case, would it not perhaps be preferable to examine realistically the specific conditions which account for the genesis and rise of the sports movement of our time, to face up to the fact that game-contests of the type which we call 'sport', like the industrial nation-states where they take place, have certain unique characteristics which distinguish them from other types, and to start the difficult task of enquiring into and explaining the nature of these distinguishing characteristics?

4

On closer inspection, it is not difficult to see that the game-contests of classical antiquity, which are often represented as the great paradigm of sport, had a number of features and grew up under conditions which were very different from those of our own game-contests. The ethos of the contenders, the standards by which they were judged, the rules of the contests, and the performances themselves differed markedly in many respects from those characteristic of modern sport. Many of the relevant writings of today show a strong tendency to minimize the differences and maximize the similarities. The result is a distorted picture of our own as well as of Greek society and a distorted picture of the relationship between them. The issues are confused not only by the tendency to treat the game-contests of antiquity as the ideal embodiment of contemporary sport but also by the corresponding expectation to find confirmation for this hypothesis in the writings of antiquity and the tendency to neglect contradictory evidence or to treat it automatically as a reference to exceptional cases.

It may be enough here to point to one of the basic features characteristic of the differences in the whole structure of game-contests of classical antiquity and those of the nineteenth and twentieth centuries. In antiquity the customary rules of 'heavy' athletic events, such as boxing and wrestling, admitted a far higher degree of physical violence than that admitted by the rules of the corresponding types of sport-contests. The rules of the latter, moreover, are very much more detailed and differentiated; they are not primarily customary rules but written rules, explicitly subject to reasoned criticism and revision. The higher level of physical violence in the games of antiquity itself was anything but an isolated datum. It was symptomatic of specific features in the organization of Greek society, especially in the stage of development reached by what we now call the 'state' organization and by the degree of monopolization of physical violence embodied in it. A relatively firm, stable and impersonal monopolization and control of the means of violence is one of the central structural traits of contemporary nation-states. Compared with it, the institutional monopolization and control of physical violence in the city-states of Greece was still rudimentary.

The clarification of problems such as these is not difficult if their investigation is guided by a clear theoretical model such as that provided by the theory of civilizing processes.[7] According to it, one expects that state formation and conscience formation, the level of socially permitted physical violence and the threshold of repugnance against using it or witnessing it, differ in specific ways at different stages in the development of societies. It is striking to find how fully the evidence in the case of classical Greece confirms these theoretical expectations. In this way, theory and empirical data together remove one of the main obstacles to the understanding of the developmental differences such as those which exist between ancient and contemporary game-contests, namely the feeling that one casts a slur on another society and lowers its human value by admitting that the level of physical violence tolerated there even in game-contests was higher, and the threshold of revulsion against people wounding or even killing each other in such a contest to the delight of spectators correspondingly lower than our own. In the case of Greece, one is thus torn between the high human value traditionally attached to its achievement in philosophy, the sciences, the arts and poetry, and the low human value which one seems to attribute to the ancient Greeks if one speaks of their lower level of revulsion against physical violence, if one seems to suggest that they were, compared with ourselves, 'uncivilized' and 'barbarous'. It is precisely the misunderstanding of the factual nature of civilizing processes, the prevailing tendency to use terms like 'civilized' and 'uncivilized' as expressions of ethnocentric value judgements, as absolute and final moral judgements—we are 'good', they are 'bad', or vice versa—that leads our reasoning into seemingly inescapable contradictions such as these.

We ourselves are brought up, in accordance with the specific social organization and control of the means of violence within the industrial nation-states of our time, with specific standards of self-control with regard to impulses of violence. We measure transgressions automatically by these standards—whether they occur in our own or in other societies at a different stage of development. Internalized, these standards afford protection and strengthen our defences against lapses in a variety of ways. A heightened sensibility with regard to acts of violence, feelings of repugnance against seeing violence committed beyond the permitted level in real life, guilt-feelings about our own lapses, a 'bad conscience', all these are symptomatic of these defences. However, in a period of incessant violence in inter-state affairs, these internalized defences against impulses to violence inevitably remain unstable and brittle. They are continuously exposed to conflicting social pressures—those encouraging a high level of self-control of violent impulses in human relations within one and the same state-society, and those encouraging a loosening of the self-control or violent impulses and even a training for violence in the relations between different state-societies. The former account for the relatively high degree of physical security, though not, of course, of psychological and other forms of security, enjoyed by citizens of more developed nation-states within their own societies. They constantly conflict with the demands made on the citizens of these states as a result of the absence of any effective monopolization and control of physical violence in inter-state relations. A double morality, a split and contradictory conscience formation, is the result.

No doubt discrepancies of this type can be found at many stages in the development of societies. The level of violence control within social groups at the tribal stage is almost always higher than that of violence control between social groups of this type. It was certainly no different in the case of the Greek city-states. But in their case the disparity between the two levels was relatively small compared with that characteristic of our own time. There is a good deal of evidence to suggest that this gradient, the disparity between the level of physical security and of both social and self-control of violent impulses, with the corresponding conscience formation reached today in intra-state relations, and the level of physical security and social regulation of overtly violent feelings and—intermittently—of overt acts of violence in inter-state relations is greater today than ever before. The level of physical security within the more advanced industrial nation-states, though it may appear low enough to those who live in them, is, in all likelihood, normally higher than in less developed state societies, while the insecurity in inter-state relations has hardly decreased. Violent inter-state conflicts at the present stage of social development are still as unmanageable for those involved in them as they always were. Standards of civilized behaviour, accordingly, are relatively low and the internalization of social taboos against physical violence, the conscience formation, is in that respect transient and comparatively unsteady. That conflicts and tensions within industrial nation-states have become—normally—less violent and somewhat more manageable is the result of a long, unplanned development; it is certainly not the merit of the present generations. But present generations are apt to regard it as such; they are inclined to sit in judgement over past generations whose conscience formation, whose level of revulsion against physical violence, for instance in the relations between ruling elites and ruled, was lower, as if their own, higher level of revulsion was simply their own personal achievement.

The level of violence to be observed in the game-contests of past ages is often judged in this manner. We often fail to distinguish between individual acts of transgression against the standards of violence control within our own society and individual acts of a similar kind committed in other societies in accordance with *their* socially permitted level of violence, in accordance with the norms of *those* societies. Thus our immediate, our almost automatic emotional response often induces us to judge societies with different standards of violence control and of revulsion against violence as if the members of these societies had been free to choose between *their* standards and *their* norms and ours, and, having had this choice, had taken the wrong decision. We enjoy, in relation to them, the same feeling of 'being better', of moral superiority often expe-

rienced in relation to individual offenders in our own society if we call
their conduct 'uncivilized' or 'barbarous', in this manner expressing our
feeling of moral superiority. We treat their adherence to social norms
which permit forms of violence that are condemned as repulsive in our
own societies as a blot on their moral character, as a sign of their inferiority as human beings. Another society is thus judged and evaluated
by us as a whole as if it were an individual member of our own. As a rule,
we do not ask and, as a result, we do not know how changes in the level
of violence control, in the social norms regulating violence, or in the
feelings associated with violence occur. Nor, as a rule, do we ask and
therefore we do not know why they occur. We do not know, in other
words, how they can be explained or, for that matter, how our own,
higher level of sensitivity with regard to physical violence, at least in intra-state relations, can be explained. At the most, we explain them
vaguely by the choice of our expressions rather than explicitly and criti-
cally, for example as a 'flow' in the nature of the groups concerned, or as
an unexplainable characteristic of their 'racial' or ethnic make-up.

5

The customary levels of violence used and permitted in the game-
contests of societies at different stages of development thus illuminate a
much wider and a very fundamental problem. A few examples may help
to give it precision.

Take the case of wrestling as performed in our own days and in antiquity. Today, the sport is highly organized and highly regulated. It is governed by an International Wrestling Federation with headquarters in
Switzerland. According to the Olympic rules of January 1967, among the
foul holds of free-style wrestling are the stranglehold, the half-strangle,
and the double nelson with pressure applied straight down or with the
use of legs. Punching, kicking, butting with the head are all forbidden. A
bout, lasting not more than nine minutes, and divided into three periods
of three minutes each with two intervals of one minute, is controlled by
a referee, three judges and a timekeeper. In spite of these very tight regulations, free-style wrestling appears to many people today as one of the
less refined, 'cruder' types of sport. Performed as a spectator sport by
professionals, a slightly rougher though often pre-arranged version is
still highly popular. But the professionals rarely inflict serious injuries on
each other. In all likelihood, the public would not enjoy seeing bones
broken and the blood flow. But the performers make a good show of
hurting one another, and the public seems to like the make-believe.[8]

Among the game-contests of the ancient Olympic Games was the pancration, a kind of ground wrestling which formed one of the most popular events. But the level of permitted violence represented by the customary duel of the pancration was very different from that permitted in contemporary free-style wrestling. Thus Leontiskos of Messana, who twice in the first half of the fifth century won the Olympic crown for wrestling, obtained his victories not by throwing his opponents but by breaking their fingers. Arrhachion of Phigalia, twice Olympic victor in the pancration, was strangled in 564 during his third attempt to win the Olympic crown, but before being killed he succeeded in breaking the toes of his opponent and the pain forced the latter to give up the struggle. The judges, therefore, crowned Arrhachion's corpse and proclaimed the dead man victor. His compatriots subsequently erected a statue of Ar-rhachion in the market-place of their town.[9] This, apparently, was the customary practice. If a man was killed in a game-contest of one of the great festivals, the dead man was crowned victor. But apart from loss of the crown—a very severe loss—the survivor was not punished. Nor, as far as one can see, was any social stigma attached to his action. To be killed or to be very severely wounded and perhaps incapacitated for life was a risk a fighter in the pancration had to take. One can assess the dif-ference between wrestling as a sport and wrestling as an 'agon' from the following summary:

> In the pancration, the competitors fought with every part of their body, with their hands, feet, elbows, their knees, their necks and their heads; in Sparta they even used their feet. The pancratiasts were allowed to gouge one another's eyes out . . . they were also allowed to trip their opponents, lay hold of their feet, noses and ears, dislocate their fingers and arms and apply strangle-holds. If one man succeeded in throwing the other, he was entitled to sit on him and beat him about the head, face and ears; he could also kick him and trample on him. It goes without saying that the contes-tants in this brutal contest sometimes received the most fearful wounds and that not infrequently men were killed! The pancration of the Spartan epheboi was probably the most brutal of all. Pausanias tells us that the contestants quite literally fought tooth and nail and bit and tore one an-other's eyes out.[10]

There was a judge but no timekeeper and no time limits. The struggle lasted until one of the opponents gave up. The rules were traditional, un-written, undifferentiated and, in their application, probably elastic. It seems that, traditionally, biting and gouging were forbidden. But before the judge could drive an offender, caught up in the fury of the battle, away from his opponent, the damage was probably done.

The old Olympic Games lasted more than a thousand years. Stan-dards of violence in fighting may have fluctuated throughout this period.

But whatever these fluctuations were, throughout antiquity the threshold of sensitivity with regard to the infliction of physical injuries and even to killing in a game-contest and, accordingly, the whole contest ethos, was very different from that represented by the type of contest which we nowadays characterize as 'sport'.

Boxing is another example. Like the pancration type of wrestling, it was very much less hedged in by rules and was therefore to a much higher extent dependent on physical strength, on spontaneous fighting passion and endurance, than sport boxing. One did not distinguish between different classes of boxers. One did not try, therefore, to match people according to their weight either in this or in any of the other contests. The only distinction made was that between boys and men. Boxers did not only fight with their fists. As in almost all forms of boxing, the legs played a part in the struggle. Kicking the shins of an opponent was a normal part of the boxing tradition in antiquity.[11] Only the hand and the upper parts of four fingers were bound with leather thongs fastened to the forearm. Fists could be clenched or fingers stretched and, with hard nails, rammed into the opponent's body and face. As time went on, soft leather thongs gave way to harder thongs specially made from tanned ox-hide.[12] These were then fitted with several strips of hard thick leather with sharp projecting edges. The statue of a seated boxer by Apollonius of Athens (first century BC), now in the Museo Nazionale delle Terme in Rome, shows the arrangement fairly clearly. But perhaps boxing is a misleading term. Not only the manner but also the aim and the ethos of this kind of fighting were different from those in sport boxing. Significantly enough, the fighting ethos of these pugilistic matches, like that of the Greek *agones* generally, was far more directly derived from the fighting ethos of a warrior aristocracy than is the case with the fighting ethos of sport contests. The latter stemmed from the tradition of a country which, more than most other European countries, developed a distinct organization of sea-warfare[13] very different from that of land-warfare, and whose land-owning upper classes—aristocracy and gentry—developed a code of behaviour less directly concerned than that of most other European upper classes with the military code of honour of the officer corps of land-armies.

Greek 'boxing', in common with the other forms of agonistic training and practice in the Greek city-states, but unlike English boxing in the eighteenth and nineteenth centuries, was regarded as a training for warfare as well as for game-contests. Philostratos mentions that the fighting technique of the pancration stood the Greek citizen-armies in good stead in the battle of Marathon when it developed into a general mêlée, and also at Thermopylae where the Spartans fought with their bare hands when their swords and spears had been broken.[14] In the time of Imperial

Rome in which he wrote, wars were no longer fought by citizen armies. They were fought by professional soldiers, by the Roman legions. The distance between military technique and the conduct of war on the one hand, and the traditional agonistic technique of the game-contests on the other hand, had become greater. The Greek Philostratos looked back to the classical age with understandable nostalgia. Perhaps even there, in the period of the hoplite armies, the fighting techniques of war and those of the game-contests were no longer quite as connected with each other as he suggests, but their connection was very much closer than that between the fighting techniques of sport-contests and the fighting techniques of warfare in the age of industrial nation-states. Philostratos was probably very near the mark when he wrote that, in former days, people had regarded the game-contests as an exercise for war and war as an exercise for these contests.[15] The ethos of the game-contests at the great Greek festivals still reflected that of the heroic ancestors as represented in the Homeric epics and perpetuated to some extent from generation to generation by their use in the education of the young. It had many characteristics of the display ethos which rules the status and power rivalries of noble elites in a great number of societies. Fighting, in games as in war, was centred on the ostentatious display of the warrior virtues which gained for a man the highest praise and honour among other members of his own group and for his group—for his kin-group or his city—among other groups. It was glorious to vanquish enemies or opponents but it was hardly less glorious to be vanquished, as Hector was by Achilles, provided one fought with all one's might until one was maimed, wounded or killed and could fight no longer. Victory or defeat was in the hands of the gods. What was inglorious and shameful was to surrender victory without a sufficient show of bravery and endurance.

It was in line with this warrior ethos that a boy or man killed in one of the Olympic boxing or wrestling matches was often crowned as victor to the glory of his clan and his city and that the survivor—the killer—was neither punished nor stigmatized. The Greek games were not ruled by a great concern for 'fairness'. The English ethos of fairness had non-military roots. It evolved in England in connection with a very specific change in the nature of the enjoyment and excitement provided by game-contests as a result of which the all-too brief pleasure in the outcome of a sports battle, in the moment of consummation or victory, was extended and prolonged by the equal pleasure and excitement, derived from what initially was foreplay, from participating in or from witnessing the tension of the game-contest itself. Greater emphasis on the enjoyment of the game-contest, and the tension-excitement it provided as such, was to some extent connected with the enjoyment of betting which, in England, played a considerable part both in the transformation of 'cruder' forms of game-contests into sports and in the development of the ethos of fairness. Gentlemen watching a game-contest played by their sons, their retainers or by well-known professionals liked to put money on one side or the other as a condiment of the excitement provided by the contest itself which was already tempered by civilizing restraints. But the prospect of winning one's bet could add to the excitement of watching the struggle only if the initial odds of winning were more or less evenly divided between the two sides and offered a minimum of calculability. All this required, and in turn was made possible by, a higher organizational level than that reached in the city-states of ancient Greece:

> The boxers of Olympia were not classified according to weight any more than the wrestlers were. There was no boxing ring, the bouts being fought on an open piece of ground inside the stadium. The target area was the head and the face . . . The fight went on until one of the two contestants was no longer able to defend himself or acknowledged defeat. This he did either by raising his index finger or extending two fingers towards his opponent.[16]

Representations on Greek vases usually show boxers in a traditional stance so close to each other that each stands with one foot forward next to or even behind that of the other. There was little scope for the footwork which enables modern boxers to move quickly, now to the right or left, now backwards, now forwards. To move backwards, according to the code of warriors, was a sign of cowardice. To avoid the enemy's blows by moving out of his way was shameful. Boxers, like warriors at close quarters, were expected to stand fast and not to give way. The defences of skilful boxers might be impenetrable; they might tire their opponents and win without receiving injuries. But if the fight took too long, a judge could order the two opponents to take and to give blow for blow without defending themselves until one of them was no longer able to continue the fight. This agonistic type of boxing, as one can see, accentuated the climax, the moment of decision, of victory or defeat, as the most important and significant part of the contest, more important than the game-contest itself. It was as much a test of physical endurance and of sheer muscular strength as of skill. Serious injuries to the eyes, ears and even to the skull were frequent; so were swollen ears, broken teeth and squashed noses. We hear of two boxers who agreed to exchange blow for blow. The first struck a blow to the head which his opponent survived. When he lowered his guard, the other man struck him under the ribs with his outstretched fingers, burst through his side with his hard nails, seized his bowels and killed him.[17]

'Of all the Olympic contests the one which is most alien to us today is boxing; no matter how hard we try we are still unable to conceive how a highly
cultivated people with such discriminating aesthetic tastes could derive
pleasure from this barbaric spectacle in which two men beat one another
about the head with their heavily mailed fists . . . until one of them acknowledged defeat or was reduced to such straits that he was unable to
continue to fight. For not only under the Romans, but under the Greeks as
well this form of contest was no longer a sport; it was a deadly serious
business . . . More than one Olympic competitor lost his life in the sta-
dium.'

This critique, made in 1882 by Adolf Boetticher, one of the early
Olympic scholars, is valid today. Like their colleagues in the wrestling and
the pancration, the boxers were determined to win at all costs.[18]

The facts are not in doubt but the evaluation is. The quotation represents an almost paradigmatic example of the misunderstanding that results from the unquestioned use of one's own threshold of repugnance in
the face of specific types of physical violence as a general yardstick for all
human societies regardless of their structure and of the stage of social development they have reached, especially the stage they have reached in
the social organization and control of physical violence: this is as significant an aspect of the development of societies as the organization and
control of 'economic' means of production. One encounters here a very
striking example of the barrier to the understanding of societies produced by the dominance of heteronomous[19] evaluations over the perception of functional interdependencies. Classical Greek sculpture ranks
highly in the value scale of our time. The types of physical violence embodied in Greek game-contests such as the pancration, according to our
value scale, receive high negative marks. The fact that we associate with
the one a high positive value, with the other a high negative value, makes
it appear to those who allow their understanding to be guided by preconceived value judgements that these data cannot possibly be connected with each other. It confronts those who judge the past in terms of
this type of evaluation with an insoluble problem.

However, if one is concerned with the sociological analysis of the connections between different aspects of the same society, one has no reason
to assume that only those manifestations of that society to which, as an
outside observer, one attributes the same value, be it positive or negative,
are interdependent. One can discover in all societies factual interdependencies between aspects to which an observer on the one hand and the
people themselves who form these societies on the other attach opposite
values. The beauty of Greek art and the relative brutality of Greek game-

contests are an example. Far from being incompatible, they were closely connected manifestations of the same level of development, of the same social structure.

The emergence of Greek sculpture from its archaic mould and the idealistic realism of the sculptures of the classical period remain incomprehensible without an understanding of the part which the physical appearance of a person played as a determinant of the social esteem in which he was held among the ruling elites of the Greek city-states. In that society it was hardly possible for a man with a weak or misformed body to reach or to maintain a position of high social or political power. Physical strength, physical beauty, poise and endurance played a very much higher part as determinants of the social standing of a male person in Greek society than they do in ours. One is not always aware that the possibility for a man who is physically handicapped to rise to, or to maintain, a position of leadership or high social power and rank is a relatively recent phenomenon in the development of societies. Because 'body image' or physical appearance ranks relatively low, much lower, for example, than 'intelligence' or 'moral character', in the value-scale which, in societies such as ours, determines the ranking of men and the whole image we form of them, we often lack the key to the understanding of other societies in which physical appearance played a much greater part as a determinant of the public image of a man. In ancient Greece this was undoubtedly the case. One can perhaps convey the difference by pointing to the fact that in our society physical appearance as a determinant of the social image of an individual still plays a very high and perhaps a growing part as far as women are concerned but with regard to men, although television may have some impact on the problem, physical appearance and particularly bodily strength and beauty do not play a very great part in the public esteem of a person. The fact that one of the most powerful nations of our time elected a paralysed man to its highest office is in this respect symptomatic.

It was different in the society of the Greek city-states. From childhood on, human beings who were weak or misformed were weeded out. Weak babies were left to die. A man who was unable to fight counted for little. It was very rare for a man who was crippled, ailing or very old to gain or to maintain a position of public leadership. The term used in classical Greek society as one of the expressions of their ideal, the term *arete*, is often translated as 'virtue'. But in fact it did not refer, as the term 'virtue' does, to any moral characteristics. It referred to the attainments of a warrior and a gentleman among which his body image, his qualification as a strong and skilled warrior, played a dominant part. It was this ideal which found expression in their sculptures as well as in their game-contests. Most Olympic victors had their statues erected in Olympia and sometimes also in their home town.[20]

It is merely another facet of the same distinguishing characteristic of Greek society during the classical age that the social position of athletes was very different from that which they hold in our own society. The equivalent of sport, the 'culture' of the body, was not to the same extent a specialism as it is today. In contemporary societies a boxer is a specialist; and if we apply the term to those who gained fame as 'boxers' in antiquity, the mere use of the word is apt to conjure up in our minds a similar picture. In fact, the men who proved their physical strength, their agility, their courage and their endurance through their victories in the great festivals, of which those at Olympia were the most famous, stood a very good chance of gaining a high social and political position in their home society if they did not already hold it. For the most part the participants in the game-contests of Olympia probably came from 'good families', from the relatively wealthy elites of their home towns, from groups of landowners and perhaps from wealthier peasant families. Participation in these game-contests demanded a long and arduous training which only relatively wealthy people could afford. A promising young athlete who lacked the money for such a training might find a wealthy patron; or a professional trainer might advance him the money. But if he gained a victory at Olympia, he brought fame to his family and his home town and had a strong chance of being counted from then on as a member of its ruling elite. Probably the most famous wrestler of classical antiquity was Milon of Croton. He gained a considerable number of victories at Olympia and other panhellenic festivals. He was a man of prodigious strength which in time became proverbial. He is also mentioned as one of the best pupils of Pythagoras and as commander of the army of his home town in its victorious battle against the Sybarites which ended in the furious mass-killing of the latter after their defeat. We find the same picture in reverse if we notice that men who today are remembered above all for their intellectual achievements, were often remembered in their own time also in connection with their attainments as warriors or athletes. Aeschylus, Socrates and Demosthenes went through the hard school of hoplite fighting. Plato had victories in some of the athletic festivals to his credit. Thus, the idealization of the warrior in Greek sculpture, the representation even of the gods in accordance with the ideal physical appearance of the aristocratic warrior, and the warrior ethos of the game contests were, indeed, not only compatible; they were closely connected manifestations of the same social group. Both are characteristic of the social position, the manner of life and the ideals of these groups. But the understanding of this factual interdependence does not impair the enjoyment of Greek art. If anything, it enhances it.[21]

# 7

A comparison of the level of violence represented by the game-contests of classical Greece, or for that matter by the tournaments and folk-games of the Middle Ages, with those represented by contemporary sport-contests shows a specific strand in a civilizing process, but the study of this strand, of the civilizing of game-contests, remains inadequate and incomplete if one does not link it to that of other aspects of the societies whose manifestations game-contests are. In short, the fluctuating level of civilization in game-contests must remain incomprehensible if one does not connect it at least with the general level of socially permitted violence, of the organization of violence-control, and with the corresponding conscience formation in given societies.

A few examples may help to bring this wider context into focus. In the twentieth century, the mass slaughter of conquered groups by the German Nazis has aroused almost world-wide revulsion. The memory of it for some time tarnished the good name of Germany among the nations of the world. The shock was all the greater because many people had lived under the illusion that, in the twentieth century, such barbarities could no longer happen. They had tacitly assumed that people had become more 'civilized', that they had become 'morally better' as part of their nature. They had taken pride in being less savage than their forefathers or than other peoples that they knew without ever facing up to the problem which their own relatively more civilized behaviour posed—to the problem of why they themselves, why their behaviour and their feelings had become a little more civilized. The Nazi episode served as a kind of warning; it was a reminder that the restraints against violence are not symptoms of the superiority of the *nature* of 'civilized nations', not eternal characteristics of their racial or ethnic make-up, but aspects of a specific type of social development which had resulted in more differentiated and stable social control of the means of violence and in a corresponding conscience-formation. Evidently, this type of social development could be reversed.

This does not necessarily imply that there are no grounds for evaluating the results of this development in human behaviour and feelings as 'better' than the corresponding manifestations of earlier developmental stages. Wider understanding of the nexus of facts provides a much better, indeed provides the only secure basis for value judgements of this type. Without it, we cannot know, for example, whether our manner of building up individual self-controls against physical violence is not associated with psychological malformations which, themselves, might appear highly barbaric to a more civilized age. Moreover, if one evaluates a more civilized form of conduct and a feeling as 'better' than less civilized forms, if one considers that mankind has made progress by arriving at one's own standards of revulsion and repugnance against forms of violence which were common in former days, one is confronted by the problem of why an unplanned development has resulted in something which one evaluates as progress.

All judgements about standards of civilized behaviour are comparative judgements. One cannot say in any absolute sense: we are 'civilized', they are 'uncivilized'. But one can say with great confidence: 'the standards of conduct and feeling of society A are more, those of society B, less civilized', provided one has worked out a clear and precise developmental gauge. The comparison between the Greek agon-contests and contemporary sport-contests provides one example. Standards of public revulsion in the face of mass murder provide another. As it showed itself in recent times, the almost universal feeling of repugnance against genocide indicates that human societies have undergone a civilizing process, however limited in scope and however unstable its results. Comparison with past attitudes show this very clearly. In Greek and Roman antiquity, the massacre of the whole male population of a defeated and conquered city and the sale into slavery of its women and children, though they might have aroused pity, did not rouse widespread condemnation. Our sources are incomplete but even they show that cases of mass slaughter recurred with fair regularity throughout the whole period.[22] Sometimes the battle fury of a long-threatened or frustrated army played its part in the wholesale massacre of enemies. The destruction of all the Sybarites they could lay their hands on by the citizens of Croton under the leadership of Milon, the famous wrestler, is a case in point. Sometimes 'genocide' was a calculated act aimed at destroying the military power of a rival states, as in the case of Argos, whose military power as a potential rival of Sparta was more or less annihilated by the wholesale destruction of all men who could bear arms on the orders of the Spartan general, Cleomenes. The massacre of the male population of Melos at the order of the Athenian Assembly of Citizens in 416 BC, vividly described by Thucydides, resulted from a figuration very similar to that which led to the Russian occupation of Czechoslovakia in 1968. The Athenians regarded Melos as part of their empire. It had a specific strategic significance for them in their struggle with Sparta. But the inhabitants of Melos did not wish to become part of the Athenian empire. Therefore the Athenians killed the men, sold the women and children into slavery, and settled the island with Athenian colonists. Some Greeks regarded war as the normal relationship between city-states. It could be interrupted by treaties of limited period. Gods, through the mouths of their priests, and writers might disapprove of massacres of this kind. But the level of 'moral' repugnance against what we now call 'genocide' and, more generally, the level of internalized inhibitions against physical violence were decidedly lower, the feelings of guilt or shame associated with such inhibitions decidedly weaker, than they are in the relatively developed nation-states of the twentieth century. Perhaps they were entirely lacking.

There was no lack of compassion with the victims. The great Athenian dramatists, above all Euripides in his *Trojan Women*, expressed this feeling with a vividness which was all the stronger because it was not yet overlaid by moral repugnance and indignation. Yet one can hardly doubt that the sale into slavery of the women of the defeated, the separation of mother and child, the killing of male children, and many other themes of violence and warfare in their tragedies possessed very much greater actuality for an Athenian public in the context of their lives than they possess for a contemporary public in the context of ours.

Altogether, the level of physical insecurity in the societies of antiquity was very much higher than it is in contemporary nation-states. That their poets showed more compassion than moral indignation is not uncharacteristic of this difference. Homer, already, disapproved of the fact that Achilles, in his grief and fury at the death of Patroclus, had not only sheep, cattle and horses but also 12 young Trojan nobles killed and burned on the funeral pyre of his friend as a sacrifice to his ghost. But, again, the poet did not sit in judgement and condemn his hero from the high throne of his own moral righteousness and superiority because he had committed the barbarous atrocity of human sacrifice. The poet's criticism of Achilles did not have the emotional colour of moral indignation. It did not cast doubt on what we call the 'character' of his hero, on his value as a human being. People do 'bad things' (*kaka erga*) in their grief and fury. The bard shakes his head but he does not appeal to the conscience of his listeners; he does not ask them to regard Achilles as a moral reprobate, a 'bad character'. He appeals to their compassion, to their understanding of the passion which seizes even the best, even the heroes, in times of stress and makes them do 'bad things'. But his human value as a nobleman and a warrior is not in doubt. Human sacrifice did not have for the ancient Greeks quite the same odour as something horrible that it has for the more 'civilized' nations of the twentieth century.[23] Every schoolboy of the Greek educated classes knew of the wrath of Achilles, of the sacrifices and the game-contests at the funeral of Patroclus. The Olympic game-contests stood in a direct line of succession from these ancestral funeral contests. It was a very different line of descent from that of contemporary sport-contests.

8

Nor, as far as one can see, was the normal level of passion and violence of the Homeric heroes and gods or, expressed differently, their normal developmental level of built-in self-control, of 'conscience', more than a few steps behind that reached in Athens during the classical period. The surviving stones, the temples and the sculptures of Greek gods and heroes have all contributed to the image of the ancient Greeks as a peculiarly even-tempered, balanced and harmonious people. The term 'classical' itself, in phrases such as 'classical antiquity', conjures up the picture of Greek society as a model of balanced beauty and equipoise which later generations can never again hope to emulate. This is a misconception.

One cannot set out here with the precision it deserves the place of classical Greece in the development of 'conscience', of internalized controls with regard either to violence or to other spheres of life. It must be enough to say that even classical Greece still represents the 'dawn of conscience', a stage where the transformation of a self-controlling conscience represented by communal images of external superhuman persons, of commanding or threatening demon-gods who told human beings more or less arbitrarily what to do and what not to do, into a relatively impersonal and individualized inner voice speaking in accordance with general social principles of justice and injustice, right and wrong, was still rather the exception than the norm. Socrates' *daimonion* was perhaps the closest approximation to our type of conscience-formation in classical Greek society but even this highly individualized 'inner voice' still had in some measure the character of a tutelary genius. Moreover, the degree of internalization and individualization of norms and social controls which we encounter in Plato's representation of Socrates was, in his time, without doubt a very exceptional phenomenon. It is highly significant that the classical Greek language lacked a differentiated and specialized word for 'conscience'. There are a number of words such as *synesis, euthymion, eusebia* and others which are occasionally translated as 'conscience', but, on closer inspection, one soon becomes aware that each of them is less specific and covers a much broader spectrum, such as 'having scruples', 'piety', and 'reverence towards god'. But a single concept as highly specialized as the modern concept of 'conscience', denoting a highly authoritative, inescapable and often tyrannical inner agency which, as part of his or her self, guides an individual's conduct, which demands obedience and punishes disobedience with 'pangs' or 'bites' of guilt-feelings, and which, unlike 'fear of the gods' or 'shame', acts on its own, seemingly coming from nowhere, seemingly without deriving power and authority from any external agency, human or superhuman—this concept of conscience is absent from the intellectual equipment of ancient Greece. The fact that this concept of 'conscience' had not yet developed in Greek society can be regarded as a very reliable index of the fact that conscience-formation in that society had not yet reached a stage of internalization, individualization and relative autonomy in any degree comparable to our own.

If one wants to understand the higher level of violence embodied in Greek game-contests and the lower level of revulsion against violence in Greek society generally, this is one of the clues that one needs. It is symptomatic of the fact that, within the social framework of a Greek city-state, individuals were still to a much higher extent dependent on others, on external agencies and sanctions as means of curbing their passions, that they could rely less on internalized barriers, on themselves alone, for controlling violent impulses, than people in contemporary industrial societies. One must add that they, or at least their elites, were already capable to a much higher extent of restraining themselves individually than their forefathers in the pre-classical age had been. The changing images of Greek gods, the critique of their arbitrariness and ferocity, bear witness to this change. If one bears in mind the specific stage in a civilizing process represented by Greek society in the days of self-ruling city-states, it is easier to understand that—compared with ours—the very high passionateness of the ancient Greeks in action was perfectly compatible with the bodily balance and equipoise, the aristocratic grace and pride in movement reflected in Greek sculpture.

As a last step, it may be useful to point briefly to one other link in the chain of interdependencies which connect the level of violence embodied in the Greek type of game-contests and of warfare with other structural characteristics of Greek society. It is quite significant for the stage which state organization had reached in the period of the Greek city-states that the protection of the life of a citizen against attacks by another was not yet treated in the same way as it is treated today, as a monopoly concern of the state. Even in Athens it was not yet treated in this manner. If a person was killed or maimed by a fellow citizen, it was, even in classical times, still a matter for his or her kinsmen to avenge and settle the account. By comparison with our own time, the kin-group still played a much larger part in protecting an individual against violence. This meant, at the same time, that every able-bodied male person had to be prepared for the defence of his kinsmen or, if it came to that, for an attack in order to help or to avenge his kinsmen. Even within a city-state, the general level of physical violence and insecurity was comparatively high. This, too, helps to account for the fact that the level of revulsion against inflicting pain and injuries on others, or of seeing it done, was lower and that feelings of guilt about acts of violence were less deeply bred into the individual. In a society so organized they would have been a severe handicap.

A few sayings of a great Greek philosopher, Democritus, may perhaps help to give a little more depth to the understanding of these differences. They are symptomatic of the common social experience of people in that situation. They show that—and they indicate why—'right' and 'wrong' cannot mean quite the same thing in a society such as ours as in a society where every individual may have to stand up for himself and for his kinsman in defence of their lives. It is right, said Democritus, according to the rules of custom to kill any living thing which has done an injury; not to kill it is wrong. The philosopher expressed these views wholly in human and social terms. There is no appeal to the gods; nor to righteousness and holiness as can be found later in Socrates' dialogue with Protagoras—if one can trust Plato. Nor, as one can see, is there any appeal for protection to law courts, to state institutions, to governments. People were, then, far more on their own with regard to sheer physical survival than we are. This is what Democritus said:

### 68 (B257)

As to animals in given cases
of killing and not killing the rule is as follows:
if an animal does wrong
or desires to do wrong
and if a man kill it
he shall be counted exempt from penalties.
To perform this promotes well-being
rather than the reverse.

### 3 (B258)

If a thing does injury contrary to right
it is needful to kill it.
This covers all cases.
If a man do so
he shall increase the portion in which he partakes of right
and security
in any [social] order.

### 5 (B256)

Right is to perform what is needful
and wrong is to fail to perform what is needful
and to decline to do so.

### 6 (B261)

If men have wrong done to them
there is need to avenge them so far as is feasible.
This should not be passed over.
This kind of thing is right and also good
and the other kind of thing is wrong and also bad.[24]

## Notes

1. This essay was previously published in Eric Dunning (ed.), *The Sociology of Sport: a Selection of Readings,* London, 1971. The theoretical framework embodied in it is closely connected with and, in fact, represents an enlargement upon, the theory of civilizing processes set out in Norbert Elias, *The Civilizing Process,* Oxford, [1994]. . . .

2. It is not possible here to enquire in greater detail into the problem why, in contrast to the almost world-wide diffusion and adoption of the 'soccer' type of English football, the diffusion and adoption of the 'rugger' type was far more limited in scope. But it may be worth mentioning that the exploration of problems such as this can provide a good deal of evidence and can serve as a test case for specific aspects of a sociological theory of sport.

3. Author's translation from Agnes Bain Stiven, *Englands Einfluß auf den deutschen Wortschatz,* Marburg, 1936, p. 72.

4. Prince Puechlser-Muskau, *Briefe eines Verstorbenen,* 9 October 1810.

5. J. G. Kohl, quoted in F. Kluge, *Ethymologisches Wörterbuch,* 17th ed., 1957, article on sport.

6. *Larousse du XIXième Siècle.*

7. Norbert Elias, *The Civilizing Process,* Oxford, [1994]. . . .

8. For a discussion of modern professional wrestling as a type of farce, see 'American Sports: Play and Dis-Play' and 'Wrestling: the Great American Passion Play' by Gregory P. Stone, in Eric Dunning (ed.), *The Sociology of Sport: a Selection of Readings,* London, 1971.

9. H. Foerster, *Die Sieger in den Olympischen Spielen,* Zwickau, 1891.

10. Franz Mezoe, *Geschichte der Olympischen Spiele,* Munich, 1930, pp. 100–1; quoted in Ludwig Dress, *Olympia: Gods, Artists and Athletes,* London, 1968, p. 83.

11. Philostratos, *On Gymnastics* (Peri Gymnastike), first half of the third century AD, ch. 11.

12. Philostratos mentions that thongs made from pig's hide were forbidden because it was believed that the injuries inflicted by them were too severe. Also that one should not punch with the thumb. It is perhaps worth mentioning these details. One should not think that the customary rules of game-contests in antiquity showed no regard at all for the participants. But rules such as these were simply handed on by oral tradition and thus still left a very wide scope for serious injuries.

13. See Norbert Elias, 'Studies in the Genesis of the Naval Profession', *British Journal of Sociology,* vol. 1, no. 4, December 1950.

14. Philostratos, *On Gymnastics,* ch. 11.

15. Ibid., ch. 43.

16. Dress, *Olympia*, p. 82.

17. Ibid.

18. Ibid., p. 81.

19. For an explanation of this term and for a discussion of problems of 'objectivity' in sociology, see Norbert Elias, 'Problems of Involvement and Detachment', pp. 217–48 below. See also Norbert Elias, *Involvement and Detachment*, Oxford, [1987].

20. One does not need to discuss here the reasons for the wave of secularization which shows itself, among other things, in the transition from the more solemn, more awe-inspiring and perhaps more expressive representations of gods and heroes in the archaic period—an example is the Medusa from the pediment of the temple of Artemis at Corcyra, sixth century BC—to the idealizing realism of the classical period where gods and heroes are represented as well-proportioned warriors, young or old, whose bodies speak, though their faces are perhaps a little empty even if, as in the case of the Delphi charioteer, the in-laid eyes and part of the colour have been preserved.

21. The extent to which the characteristics of an earlier stage in the development of state organization, especially in the monopolization and control of physical violence, affects all human relationships, shows itself, among other things, in the frequency with which Greek legends refer to conflicts between father and son. So far as Greek society is concerned, Freud was probably misled in his interpretation of the Oedipus legend or, at least, he saw only one side of the picture, that of a single individual, the son. In the context of Greek society, one cannot help but notice the specific social figuration reflected in this, as in other, related Greek legends. One cannot help questioning the relationship between the son and the father, the young king and the old king, from the father's side as well as from the son's side. From the son's side it may well be, as Freud said, tinged with jealousy over the father's possession of the wife—and, one may add, with fear of the father's physical strength and power. Seen, however, from the father's side, as reflected in Greek legends, the old king's fear and jealousy of the son plays an equal part in the relationship between the two. For, inevitably, the father will grow older and physically weaker, the son, weak as a little child, will grow physically stronger and more vigorous. In ancient times, when the well-being of a whole community, of a clan or a house, was not only factually but—in the imagination of the members of such groups—magically bound up with the health and vigour of the king or the leader, the older man was often ritually killed when he grew older, when his strength and vigour departed, and replaced by one of his sons, the young king. Numerous Greek legends show that the young son, the future heir, had to be hidden from the wrath and persecution of his father while he was still young and that he usually had to be educated by strangers. Thus, 'we know', according to a recent study (Edna H. Hooker, *The Goddess of the Golden Image, in Parthenos and Parthenon, Greece and Rome*, supplement to vol. X, Oxford, 1963, p. 18), 'that royal children in primitive agrarian communities were in constant danger as a potential threat to the king's tenure of his throne or sometimes to a stepmother's ambition for her own sons. Few princes in Greek myth and legend were brought up at home. Some were sent to the Centaur, Cheiron; but most were exposed with tokens of their origin to be reared by strangers.'

King Laius exposed his son Oedipus, fearing that he would be killed by him. Zeus was reared by nurses and brought up in secrecy because his father Kronos felt that he was a menace and tried to kill him. Zeus himself, like Jahwe, was afraid that man would learn to participate in his magical knowledge and violently punished the younger man, Prometheus, who had dared to steal fire from heaven and to give it to people.

It may well be that the escalation of mutual rivalry and jealousy as one ingredient in the complex relationship between father and son, the peculiar process whose reflections we find in Greek and in many other legends, no longer play the part in a society where even male relatives no longer endanger one another's lives, where the state has monopolized the right to use physical violence, that it once played in societies where fathers could kill or expose their children. It would require more figurational investigations of fathers and sons in order to find out to what extent the son's feeling of rivalry and jealousy of the father, as discovered in his patients by Freud, is at the same time a reaction to the father's feeling of rivalry and jealousy of the son. But if one considers Greek legends, above all the Oedipus legend itself, one can hardly doubt the double-sidedness, the reciprocal feelings of rivalry which play a part in the relationship between father and son. The use made of this legend as a theoretical model seems incomplete as long as the part played by the dynamics of this figuration, by the reciprocity of feelings between a son who, from being weak got stronger, and a father who, from being strong gets weaker, is more fully investigated. In societies where physical strength and power played a much larger part than they do today in the relationships within as well as outside a family, this figuration must have had very great and by no means only unconscious significance. Seen in this context, the Oedipus legend reads like a legend designed to threaten sons that they will be punished by the gods if they kill their fathers. However, the salient point about the legend is probably not, in the first place, the killing of the old king by or in favour of the young king but the breaking of the incest taboo, of the prohibition of the son's intercourse with his mother which, of course, is a much older social prohibition than that against killing the father. In this respect, the Oedipus myth evidently symbolizes a relatively late stage in the development of a society in which, at an earlier stage, neither the killing of the young son nor the killing of the old father was a crime. These legends, thus, can help us to understand a type of human relationship which existed at a stage of social development when the organization which we how call the 'state' was still in its infancy, and when the physical strength of a person, his capacity to ensure his survival through his own fighting power, was a major determinant of all types of human relationships, including that between father and son.

22. Pierre Ducrey, *Le Traitement de Prisonniers de Guerre dans la Grèce antique,* Ecole Française d' Athènes, Travaux et Memoires, Fas. XVIII, Paris, 1968, pp. 196 ff.

23. Fr. Schwenn, *Die Menschenopfer bei den Griechen und Romern,* Giessen, 1915.

24. I am quoting these fragments in the translation which Eric A. Havelock has published in his book, *The Liberal Temper in Greek Politics,* New Haven and London, 1964, pp. 127–8. I think his attempt at conveying to a contemporary English-speaking reader the meaning of these fragments, as far as that is possible, succeeds rather well. He also shows, more clearly perhaps than many other writers, that the stress which Plato and Aristotle laid on the central authority of the state as the primary issue of political problems is often wrongly regarded as characteristic of the ancient Greeks in general, whereas in fact this stress is, at most, characteristic of a late and perhaps only the last phase in the development of the independent Greek city-states. I cannot quite agree, however, with Professor Havelock's interpretation of the teachings of philosophers such as Democritus as 'liberal'. Liberalism as a political philosophy presupposes a very highly developed state organization even though it is aimed at preventing too great an interference of the representatives of the state into the affairs of its individual members. The self-reliance of the individual which Democritus advocates, on the other hand, is characteristic of a stage of development in which an individual and his kin-group cannot yet count on the protection of a reasonably effective and impersonal state organization. It is not really a 'liberal' idea that men have a right and a duty to avenge themselves and to kill their own enemies.

# 11

## The Changing Balance of Power between the Sexes in Ancient Rome

### 1

Does it seem a bit incongruous that I propose to talk about the changing balance of power between men and women? No doubt it is more usual to apply the term balance of power to the relationship of states. They, powerful states, often confront one another armed to the teeth. If one of them increases its lethal equipment, the balance of power changes in its favour. A rival power may feel threatened and, in turn, increase its own armament, thus restoring the balance of power. But men and women, locked in wedlock or free, rarely confront each other armed to the teeth. Does it make sense to speak in their case too of a changing balance of power? I think it does. A few examples may illustrate why.

From time to time I used to encounter in the streets of London an elderly Indian gentleman. His wife, dressed according to Indian fashion in a saree, walked demurely two or three steps behind him. They seemed to converse with each other avidly. But they did not look at each other. He spoke to her in a low voice without turning his head, as if addressing the empty air before him, while she conveyed her response to him without lifting her eyes but sometimes with obvious energy.

This, as I saw it, was a living example of an uneven balance between the sexes and, possibly, also for what has been termed 'harmonious inequality' (see van Stolk and Wouters, 1985: Ch. 5). It shows in particular that we are confronted here with a kind of inequality that has been codified by the society in question in such a way that it became not only custom but also habit, part of the social habitus of individuals. The restraint exerted by social custom has largely turned into second nature and, thus, into self-restraint. A man and a woman brought up according to this tradition could not easily break with it without losing self-respect

From *Theory, Culture and Society* 4, nos. 2–3 (1987): 287–316 as well as the respect of their own group—even though in the busy streets of London the custom looked a little odd.

Seeing it I could not help remembering other perhaps even more telling examples of an uneven balance of power between the sexes represented by an inescapable social code. There was the terrifying custom which required a Brahman widow to be burnt alive on a funeral pyre together with her dead husband. In this case custom enshrined a balance of power between the sexes which was so uneven that a wife had to follow her husband into death as if she were his possession.[1] As a woman she was not regarded as a person in her own right, was not allowed to have a life of her own. Again, Chinese custom demanded that women should bandage their feet so tightly that they became crippled. As a result, women could no longer walk properly and lost much of their freedom of movement. In all these cases wives in any particular family might have had greater strength of character than their husbands and thus individually have gained a commanding position in the ordering of family-affairs. In society at large, however, men as a social group commanded much greater resources of power than women. Hence the ruling social code relegated women unequivocally to a subordinate and inferior position compared to men.

## 2

It is striking that the traditional code of conduct of the European upper and middle classes, in that respect, was rather ambiguous. For a long time, in fact at least till the nineteenth century, married women in most European countries had no right to own property. As a rule the law cast a more lenient eye on male than on female adultery. Sex-relations of unmarried males up to a point were usually condoned, of unmarried females severely condemned and stigmatized. Yet, while in these and other respects the traditional European code of conduct reflected an uneven balance of power in favour of men, in other respects the picture was different.

Stringent rules demonstrating in public that women were men's property or at least socially inferior to men, such as those represented by the examples I have given, were absent from the European code of good behaviour. Surprisingly, it demanded instead that men should publicly treat women in a way usually accorded to socially superior and more powerful persons. According to this code self-respecting men were supposed to stand back at a door and to allow women to pass through it before them. Men were not supposed to sit down at table before ladies were seated. Greeting rituals differed in some respects from country to country, but they were usually tilted in favour of the ladies. In some cases it was in their power to greet or not to greet a male acquaintance in the street; in other a full lifting of the hat and a deep salutation was required of a gentleman if he passed a lady of his acquaintance in the street. And there was the most obvious sign of social subordination, once to be found in a ceremonial encounter between a sovereign and his subject, the kissing of the hand. In some European societies, kissing a lady's hand formed an integral part of the greeting ceremony which a gentleman had to perform on visiting or leaving a lady's house and even when meeting her in the street. In a somewhat abbreviated form it can still be found to this day in well-bred circles of some Central European countries. There are other examples. I can disregard them here.

As one may see, this code of conduct required that women in public should be treated by men as persons of a higher social standing. The contrast to the andrarchic[2] codes mentioned before which require public demonstration of women's social inferiority could not be greater. Even at a brief glance the problem one encounters here is quite obvious. The European code of good behaviour embodied some marked gynarchic features, despite its overall andrarchic condition. A code once so widely observed as this one was in European and colonized societies in other continents is never merely a product of accident or whim. It always represents, as it were, a crystallization of the development and consequently of the changing power-structures of the countries where it is—or was— in use. The walking ritual of the Indian couple, the burning of Brahman widows, reflected such an uneven balance of power between the sexes that women were constantly compelled to demonstrate their inferior position through their conduct. The European code of which I have just given a few examples was in that respect more equivocal. So far, it presents an open and, in a way, surprising problem. I can here only introduce this problem which may sharpen our perception of the wide variety of power relationships in this and in other areas. I also do not want to deprive people who love unsolved puzzles of the joy of discovery.

The concept of a balance of power permits, as one may see, the conceptualization of shades and grades in the power differentials of human groups. Tradition has confined us too long to simple static polarities, such as rulers and ruled, where one obviously needs the imagery of a gliding approach, the ability to say 'more' or 'less'. Both the Indian and the European codes of conduct of which I have spoken represent a balance of power between the sexes tilted in favour of men. But the power differentials between the sexes in a case where public opinion could compel widows to be burned alive were evidently far greater than they were in the case of nineteenth-century women such as Ibsen's Nora or Galsworthy's

Irene who, although male dominated, had already a chance of resistance. And the odd gynarchic clues in the intrinsically andrarchic European code, too, show the need for a differentiated vocabulary.


3

The European tradition, as a continuous development, goes back to Near-Eastern and Greco-Roman Antiquity. One can trace it from there via the Middle Ages to modern times. However, continuous as it was, the process of change did not have the character of a simple unilinear development. With regard to the balance of power between the sexes the change did not lead from utter subjection of women in the early days to a gradual lessening of the inequality. Instead one discovers within the millennial development several spurts towards a lessening of the social inequalities between women and men—mostly within single social strata and, maybe, with simultaneous or subsequent counter-spurts.

One of these spurts, that which occurred in the time of the Roman Republic and the early Empire, led from extreme social subjection of women to men before and within married life to a condition of virtual equality between the sexes within married life. This rather surprising development, the first of its kind within a state society as far as I know, influenced marriage customs throughout the Roman Empire. Moreover, it was not without influence upon the marriage conception of the early Christian Church even though many of its representatives favoured the restoration or preservation of the older sex-inequality. It is still open to investigation whether and how far this first great spurt towards a more even balance of power between the sexes in their married life had a direct influence on the later European development. But the Roman development also demands attention for its own sake. The question of the conditions responsible for spurts in the direction of greater equality between men and women is of relevance far beyond the period of this early example, even though at the moment only the outlines of a solution come into view.


4

If one tries to understand the relationship between men and women in early Roman times, one has to lay aside many of the familiar concepts used in one's own time. We still use the term family derived from the Latin *familia* but the unmistakable kinship of the words can easily conceal the very wide differences of their meaning. The same goes for matrimony and many other contemporary words with a Latin ancestry.

The legal documents of the Roman state preserve for us, with regard to marriage or sex-relations and to many other aspects of social life, customs and norms characteristic of the pre-state or tribal phase in the development of the human group now known as Romans. A structural characteristic of the Roman state, of which more shall be said later, accounts for this survival of pre-state conditions in the laws and customs of a state society. In the case of marriage customs the continued existence of pre-state conditions in the Roman Republic finds confirmation in the similarity of these Roman customs to those of other Indo-Germanic tribal groups that much later, often almost a thousand years later, made their entrance into the written documents of European history. Thus the early Roman custom of a marriage by purchase, in Latin *coemptio*, has its counterpart in the Germanic marriage by means of a *kaup*.[3] Moreover the famous story about the Romans abducting by force women from the neighbouring Sabines can serve as a useful reminder that in these earlier stages women were often difficult to come by if those of one's own clan were taboo or perhaps if female infants were more neglected than male ones. Hence, young men took their wives from outside. They took them by force—that is, if they possibly could—and gave something in exchange—or, in other words bought them—if they had to. To interpret Roman law without regard for sociological consistency can be misleading. Acquiring a wife by purchase appeared in Roman law as one of the standard forms of marriage just as it appeared again many centuries later in the Latin transcription of previously unrecorded customs when migrating Germanic tribes settled down in an early form of statehood.[4]

In Roman society unmarried women, from early days onwards, were passive objects of a violent act or of a transaction between males of different kin-groups. But in time there occurred a significant change, perhaps after a period of transition. The rough warrior nobles of the earlier Roman period were transformed, thanks to the booty of successful wars and the exploitation of subjugated peoples, into a small, immensely wealthy aristocratic oligarchy that ruled a vast and still expanding empire. In this way they reached, over the generations, a higher level of civilization. Marriages of daughters, and frequently also of sons, from grand families now became largely a matter of dynastic politics, of the rivalry for power and status among the members of senatorial families. In earlier times, the husband paid the family or tribe unit for a marriageable daughter, possibly because such daughters were then relatively scarce. Later on, it was the grand families of the senatorial oligarchy who paid desired suitors of their daughters, who by then had possibly become less scarce, in the form of a dowry. In Roman law, regulations deriving from different stages of development, such as marriage on the basis of payment or dowry, are often to be found side-by-side. But it is unlikely that the social institutions and customs themselves, to which these regulations relate, continued to exist together.

5

One can recognize more clearly the developmental line of the relationship between the sexes in the Roman Republic if one reconstitutes for one's understanding the sequential order of events starting from the earlier phases. It is these which are perhaps most alien to people living in one of the internally pacified nation-states of our days.

On the way from tribe to state, superior physical force, especially in the case of men, was one of the main requirements for the survival of a group or an individual, even in everyday life. The social inferiority of women in early Rome, and also quite certainly a long time prior to the legendary foundation of the city, was therefore intimately connected to their relative physical weakness. Some women may have been stronger than some men, but as a social group women were inferior to men in terms of physical strength and the associated awareness of their own strength. They were in need of protection in times of pregnancy and birth and, in addition, particularly disadvantaged once relatively heavy iron weapons came into use.

In fact, one cannot understand the extreme power inferiority of women indicated by male customs such as buying—with goods or money—a wife from her male relatives if one does not take into account that this was characteristic of a phase in the development of human societies when war and other forms of violence between human groups, in comparison with today, were much more ubiquitous, when the survival of a group depended to a great extent on the strength or fighting skill of its members and especially of the males. These capacities were consequently decisive for the status and rank of people. In a society of this type, a warrior society, women, not considered fit for fighting, were also not considered as self-ruling human beings. Whether a man took a woman from her male relatives by force, whether he bought her for a price, it meant in effect that a wife was her husband's property. As with his other possessions, he could do with her as he liked.[5]

Perhaps one can understand better why *familia* in the Roman tradition did not mean what family means to us, the unit of husband, wife and children with relative moderate inequality or a virtual equality between the sexes. Traditionally the Roman term *familia* referred to the whole household and to all possessions of a ruling male including his wife, his children, his cattle and his slaves. The difficulty one sometimes has today in understanding the Roman concept of *familia* is closely connected with the failure to see the connection between the present structure of a family and the present structural characteristics of the organization we call the state. In the more developed societies of the twentieth century, many of the functions formerly performed by the head of a large kinship-group or by that of a large household, including the functions of internal pacification, of judging internal conflicts and above all of leading defensive or offensive fights for survival with other groups, are now firmly vested in the government of the state. In the early days of the Roman Republic the state level of integration had relatively little autonomy and few power resources of its own in relation to the patrician elders, the heads of households, the *patres familias*. The senate was an assembly of these ruling clan fathers. To whom could a wife turn if she was beaten by her husband or if he neglected her for the sake of a concubine? It was conceivable that the men of her own family-group might intervene on her behalf, but that depended very much on the effective power resources of her own group, military as well as economic, in relation to those of her husband's kin-group. In the early phases of the Republic no central authority existed that was strong enough to impose its will or its law on powerful heads of patrician families.

Thus it was not the relative physical weakness of women as such which accounted for the great power differentials between men and women and, following from that, the great social inferiority of the latter, but the structure of a society where of all the human faculties, muscle and fighting power had a social function of the highest order.

Besides fighting potential it was only the possession of magical powers that formed a similarly important source of social power—the priestly function hence stood alongside the warrior function. The Romans, however, were the heirs of a tribal tradition in which the rivalry between priests and warriors had largely been decided in favour of the warriors. Every family group had its own family gods. In relation to them it was the leading warrior, the ruler of the clan, in short the *pater familias,* who also exercised the functions of a priest. The Romans had also, of course, from an early stage, communal gods and goddesses. One of these goddesses had its own priestesses. These, the Vestals, occupied an extraordinary position among the women of Rome, in particular in earlier times, on account of their magical powers and their relationship to the spirit world. The price for this was the renunciation of marriage, and any contact with men in general.

# 6

The other women of the Roman upper classes, at least up to the end of the second Punic war, led a very confined life. Until the Roman state acquired an effective monopoly of physical force or had officials who were willing and able to enforce the law and decisions of the courts—if necessary against the opposition of the most powerful families—women depended wholly on the protection offered by their male relatives. These men therefore ruled the women of Rome, at least until the defeat of Carthage—and longer still in Roman law. The Roman Republic was, and remained until its late stages, a warrior state. The women of Rome, who were excluded from military and civil service, held the characteristic position of an outsider group in relation to the state. For a long time they were perceived by men as half-persons, as lesser-kinds of human beings.

Nothing is more significant in that respect than the fact that Romans were not in the habit of giving their women, as they did in the case of men, a personal name. All they had to distinguish them from each other was a female form of the name of their father's kin-group, of his *gens* or clan. If a father belonged to the house of the Claudians, all his daughters were called Claudia. The only way to distinguish them was by adding 'the elder' or 'the younger', 'the first' or 'the second'. Men did not see women as individuals in the same sense as they perceived themselves as such and thus required for women no personal name.

For a long time Roman women were in fact as they were in law always under the privilege, one could even say in the possession, of a man. Prior to the late second and perhaps even to the first century BC they had no independent existence. They were under the tutelage of their father, their brother or other male members of their own family.

There were two well-known forms of marriage in the Roman upper class: one in which the control of a woman was handed over to her husband, marriage *cum conventione in manum mariti,* the other without transfer of the tutelage over a woman from her own family to her husband. The difference in course of time assumed great importance, for the second of these two forms of marriage, that in which control over a woman remained with her own family and was not given into the hands of her husband, became eventually, and particularly after the final defeat and destruction of Carthage, the lever by means of which married women were able to free themselves in fact and then also in law from the control of any man and to act as individuals in their own right. But that rather surprising process of emancipation was a gradual process; in all likelihood a condition of equality in marriage was fully established and widely accepted only in the late second and perhaps not before the turn of the first century BC.

In order to see this emancipatory development in better perspective, it may be useful to sum up the major disabilities from which women suffered during the earlier stages of the Republic. Women could not own property. As they themselves were initially a kind of property of the men of their family or of their husband, this is quite understandable. A woman could not divorce on her own initiative, but her husband could divorce her. Women were apparently forbidden to drink wine. Next to adultery, the drinking of wine was often mentioned as a reason why a husband divorced his wife.

## 7

Perhaps it is necessary to add that a Roman marriage did not require legitimation or registration through a religious or a state authority.[6] The Roman Republic did not have the institutional means for bringing people's sexual life and thus also marriage under state control. No offices existed where a marriage or, when it came, a divorce could be registered. As Roman state authorities gradually achieved greater autonomy in relation to the powerful family units, they repeatedly tried to gain some control over the married life of the upper classes. The sex life of the people remained, as far as one can see, solely a matter for the people, outside official concern. Marriage in Republican Rome was still largely an institution at the pre-state level, an affair of clans, of family units or as we express it, a private institution. It originated, as I have already mentioned, from the transaction between the men of a woman's family group and the prospective husband or perhaps his family group.

The same goes for divorce. The legitimizing agency of marriage or divorce was a circle of relatives, of friends, sometimes of neighbours, of representatives of the local community. A little regarded Roman institution, characteristic of the pre-state, confirms this. If a husband wanted to divorce his wife he could call together a *iudicium domesticum*, a meeting of relatives and friends which presumably acted as a more or less informal legitimizing agency of the divorce, but which probably could also discuss the whole matter and mediate between husband and wife. Even when the Roman state developed some institutions of its own, such as that of the censors, who could deal with matrimonial affairs, these officers continued to rely on this older pre-state institution. Thus the censors in 307 BC removed a member of the Senate because he had divorced his wife without calling together a *consilium amicorum* (Val. Max., II: 9, 2). Again Augustus, anxious to curb the easy and informal form of divorce which had become customary in the late Republic and which gave wives the same right as their husbands to end their marriage at will, published a law according to which a divorce could only be recognized as valid if it was formally declared in the presence of seven witnesses. In a way that was a revival of the old 'council of friends'. But the emperor's decree apparently had little effect on the prevailing practice. At that stage the organizational techniques and perhaps even the financial resources available to the state authorities were not yet adequately developed for the bureaucratic tentacles to extend to the marital sphere.

Thus the change in the balance of power between husbands and wives which occurred in the development of Roman society was not in the first instance brought about by a deliberate change of legislation. It was in the first instance a change of custom indicating a wider change in society at large. In fact one might say that the change took place within the framework of the traditional legislation simply by re-interpreting it or by making a different use of old legal prescriptions and with a minimum of additional legislation so as to suit changing customs. With regard to their formal laws Romans were more conservative than with regard to their customs.

8

There is no lack of non-legal evidence to indicate the extent and the direction of the change. See, for example, the epitaph on the tombstone of a Roman wife from the second century BC (Dessau, 1954: No. 8403, quoted in Finley, 1968: 130):

> Hospes, quod deico, paullum est, asta ac pellege.
> heic est sepulcrum hau pulcrum pulcrai feminae.
> nomen parentes nominarunt Claudiam.
> suom mareitum corde deilexit souo.
> gnatos duos creavit. horunc alterum
> in terra linquit, alium sub terra locat.
> sermone lepido, tum autem incessu commodo.
> domum servavit. lanam fecit. dixi. abei.

> Friend, I have not much to say; stop and read it. This tomb, which is not fair, is for a fair woman. Her parents gave her the name Claudia. She loved her husband in her heart. She bore two sons, one of whom she left on earth, the other beneath it. She was pleasant to talk with, and she walked with grace. She kept the house and worked in wool. That is all. You may go.

This epitaph was obviously composed or ordered by the husband or another kinsman of the deceased woman. Quite a number of such inscriptions have been discovered. They all tell the same story. Much of this text is conventional. It represents a Roman husband's prescription for a woman considered to be a good wife. But the laconic brevity of this particular epitaph may also strike an individual note. It is as if the man who ordered this inscription had heard the rumblings of the change to come and said with some defiance: that is how this woman was and, by God, that is how a woman ought to be.

The women of that age, as Finley (1968: Ch. 10: 'The Silent Women of Rome') pointed out, were silent—i.e. silent for us. But from the little we know it is quite clear that during the second and first centuries BC some kind of public controversy took place among men about the position of women in Roman society, some men advocating a change, some resisting it with all their might. Of the latter's voices, particularly that of Cato's, some fragments have been preserved. Thus it was reported that Cato said: 'Roman men rule the world and are ruled by women'. Men who opposed the changes mainly spoke of their negative aspects. They referred to the growing immorality, to the licentiousness of men and women and to the arrogance of the latter. Thus the age in which Romans reached a condition of civilization which enabled them to emulate Greeks in the elegance of speech, in the sensitivity of feeling and taste, in art and literature, was also an age from which many of them looked back with nostalgia and anger to the Roman past as a better age when men and women lived an austere life and were always virtuous.

From a distance it is easier simply to seek a better understanding of what actually happened. Thus it is perhaps useful (taking up an earlier point) to sum up some of the salient aspects indicative of the balance of power between men and women of the Roman upper classes before the change set in, and to confront them with the new setting. The change did not come suddenly; it was a gradual change. But the turning point was, as I have said, before the final defeat and destruction of Carthage which made Rome's hegemonial position in the Mediterranean almost irrevocable.

According to the old order unmarried women were always under the control of male members of their family. A husband was chosen for them in accordance with the interests of their family. On marrying, control over them could either be transferred to the husband or remain with their own male relatives. Women had, in this long period as far as we know, no property of their own, little education and no right to divorce their husband on their own initiative. While extra-marital relations of men were taken for granted, those of wives could ruin their whole social existence.

The emancipatory change made itself felt in the second half of the second century and matured in the course of the first century BC. One of its symptoms was that unmarried daughters participated more freely in the educational opportunities open to their brothers. Some of them became early acquainted with Greek literature, science and philosophy, could converse with educated young men on equal terms and were used to looking beyond the household duties of the traditional Roman matron.

An essential of the new order was above all a married woman's possession of her own property. As before young women were married in accordance with the dynastic interests of their families. But divorce, which had always been an easy and informal affair for men, now also became an easy and informal matter for women. The wife as well as the husband could say: 'I wish to divorce you'. Probably with the help of their freedmen who acted as their men of business, each took his or her property when they left each other, and that was that.

Moreover, while in the case of a young previously unmarried woman, as a rule family policy decided the choice of her husband, after a divorce it was usually left to a woman herself to decide whether she wanted to marry again and if so whom she wanted to marry. In addition, while in former days society only tolerated extra-marital relationships of married men, which in fact were taken for granted, society now also tolerated, within narrower limits, extra-marital relationships of young married women, provided they were pursued with appropriate discretion. It was said of Augustus that he divorced his first wife because she protested against his extra-marital affairs. It was also said that Tiberius, the son which Livia, Augustus' second wife, had from her first marriage, was actually the product of a clandestine affair which he had with Livia during her first marriage. In former days the mere suspicion of adultery would have disgraced a Roman matron. In the late Republic and then in the Empire such stories were frequently bandied about. Rome gossiped with gusto and no one was apparently the worse off.

# 9

Catullus' Claudia, to whom he addressed some of his most beautiful love poems, was a married woman when he fell in love with her. He was a provincial of middle class descent, she was a great lady, member of one of the oldest aristocratic houses of Rome, the *gens Claudia*. It was a type of love-relationship which, as far as we know, was new to Rome. It sheds light on changes in both the balance of power between the sexes and Roman society.

A young man of great talent was deeply attached to a grand lady who, while still young, was older than he and superior in rank, elegance, experience, and savoir vivre. Catullus, possibly the foremost lyrical poet in the Roman republic, loved her passionately. If we can believe his poems, she answered his love and granted him, as it is called, her favours. She then turned away from him. Did they become the object of gossip? Was she tired of him? But he continued to love her, and at the same time despised her for having toyed with him. His words *odi et amo* have been ringing in our ears for centuries. He threw these words into her face: 'I love you and I hate you'—possibly the first time that a man gave expression to the possible ambivalence of feelings. Catullus died young. It is believed that Claudia's house in Rome has been discovered, containing pictures of the mystery cults then fashionable in Rome. Rumour has it that she had friendly relations with Cleopatra when the queen of Egypt came to visit Caesar in Rome. Her husband died long before her; apparently she did not remarry.

Relationships, as that between Catullus and Claudia, a gifted, socially inferior young man, and a socially superior, older woman, became much more frequent many centuries later in the time of courtly love and of court society generally (cf. Elias, 1983, 1994). There it became, in some cases, almost a standardized form of relationship between women and men. In Rome, it represented merely one of a number of possible novel forms of relationships between the sexes. It brought with it, as can be seen, a new range of emotions and a heightened sensitivity, which expressed itself, for example, in the new receptivity for the meaning and tone of poems among the Roman public. As was the case later in courtly, and then Baroque, poems, Catullus' had also not been intended for an anonymous public but represented what we now, slightly derogatively, call 'occasional poems'. They arose from a specific, both personal and social, situation and were intended for a known audience. Catullus' poetry clearly exhibits a specific expression of a changed relationship between men and women. In comparison with early Rome, when women were subject to men, this change in the relationship between the sexes becomes more evident. Now, in relationships of the kind between Claudia and Catullus, the woman is quite unequivocally in a stronger position than the man. In some of his poems Catullus fights hopelessly for a love that will not die. He abuses the husband of the woman he loves and tells her how much he despises her. The changed balance of power between the sexes gives rise to very new forms of struggle between them. Catullus' poems are a lasting evidence of this.

## 10

The virtual equality between husband and wife in Roman marriages was quite unique and of great consequence for the future. As far as we know today, this was the first time in the development of state-societies that married women could take charge of their own lives, as previously only men could. This went hand-in-hand with a higher level of self-discipline in the dealings of married men and women with each other. It found expression in Rome in a peculiar aspect of upper-class marriages which is worth mentioning.

Although examples of affection and warmth of feeling between husband and wife were not lacking in Roman society, one cannot help feeling that the Roman tradition also helped to foster a curious aloofness between the marriage partners. One has the impression that ladies of the senatorial classes often identified themselves far more closely with their own lineage than with that of their husbands. They remained after all part of the noble house into which they had been born for life, while marriages might be transient. Also, some evidence points to the fact that the noble women of Rome, like women in many other societies, formed a social network of their own, clearly distinct from that of men, but like the latter with their own relational channels and conventions.

I can perhaps illustrate the existence of women as a distinct social group, as a social network with conventions of its own by means of an example. It may also be of help as an example of the new type of women, more precisely of the changed social habitus or personality structure of women which came to the fore in the late second and the first century BC and which persisted in Rome till late into the Christian era. The difference from the type of woman represented by the epitaph I have quoted before, the type of woman whose life was confined to the household and the service of her husband, is striking. No less striking is the difference between this ancient Roman and the present form of marriage indicated by the following episode.

During the Roman civil war in the latter half of the first century BC, when Octavian, later the emperor Augustus, Mark Anthony and Lepidus ruled the Roman state together as a dictatorial triad, they imposed an immense levy on 1400 particularly rich wives and close female relatives of their outlawed and proscribed opponents. These ladies decided to approach the lawmakers and rulers of the state, as was probably customary for Roman women, indirectly by visiting and asking for the help of the mothers and wives of the dictators. While they were received in a friendly manner by the ladies of Octavian's and Lepidus' household, they were loudly attacked and repulsed by Fulvia, Anthony's wife. The aggrieved ladies therefore decided on the unusual step of going together to the forum to explain publicly their objections to the dictators who were holding a public meeting there. Although not for men, it was certainly for women—even for a group of patrician ladies—a very unusual step. But their own male relatives were outlawed and abroad. So they took it upon themselves to explain their grievance to the dictators in the presence of the people assembled at the forum.

Normally women did not take part in the assemblies held and in the political decisions taken at the forum. A group of great Roman ladies appearing at the forum before the rulers of the state was an unusual sight. Although it has been reported to us by a later historian of antiquity, the whole scene is of great significance if one wants to understand the singular character of the relationship and, in particular, of the balance of power between men and women in the Roman upper classes. In some respects, as one shall see, this relationship was different from those known to people today from their own experience. It does not matter very much that the report we have was written quite some time after the event. It was still written for a reading public of the ancient world for whom a relationship between women and men as described was probably not unfamiliar, and was certainly less strange than it might appear today.

The large group of Roman ladies appeared at the forum, and the crowd, we are told, respectfully opened a way for them. Even the guards, the police of that age, lowered their weapons so that the ladies could appear before the three dictators who were probably as surprised as the mass of the people at the unusual sight of women appearing at the forum. According to the report, we gather the dictators were angry, but one of the ladies, Hortensia, the daughter of a famous orator, had started to address them in the traditional manner and as the crowd appeared to be on the side of the ladies, the triumvirs decided they could not use violence against them and listened to Hortensia's address. This, briefly, was the line of argument attributed to her. It was, in the old Roman manner, clear and succinct.

She first explained why they had taken the extraordinary step of addressing the highest magistrates of the state personally. As was customary for women of rank who wished to address a petition to the magistrates they had first approached the ladies of their household, but they were treated by Fulvia, the wife of Anthony, in an unbecoming manner. Hortensia declared that it was Fulvia who drove them to the forum. They, the triumvirs, had already deprived them of their father, of all their male relatives. If they now took away their property as well, they would reduce them all to a condition which was not in keeping with their birth, their way of life and their sex.

> 'If we have done you wrong', she continued, 'as you say our husbands have, proscribe us as you have them. But if women have not voted any of you public enemies, have not torn down your houses, destroyed your army, or led another one against you; if we have not hindered you in obtaining offices and honours—why do we share the penalty when we did not share the guilt?
>
> 'Why should we pay taxes when we have no part in the honours, the

commands, the state-craft, for which you contend against each other with
such harmful results? Because this is a time of war, do you say? When have
there not been wars, and when have taxes ever been imposed on women,
who are exempted by their sex among all mankind? Our mothers did once
rise superior to their sex and made contributions when you were in danger
of losing the whole empire and the city itself through the conflict with the
Carthaginians. But then they contributed voluntarily, not from their
landed property, their fields, their dowries or their houses, without which
life is not possible to free women, but only from their own jewellery and
even these not according to fixed valuation, not under fear of informers or
accusers, not by force and violence, but what they themselves were willing
to give. What alarm is there now for the empire or the country? Let war
with the Gauls or Parthians come, and we shall not be inferior to our
mothers in zeal for the common safety; but for civil wars may we never
contribute, nor ever assist you against each other! Neither Marius nor
Cinna imposed taxes upon us. Nor did Sulla, who held despotic power in
the state, do so, whereas you say that you are re-establishing the com-
monwealth.'

   While Hortensia thus spoke the triumvirs were angry that women
should dare to hold a public meeting when the men were silent; that they
should demand from magistrates the reasons for their acts, and themselves not so much as furnish money while the men were serving in the
army. They ordered the lictors to drive them away from the tribunal,
which they proceeded to do until cries were raised by the multitude outside, when the lictors desisted and the triumvirs said they would postpone
till the next day the consideration of the matter. On the following day they
reduced the number of women, who were to present a valuation of their
property, from 1400 to 400, and decreed that all men who possessed more
than 100,000 drachmas, both citizens and strangers, freedmen and
priests, and men of all nationalities without a single exception, should
(under the same dread of penalty and also of informers) lend them at interest a fiftieth part of their property and contribute one year's income to
the war expenses. (*Appian's Roman History: The Civil War,* 4: 32–4)

As Appian described it about two centuries later the episode is in-
triguing. Like other historians of Antiquity he may have used older
sources for his account of the Roman civil wars. Like others he used his
imagination. The historians' licence allowed him to enliven his narrative, as Thucydides and Livy did, by means of invented speeches and con-
versations. He may or may not have found in his sources a description of
the appearance before the three rulers of a group of noble ladies. But he
wrote for inhabitants of the Roman empire. His capacity to invent was
limited by what his public was likely to know about the conduct and feelings of Roman women and their marital relationships. To today's readers it may seem strange that the wives and daughters, the female relatives

of men outlawed and perhaps threatened with death, should stay quietly in Rome quite certain, as it appears, that no harm would be done to them while their men were in hiding as deadly enemies of the ruling group. Evidently it was not so strange in a Roman context. One could say with some justification that men and women formed two distinct sub-classes of the ruling classes in Roman society, and certainly not only there.

Whatever the historical accuracy of Appian's report may have been, its sociological relevance is considerable. Women in Rome, once entirely subject to the rule of men, had become, in late Republican and in early imperial times, self-ruling human beings in their marriages. That they had independent means, an income of their own, played a large part in their personal, social and thus also in their marital independence. Within their married lives they had gained for themselves full equality with their husbands. Like their husbands they could end their marriage at will or by mutual consent.

I have spoken of a certain aloofness in the attitude to each other of husbands and wives. This is an example. One need not doubt that relations of love, of affection, of great warmth of feeling between husband and wife existed in Roman society as elsewhere. Yet, Roman women of the upper-classes were, as one can see here, almost completely excluded from that sphere of life which in Republican times formed the centre of gravity of the activities and ambitions of many men. They were largely excluded from participation in the affairs of state. In imperial times, of course, most men of the senatorial classes were equally excluded from this sphere. Thus, this episode shows features of marital relationships in late Republican and early imperial times which are significant for an understanding of the changing balance between the sexes. It shows the independence of women regarding their property, even though perhaps in an idealized manner. On the other hand, it may be indicative for the limits of this independence that convention decreed that women who wished to put forward a petition or to influence the magistrates should visit, and confer with, the ladies of the magistrates' household and try to influence the husbands through their wives and daughters. That was an example of the women's network of which I have spoken before.[7]

The fact that married women in Rome, probably for the first time in the development of a state, reached full equality with their husbands and like them could end their marriage by consent and perhaps at will had far reaching consequences; its influence on marriage relations can be felt till late imperial times, and on Roman and Church law till far into the Middle Ages. However, this Roman marriage relationship had aspects which were different from an egalitarian relationship of our age. To remember that is perhaps useful.[8]

In the development of European societies one may also encounter a stage when men and women in certain respects formed different social groups. There were spheres in the life of men from which women were excluded and vice versa. But in European societies this separation of social spheres and the formation of distinctively separate male and female groups usually went hand in hand with a very pronounced inequality between the sexes in married life. In Roman society it went hand in hand with virtual equality in married life. The episode I have just quoted can serve as an illustration.

There were other Roman reports of women joining each other in segregated groups, in religious groupings, even in the form of a women's senate and in other ways which confirm the impression that a separate women's social circuit was and remained even in the Christian era a standing feature of Roman life. Rich women had few household duties. Close ties with their own family, possibly attachment but also some aloofness between husband and wife, and a woman's own social network—these features together make a fairly consistent picture.


## 11

Something has to be said about the reasons for this development of a less uneven balance of power between the sexes in the Roman state. One may keep in mind that in the development of human societies events judged to be bad often follow from others judged to be good, and good events from bad ones. If one looks for explanations, therefore, it is better to cast aside wishes and values of this kind and to content oneself with a simple discovery of what happened and why.

Rome underwent in the course of four or five centuries a development which transformed a city-state into the capital of a vast empire. Rome's leading group, its senatorial class, largely responsible for this transformation, underwent a corresponding change. From being a class of peasant warriors it became a class of aristocratic holders of high military and civil offices owning immense estates and much else besides. Hortensia's speech before Octavian and Mark Anthony contains an account of the kind of property which enabled a noble lady to lead an independent life appropriate, as she said, to her social rank. A lady derived her income mainly from landed property which included, as a matter of course, an army of labouring slaves and of freedmen as supervisors and administrators. In addition, a lady possessed a large treasure of jewellery, partly for use and partly, no doubt, as reserve for a rainy day.

The gradual accumulation of great wealth in the hands of the aristocratic families of Rome was the first reason one has to mention for a change in the husband-wife relationship. But one cannot quite understand the connection if one considers the accumulation of wealth as the fruit of commerce and other economic activities.

The Roman nobility was anything but a ruling group of merchants. It was essentially a warrior nobility, later an aristocracy of holders or former holders of the highest military and civil offices. The growing wealth of Rome like that of many other state societies of Antiquity was derived from successful wars. War booty, the sale of prisoners of war as slaves, tribute from subject peoples, wealth amassed as governor or military commander of provinces, these and other positional chances of a similar type were the sources which made Rome rich. From the ruling classes, who kept the greater part to themselves, some portions of the wealth trickled through to the other classes. Bread and circuses, the free distribution of grain to all Roman citizens and the free access to gladiatorial games paid for by the wealthy, these were two of the ways in which the mass of the Roman citizens participated in the growing wealth of the upper classes. It is an open question whether it is at all possible to talk of an autonomous economic development of the state. As far as Rome is concerned, it certainly is not the case.

One of the main levers of change in the relation between husband and wife was the transition from a condition where women were in effect part of their husband's property and as such did not have any property of their own to a condition where women became owners of property in their own right. As I have already mentioned the transformation came about mainly by a change in custom and with a minimum of legal changes. The legal prescription which allowed this change in custom was the rule according to which a woman could be married without transfer to her husband of the male tutelage over her and thus also over her property. In that case the tutelage and control over a married woman remained in the hands of her father or, in the case of his death, of one of her uncles or brothers.

What appears to have happened as time went on and as the wealth of the Roman aristocracy increased, sometimes by leaps and bounds, was this: It became customary in these high-ranking circles to endow daughters with property of their own in addition to the indispensable jewellery. When the daughter was married the husband received a dowry of which he might have the usufruct or perhaps even the possession, but the property of his wife remained formally under the control of his wife's male relatives. In course of time it became customary for the male relatives of a married woman not to make use of their prerogative to control her and her property. In all likelihood these men were wealthy enough, and thus it became customary for married women to treat the property handed over to them by their family as their own, to control it themselves. Thus the legal prescription of a marriage *sine coventione in manum mariti* became the main vehicle for a change in custom which gave married women de facto control over property. But there were also some new pieces of legislation which aided the process, for example, a law which allowed women to inherit property left to them.

## 12

However, this change in custom could not have been effected without a change in the structure of the Roman state. It was one of the characteristic developments in Rome as in a number of other states that in its course jurisdiction became more impartial, less influenced by the differences in power and status of accuser and accused, and law-enforcement institutions became more effective. This aspect of the state formation process played a decisive part in the development of greater marital equality between the sexes. For as long as a husband could use his greater influence over law courts and law enforcement officers, or simply his greater physical strength, to wrest from his wife the control over her property, women were bound to remain in a position of social inferiority. Cato, in one of his characteristic utterances, observed that in his time women kept control over their property to themselves instead of handing it over to their husbands. At the most they lent to their husband. Then, after a while, when he was tardy with his payments they got impatient and sent the law officers after him.

Thus, one of the decisive conditions which made possible the rise of married women to greater equality with their husbands was a development of law-enforcement which protected women from the wrath and threats from a physically stronger husband, and which ensured the safety of a person as well as a person's possessions whether that person was a woman or a man.

Perhaps it is useful in this context to remember the story of yet another Appius Claudius of an earlier and rougher age, when the people's demand for participation in the affairs of the state was rising and the warrior nobility tried to stem the flood in the usual way, by means of a dictatorship, in this case an autocratic regime headed by a board of ten. Appius Claudius was its head, as told by Dionysius of Halicarnassus (Dion. Hal. IX: 28, quoted in Kiefer, 1953: 10). The story is almost certain legendary. Yet it has features which are consistent with, and characteristic of, a period in which the law is used to enforce an orderly conduct of the people while the upper classes, as the most powerful group, feel themselves to be above the law.

Appius Claudius fell violently in love with a beautiful Plebeian woman called Virginia. He could not marry her. Regular marriages could not be contracted between nobles and girls from the people. So he sent the woman who brought her up much money and suggested some ways that would allow him to seduce the girl. There is one sentence in the record of this story which has the true ring of the age. He directed his messengers not to tell the woman who was in love with the girl but only to say that he was one of those who could harm or help anyone he wished. When he did not succeed he used force. He had the girl abducted by his agents. When her father and her fiancé protested, Appius Claudius declared that her mother was one of his slaves. At this point her father recognized that he could not win against the powerful man who said that he loved his daughter. He asked for permission to take leave from his daughter. He embraced her and manoeuvred her gently to the front of an open butcher shop, seized one of the knives and stabbed her to death.

The story looks suspiciously similar to the much more famous story of Lucretia. In the one case the death of the endangered girl was the legendary prelude to the liberation of Rome from the rule of an alien king, and thus the event achieved fame. In the other case it foreshadowed the end of the unrestrained rule of warrior nobles who felt themselves to be above the law. Since the nobles remained in power Virginia became less famous than Lucretia. Though legendary, the story of Virginia illustrates an aspect of the state formation process which played a central part in the changing balance of power between the sexes not only in Rome but also in other societies. One of the conditions for lessening the inequality between men and women in a society was the growth of a state organization, particularly of its legal and law-enforcement institutions which could prevent men from using either their strength or their influence in order to impose their will upon women.

There is no need here to go into the question of how and why a state develops in this way. In time the rule of the Roman upper class, which continued (with a number of concessions to the wealthier middle classes and the mass of the people from the very beginning—*ab urbe condita*) until it was replaced by the rule of emperors, ceased to be a largely arbitrary regime and became a class rule constrained by an elaborate body of laws.

However, one further factor which worked as a lever towards greater equality of wives and husbands deserves to be mentioned. Rome had already undergone in Republican times an unmistakable civilizing spurt, even though its rise was largely due to successes in war. The reception of Greek culture and the novel Roman creativity in literature, historiography and philosophy which presupposed a growing sensitivity of the reading public were symptoms of this spurt. So was a greater refinement in manners and in love. Ovid's 'Ars Amatoria' bears witness to the fact. It may not correspond to present standards of sexual sensitivity, but it certainly speaks of an advance in refinement between the sexes and of a greater measure of restraint in men's approaches to women.

In contrast to the old days women were now in fact, and were seen by men as, human beings in their own right. One cannot quite understand why in Roman society the custom which initially placed women and their property under the tutelage of men gradually lapsed if one does not refer to this civilizing spurt as one of the conditions for this change. Once the stage of greater equality between women and men in their married life had been reached in Rome, it was maintained for a surprisingly long time, even when the state organization—particularly in the Western part of the Roman Empire—and thus the conditions of the level of civilization that had been achieved began to deteriorate.


13

Again and again in the development of humanity one encounters innovations of great consequence which in later times are no longer recognizable as such because they are taken for granted; they have come to be accepted as self-evident or maybe simply as rational. That women attained in married life a position of equality with men was a case of this kind. It was a Roman innovation. However, it did not mean that women attained a position of equality with men in other areas of Roman society. Women in Rome were, and remained, excluded from military and civil offices. It is difficult to say whether in Roman times women ever participated in long-distance commerce or tax-farming, but it is not very likely, nor as far as one can see did Roman women actively participate in the production of literature, art, philosophy, science or in the writing of history. All these spheres of human activity, as far as one can tell, in Roman times remained, with minimal exceptions, the preserve of men. Yet, in terms of the development of humanity, it was a great innovation and a fact of great consequence that in the late Roman Republic women attained a position of equality with their husbands in married life and retained that position for many centuries during the time of the Roman emperors.

It was a fact of great consequence mainly for two reasons. While in the early Republic—as in many other early state societies—married women were not perceived and were not treated as self-ruling human beings, as individuals in their own right, but rather as possessions or adjuncts of their husbands, the custom which established itself in the late Republic and was maintained in the heyday of the Empire enabled women to develop into what we now call individuals—they were capable of taking independent decisions and of acting on their own. For several centuries one gets glimpses of independent-minded women in Roman society. They disappeared in the West, as one might expect, as the state's monopoly of physical force was eroded as migrant tribes roamed over the countryside and assailed the cities, while in some cases local strongmen, the precursors of feudal lords, organized local opposition and provided a kind of protection. The native customs of the Germanic invaders attributed to women an inferior position akin to the 'norms' which prevailed among the Romans in earlier days.[9] This, as one may assume, contributed to the erosion of the more egalitarian marriage tradition.

However, as long as the emperors and their legions were able to maintain the internal peace—the *Pax Romana*—within the whole empire, the tradition of a relatively egalitarian form of marriage seems to have persisted among the wealthier urban classes of the Roman empire. That was one of the ways in which the innovation of the late Republic proved of great consequence. It had grown into the fabric of Roman society as a custom and maintained itself as such with considerable tenacity.

A short series of examples may help to illustrate the fact that the custom had formed deep roots. Perhaps I should mention once more that what had appeared first as a Roman custom eventually became codified as part of the Roman law. Two aspects played a crucial part as preconditions of the egalitarian character of marriage; both had probably at first developed in social practice. The first of these aspects was the independence of wives as well as of husbands with regard to their own property. The second aspect, no less important, was the essentially voluntary character of the marriage association. Its principal safeguard was the ability of each marriage partner, wife as well as husband, to declare that he or she wished to end the marriage relationship. In that respect the marriage customs of the late Roman Republic and the earlier Empire went further than the legal regulations of many present-day societies.

In the late Roman Republic marriage among the upper classes apparently became more and more a voluntary association of a woman and a man, maintained by the consent of both. As custom transformed itself into law, especially in imperial times, a whole host of legal prescriptions grew up, gradually limiting the voluntary character of the marriage association though never actually destroying it. It contrasted sharply with the teaching of the early Church which in principle demanded that a marriage should be regarded as a lifelong association and as indissoluble as long as both partners lived. Roman law provided for several forms of divorce. There was the *divortium bona gratia*, a one-sided form of divorce for a variety of reasons which had not to include any wrongdoing on the part of the other partner. There was also the *divortium consensu,* which allowed wife and husband to divorce each other by mutual consent. If the two people agreed, it was, in the early imperial period as well, not too difficult to find a legal reason for divorce to suit their own case. Neither of these two forms of divorce entailed financial disadvantage for either husband or wife. There were other legal forms of divorce based on misdemeanour or disability of one marriage partner with financial losses for the latter. But there is no need here to go into the details.

The Christian emperors, from the time of Constantine, tried to sharpen the teeth of marital law and, among other things, to make divorce less easy again. A law of the emperor Justinian (Nov. 117, c. 10., quoted in Geffcken, 1894: 25) went so far as to prohibit divorce by consent except in cases in which both sides wanted to enter a monastery. Already Justinian's successor, Justin II, so we are told, was compelled to withdraw the law because the complaints about attacks and poisoning among married people had grown in a terrifying manner. Apparently the Christian emperors were more successful in their attempt at restricting the possibility of divorce as a result of a one-sided declaration of one partner. Emperor Constantine published in 331 a legal innovation which tried to reform the *repudium iustum* by eliminating this kind of legal repudiation in the case of minor reasons and confining it to a small number of very weighty reasons. It is interesting to see what they were. A woman should have the right to divorce her husband if he was a murderer, a poisoner or a violent violator of graves. A husband should be able to divorce his wife only for such reasons as adultery, female pimping or poisoning. One can see a note of inequality creeping in. A man's adultery obviously was not one of the reasons why, according to Constantine's law, a wife should be able to divorce her husband.

One cannot detect in the code of Roman law left by the emperors up to the time of Justinian a return to the earlier state of inequality which allowed only the husband to end the marriage by means of divorce. In spite of increasing restrictions Roman divorce law continued to maintain the equality of the marriage partners in so far as both wives and husbands were given the right to initiate divorce. Women continued to be considered in Roman law, like men, as persons in their own right. It also showed itself in the fact that among the wealthier classes marriage by consent of both partners had gained ground in the empire. Like divorce, the conclusion of a marriage in the Roman empire remained, despite all marriage laws, an affair of the families or individuals concerned, although state intervention, whether successful or not, continued to increase during the empire. It required no state registration, nor any church service. The introduction of the bride into the bridegroom's home—*deductio in domum*—was the ceremony broadly corresponding to what we now call a wedding.

# 14

The young Christian Church, while struggling to Christianize the society of the Roman Empire, became in its turn romanized. The absorption by some of the Church fathers of the demand that a marriage should have the consent of both partners—i.e. of the woman, too—was a symptom of this. But the situation was more complex.

However, the newly established Frankish, Anglo-Saxon and other Germanic kingdoms, as one might expect, carried marriage customs characteristic of an earlier stage of development and not unlike those prevalent among the Romans themselves when they emerged from their tribal stage, but very different from the marriage customs prevalent in the urban Roman societies of their own time. In the Germanic kingdoms marriage by force or by purchase, i.e. without the consent of the woman concerned, was still widely practised. The *leges barbarorum* bear witness to the fact. Thus one of them from the early seventh century AD stated:

> If someone abducts a young woman by force he is to pay to the owner fifty shillings and to buy afterwards from this owner his consent (sc. to the marriage). (Giesen, 1973: 27 n. 43)

This, indeed, is reminiscent of prescriptions from the early Roman period. Yet what may seem to be a simple return to an earlier stage occurred in this case under very different conditions. The Roman heritage was not entirely lost. It was to some extent carried forward by the romanized Church.

I have spoken before of two ways in which the development of the relationship between the sexes in Roman antiquity left its mark on the later development. The marriage customs of the Romans, although they survived to some extent in the East, perished in the upheavals which followed the disintegration of the West Roman empire. But a code of Roman law survived. Even though its prescriptions became dormant for a time, after a long interval—following the development of an appropriate new state formation—Roman law was again unearthed and studied. It was taken up as an appropriate model by the administration of the newly centralized states, and thus again became selectively effective.

It had also left its mark on the law of the Church. In accordance with Roman customs the Church developed the doctrine that consensus of both, the woman and the man, was necessary for a valid marriage. But until the twelfth century it remained an open question whether verbal consent or *capula carnalis* constituted the decisive act which gave validity to a marriage. The theological school of Bologna favoured the latter view; the theological school of Paris, and in particular Peter Lombard, argued in favour of the former view. The school of Paris carried the day with the argument that decisive for a valid marriage was the consent of both partners, normally before witnesses. That is a very good example of the way in which, with the help of written texts, the development of an earlier age, even though the knowledge it had produced became dormant and ineffectual for a time, could once more make its influence felt when the development of society as a whole offered the right conditions for it.

## 15

Historical study of the past, directed as it is towards the particular, often impedes comparisons; sociological study facilitates them. In our own time a lively discussion is taking place with regard to the balance of power between the sexes. But there is a tendency to consider changes in the balance of power between the sexes in a wholly voluntaristic manner, as if it depended entirely on the goodwill, or alternatively the ill will, of the people concerned. Undoubtedly to go back from the present times to consider the changing balance of power between the sexes within the framework of a state society which to some extent is very different from the present one requires a certain capacity for detachment. But if one is willing to make a little effort to distance oneself from contemporary issues, one may perhaps find such a sociological way of dealing with past changes in the balance of power between the sexes helpful in understanding present problems. In that way one may understand better that changes in the balance of power between the sexes can never be effected or understood without regard to the overall development of society.

It has become apparent for instance that the effectiveness of the state in protecting the person as well as the income or property of women was one of the factors responsible for changes in the balance of power between the sexes. I also believe it to be an important factor today. It is useful to remember that at one time the condition of equality which married women had reached was whittled down and eroded when the central monopoly of physical force, one of the central pieces of a state organization, broke down when local strongmen or invaders from outside took over and violence and insecurity again spread over the whole state society.

Finally, the Roman example can show how closely the relative parity between men and women is connected with the developmental stage of civilization. Sensitivity on the part of men for the condition of women and vice versa, a relatively high level of well-tempered self-restraints or, in other words, a civilizing spurt was one of the conditions for the emergence and maintenance of more egalitarian forms of sex relations in ancient Rome. *Mutatis mutandis,* the same holds true, I think, in our own time.

## Notes

Lecture in Bologna, 14 September 1985 (*'Lettura' del Mulino,* 1985). The original English manuscript has been edited according to the revised German version in the *Kölner Zeitschrift für Soziologie und Sozialpsychologie,* 38 (1986): 425–49.

1. The Imperial British Administration had some difficulty in abolishing this custom.

2. The traditional concepts patriarchal and matriarchal cannot be used in this context. They refer to men in their capacity as fathers, to women in their capacity as mothers. I prefer the terms 'andrarchic', meaning men-dominated, and 'gynarchic' meaning women-dominated to the more traditional concepts because men's rule is not necessarily, and is certainly not in this case, identical with fathers' rule, nor women's rule with mothers' rule.

3. A marriage was to a large extent dependent on the relationship between self-ruling tribal groups. In the incessant struggle for survival in which such groups lived at an earlier stage, a marriage between a daughter of one group and the son of another was a means of binding the two groups to each other as allies and friends. A marriage, and the marriage gift which always seems to have accompanied such a marriage, was designed to establish peace and friendship between two groups. If the gift was accepted by another group, it was a sign that its members were willing to enter into such a bond. If the gift was refused, it was a sign that they were not willing to enter into friendly and peaceful relationships. It is important to understand that the woman herself was a gift which one kinship group gave to another as she was likely to bear children for the other group. But the women-giving group expected a counter-gift. In that sense the early form of marriage can be described as a marriage by purchase.

4. An example which, in an attenuated form but still quite vividly, illustrates the concept of a woman as part of the common possessions of the males of a kin-group is the following legal regulation: if a man wishes to marry a widow he has to pay each of her male relatives up to the fifth or sixth grade a specified amount of money. It was larger in the case of her father or brothers than for her uncles or cousins and diminished by degrees. At the stage of development kin-groups of this type, for which adequate names are difficult to find in the vocabulary of an industrial nation state— 'extended family' is an ethnocentric misnomer—probably still had the functions and characteristics of a survival unit. Their members, in all likelihood, stood up for each other in case of attack and if necessary revenged one another. It was probably in connection with kin-groups of this type that churchmen sometimes extended the incest taboo to relatives of the sixth (or seventh) grade.

5. Roman law has preserved for us another form of marriage. A man could acquire rights over a woman through continuous use. He could claim her as his own, apparently without paying a price for her, because he had used her for himself for some time.

6. Quite similar conditions are to be found in medieval German society up to the thirteenth century and partially beyond it. (Cf. for these conditions and for the changes setting in at that time: Michael Schröter, '*Wo zwei zusammenkommen in rechter Ehe . . .': Sozio- und psychogenetische Studien über Eheschließungsvorgänge vom 12. bis 15. Jahrhundert,* 1985; and also Schröter's article 'Marriage' [1987].)

7. The assumption that women did not have to pay taxes, if confirmed, would obviously be of great interest. But I have no confirmation. One also wonders whether the freedom from taxes of women may have been in danger in Appian's times.

8. Today women, almost as a matter of course, are expected to support the party and thus the political ideology which is likely to carry their husbands to high office and husbands are expected to do the same if their wives embark on a political career. What is more, in the multi-party states of our age, politicians in high office have to give the impression to society that they are a living example of what is believed to be the ideal husband-wife relationship. They have to give that impression at the risk of losing votes, of seriously damaging the career chances of a politically active marriage partner. While in practice a relatively egalitarian husband-wife relationship often requires a continued effort of stabilization, the politicians of our age have to project to the outer world a picture of almost effortless marital stability and identification. No such requirements were made on politically active men in ancient Rome or even on women. Catullus' Claudia actively supported Caesar's and her own brother's populist faction while her husband sympathized with the conservatives of his age. But then Roman society at the time of the Republic was anything but a democratic society. It was an aristocratic oligarchy.

9. The term 'norm' is frequently misused today. Sociologists, too, use it often in a philosophical manner as though it referred to unchanging, metaphysical data of unknown origin which somehow float about over and above human beings. Here it is seen differently. Whatever it is that could be regarded as the norm governing the conduct of husbands in ancient Rome appears on closer inspection as a retrospectively abstracted rule of customs that developed in an unplanned way; e.g. the 'rule' of equality between men and women in the case of divorce. Such a norm can only be understood and explained with the help of a process-sociological reconstruction, that is a reconstruction of the preceding inequality of the partners and of the process that led from it to later equality. And since it is the shifts in power between and within states or tribes that are at the centre of these processes, one could say perhaps more generally: norms change with power relations.

# References

Dessau, Hermannus (1954) *Inscriptiones Latinae selectae*. 2nd ed. Berlin.

Elias, Norbert (1983) *The Court Society*. Oxford: Basil Blackwell.

Elias, Norbert (1994) *The Civilizing Process*. Oxford: Blackwell.

Finley, M. I. (1968) *Aspects of Antiquity*. London: Chatto and Windus.

Geffcken, Heinrich (1894) *Zur Geschichte der Eheschließung vor Gratian*. Leipzig.

Giesen, Dieter (1973) *Grundlagen und Entwicklung des englisches Eherechts in der Neuzeit bis zum Beginn des 19. Jahrhunderts*. Bielefeld.

Kiefer, Otto (1953) *Sexual Life in Ancient Rome*. London.

Schröter, Michael (1985) 'Wo zwei zusummenkommen in rechter Ehe . . .': *Sozio- und psychogenetische Studien über Eheschließungsvorgänge vom 12. bis 15. Jahrhundert*. Frankfurt a.M.

Schröter, Michael (1987) 'Marriage', *Theory, Culture and Society* 4, no. 2–3: 317–22.

van Stolk, Bram and Wouters, Cas (1985) *Vrouwen en tweestrijd*. 2nd ed. Deventer.

# III

## KNOWLEDGE

# 12

# Involvement and Detachment

> OLD LADY: Are you not prejudiced?
> AUTHOR: Madame, rarely will you meet a more prejudiced man nor
> one who tells himself he keeps his mind more open. But cannot that be
> because one part of our mind, that which we act with, becomes
> prejudiced through experience, and still we keep another part
> completely open to observe and judge with?
> OLD LADY: Sir, I do not know.
> AUTHOR: Madame, neither do I and it may well be that we are talking
> nonsense.
> OLD LADY: That is an odd term and one I did not encounter in my
> youth.
> AUTHOR: Madame, we apply the term now to describe unsoundness in
> abstract conversation, or, indeed, any overmetaphysical tendency in
> speech.
> OLD LADY: I must learn to use these terms correctly.
>                                          E. Hemingway, *Death in the Afternoon*

## 1

One cannot say of a person's outlook in any absolute sense that it is detached or involved (or, if one prefers, "irrational", "objective" or "subjective"). Only small babies, and among adults perhaps only insane people, become involved in whatever they experience with complete abandon to their feelings here and now; and again only the insane can remain totally unmoved by what goes on around them. Normally adult behaviour lies on a scale somewhere between these two extremes. In some groups, and in some individuals of these groups, it may come nearer to one of them than in others; it may shift hither and thither as social and mental pressures rise and fall. But social life as we know it would come to an end if standards of adult behaviour went too far in either direction. As far as one can see, the very existence of ordered group life depends on the interplay in people's thoughts and actions of impulses in both directions, those that involve and those that detach keeping each other in

From *Involvement and Detachment* (1987), pp. 3–34; originally published in *British Journal of Sociology* 7, no. 3 (1956): 226–52 check. They may clash and struggle for dominance, or compromise and form alloys of many different shades and kinds—however varied, it is the relation between the two which sets people's courses. In using these terms,[1] one refers in short to changing equilibria between sets of mental activities which in humans' relations with other humans, with non-human objects and with themselves (whatever the other functions of these mental activities may be) have the function to involve and to detach.

As tools of thinking, therefore, "involvement" and "detachment" would remain highly ineffectual if they were understood to adumbrate a sharp division between two independent sets of phenomena. They do not refer to two separate classes of objects; used as universals they are, at best, marginal concepts. In the main, what we observe are people and people's manifestations, such as patterns of speech or of thought, and of other activities, some of which bear the stamp of higher, other of lesser detachment or involvement. It is the continuum that lies between these marginal poles that presents the principal problem. Can one determine with greater accuracy the position of specific attitudes or products of people within this continuum? One might, impressionistically, say, for example, that in societies like ours people tend to be more detached in their approaches to natural than to social events. Can one trace, at least summarily, criteria for different degrees of detachment and involvement? What in fact is meant, what does it imply, if one says that in societies such as ours, with a relatively high degree of industrialization and of control over non-human forces of nature, approaches to nature are on the whole more detached than those to society? The degree of detachment shown by different individuals in similar situations may differ greatly. Can one, nevertheless, speak, in this respect, of different degrees of detachment and involvement regardless of these individual variations?


## 2

The way in which individual members of a group experience whatever affects their senses, the meaning which it has for them, depends on the standard forms of dealing with, and of thinking and speaking about, these phenomena which have gradually evolved in their society. Thus, although the degree of detachment shown in one's encounter with natural forces may vary from individual to individual and from situation to situation, the concepts themselves which, in societies like ours, all individuals use in thinking, speaking and acting—concepts like "lightning", "tree" or "wolf" no less than "electricity", "organism", "cause and effect" or "nature"—in the sense in which they are used today, represent a relatively high degree of detachment; so does the socially induced experience of nature as a "landscape" or as "beautiful". The range of individual variations in detachment, in other words, is limited by the public standards of detachment embodied in modes of thinking and speaking about nature and in the widely institutionalized use of natural forces for human ends. Compared with previous ages, control of emotions in experiencing nature, as that of nature itself, has grown. Involvement has lessened, but it has not disappeared. Even scientific approaches to nature do not require the extinction of other more involved and emotive forms of approach. What distinguishes these from other less detached approaches is the manner in which tendencies towards detachment and towards involvement balance each other and blend.

Like other people, scientists engaged in the study of nature are, to some extent, prompted in the pursuit of their task by personal wishes and wants; they are often enough influenced by specific needs of the community to which they belong. They may wish to foster their own career. They may hope that the results of their inquiries will be in line with theories they have enunciated before or with the requirements and ideals of groups with which they identify themselves. But these involvements, in the natural sciences, determine as a rule nothing more than the general direction of inquiries; they are, in most cases, counterbalanced and checked by institutionalized procedures which compel scientists, more or less, to detach themselves, for the time being, from the urgent issues at hand. The immediate problems, personal or communal, induce problems of a different kind, scientific problems which are no longer directly related to specific persons or groups. The former, more narrowly timebound, often serve merely as a motive force; the latter, the scientific problems which they may have induced, owe their form and their meaning to the wider and less time-bound continuum of theories and observations evolved in this or that problem area by generations of specialists.

Like other human activities, scientific inquiries into nature embody sets of values. To say that natural sciences are "non-evaluating" or "value-free" is a misuse of terms. But the sets of values, the types of evaluations which play a part in scientific inquiries of this type differ from those which have as their frame of reference the interests, the well-being or suffering of oneself or of social units to which one belongs. The aim of these inquiries is to find the inherent order of events as it is, independently not of any, but of any particular, observer, and the importance, the relevance, the value of what one observes is assessed in accordance with the place and function it appears to have within this order itself.

In the exploration of nature, in short, scientists have learned that any direct encroachment upon their work by short-term interests or needs of specific persons or groups is liable to jeopardize the usefulness which their work may have in the end for themselves or for their own group. The problems which they formulate and, by means of their theories, try to solve have in relation to personal or social problems of the day a high degree of autonomy; so have the sets of values which they use; their work is not "value-free", but it is, in contrast to that of many social scientists, protected by firmly established professional standards and other institutional safeguards against the intrusion of heteronomous evaluations.[2] Here, the human primary tendency to take the short route from a strongly felt need to a precept for its satisfaction has become more or less subordinate to precepts and procedures which require a longer route. Natural scientists seek to find ways of satisfying human needs by means of a detour—the detour via detachment. They set out to find solutions for problems potentially relevant for all human beings and all human groups. The question characteristic of involvement—"What does it mean for me or for us?"—has become subordinate to questions like "What is it?" or "How are these events connected with others?" In this form, the level of detachment represented by the scientist's work has become more or less institutionalized as part of a scientific tradition reproduced by means of a highly specialized training, maintained by various forms of social control and socially induced emotional restraints; it has become embodied in the conceptual tools, the basic assumptions, the methods of speaking and thinking which scientists use.

Moreover, concepts and methods of this type have spread, and are spreading again and again, from the workshops of the specialists to the general public. In most industrial societies, impersonal types of explanations of natural events and other concepts based on the idea of a relatively autonomous order, of a course of events independent of any specific group of human observers, are used by people almost as a matter of course, though most of them are probably unaware of the long struggle involved in the elaboration and diffusion of these forms of thinking.

Yet, here too, in society at large, these more detached terms of thinking represent only one layer in people's approaches to nature. Other more involved and emotive forms of thinking about nature have by no means disappeared.

Thus in falling ill one may find one's thoughts stray again and again to the question, "Who is to blame for this?" The childhood experience of pain as the outcome of an attack, and perhaps a certain urge to retaliate, may assert themselves even though under the pressure of an overgrown conscience the attack may appear as deserved, so that one may come to feel, rightly or wrongly, that one has only oneself to blame for it. And yet one may accept at the same time the doctor's more detached dictum that this illness followed primarily from a completely blind biological course of events and not from anybody's intentions, not from conscious or unconscious motives of any kind.

More involved forms of thinking, in short, continue to form an integral part of our experience of nature. But in this area of our experience they have become increasingly overlaid and counterbalanced by others which make higher demands on people's faculty of looking at themselves, as it were, from outside and of viewing what they call "mine" or "ours" as part systems of a larger system. In experiencing nature humans have been able, in the course of time, to form and to face a picture of the physical universe which is emotionally far from satisfactory, which, in fact, seems to become less and less so as science advances, but which at the same time agrees better with the cumulative results of systematic observations. They have learned to impose upon themselves greater restraint in their approaches to natural events, and in exchange for the short-term satisfactions which they had to give up they have gained greater power to control and to manipulate natural forces for their own ends, and with it, in this sphere, greater security and other new long-term satisfactions.

## 3

Thus in public approaches to nature, people have travelled a long way (and have to travel it again and again as they grow up) from the primary, the childhood patterns of thinking. The road they have travelled is still far from clear. But one can see in broad outline some of its characteristic patterns and mechanisms.

When humans, instead of using stones as they found them against enemies or beasts, with greater restraint of their momentary impulses, gradually changed towards fashioning stones in advance for their use as weapons or tools (as we may assume they did at some time), and when, increasing their foresight, they gradually changed from gathering fruits and roots towards growing plants deliberately for their own use, it implied that they themselves as well as their social life and their natural surroundings, that their outlook as well as their actions, changed. The same can be said of those later stages in which changes in human thinking about nature became more and more the task of scientific specialists. Throughout these developments the mastery of people over themselves, as expressed in their mental attitudes towards nature, and their mastery over natural forces by handling them, have grown together. The level and patterns of detachment represented by public standards of thinking about natural events were in the past and still are dependent on the level and the manner of control represented by public standards of manipulating them, and vice versa.

For a very long time, therefore, in their struggle with the non-human forces of nature, humans must have moved in what appears in retrospect as a vicious circle. They had little control over natural forces on which they were dependent for their survival. Wholly dependent on phenomena whose course they could neither foresee nor influence to any considerable extent, they lived in extreme insecurity, and, being most vulnerable and insecure, they could not help feeling strongly about every occurrence they thought might affect their lives; they were too deeply involved to look at natural phenomena, like distant observers, calmly. Thus, on the one hand, they had little chance of controlling their own strong feelings in relation to nature and of forming more detached concepts of natural events as long as they had little control over them; and they had, on the other hand, little chance of extending their control over their non-human surroundings as long as they could not gain greater mastery over their own strong feelings in relation to them and increase their control over themselves.

The change towards greater control over natural phenomena appears to have followed what in our traditional language might be called "the principle of increasing facilitation". It must have been extremely difficult for people to gain greater control over nature as long as they had little control over it; and the more control they gained, the easier it was for them to extend it.

Nothing in our experience suggests that part-processes of this kind must always work in the same direction. Some of the phases in which they went into reverse gear are known from the past. Increasing social tensions and strife may go hand in hand with both a decrease of people's ability to control, and an increase in the fantasy-content of their ideas about, natural as well as social phenomena. Whether feedback mechanisms of this kind work in one or in the other direction depends, in short, on the total situation of the social units concerned.

## 4

Paradoxically enough, the steady increase in the capacity of humans both for a more detached approach to natural forces and for controlling them, and the gradual acceleration of this process, have helped to increase the difficulties which they have in extending their control over processes of social change and over their own feelings in thinking about them.

Dangers threatening people from non-human forces have been slowly decreasing. Not the least important effect of a more detached approach in this field has been that of limiting fears, of preventing them, that is, from irradiating widely beyond what can be realistically assessed as a threat. The former helplessness in the face of incomprehensible and unmanageable natural forces has slowly given way to a feeling of confidence, the concomitant, one might say, of increasing facilitation, of people's power to raise, in this sphere, the general level of well-being and to enlarge the area of security through the application of patient and systematic research.

But the growth of people's comprehension of natural forces and of the use made of them for human ends is associated with specific changes in human relationships; it goes hand in hand with the growing interdependence of growing numbers of people. The gradual acceleration in the increment of knowledge and use of non-human forces, bound up, as it is, with specific changes in human relations, has helped, in turn, to accelerate the process of change in the latter. The network of human activities tends to become increasingly complex, far-flung and closely knit. More and more groups, and with them more and more individuals, tend to become dependent on each other for their security and the satisfaction of their needs in ways which, for the greater part, surpass the comprehension of those involved. It is as if first thousands, then millions, then more and more millions walked through this world with their hands and feet chained together by invisible ties. No one is in charge. No one stands outside. Some want to go this way, others that. They fall upon each other and, vanquishing or defeated, still remain chained to each other. No one can regulate the movements of the whole unless a great part of them are able to understand, to see, as it were, from outside, the whole patterns they form together. And they are not able to visualize themselves as part of these larger patterns because, being hemmed in and moved uncomprehendingly hither and thither in ways which none of them intended, they cannot help being preoccupied with the urgent, narrow and parochial problems which each of them has to face. They can only look at whatever happens to them from their narrow location within the system. They are too deeply involved to look at themselves from without. Thus what is formed of nothing but human beings acts upon each of them, and is experienced by many as an alien external force not unlike the forces of nature.

The same process which has made people less dependent on the vagaries of nature has made them more dependent on each other. The changes which, with regard to non-human forces, have given people greater power and security have increasingly brought upon them different forms of insecurity. In their relations with each other, people are again and again confronted, as they were in the past in their dealings with non-human forces, with phenomena, with problems which, given their present approaches, are still beyond their control. They are incessantly faced with the task of adjusting themselves to changes which, though perhaps of their own making, were not intended by them. And as these changes frequently bring in their wake unforeseen gains for some and losses for others, they tend to go hand in hand with tensions and frictions between groups which, at the same time, are inescapably chained to each other. Tests of strength and the use of organized force serve often as costly means of adjustment to changes within this tangle of interdependencies; on many of its levels no other means of adjustment exist.

Thus, vulnerable and insecure as people are under these conditions, they cannot stand back and look at the course of events calmly like more detached observers. Again, it is, on the one hand, difficult for men in that situation to control more fully their own strong feelings with regard to events which, they feel, may deeply affect their lives, and to approach them with greater detachment, as long as their ability to control the course of events is small; and it is, on the other hand, difficult for them to extend their understanding and control of these events as long as they cannot approach them with greater detachment and gain greater control over themselves. Thus a circular movement between inner and outer controls, a feedback mechanism of a kind, is at work not only in people's relations with the non-human forces of nature, but also in their relations with each other. But it operates at present in these two spheres on very different levels. While in people's relations with non-human forces the standard of both the control of self and that of external events is relatively high, in relations of people with people the socially required and socially bred standard of both is considerably lower.

The similarities between this situation and that which humans had to face in past ages in their relations with the forces of nature are often obscured by the more obvious differences. We do already know that people can attain a considerable degree of control over natural phenomena impinging upon their lives and a fairly high degree of detachment in manipulating and in thinking of them. We do not know, and we can hardly imagine, how a comparable degree of detachment and control may be attained with regard to social phenomena. Yet for thousands of years it was equally impossible for those who struggled before us to imagine that one could approach and manipulate natural forces as we do. The comparison throws some light on their situation as well as on ours.

5

It also throws some light on the differences that exist today between the standards of certainty and achievement of the natural and the social sciences. It is often implied, if not stated explicitly, that the "objects" of the former, by their very nature, lend themselves better than those of the latter to an exploration by means of scientific methods ensuring a high degree of certainty. However, there is no reason to assume that social data, that the relations of persons, are less accessible to human comprehension than the relations of non-human phenomena, or that people's intellectual powers as such are incommensurate to the task of evolving theories and methods for the study of social data to a level of fitness comparable to that reached in the study of physical data. What is significantly different in these two fields is the situation of the investigators and, as part of it, their attitudes with regard to their "objects"; it is, to put it in a nutshell, the *relationship between "subjects" and "objects"*. In this relationship, if situation and attitudes are taken into account, the problems and the difficulties of an equal advance in the social sciences stand out more clearly.

The general aim of scientific pursuits is the same in both fields; stripped of a good many philosophical encrustations it is to find out in what way perceived data are connected with each other. But social as distinct from natural sciences are concerned with conjunctions of persons. Here, in one form or the other, people face themselves;[3] the "objects" are also "subjects". The task of social scientists is to explore, and to make people understand, the patterns they form together, the nature and the changing configuration of all that binds them to each other. The investigators themselves form part of these patterns. They cannot help experiencing them, directly or by identification, as immediate participants from within; and the greater the strains and stresses to which they or their groups are exposed, the more difficult is it for them to perform the mental operation, underlying all scientific pursuits, of detaching themselves from their role as immediate participants and from the limited vista it offers.

There is no lack of attempts in the social sciences at detaching oneself from one's position as an involved exponent of social events, and at working out a wider conceptual framework within which the problems of the day can find their place and their meaning. Perhaps the most persistent effort in that direction has been made by the great pioneering sociologists of the nineteenth and early twentieth centuries. But their work also shows most conspicuously the difficulties which, under present conditions, stand in the way of such an attempt. On the other hand, they all attempted to discover, from one angle or the other, the inherent order of the social development of mankind, its "laws", as some of them called it. They tried to work out a comprehensive and universally valid theoretical framework, within which the problems of their own age appeared as specific problems of detail and no longer as the central problem from which those of other ages received their relevance and their meaning. And yet, on the other hand, they were so deeply involved in the problems of their own society that they often viewed, in fact, the whole development of people's relations with each other in the light of the hopes and fears, the enmities and beliefs resulting from their role as immediate participants in the struggles and conflicts of their own time. These two forms of approach—one, more involved, which made them see the development of human society as a whole in the light of the pressing problems of their own time, and the other, more detached, which enabled them to visualize the short-term problems of their own time in the light of the long-term development of society—were so inextricably interwoven in their work that, in retrospect, it is difficult to sift one from the other, and to sort out their contribution to the development of a more universally valid system of theories about people in society from ideas relevant only as an expression of their own ideals and idiosyncrasies in the struggles of a particular historical period.

Since then, a good deal more factual material about social phenomena has been brought to light. The elaboration of a more impersonal body of theories, and their adjustment to a widening range of observed facts brought to light under their guidance, have considerably advanced in some social sciences, and advanced in some more than in others.[4] To a greater or lesser extent, research in all human sciences still tends to oscillate between two levels of consciousness and two forms of approach, the one more akin, one might say, to a simple geocentric, the other more to a heliocentric, approach. And the constant upsurge of the former in connection with acute social and political tensions effectively bars in most social sciences the steady continuity of research which has become so marked a characteristic of many natural sciences. The pressure of short-term problems which can no longer be solved in traditional ways, of social problems which appear to require for their solution procedures evolved and employed by scientific specialists, has increased together with the complexity of human relations itself. Fragmentation of social research has grown apace. Even as an aim of research, the idea of a wider theoretical framework connecting and unifying the problems and results of more limited inquiries has become more remote; to many it appears unattainable, to others, in addition, undesirable. For the immediate difficulties of people springing up in their own midst from the unmanageable forces of social change, from conflicts and frictions among themselves, have remained exceedingly great. The strength of involvement, within the social context of men's lives, if it has not actually increased, has hardly lessened.

Hence, whatever else may have changed since the days of pioneering sociologists, certain basic characteristics of the social sciences have not. For the time being, social scientists are liable to be caught in a dilemma. They work and live in a world in which almost everywhere groups, small and great, including their own groups, are engaged in a struggle for position and often enough for survival, some trying to rise and to better themselves in the teeth of strong opposition, some who have risen before trying to hold on to what they have, and some going down.

Under these conditions, the members of such groups can hardly help being deeply affected in their thinking about social events by the constant threats arising from these tensions to their way of life or to their standards of life and perhaps to their life. As members of such groups, scientific specialists engaged in the study of society share with others these vicissitudes. Their experience of themselves as upholders of a particular social and political creed which is threatened, as representatives of a specific way of life in need of defence, like the experience of their fellows, can hardly fail to have a strong emotional undertone. Group images, those, for instance, of classes or of nations, self-justifications, the cases which groups make out for themselves, represent, as a rule, an amalgam of realistic observations and collective fantasies (which, like the myths of simpler people, are real enough as motive forces of action). To sift out the former from the latter, to hold up before these groups a mirror in which they can see themselves as they might be seen, not by an involved critic from another contemporary group, but by an inquirer trying to see in perspective the structure and functioning of their relationship with each other, is not only difficult in itself for anyone whose group is involved in such a struggle; expressed in public, it may also weaken the cohesion and solidarity feeling of the group and, with it, its capacity to survive. There is, in fact, in all these groups a point beyond which none of its members can go in his or her detachment without appearing and, so far as their group is concerned, without becoming, a dangerous heretic, however consistent their ideas or their theories may be in themselves and with observed facts, however much they may approximate to what we call the "truth".

And yet, if social scientists, although using more specialized procedures and a more technical language, are in the last resort not much less affected in their approach to the problems of society by preconceived ideas and ideals, by passions and partisan views, than the man in the street, are they really justified in calling themselves "scientists"? Does any statement, any hypothesis or theory, deserve the epithet "scientific" if it is ultimately based on dogmatic beliefs, on *a priori* assumptions, on ideas and evaluations which are impervious to arguments based on a more systematic and dispassionate examination of the available evidence? Can social scientists make any specific contribution to the solution of major problems, even of their own groups, of their own country, class, profession or whatever it is, if they accept as the self-evident foundation of their theories some of the religiously held creeds and norms of one or the other of these groups, so that the results of their studies are destined from the start to agree, or at least not to disagree, with the basic tenets of these communal beliefs? Without greater detachment and autonomy of thinking, can they hope to put in the hands of their fellow-humans more fitting tools of thinking and more adequate blueprints for the handling of social and political problems—more adequate blueprints than those handed on unreflectingly from generation to generation or evolved haphazardly in the heat of the battle? And even if they do not accept such beliefs unquestioningly, are they not often impelled to use them as the general frame of reference for their studies simply by sentiments of solidarity, of loyalty or perhaps of fear? Are they not sometimes only too justified in thinking that it might weaken a cause which they regard as their own if they were to subject systematically the religiously held social creeds and ideals of one of their own groups to a more dispassionate scientific examination, that it might put weapons in the hands of opponents or that, as a result, they themselves might be exposed to ostracism, if to nothing worse?

The dilemma underlying many of the present uncertainties of the sciences of humans is, as one can see, not simply a dilemma of this or that historian, economist, political scientist or sociologist (to name only some of the present divisions); it is not the perplexity of individual social scientists, but that of social scientists as a professional group. As things stand, their social task as scientists and the requirements of their position as members of other groups often disagree; and the latter are apt to prevail as long as the pressure of group tensions and passions remains as high as it is.

The problem confronting them is not simply to discard the latter role in favour of the former. They cannot cease to take part in, and to be affected by, the social and political affairs of their groups and their time. Their own participation and involvement, moreover, is itself one of the conditions for comprehending the problems they try to solve as scientists. For while one need not know, in order to understand the structure of molecules, what it feels like to be one of its atoms—in order to understand the functioning of human groups one needs to know, as it were, from inside how human beings experience their own and other groups, and one cannot know without active participation and involvement.

The problem confronting those who study one or the other aspects of human groups is how to keep their two roles as participant and as inquirer clearly and consistently apart and, as a professional group, to establish in their work the undisputed dominance of the latter.

This is so difficult a task that many representatives of social sciences, at present, appear to regard the determination of their inquiries by preconceived and religiously held social and political ideals as inevitable. They often seem to consider these heteronomous foundations of their pronouncements as characteristic, not of a specific situation and, within it, of a specific dilemma, but of their subject-matter as such. The latitude they allow each other in their use of dogmatic ideals and evaluations as a basis for the setting of problems, the selection of material and the construction of theories is very wide—and is apt to become wider still whenever the pressure of tensions and passions mounts in society at large.

# 6

The chance which social scientists have to face and to cope with this dilemma might be greater if it were not for another characteristic of their situation which tends to obscure the nature of these difficulties. This is the ascendancy gained, over the centuries, by a manner or style of thinking which has proved highly adequate and successful in men's dealings with physical events, but which is not always equally appropriate if used in their dealings with others. One of the major reasons for the difficulties with which people have to contend in their endeavour to gain more reliable knowledge about themselves is the uncritical and often dogmatic application of categories and concepts, highly adequate in relation to problems on the level of matter and energy, to other levels of experience and, among them, to that of social phenomena. Not only are specific concepts of causation or of explanation formed in this manner generalized and used almost as a matter of course in inquiries about human relations; this mechanical diffusion of models expresses itself, too, for example, in the widespread identification of "rationality" with the use of categories developed mainly in connection with experiences of physical events, and in the assumption that the use of other forms of thinking must necessarily indicate a leaning towards metaphysics and irrationality.

The same tendency towards over-generalizing shows itself in many current ideas of what is and what is not scientific. By and large, theories of science still use as their principal model the physical sciences—often not in their contemporary, but in their classical form. Aspects of their procedures are widely regarded as the most potent and decisive factor responsible for their achievements and as the essential characteristic of sciences generally. By abstracting such aspects from the actual procedures and techniques of the physical sciences, one arrives at a general model of scientific procedure which is known as "the scientific method". In name, it represents the distinguishing characteristics common to all scientific, as distinct from non-scientific, forms of solving problems. In fact, it often constitutes a curious compound of features which may be universal with others characteristic of the physical sciences only and bound up with the specific nature of their problems. It resembles a general concept, "animal", formed without reference to the evolutionary diversity and connections of animal species from a rather restricted observational field, so that structures and functions common perhaps to all animals, as distinct from non-living things and from plants, mingle in it with others characteristic only of certain types of animals—of, say, mammals or of vertebrates.

The assumption is that in this generalized form "the scientific method" can be transferred from the field where it originated, from the physical sciences, to all other fields, to biological as well as to social sciences, regardless of the different nature of their problems; and that wherever it is applied it will work its magic. Among social scientists in particular it is not uncommon to attribute difficulties and inadequacies of their work to the fact that they do not go far enough in copying the method of physical sciences. It is this strong concentration of their attention on problems of "method" which tends to obscure from their view the difficulties that spring from their situation and from their own approaches to the problems they study.

The superior achievement and status of the physical sciences itself constitutes a highly significant factor in the situation of those who work in the field of social sciences. If, as participants in the life of a turbulent society, they are constantly in danger of using in their inquiries preconceived and immovable social convictions as the basis for their problems and theories, as scientists they are in danger of being dominated by models derived from inquiries into physical events and stamped with the authority of the physical sciences.

The fact that people confronted with the task of formulating and exploring new sets of problems model their concepts and procedures on those which have proved their worth in other fields is in no way surprising or unique. It is a recurrent feature in human history that new crafts and skills, and among them new scientific specialisms, in the early stages of their development, continue to rely on older models. Some time is needed before a new group of specialists can emancipate itself from the ruling style of thinking and of acting; and in the course of this process their attitude towards the older groups, as in other processes of emancipation, is apt to oscillate. They may go too far for a while and may go on too long in their uncritical submission to the authority and prestige of the dominant standards; and then again, they may go too far in their repudiation and in their denial of the functions which the older models had or have in the development of their own. In most of these respects the emergence of the younger social sciences from under the wings of the older natural sciences follows the usual pattern.

But there can rarely have been a situation in which the gradient between the comparatively high level of detachment manifest in the older branches of knowledge and the much lower represented by the younger branches was equally steep. In the physical sciences, it is not only the development and use of a specific method for the solution of problems and the testing of theories, but the framing of problems and theories itself, which presupposes a high standard of detachment. The same method transferred to social sciences is not infrequently used for the exploration of problems and theories conceived and studied under the impact of strong involvements. Hence the use, in social sciences, of a method akin to that evolved in the physical sciences often gives to the former the appearance of a high level of detachment or of "objectivity" which those who use this method are in fact lacking. It often serves as a means of circumventing difficulties which spring from their dilemma, without facing it; in many cases, it creates a façade of detachment masking a highly involved approach.

As a result, a crucial question is often regarded as sealed and solved which in fact is still in abeyance: the question of which of the procedures and techniques of the physical sciences are commensurate to the task of social sciences and which are not. The abstraction from these specific procedures of a general model of the scientific method, and the claim often made for it as the supreme characteristic of research that is scientific, have led to the neglect, or even to the exclusion from the field of systematic research, of wide problem areas which do not lend themselves easily to an exploration by means of a method for which the physical sciences have provided the prototype. In order to be able to use methods of this kind and to prove themselves scientific in the eyes of the world, investigators are frequently induced to ask and to answer relatively insignificant questions and to leave unanswered others perhaps of greater significance. They are induced to cut their problems so as to suit their method. The exclusive and seemingly final character of many current statements about the scientific method finds expression in the strange idea that problems which do not lend themselves to investigations by means of a method modelled on that of the physical sciences are no concern of people engaged in scientific research.

On closer investigation, one will probably find that the tendency to consider a highly formalized picture of this one set of sciences and their method as the norm and ideal of scientific inquiries generally is connected with a specific idea about the aim of sciences. It is, one might think, bound up with the assumption that among propositions of empirical sciences, as among those of pure mathematics and related forms of logic, the only relevant distinction to be made is that between propositions which are true and others which are false; and that the aim of scientific research and of its procedures is simply and solely that of finding the "truth", of sifting true from false statements. However, the goal towards which positive sciences are striving is not, and by their very nature cannot be, wholly identical with that of fields like logic and mathematics, which are concerned with the inherent order of certain tools of thinking alone. It certainly happens in empirical investigations that people make statements which are simply found to be false. But often enough rough dichotomies like "true" and "false" are highly inadequate in their case. People engaged in empirical research often put forward propositions or theories whose merit is that they are truer than others or, to use a less hallowed term, that they are *more* adequate, *more* consistent, both with observations and in themselves. In general terms, one might say it is characteristic of these scientific as distinct from non-scientific forms of solving problems that, in the acquisition of knowledge, questions emerge and are solved as a result of an uninterrupted two-way traffic between two layers of knowledge: that of general ideas, theories or models and that of observations and perceptions of specific events. The latter, if not sufficiently informed by the former, remains unorganized and diffuse; the former, if not sufficiently informed by the latter, remains dominated by feelings and imaginings. It is the objective of scientists, one might say, to develop a steadily expanding body of theories or models and an equally expanding body of observations about specific events by means of a continuous, critical confrontation leading to greater and greater congruity with each other. The methods actually used in empirical investigations inevitably vary a good deal from discipline to discipline in accordance with the different types of problems that present themselves for solution. What they have in common, what identifies them as scientific methods, is simply that they enable scientists to test whether their findings and pronouncements constitute a reliable advance in the direction of their common objective.

# 7

Is it possible to determine with greater precision and cogency the limitations of methods of scientific research modelled on those of the physical sciences? Can one, in particular, throw more light on the limits to the usefulness of mathematical or—as this term is perhaps too wide in this context—of quantifying models and techniques in empirical researches? At the present state of development, the weight and relevance of quantifying procedures clearly differ in different problem areas. In some, above all in the physical sciences, one can see today no limit to the usefulness of procedures which make relations of quantities stand for the non-quantitative aspects of the relations of data; the scope for reducing other properties to quantities and for working out, on the basis of such a reduction, highly adequate theoretical constructs appears to be without bounds.

In other fields of research the scope for similar reductions is clearly very much narrower; and theoretical constructs based on such reductions alone often prove far less adequate. Have problem areas which do not lend themselves as well as the physical sciences to the application of quantifying methods of research, certain general properties which can account for such differences in the scope and relevance of quantifying procedures as instruments of research?

It is possible to think that this problem itself can be readily solved in terms of quantities alone. As one passes from studies of matter and energy and its various transformations to those of organisms and their development as species and individuals, and again to studies of people as societies and individuals (in not quite the same sense of the word), according to a not uncommon view the problems which one encounters become more complex; the greater complexity is often thought to follow from the fact that the number of interacting parts, factors, variables or suchlike increases as one moves from the study of inorganic matter to those of organisms and of people; and as a result of this increase in numbers, so the argument seems to run, measurements and mathematical operations generally become more and more complicated and difficult. If one accepts the idea that it is the aim of scientific investigations everywhere to explain the behaviour of composite units of observation by means of measurements from that of their simpler constituent parts, each of the variables affecting the behaviour of such a unit would have to be measured by itself so as to determine the quantitative aspects of its relations with others. The greater the number of variables, the greater would be the number of measurements and the more complicated would be the mathematical operations necessary to determine their interplay. In the light of this hypothesis, the demands made on the resources in manpower, in computing machines, in mathematical techniques and in money and time would progressively increase from one set of sciences to the other with the increase in the number of factors that has to be taken into account. More and more, these demands would become prohibitive, and research on quantitative lines alone would no longer be possible. According to this view, it is for that reason that one has to resign oneself to the use of less precise and less satisfactory methods of investigation in many fields of study.

In a way, this approach to the observable limitations of quantifying methods in research is itself not uncharacteristic of the manner in which forms of thinking most serviceable in the exploration of physical data become distended into what almost represents a general style of thinking. The choice of a heap of more and more factors or variables as a model for increasing complexity is determined by a general expectation which is evidently based on experiences in physical research, but which tends to assume the character of an *a priori* belief: by the expectation that problems of all kinds can be satisfactorily solved in terms of quantities alone.

However, the area within which this expectation can be safely used as a guide to the formulation of problems and theories has very definite limits. The properties of different units of observation characteristic of different disciplines are affected not only by the number of interacting parts, variables, factors or conditions, but also by the manner in which constituents of such units are connected with each other. Perhaps the best way to indicate briefly this aspect of differences is the hypothetical construction of a model of models which represent different frames of reference of scientific problems in a highly generalized form, as composite units arranged according to the extent of interdependence of their constituents or, more generally, according to the degree of organization which they possess.

Arranged in this manner, this continuum of models would have one pole formed by general models of units, such as congeries, agglomerations, heaps or multitudes, whose constituents are associated with each other temporarily in the loosest possible manner and may exist independently of each other without changing their characteristic properties. The other pole would be framed by general models of units such as open systems and processes which are highly self-regulating and autonomous, which consist of a hierarchy of interlocking part-systems and part-processes, and whose constituents are interdependent to such an extent that they cannot be isolated from their unit without radical changes in their properties as well as in those of the unit itself.

Between these two poles would be spaced out intermediary models[5] graded according to the degree of differentiation and integration of their constituents.

As one moves along this continuum of models from paradigms of loosely composed units to others of highly organized units, as models of congeries step by step give way to those of self-regulating open systems and processes with more and more levels, many of the devices developed for scientific research into units of the first type change, or even lose, their function. In many cases, from being the principal instruments and techniques of research, they become, at the most, auxiliaries.

Less adequate, in that sense, becomes the concept of an independent variable of a unit of observation which is otherwise kept invariant and, with it, the type of observation and experimentation based on the supposition that what one studies is a heap of potentially independent variables and their effects.

Less adequate, too, becomes the concept of a scientific law as the general theoretical mould for particular connections of constituents of a larger unit. For it is one of the tacit assumptions underlying both the conception and the establishment of a scientific law, that the phenomena of which one wishes to state in the form of a law that the pattern of their connection is necessary and unchanging do not change their properties irreversibly if they are cut off from other connections or from each other. The type of relationship whose regularity can be fairly satisfactorily expressed in the form of a law is a relationship which is impermanent, though it has a permanent pattern: it can start and cease innumerable times without affecting the behaviour of other constituents of the larger nexus within which it occurs, or the properties of the larger nexus itself. General laws for particular cases, in short, are instruments for the solution of problems whose referential frame is conceived as a congeries.[6]

The more the framework of problems resembles in its characteristics a highly self-regulating system and process, the greater in other words the chance that constituents are permanently connected with each other so that they are bound to change their properties irrevocably if these connections are severed, the more likely is it that laws assume a subsidiary role as tools of research; and the more does one require, as the paramount vehicle for exploring and presenting regularities of part-connections, system- and process-models clearly representative of the fact that part-events are linked to each other as constituents of a functioning unit without which they would not occur or would not occur in this manner.

Nor do those time-honoured intellectual operations known as induction and deduction retain quite the same character throughout this continuum of models. In their classical form they are closely linked with intellectual movements up and down between discrete and isolated universals, which may be general concepts, laws, propositions or hypotheses, and an infinite multitude of particular cases which are also conceived as capable of preserving their significant characteristics if they are studied in isolation independently of all other connections.

When models of multitudes become subordinate to models of highly organized systems, another type of research operation gains greater prominence, modifying to some extent those of induction and deduction, namely movements up and down between models of the whole and those of its parts.

It is difficult to think of any well established terms expressing clearly the differential qualities and the complementary character of these two operations. Perhaps one might call "analytical" those steps of research in which the theoretical representation of a system is treated more or less as a background from which problems of constituent parts stand out as the prime object of research and as a potential testing-ground for theoretical representations of the whole; and one might call "synoptic" (not to say "synthetic") those steps which are aimed at forming a more coherent theoretical representation of a system as a whole as a unifying framework and as a potential testing-ground for relatively uncoordinated theoretical representations of constituent parts. But whatever the technical terms, one can say that the solution of problems whose framework represents a highly integrated unit depends in the long run on the coordination and balance between steps in both directions.

In the short run, synopsis may be in advance of analysis. Its theoretical results have in that case, at the worst, the character of speculations; at the best, if they are conformable to a larger body of observational and theoretical fragments, that of working hypothesis. Many of the ideas put forward by the pioneering sociologists of the nineteenth century, preoccupied as they were with the process of mankind as a whole, illustrate this stage. Or else analysis may be in advance of synopsis. In that case, knowledge consists of a plethora of observational and theoretical fragments for which a more unified theoretical framework is not yet in sight. A good deal of the work done by sociologists during part of the twentieth century can serve as an illustration of that stage. Many of them, in reaction from the more speculative aspects of the work done by the system-builders which preceded them, became distrustful of any overall view and of the very idea of "systems" itself; they confined themselves more and more to the exploration of isolated clusters of problems which could be explored as nearly as possible by methods used by representatives of other sciences, though they themselves lacked what these others already possessed: a more unified, more highly integrated system of theoretical constructs as a common frame of reference for isolated studies of part-connections.

In the case of units of observation such as multitudes and populations, it is an appropriate aim of research to develop theoretical models of a composite unit as a whole by treating it as the sum total of its components and by tracing back its properties to those of its parts. But this reduction of the whole to its parts becomes increasingly less appropriate if one moves within the continuum of models towards more highly organized units. As the constituents of such units lose their identity if their connection with others is broken off—as they become and remain what they are only as functioning parts of a functioning system of a specific type, or even of an individual system—the study of temporary isolates is useful only if its results are again and again referred back to a model of their system; the properties of parts cannot be adequately ascertained without the guidance provided by a theoretical model of the whole. At an early stage in the development of a particular field of problems, such models, like maps of largely unexplored regions, may be full of blanks and perhaps full of errors which can be corrected only by further investigations of parts. But however much one or the other may lag behind, studies on the level of the whole system and studies on the level of part-units are greatly impeded if they cannot rely on a measure of correspondence and coordination which allows scientists to move the focus of their observations and reflections freely from one level to the other.

8

The difficulty is that there are often more than two levels to be considered. Highly structured systems and processes often have parts which are also systems and processes; and these in turn may have parts which again are developing systems, though with a smaller measure of autonomy. In fact, such systems within systems, such processes within processes, may consist of many levels of varying relative strength and controlling power interlaced and interlocked with each other; so that those who are digging up knowledge on one of them stand in need of free channels of communication with others who are working in the many

galleries above and below and, at the same time, of a clear conception of
the position and functions of their own problem area, and of their own
situation, within the whole system. In practice, such lines of communication are often deficient or non-
existent. Problems on different levels are frequently investigated by dif-
ferent groups of specialists who hardly look beyond their particular
pitch. Many of them draw from limited experiences with problems characteristic of one level, or merely of one of its aspects, inferences for the
solution of problems whose frame of reference comprises many levels or
perhaps the whole system. And if one of these groups, if—as has in fact
happened—specialists for the study of units which represent a relatively
low level of organization, such as physicists, are greatly in advance of
others in the exploration of their level and the development of corresponding techniques, the unselective imitation of their models and
methods in studies of more highly organized units is likely to give rise to
a welter of misconceived problems.

For not only the whole system, but also each of its constituent systems, may display patterns of connections and regularities which are different and which cannot be deduced from those of their constituent
systems. Theoretical models and methods of research designed for the
study of units which are less differentiated and integrated can be, therefore, at best, only partially appropriate as means of research into more
highly organized units, even if the latter contain the former, or homologues of the former, as constituent parts.

There are many instances of the difficulties that can ensue from the
application of models designed for the study of part-systems at one level
of organization to that of systems at another level or of the paramount
system as a whole.

Take, for example, the old controversy about the usefulness of physical systems such as machines as explanatory models for biological systems such as animals and humans. If one adheres to the traditional way
of thinking, one can usually perceive only two possible solutions to the
focal problem of this controversy. One can either accept physical systems of one kind or the other as complete models for organisms and assume, explicitly or not, that an organism as a whole is a set of physical
events on exactly the same level as physical events outside organisms. Or
one can adopt vitalistic models and assume that special non-physical
forces are at work in organisms which account for the observable differences between living and non-living systems.

In order to accept either of these two alternatives, one has to stretch a
good many points. As in other cases in which it is difficult, not simply to

find a solution for a problem, but to think of any possible model for a solution which would fit the available evidence reasonably well, it is the type of available models rather than the evidence which requires re-examination. The difficulties with which people have met, at least since the days of Descartes, in tackling the question of whether or not living systems can be adequately explained by analogies with non-living systems, are closely bound up with the tradition of thinking which decrees that the behaviour of whole units has to be explained from that of their parts. It becomes less difficult to conceive of a more fitting model for the solution of this question if it is accepted that there are types of problems which require a different approach—problems which can be brought nearer solution only if one is aware that the units under observation have properties which cannot be inferred from those of their parts.

Human-made machines, as we know them, are homologues not of all, but only of some, levels in the hierarchic order of open systems represented even by animals of a simpler type. As each system of a higher order may have properties different from those lower-order systems which form its parts, and as animals rising in the evolutionary scale represent systems within systems on a steadily rising number of levels, one would expect the behaviour and characteristics of organisms to correspond only partially to those of machines or of chains of chemical reactions; one would expect organisms to display characteristics which are only in some regards similar to, but in others different from, physical systems, and yet to reveal themselves as nothing but heaps of physical particles if their many-levelled organization is destroyed or if component parts are studied in isolation.

But one could no longer expect, in that case, that all problems of organisms will be solved in the end by analogies with machines or with other physical systems, and that biological sciences will gradually transform themselves into physical sciences. In living systems physical processes are patterned and organized in a way which induces further patterning and organizing of these processes. Even if people should succeed in constructing artefacts with very many more and much higher levels of organization and control than those of any known machine, artefacts which could build and rebuild their own structure from less highly organized materials, which could grow and develop, feel and reproduce themselves, one would have to apply to their construction and to their study biological as well as physical categories and models.

In controversies between vitalists and mechanists, both sides take it more or less for granted that the model of explanation according to which studies in the properties of parts are expected to provide the key for the problems presented by those of the whole is a universal model. In fact, it is a specific and partial model appropriate only to the study of units on a relatively low level of organization.[7]

Or take the much discussed question of the relationship between the behaviour of higher animals and that of humans. Attempts to explain the latter in terms of the former are not uncommon. Yet, again, one cannot comprehend the functioning and structure of systems which embody a higher level of organization and control only in terms of others which are less highly organized, even if the former are the descendants of the latter. While people function partly as other animals do, as a whole they function and behave in a way no other animal does.

The change towards greater cortical dominance (to mention only one aspect of these differences) provides a useful illustration of the way in which an increase in the controlling and coordinating power of a part-system on a very high level in the hierarchy of interlocking systems goes hand in hand with changes in the equilibrium and the functioning of systems on all levels, and with a transmogrification of the overall system itself. It is to differences such as these that one will have to turn in order to establish more clearly and more firmly that—and why it is so that—the sciences of humans cannot be expected to transform themselves, sooner or later, into a branch of the biological sciences, even though results of studies into aspects of humans within the competency of the latter form an integral element of the former.

Finally, similar problems and similar difficulties can be found, again on a different level and in a different form, in the long-drawn-out dispute about the relationship of "individual" and "society". Again, one seems to be left with the choice between two equally unsatisfactory alternatives. However much one may try one's hand at some kind of compromise, on the whole, opinions are so far arrayed in two more or less irreconcilable camps. One can place oneself nearer those who think of societies as heaps or masses of individual people and of their properties and their development, simply as the outcome of individual intentions and activities; and one can place oneself nearer those who think of societies, of social processes in all their various aspects, more or less as if they existed in some sense outside and apart from the individual people by whom they are formed.

Common to both sides, again, is a style of thinking, an idea as to how phenomena ought to be explained, which has been found most serviceable in men's attempts to explain, and to gain control over, physical events. But in this case the impasse is not only due to the uncritical transfer of models of thinking from one field to another. Attempts to work out better theoretical models for the relationship of individual and society suffer even more from the fact that this relationship has become, in our age, one of the focal points, if not *the* focal point, in the clash of value systems, of social beliefs and ideals which divide some of the most powerful groupings of men. In society at large, the question of what the rights and duties of individuals in society *ought* to be, or whether the well-being of society *ought* to be considered as more important than that of individuals, and other questions of this kind, are evocative of a wide range of practical issues which are highly controversial. Answers to such questions form in many cases the shibboleth by which followers of different social and political creeds recognize friend and foe. As a result, reinforced as it constantly is by tensions and passions of rivalling groups, the question as to what the relationship of individual and society ought to be tends to mask and to muffle in discussions and studies the question as to what kind of relationship it actually is—so much so that the simple question of fact often appears to be almost incomprehensible. And as it happens that this factual question is representative of one of the basic problems of the social sciences, the difficulties which stand in the way of any attempt to distinguish and to detach it clearly from the topical social and political questions which are often expressed in similar terms, constitute one of the major barriers to the further development of the social sciences, and particularly to that of sociology.

What has been said, so far, about other types of part-whole relationships can be of some help, if not in solving, at least in clarifying this problem. In many respects the relationship between people as individuals and people as societies differs from these other types. It is quite unique, and not all its features fit entirely in the schema of a part-whole relationship. At the same time, it shows many of its characteristics and presents many of the problems generally associated with it.

All societies, as far as one can see, have the general characteristics of systems with sub-systems on several levels of which individuals, as individuals, form only one. Organized as groups, individuals form many others. They form families; and then again on a higher level, as groups of groups, villages or towns, classes or industrial systems and many similar structures which are interlocked and which may form with each other an overall system, such as tribes, city-states, feudal kingdoms or nation-states, with a dynamic power equilibrium of its own. This, in turn, may form part of another less highly organized, less well integrated system; tribes may form with each other a federation of tribes, nation-states a balance-of-power system. In this hierarchy of interlocking social units the largest unit need not be the most highly integrated and organized unit; so far in the history of humanity it never has been. But whatever form it may take, that system in the hierarchy of systems which constitutes the highest level of integration and organized power is also the system which has the highest capacity to regulate its own course. Like other open systems, it can disintegrate if the pressure of tensions from within or without becomes too strong. As long as its organization remains more or less intact, it has a higher degree of autonomy than any of its constituents.

And it is the structure and development of this system which in the last resort determine those of its part-systems, including those of its individual members. Different levels in this hierarchy of systems, such as individuals as such or as families or classes, have a greater or smaller measure of autonomy; they may, for example, cooperate or they may fight with each other. But the scope for autonomous actions varies with the properties of the paramount system as well as with the location of part-units within it; and so does the basic personality structure of its individual members. For on the properties and the development of this system depend those of the institutionalized set of relationships which we call "family"; this, in turn, induces the organization and integration of functions in individual children who as adults will be called upon to carry on, to develop and perhaps to change the institutions of the paramount system which, by means of this and of other homeostatic devices, is enabled to perpetuate at least some of its distinguishing characteristics.

Thus unique as the relationship of "individual" and "society" is, it has this in common with other part-whole relationships characteristic of highly organized, self-regulating systems: that the regularities, the attributes and the behaviour of systems on different levels, and above all those of the paramount system itself, cannot be described simply in terms appropriate to those of their parts; nor can they be explained as effects of which their constituents are the cause. And yet they are nothing outside and apart from these constituents.

Those who approach social phenomena, wittingly or unwittingly, as if societies were nothing but heaps of individual people, and who try to explain the former in terms of the latter, cannot conceive of the fact that groups formed by individuals, like other organizations of part-units, have properties of their own which remain unintelligible for an observer if his attention is focused on individual people as such and not, at the same time, on the structures and patterns which individuals form with each other.

Those who approach social phenomena, wittingly or not, as if these phenomena existed independently of the individuals by whom they are formed, are usually aware of the fact that phenomena of this kind have their irreducible regularities. But expecting, as they have been trained to expect, that the regularities of composite units can be deduced from those of their parts, and perhaps puzzled by the fact that they cannot deduce the social regularities which they observe simply and clearly from individual regularities, they tend to fall into a manner of speaking and thinking which suggests that social phenomena exist in some sense independently of individual people. They tend to confuse "having regularities of their own" with "having an existence of their own", in the same way in which the fact that organisms have regularities which cannot be deduced from those of unorganized physical events is often interpreted as a sign that something in organisms has an existence independent of physical events. Here as elsewhere, the inability to think in terms of systems leaves people with the choice between two equally unpalatable alternatives—that between atomistic and hypostatic conceptions.

Some problems cannot be brought nearer solution mainly because one has not sufficient facts to go on, others mainly because, as problems, they are misconceived: general ideas, types of classes, the whole manner of thinking, may be malformed or simply inadequate as a result of an uncritical transfer of intellectual models from one context to another. Some of the difficulties encountered in social sciences are of this type. They are due to insufficiencies, not so much in the knowledge of facts as in the basic ideas, categories and attitudes used in making observations of, and in handling, facts. Since people conceived the idea that one might explore not only physical but also social phenomena, as it were, scientifically, those who tried to do so have always been more or less under the influence of two types of models developed, in different contexts, by two more powerful groups: models of setting and solving problems about social phenomena current in society at large, and those of dealing with problems about "nature" developed by natural scientists. It is a question of how far either of these two types of model is suited to scientific inquiries into social phenomena. By raising it, one adumbrates the need for re-examination of a wider problem: that of the nature and acquisition of human knowledge generally.

Models of the first type are often used unintentionally by social scientists. They are concerned with phenomena from a sphere of life in which the contingency of unmanageable dangers is continuously high; it is difficult for them to disengage the ideas and concepts they use in their specialized work as scientists from those used day by day in their social life. The hypothetical model used for the study of problems of this kind is a continuum of which one marginal pole is formed by properties of persons and their situation characteristic of complete involvement and complete lack of detachment (such as one might find in the case of young babies), and the other of properties characteristic of complete detachment and a zero-point of involvement.

Models of the second type, those of natural sciences, are often, though not always, copied deliberately by social scientists; but they do not always examine, at the same time, in what respect these models are consonant with their specific task. Pressed by uncertainties not unconnected with the strength of their involvements, they are apt to seize upon these models as ready-made and authoritative means for gaining certainty, often enough without distinguishing clearly whether it is certainty about something worth knowing or something rather insignificant which they have gained in this way. As one has seen, it is this mechanical transfer of models from one scientific field to another which often results in a kind of pseudo-detachment, in a malformation of problems and in severe limitations of topics for research. The hypothetical model used for the study of problems of this kind is a continuum of models of composite units arranged according to the degree of interdependence of part-units. By and large, problems of the physical sciences have as their frame of reference concepts of units with a relatively low degree of organization. Problems referring to units of an equally low degree of organization—for example, to populations in the statistical sense of the word—are not lacking in the social sciences. But in their case units of this type are always parts of other far more highly organized units. Types of concepts, of explanations and procedures used for inquiries into the former are, at best, only of limited use in scientific studies of the latter; for in their case, in contrast to that of units of low organization, the knowledge one has gained about properties of isolated parts can only be assessed and interpreted in the light of the knowledge one has gained of properties of the whole unit.

If it is difficult for social scientists to attain greater autonomy of their scientific theories and concepts in relation to public creeds and ideals which they may share, it is no less difficult for them to gain greater autonomy in the development of their scientific models in relation to those of the older, more firmly established and successful physical sciences. The crucial question is whether it is possible to make much headway towards a more detached, more adequate and autonomous manner of thinking about social events in a situation where people in groups, on many levels, constitute grave dangers for each other. Perhaps the most significant insight to be gained from such reflections is the awareness of what has been named here, inadequately enough, the "principle of increasing facilitation": the lower the social standards of control in manipulating objects and of detachment and adequacy in thinking about them, the more difficult is it to raise these standards. How far it is possible under present conditions for groups of scientific specialists to raise the standards of autonomy and adequacy in thinking about social events and to impose upon themselves the discipline of greater detachment, only experience can show. Nor can one know in advance whether or not the menace which human groups on many levels constitute for each other is still too great for them to be able to bear, and to act upon, an overall picture of themselves which is less coloured by wishes and fears and more consistently formed in cross-fertilization with dispassionate observation of details. And yet how else can one break the hold of the vicious circle in which high affectivity of ideas and low ability to control dangers coming from people to people reinforce each other?

## Notes

1. It is still the prevalent practice to speak of psychological characteristics and of social characteristics of people not only as different, but as separable and, in the last resort, independent sets of properties. And if this is the assumption underlying one's form of discourse, terms like "involved" and "detached", as they are used here, must appear as equivocal and vague. They have been chosen in preference to other perhaps more familiar terms precisely because they do not fall in line with linguistic usages which are based on the tacit assumption of the ultimate independence of psychological and social properties of humans. They do not suggest, as some current scientific concepts do, that there are two separate sets of human functions or attributes, one psychological and one social in character, which communicate with each other only occasionally during a limited span of time with a definite beginning and a definite end by means of those one-way connections which we call "causes-and-effects", and then withdraw from each other until a new causal connection is established again with a definite beginning and a definite end.

Both these terms express quite clearly that changes in a person's relation with others and psychological changes are distinct but inseparable phenomena. The same holds good of their use as expressions referring to people's relation to "objects" in general. They seem preferable to others which, like "subjective" and "objective", suggest a static and unbridgeable divide between two entities, "subject" and "object". To give a brief and all too simple example of their meaning in this context: a philosopher once said, "If Paul speaks of Peter he tells us more about Paul than about Peter." One can say, by way of comment, that in speaking of Peter he is always telling us something about himself as well as about Peter. One would call his approach "involved" as long as his own characteristics, the characteristics of the perceiver, overshadow those of the perceived. If Paul's propositions begin to tell more about Peter than about himself the balance begins to turn in favour of detachment.

2. This concept has been introduced here in preference to the distinction between scientific procedures which are "value-free" and others which are not. It rather confuses the issue if the term "value", in its application to sciences, is reserved to those "values" which intrude upon scientific theories and procedures, as it were, from outside. Not only has this narrow use of the word led to the odd conclusion that it is possible to sever the connection between the activity of "evaluating" and the "values" which serve as its guide; it has also tended to limit the use of terms like "value" or "evaluation" in such a way that they seem applicable only in cases of what is otherwise known as "bias" or "prejudice". Yet even the aim of finding out the relatedness of data, their inherent order or, as it is sometimes expressed, at approximating to the "truth", implies that one regards the discovery of this relatedness or of the "truth" as a "value". In that sense, every scientific endeavour has moral

implications. Instead of distinguishing between two types of sciences, one of which is "value-free" while the other is not, one may find it both simpler and more apposite to distinguish in scientific pronouncements between two types of evaluations, one autonomous, the other heteronomous, of which one or the other may be dominant.

3. The problem of "facing oneself" is no doubt far more complex than can be shown here. It plays its part in explorations of nature as well as in those of society. For humans form part of both. Every major change in people's conception of nature, therefore, goes hand in hand with a change of the picture they have of themselves. So does any change in their conception of the social universe. Success and failure of any attempt to change from a more involved to a more detached view of social phenomena are bound up with the capacity of people to revise the picture they have of themselves in accordance with the results of more methodical studies, and often enough in a way which runs counter to deeply felt beliefs and ideals. In that respect the problem of increasing detachment in the social sciences is hardly different from that which plays its part in the development of the natural sciences.

However, it must still be regarded as an open problem how far people are capable of "facing themselves", of seeing themselves as they are without the shining armour of fantasies shielding them from suffering past, present and future. It is fairly safe to say that their capacity to do so grows and declines with the degree of security which they enjoyed and enjoy. But it probably has its limits.

However that may be, at present such problems can be discussed only in societies which demand and produce a high degree of individualization and in which people are being brought up to experience themselves, more perhaps than ever before, as beings set apart from each other by very strong walls. There can be little doubt that the picture of self which is thus built up in the growing person makes it rather difficult to envisage oneself in a more detached manner as forming patterns with others, and to study the nature and structure of these patterns as such.

4. The evident differences in the levels of development of different social sciences have perhaps not attracted quite the attention they deserve as a subject of research. Like the differences in the development of natural and social sciences generally, they are relevant to any theory of knowledge and of sciences.

To set out here more comprehensively the problems raised by such differences would require an exposition of the wider theory of knowledge implied in these observations on detachment and involvement; it would require fuller elaboration of the general conceptual framework that has been used here and within which, as one has seen, the development of scientific thinking, as of thinking in general, and that of changes in the situation of those who think, instead of being allotted to largely independent fields of studies, are linked to each other as different, but inseparable and interdependent, facets of the same process. Only with the help of such an integrating framework is it possible to determine with greater precision different stages and levels of thinking and knowing, whether or not one adopts concepts like "level of detachment", "level of fitness", "level of control" and others which have been used here.

On these lines, one might say, for example, that, under present conditions, anthropologists have a better chance of developing theories on human relations to a higher level of fitness than, say, those engaged in the study of highly differentiated societies to which they themselves belong or which are antagonists or partners of societies to which they belong; they have a better chance, not only because it is easier to survey, and to form relatively fitting theories about, social units which are small and not too complex in structure, but also because the investigators themselves are, as a rule, less directly involved in the problems they study. Anthropologists, in most cases, study societies to which they do not belong, other sociologists mostly societies of which they are members.

But in saying this, one refers only to one facet of the relationship between the mode of thinking and the situation of those who think. To complete the nexus one would have to add that the more detached theoretical tools of thinking which anthropologists have a chance to build up in accordance with their specific situation, can themselves act, within certain limits, as a shield against the encroachment upon their scientific work, and perhaps even on their personal outlook, of more involved, more emotive forms of thinking, even if tensions mount between social units to which they belong as participant members and others in relation to which they play mainly the part of investigators.

Here, too, in comparative studies on the development of social sciences, it may be more appropriate and more profitable to focus on the relations of observers and observed than on either of them or on "methods" alone.

5. Even in the elementary form in which it is presented here, such a serial model may help to clarify the confusion that often arises from an all too clear-cut dichotomy between congeries and systems. Not all frames of reference of physical problems cluster narrowly around the congeries pole of the model. Not all frames of reference of biological or sociological problems have their equivalent close to the other pole. They are, in each of these areas of inquiry, more widely scattered than it is often assumed. And although, in each of these areas, their bulk can probably be assigned to a specific region of the serial model, frames of reference of the problems of different disciplines, projected on this model, frequently overlap.

6. In the case of the second law of thermodynamics, an experimental and statistical law has been interpreted as a statement about qualities possessed by the referential system as a whole, that is, by the physical universe. However, if one may use experiences in other fields as a model, it is not always safe to assume that properties observed as those of constituent parts of a system are also properties of the system as a whole. Whether or not one is justified, in this case, to assume that regularities observed in a part-region of a system, in a part-region of both time and space, can be interpreted as regularities of the whole system, only physicists are entitled to judge.

However, these general considerations about laws are hardly affected by this case. In physics as in other scientific disciplines the referential framework of problems is far from uniform. Although, in the majority of cases, the units of observation are simply conceived as heaps, there are others in which they are envisaged as units endowed with properties approaching to those of systems. But compared with the models of systems and processes developed in some of the biological and some of the social sciences, those which have been produced in physical sciences show, on the whole, a relatively high independence of parts and a relatively low degree of organization.

This may or may not account for the fact that although the status of laws, in the classical sense of the word, has to some extent declined in the physical sciences with the ascendance of models which have some of the characteristics of systems, the change does not appear to be very pronounced. What apparently has become more pronounced is the implied expectation that the diverse laws discovered in studies of isolated connections will eventually coalesce and form with each other a comprehensive theoretical scaffolding for the behaviour of the overall system as a whole. Perhaps it is not yet quite clear why one should expect that the unconnected clusters of connections whose regularities one has more or less reliably determined will subsequently link up and fall into pattern. To expect that they will do so, at any rate, means assuming that in the end all congeries including that of energy-matter will turn out to be systems of a kind, or aspects and parts of systems.

7. One need hardly say that the same argument holds good with regard to the old dispute about the relationship of what is traditionally called "body" and "mind". In this case

too proposals for the solution of the problem on purely physical and on metaphysical lines are usually representative of the same style of thinking, and equally inept. They may be monistic or dualistic; they may credit the "mind" with qualities of "matter", or "matter" with qualities of the "mind"—all these propositions trying to account for the whole in terms of its parts.

# 13

## Observations on Gossip

Gossip . . . has always two poles, those who gossip and those about whom they gossip. In cases in which subjects and objects of gossip belong to different groups, the frame of reference is not only the group of gossipers but the situation and structure of both groups and their relationship with each other. Without this wider frame of reference the crucial question why group gossip can ever be, as it was in the case of "village" gossip about Estate people, an effective device for wounding and humiliating members of another group and for ensuring one's ascendency over them cannot be answered.

A good deal of what "villagers" habitually said about Estate families was vastly exaggerated or untrue. The majority of Estate people did not have "low morals"; they did not constantly fight with each other, were not habitual "boozers" or unable to control their children. Why were they powerless to correct these misrepresentations? Why could they be put to shame if a "villager" used in their presence a humiliating code word, symbol of their lower status such as "rat alley"? Why could they not shrug it off or retaliate with an equally massive flood of insinuations and distortions?

Some of the organisational explanations have already been mentioned. The "villagers" were more united than Estate people; in relation to them they closed their ranks, and their unity lent strength and veracity to their statements about the Estate people however out of tune they were in relation to the facts. The Estate people could not retaliate because they had not the power. But in order to see the configuration in depth, one has to include in one's picture in addition to its organisational aspects, such as the monopolisation of key positions by members of the old families' network, also its personal aspects. The majority of the Estate people could not retaliate because, to some extent, their own conscience was on the side of the detractors. They themselves agreed with the "village" people that it was bad not to be able to control one's children or to get drunk and noisy and violent. Even if none of these reproaches could be applied to themselves personally, they knew only too

From *The Established and the Outsiders*, pp. 101–5

well that they did apply to some of their neighbours. They could be shamed by allusions to this bad behaviour of their neighbours because by their living in the same neighbourhood the blame, the bad name attached to it, according to the rules of affective thinking, was automatically applied to them too. In their case, as in so many others, blemishes observable in some members of a group were emotionally transferred to all members of the group. The rejecting gossip of the "village", all the open or whispered expressions of reproach and contempt levelled against the Estate people, had power over them, however decent and orderly they were in their own conduct, because part of themselves, their own conscience, agreed with the "villagers'" low opinion of their neighbourhood. It was this silent agreement which paralysed their ability to retaliate and to assert themselves. They could be put to shame if someone called out a derogatory name applied to the group to which they belonged or accused them, directly or indirectly, of misdeeds and bad qualities which, in fact, could be found in their group only among the "minority of the worst".

The attribution of blame or for that matter of praise to individuals who, individually, have done nothing to deserve it, because they belong to a group which is said to deserve it, is a universal phenomenon. People can often disarm or silence others with whom they disagree or fight by throwing in their teeth some disparaging and vilifying group name or pieces of shameful gossip which refer to their group provided they themselves belong to a group which successfully claims a superior status compared to that of their opponents. In all these cases the objects of the attack are unable to hit back because, though personally innocent of the accusations or reproaches, they cannot discard, not even in their own mind, the identification with the stigmatised group. Vilifications setting in motion the socially inferior group's own sense of shame or guilt feelings with regard to some inferiority symbols, some signs of the worthlessness attributed to them and the paralysis of their power to strike back which goes hand in hand with it, thus form part of the social apparatus with which socially dominant and superior groups maintain their dominion and their superiority over socially inferior groups. Individual members of the inferior group are always supposed to be tarred by the same brush. They cannot escape from the group stigmatisation individually, just as they cannot escape individually from the lower status of their group. One often speaks and thinks today as if individuals in contemporary societies were no longer bound to their groups as tightly as individuals were in former days when they were bound to clans, tribes, castes or estates and were judged and treated accordingly. But the difference is at the most a difference of degrees. The example of the Estate people in Winston Parva showed, in miniature, the extent to which the fate of individuals, through identification by others and by themselves, can be dependent even in contemporary societies on the character and situation of one of their groups. Merely by living in a specific neighbourhood individuals were judged and treated, and to some extent judged themselves, in accordance with the image which others had of their neighbourhood. And this dependence of individuals on the standing and the image of groups to which they belong, the profound identification of the former with the latter in the assessment of others and in their own self-esteem, is not confined to social units with a high degree of individual social mobility such as neighbourhoods. There are others, such as nations, classes or ethnic minority groups, where the bonds of identification of individuals with their group and their participation by proxy in the collective attributes are far less elastic. The collective disgrace attached to such groups by other more powerful groups and embodied in standard invectives and stereotyped blame-gossip usually has a deep anchorage in the personality structure of their members as part of their individual identity and as such cannot be easily shaken off.

And an equally deep anchorage in the personality structure of individuals has its counterpart, the belief in the collective grace or virtue which many groups attribute to themselves and which may be attributed to them by other groups whom they regard as inferior. The mild form of such a group charisma which the "villagers"—particularly the members of the old families' network—felt they possessed is an example. It formed a focal point of the image they had of themselves—not as single individuals, but as a collective, as members of this particular group. It helped to make their life together and their endeavour to preserve it more meaningful.

But the group charismatic claim performed its binding function—its function as group preserver—as in other cases only by setting up sharp barriers against other groups whose members were, according to it, for ever excluded from participation in the grace and virtues attributed to those who belonged. By thus elevating the group's own members, the group charisma automatically relegated members of other interdependent groups to a position of inferiority. The group charisma claimed by the old "village" group had its sting. It did not simply help to define the boundaries between those who belonged and those who did not belong. It also had the function of a weapon which held outsiders at bay, which helped to preserve the purity and integrity of the group. It was a weapon of defence as well as a weapon of attack. It implied that it was a sign of disgrace not to participate in the grace and the specific virtues which the members of the distinguished group claimed for themselves. What one observed in the "village" was only a moderate small-scale example of a pattern which one can observe, often in a much more tense and virulent form, in the relation of many old established groups, nations, classes, ethnic majorities, or whatever their form may be, to their outsider groups whether they are effectively kept in their place or are already rising. Everywhere group charisma attributed to oneself and group disgrace attributed to outsiders are complementary phenomena. And, as in the "village", everywhere these twin phenomena find their expression in stereotyped forms of praise for oneself and of blame, of group invectives and group abuse, directed against the outsiders. Even the least "worthy" members of charismatic groups tend to claim for themselves by identification characteristics and values attributed to the whole group and to be found in practice perhaps only as attributes of the "minority of the best".

Once more one can see how closely the structure of gossip is bound up with that of the gossiping group. What has been observed before as "praise gossip" veering towards idealisation and "blame gossip" veering towards stereotyped abuse are phenomena closely connected with the belief in one's own group charisma and the others' group disgrace. In old established groups, in groups where young people and perhaps their parents and parents' parents have absorbed such beliefs with the corresponding symbols of praise and abuse from childhood on, positive and negative group images of this kind deeply impregnate the individual's personal image. The collective identity, and as part of it the collective pride and the group charismatic claims, help to fashion his individual identity in his own as well as in other people's experience. No individual grows up without this anchorage of his personal identity in the identification with a group or groups, even though it may remain tenuous and may be forgotten in later life, and without some knowledge of the terms of praise and abuse, of the praise gossip and blame gossip, of the group superiority and group inferiority which go with it.

# 14

## Time and Timing

This is an essay on time, but it is not concerned with time alone. One may notice soon enough that it also deals with a wider problem. For the perception of events which happen one after another as a 'sequence in time' presupposes the emergence within the world at large of beings, such as humans, who are capable of remembering distinctly what happened earlier and of seeing it in their minds' eyes as a single picture, together with what happened later and what is happening now. To perceive time, in other words, requires focusing-units (humans) capable of forming a mental picture in which events A, B, C, following one after another, are present together and yet, at the same time, are seen clearly as not having happened together; it requires beings with a specific potential for synthesis which is activated and patterned by experience. The potential for this kind of synthesis is a property peculiar to human beings; it is characteristic of their way of orienting themselves. Humans orient themselves less than any other creature we know by means of unlearned reactions and, more than any other creature, by perceptions which are patterned by learning, by previous experiences, not only of each human being individually, but also of long chains of human generations. This capacity for intergenerational learning, for handing on experiences of one human generation to another in the form of knowledge, is the basis of the gradual improvement and extension of their means of orientation over the centuries.

That which one today conceptualizes and experiences as 'time' is just that: a means of orientation. As such, it had to be evolved through experience in a long intergenerational process of learning. There is ample evidence to show that human beings did not always experience connections of events in the manner now symbolically represented by the concept 'time'. The potential for synthesis with which they are equipped had to be activated and patterned by experience and, specifically, by a long line of intergenerational experiences, before humans were capable of having the kind of mental picture of time-sequences which we now possess. In other words, humankind's experience of what is now called 'time' has

From *Time: An Essay*, pp. 37–58

changed in the past and continues to change today; it has changed and is changing, moreover, not in a random or historical manner, but in a structured and directional manner which can be explained. The task of this essay is to show, in broad outline, some aspects of the structure and direction of these changes and to indicate how one might set about explaining them. Basically, the salient points of this programme are simple enough.

1. From Descartes to Kant and beyond, the dominant hypothesis concerning time was based on the assumption that humans were endowed, as it were by nature, with specific ways of connecting events, of which that of time was one. It was assumed, in other words, that the synthesis of events in the form of time-sequences patterned humankind's perception prior to any experience and was, therefore, neither dependent on any knowledge available in their society nor acquired through learning. The assumption of such a 'synthesis *a priori*' implied that humans possessed not only a *general* capacity for establishing connections, but also a compulsory capacity for making *specific* connections and for forming corresponding concepts such as 'time', 'space', 'substance', 'natural laws', 'mechanical causation' and others, which were thus made to appear as unlearned and unchanging.

I am going to show that this hypothesis is untenable. Humans possess, as part of their natural endowment, a general potential for synthesis, that is, for connecting events, but all the specific connections which they establish and the corresponding concepts used by them in their communications and reflections are the result of learning and experience, not simply of each individual human being, but of a very long line of human generations handing on knowledge and learning from one to the other: an individual life is far too short for the learning process needed in order to acquire the knowledge of specific connections such as those represented by concepts like 'cause', 'time' and others of equal universality. The philosophical view that people connect events in the form of 'time', as it were, automatically and without any learning, by means of a 'synthesis *a priori*' as a gift of their native reason, was due partly to the limited evidence available to—or used by—Descartes, Kant and others who followed in their footsteps, and partly to their concept of experience: when speaking of experience, they had in mind only the experience of a single person conceived as a totally autonomous entity and not the experience and knowledge of humankind as it grows over the centuries.

2. The idea that people have always experienced the sequences of events which one now experiences as time-sequences in the manner which predominates today—namely, as an even, uniform and continu-

ous flow—runs counter to evidence we have from past ages as well as from our town. Einstein's correction of the Newtonian time-concept is a contemporary example of the way in which the concept of time can change. Einstein made it clear that the Newtonian hypothesis of time as a unitary and uniform continuum throughout the whole of the physical universe was untenable. If one takes the trouble to look at earlier stages in the development of human societies one can find ample evidence of corresponding changes in people's experience and conceptualization of what we now call 'time'. As used today, 'time' is a concept at a high level of generalization and synthesis[1] which presupposes a very large social fund of knowledge about ways of measuring time-sequences and about their regularities. At an earlier stage people evidently could not have had this knowledge—not because they were less 'intelligent' but because this knowledge, by its very nature, required a long time to develop.

Among the earliest time-meters were the movements of the sun, moon and stars. We have a very clear picture of the connections and regularities of these movements; our ancestors had not. If one goes back far enough one encounters stages where people were not yet in a position to link the varied and complex movements of the heavenly bodies to each other in the form of a relatively well-integrated unitary picture. They experienced a great mass of single items without clear connections or, at the most, rather unstable fantasy connections. If one has no firm yardstick for timing events one cannot have a concept of time akin to ours. Furthermore, at an earlier stage people communicated with each other— and thought—in what are often called today more 'concrete' terms. As no concept can be, properly speaking, regarded as 'concrete', it would probably be more correct to speak of 'particularizing' or 'low-level' abstractions. There were stages at which people used the concept 'sleep' where we would speak of 'night', the concept 'moon' where we would speak of 'month', the concept 'harvest' or 'produce of the year' where we would speak of 'year'. One of the difficulties one encounters in an essay on time is the absence of a developmental theory of abstraction. The changes just mentioned from particularizing to generalizing abstractions are among the most significant developmental changes one encounters in this context, but there will not be enough room here to enlarge upon it. Moreover, specific time-units such as 'day', 'month', 'year', etc., which now flow smoothly into each other in accordance with our calendar and with other time regulations, did not always do so in the past. In fact, it is the development of time-reckoning in social life and of a relatively well-integrated grid of time-regulators such as continuous clocks, continuous yearly calendars and era time-scales girding the centuries (we live in the 'twentieth century Anno Domini') which is an indispensable condition of the experience of time as an even, uniform flow. Where the former is lacking the latter is lacking too.

3. A model of the development of time-concepts enables one to see more clearly the growth of the relative autonomy of society within nature. There are earlier stages where the social enclave within nature built by humans is small. The interdependence between these enclaves and what we now call, in our self-centered manner, 'our environment' is obvious and direct. The balance of power between human groups forming these enclaves and non-human nature is weighted more strongly in favour of the latter; and the timing of social events is largely dependent on observations about recurrent, natural and non-human events. As the human enclaves grow in size as well as in relative autonomy—in the course of processes such as urbanization, commercialization and mechanization—their dependence on human-made devices with the function of time-meters and time-regulators grows and that on non-human, natural time-meters such as the movements of the moon, the changing seasons, the coming and going of the tides, diminishes. In the highly urbanized and industrialized societies of our age the relationship between the changing calendar-units and the changing seasons, while not entirely disappearing, becomes more indirect and tenuous, and, in some cases, such as that between the month and the movements of the moon, it has more or less vanished. People live, to a much greater extent, within a world of symbols of their own making. The relative autonomy of their social enclaves, without ever becoming absolute, has vastly increased. One may add that the development in that direction is anything but irreversible, neither is it straight; there are many reversals, detours and zig-zag movements. Moreover, given the multifarious nature of humankind's development, one can encounter developmental sequences in the direction towards autonomy, recurring at very different dates within the era time-scale used today. Structurally equivalent stages, e.g. those with hardly any or with no human-made timing devices, may be encountered before, as well as after, the nineteenth century of the presently used era time-scale. A reminder of the fact that the autonomy of people's social enclaves, though it can increase, is always relative may help to counter a grossly misleading habit of thinking which has grown among us. We are apt to think and to speak in terms which suggest that 'society' and 'nature', 'subject' and 'object', exist independently of each other. This is a fallacy which is hard to combat without a long-term perspective.

4. In discussions about the problem of time one is liable to be misled by the substantival form of the term. I have pointed out elsewhere[2] that the convention of speaking and thinking in terms of reifying substantives

can gravely obstruct one's comprehension of the nexus of events. It is reminiscent of the tendency of the ancients, which has by no means entirely disappeared today, to personify abstractions. Just actions became the goddess Justitia. There are plentiful examples of the pressure which a socially standardized language puts on the individual speaker to use reifying substantives. Take such sentences as: 'The wind is blowing' or 'The river is flowing'—are not the wind and blowing, the river and flowing, identical? Is there a wind that does not blow, a river that does not flow?

The case is similar with the concept of time. Here, too, Western linguistic tradition has transformed an activity into a kind of object. But in the case of time the activity represented by the verbal form of the word is not a natural but a social activity. Perhaps it is easier to recognize this fact if one uses a language such as English which offers those who speak it a verbal as well as the substantival form. The Oxford Dictionary quotes the sentence from Bacon: 'There is surely no greater Wisdom than to time the Beginnings and Onsets of things.' Or from more recent times, 'to time' is defined as: 'To adjust the parts of (a mechanism) so that a succession of movements or operations takes place at the required intervals and in the desired sequence' (1895). The verbal form 'to time' makes it more immediately understandable that the reifying character of the substantival form, 'time', disguises the instrumental character of the activity of timing. It obscures the fact that the activity of timing, e.g. by looking at one's watch, has the function of relating to each other the positions of events in the successive order of two or more change-continua.

Languages which lack a verbal form corresponding to the English 'to time' offer to members of the societies where these languages are spoken only expressions such as 'to determine the time' or 'to measure the time'. That still suggests the existence of a thing called time which one can measure or determine. Linguistic habits are therefore misleading for reflection. They constantly reinforce the myth of time as something which in some sense exists and as such can be determined or measured even if it cannot be perceived by the senses. On this peculiar mode of existence of time one can philosophize tirelessly, as had indeed been done over the centuries. One can entertain oneself and others with speculations on the secret of time as a master of mystery, although there actually is no mystery.

It was Einstein who finally set the seal on the discovery that time was a form of relationship and not, as Newton believed, an objective flow, a part of creation such as rivers and mountains which, although invisible, was like them independent of the people who do the timing. But even Einstein did not probe deeply enough. He too did not entirely escape the pressure of word-fetishism, and in his own way gave new sustenance to the myth of reified time, for example, by maintaining that under certain circumstances time could contract or expand. He discussed the problems of time only within the limited terms of reference of a physicist. But a critical examination of the concept of time requires an understanding of the relation between physical time and social time or, in other words, between timing in the context of 'nature' and in that of 'society'. But this was not his task, nor did it fall within the competence of a physicist.

5. The steady expansion of human societies within the non-human, the 'earthly' sector of the universe, as mentioned before, has led to a mode of discourse which gives the impression that 'society' and 'nature' exist in separate compartments. The divergent development of natural and of social sciences has reinforced this impression. The problem of time, however, is one which we cannot hope to solve so long as physical and social time are examined independently of each other. If one translates 'time' into its verbal form and examines the problem of timing, one can see at once that the timing of social events and of physical events cannot be entirely separated. With the development of human-made time-meters, the relative autonomy of social timing in relation to the timing of non-human physical events increased; their connection became more indirect but it was never broken—it is, in fact, unbreakable. For a long time, however, the social requirements of people provided the impetus for time-measurements of the 'heavenly bodies'. It is not difficult to show how much the development of the latter, in spite of all reciprocity, was and remained dependent on that of the former.

Unless one keeps in mind the unbreakable relationship between the physical and the social levels of the universe—unless one learns, in other words, to perceive human societies as emerging and developing *within* the larger non-human universe—one is unable to attack one of the most crucial aspects of the problem of time. One can present it briefly in the following manner: in the context of physics and, thus, of the ruling tradition of philosophy, 'time' appears as a concept at a very high level of abstraction, whilst in the practice of human societies 'time' is a regulatory device with a very strong compelling force, as one can readily see if one is late for an important appointment. The conventional tendency to explore 'nature' and 'society' and, therefore, the physical and the sociological problems of 'time' as if they were completely independent of each other thus gives rise to a seemingly paradoxical problem which, as a rule, is tacitly swept under the carpet in discussions about 'time': how is it possible that something which appears, in general reflections, as a high level abstraction can exercise a very strong compulsion on people? To date, enquiries into the sociology of time are almost non-existent. The fact that time is still largely discussed in the traditional philosophical manner, even by sociologists, has something to do with it. Another reason is that studies in the sociology of time cannot be very productive as long as they are tied to a short-term perspective. They can come into their own only within the framework of a developmental and comparative approach guided by a long-term perspective.

6. Many familiar figures of speech, as has been noted, give the impression that time is a physical object. Simply by speaking of 'measuring' time one makes it appear as if time is actually a physical object like a mountain or a river, the dimensions of which can be measured. Or consider the expression 'in the course of time'; it almost suggests that people, or perhaps the whole world, were swimming in a river of time. In this case as in others the substantival form of the concept of time undoubtedly contributes much to the illusion that time is a kind of thing existing 'in time and space.' The verbal form makes it easier to avoid this illusion. It makes it clear that time-measuring or synchronization is a human activity with quite specific objectives, not merely a relationship but a capacity for establishing relationships. The question is: Who in this case relates what, and to what end?

The first step towards an answer is relatively simple: the word 'time' one might say, is a symbol of a relationship that a human group, that is, a group of beings biologically endowed with the capacity for memory and synthesis, establishes between two or more continua of changes, one of which is used by it as a frame of reference or standard of measurement for the other (or others).

The ebb and flow of the tide, or the rising and setting of the sun and moon, can serve as socially standardized continua of changes of this kind. If these crude natural sequences are found too imprecise for their purposes, people can on their own initiative establish more exact and reliable sequences as a standard for other sequences. Clocks are precisely this; they are nothing other than human-made physical continua of change which, in certain societies, are standardized as a framework of reference and a measure for other social or physical continua of changes.[3]

To relate different continua of changes to each other as 'time' is therefore to link at least three continua: the people who connect, and two or more continua of changes, one of which takes on, within particular societies, the function of a standard continuum, a framework of reference, for the other. Even if an individual member of such a group uses *himself* as the frame of reference, as in the case in which one uses one's own life as the standard continuum for timing other events, the relationship is functionally three-polar: there is oneself as the person who integrates and times; there is oneself perceived as a continuum of changes from birth to death and, in that capacity, used as a standard continuum; and there is the host of other changes which one measures in terms of the span of one's own life—of oneself as a continuum of changes.

To avoid misunderstanding, I may add that it is only in quite highly in-dividualized societies that a person is capable of timing events in terms of his own life as a standard continuum. In these societies, not only does each person stand out more distinctly from all others as a uniquely pat-terned individual, but each person is also able to time his own life very exactly as a continuum of changes in terms of another socially agreed standard continuum, such as that of the sequence of calendar years. It is at a somewhat later stage in the development of human societies that men encounter the problem and are capable of working out a relatively well-fitting time-reckoning in terms of an era, such as the Greek dating of events in terms of the sequence of olympiads, the Roman counting of years '*ab urbe condita*', or the corresponding Jewish and Christian era-timing.

In societies where no long-term era-calendar exists as a man-made standard continuum such as these, people—understandably—are un-able to say when they were born or how old they are except in terms of single events such as 'when the great storm came' or 'just before the old chief was killed'. They have, in this case, no social standard continuum as frame of reference for the continuum of changes which each of them is himself. Thus, whenever one uses, in societies such as ours, one's own in-dividual life as a frame of reference for timing other changes, one also uses implicitly a socially evolved continuum of changes, the era-reckon-ing of calendar years, as standard for a continuum which oneself is.

Time-relations, as one can see, are many-layered relationships of con-siderable complexity. One may experience some difficulty in distancing oneself from the homely metaphors which make 'time' appear as a thing, or the widely accepted notion that time can be used as a kind of football for philosophical fantasies, since nothing definite can be said about it. But in the long run one will find it more rewarding to adopt a mode of thinking which reveals 'time' to be a conceptual symbol of a gradually advancing synthesis, a setting-up of fairly complex relationships be-tween continua of changes of various kinds.

In its most elementary form, 'timing' means determining whether a change—which may be recurrent or non-recurrent—happens before, after, or simultaneously with another. If it is a sequence of changes it may mean answering questions such as that of the length of the interval be-tween them in terms of a socially agreed timing standard, such as the in-terval between two harvests, or between one new moon and another. On a more differentiated level, one may time the interval between the start and finish of a run, a reign, a human life or between what we call 'antiquity' and 'modern times' in terms of a socially agreed standard continuum of changes. How far human groups can 'time' events and can, thus, experience them in terms of 'time' depends on the extent to which they encounter in their social practice problems which require timing and on that to which their social organization and their knowledge enable them to use one set of changes as a standard for another.

7. 'When shall we do it?' This is the primary question in response to which people set out on the adventure of timing. The point of departure, that which one endeavours to time, is in the first place always one's own activities and, in the earlier stages, primarily one's own activities as a group. However, in a sense, people 'time' their activities at a stage where they are not yet confronted with problems which find expression in explicit and articulate *when*-questions. Timing in these stages is passive; it is hardly reflected on and conceptualized as such and, to some extent, passive timing remains with us. Thus one may time one's activities more or less in accordance with the prompting of one's own animalic urges: one may eat when hungry and go to sleep when tired. In our type of society these more animalic cycles are regulated and patterned in accordance with a differentiated social organization which compels people, up to a point, to discipline their physiological clockwork in terms of a social clockwork. This is far less the case in relatively simple societies; there the regulation and patterning of the physiological clockwork (as far as one can call it 'regulation') depends more directly on the extent to which non-human nature, or, in some cases, other humans on whom one can prey, allow or withhold the satisfaction of one's needs. In these societies men may go hunting when they feel hungry and may stop exerting themselves when they have eaten enough. Or, on a slightly higher level in the sequence of passive timing, they may go to sleep when it gets dark and get up when the sun rises. Conceptualization may be in terms of 'sleep' rather than in terms of 'night'. There are, thus, stages in the development of human societies where men have hardly any social timing problems which require an active synchronization of their own communal activities with other changes in the universe.

The scenario becomes markedly different when people engage in actively producing their food. Agriculture, the utilization of domesticated plants, is a good example. At this stage, problems of active timing (in addition to passive timing) and, thus, of active, social and personal control become more pronounced. For by controlling and utilizing vegetation, men become subject to a previously unknown discipline imposed on them by the requirements of the domesticated vegetation on which they have become dependent for their food supply. An example taken from the nineteenth-century history of a small African people may illustrate the point. It indicates briefly one of the problems which induce early agriculturalists to evolve forms of active timing:

> Another work that the . . . priest was in duty bound to do, was to watch the seasons in order to enable him to announce or proclaim to the public in general the time for solving wheat, and also that concerning the celebration of their festivals.
>
> On account of the former he had to go to the top of one of the sentinels facing east to watch the sunrise every morning. It is said that there is a table mountain . . . on the east . . . and when the sun is seen to rise exactly behind this Table-Mountain, then the first rain in that week was considered enough for sowing. The next morning after the rain the priest would give an alarm that would be re-echoed throughout the mountain home. After this you would see the farmers and their families running down the mountain with their hoes and baskets to join or share in the labour. This is the alarm:
>
> > Throw away poverty or
> > Famine is over
> > Although never is it said
> > Day or night;
> > I am to say it now
> > In order to be sent away
> > To the land of suffering.
>
> You would hear people sounding this alarm when sowing was going on, but after, he or she who dared to say this verse, to use the magical formula for sending Famine to the land of suffering, would be severely punished or, worst of all, sent away into slavery.
>
> Now in order to enable him also to tell the people exactly of their mid-yearly celebrations of their festivals, the Priest had to go to another rock facing West, at the sight of every New Moon to make a mark there with a stone or put a cowry into a pot set there for the purpose. Nobody had to touch this besides the priest or his assistant . . .[4]

The quotation illustrates most vividly the time-experience of people at a relatively early agricultural stage. It is determined by their practical social needs. It is, in that sense, strictly self-centered—not in terms of an individual self, but in terms of the group which experiences a timing problem. The priest observes the passage of sun and moon not because he is interested in astronomy but because these changing lights in the sky, and through them perhaps some unseen powers, tell him *when* his people should begin their sowing and *when* they should celebrate their cult festivals with rituals and sacrifices and, perhaps, with singing and dancing so as to enlist the help of their gods in the production of food and in warding off all kinds of danger. At this stage, food production and cult activities are still closely related. Together, they are among the first social foci which present people with problems of active timing. Passive timing requires no decision; active timing does. The crucial point is the coordination of the continuous round of social practices with the continuous round of changes in non-human nature. For example, last year's harvest stored for the lean months may be almost exhausted. Although perhaps supplemented by meat from animals killed by hunters or by wild roots collected here and there, for a full larder one would have to wait until the next harvest. Given the, for people, unmanageable cyclical change of the seasons and the relatively more manageable rhythm of plant growth, the question one has to decide is: when should one start sowing? In the West African setting, that means: when will the dry season give way to the rainy season? Is the rain that has fallen its harbinger, or is it a false start? Now the sun, through the mouth of the priest, has given the answer; and the people rejoice. They themselves are probably not very concerned with the question as to how their priest has arrived at an answer. They have not yet a sense of 'time' in the abstract, as something that is passing. They are concerned with their immediate problems, such as that of their decreasing stores. There are certainly societies at a comparable level of development at which such experiences have not yet crystallized into regulating concepts at the comparatively high level of abstraction, such as 'month', 'year' or, for that matter, 'time'. Their concepts are much more closely linked to the recurrent cycles of their tangible needs, of transient satisfactions giving way to renewed needs and the quest for further satisfactions in an unending round.

Timing at this stage has still very much more the character of taking omens than that of looking at an impersonal clockwork in the sky. Only gradually will it take its place and its meaning somewhere between these two poles. Moreover, abstract counting by means of numerals alone is still difficult or entirely absent. Hence the priest tries to remember how often a new moon is seen in the sky after the hot dry winds appear to have come to an end, by putting a cowrie shell in a pot every time he observes a new moon passing a particular spot. The size of the heap of cowrie shells tells him roughly whether the right time for sowing has come. It may be hard to imagine, today, human life at a stage where the knowledge of abstract counting in our manner has not been evolved—as hard as it is to imagine a stage at which people have not yet evolved the continuous timing and dating techniques which are the condition of our experience of 'time' as a continuous flow. But it is well worth making the effort.

8. This episode from the history of a small hill-people shows many

structural characteristics of relevance to a sociology of time. In sociological terms, time has a coordinating and integrating function. During earlier stages, the social function of coordination and integration is usually exercised by certain central figures, such as priests or kings. Coordination through knowledge of the 'right time' for doing things, in particular, is for a long time the special social function of priests. One can see it here. Priests are freed form the labour of growing their own food. They have more time for observing the movements of the changing lights in the sky. Already in this small African village-state the priest possesses, by virtue of his secret knowledge about finding the 'right time', sufficient power and authority to decide for the members of his society when the communal food-producing activities or, alternatively, the seasonal cult-actions should begin.

This is not an isolated case. Almost everywhere in the long development of human societies priests were the first specialists in active timing. When larger and more complex state-societies developed, priests usually shared the social function of determining when certain social activities should be undertaken—in an often uneasy partnership—with secular state authorities. When the struggles for supremacy between priests and kings went in favour of the latter, the setting of time, like the coining of money, became one of the monopolies of the state.[5] Yet even then priests remained for a long time specialists in timing procedures. In Assyria, for instance, priestly observers of the sky had to inform the king when a new moon had been actually seen by them in their special 'observatories'; for the more abstract anticipatory calculation of the moon's circuit around the earth was still beyond people's reach. In Athens a special priestly functionary, the Hieromnemon, an elected member of the highest ruling body, was concerned with the redaction of the new calendar from year to year (and Aristophanes probably got a big laugh from his audience by asking the new Hieromnemon to see to it that the days of the social calendar he had to fix were better synchronized with the visible cycles of the moon than were those of his predecessors). Caesar consulted the Pontifex Maximus when he wanted to improve the old calendar; it had got out of tune with the observable movements of the heavenly bodies and he evidently felt that it was a ruler's task to provide a well-functioning timing and dating framework for all civic activities.

Not surprisingly, the need for an orderly and unified time-reckoning varied in accordance with the growth and decline of state-units, with the size and the degree of integration of their peoples and territories and the corresponding degree of differentiation and length of their commercial and industrial ties. The juridical institutions of states required unified time-meters commensurate with the complexity and diversity of the cases which came before them. With growing urbanization and commercialization, the problem of synchronizing the growing number of human activities and of having a smooth-running continuous time-grid as a common frame of reference for all human activities became more urgent. It was one of the functions of central authorities, whether secular or clerical, to provide it and to see that it functioned. The orderly, recurrent payment of taxes, interest, wages and the fulfillment of many other contracts and obligations depended on it; and so did the many holy days—or holidays—when people rested from their labours. One can see very clearly how, under the pressure of these needs, church and state authorities, the holders of the monopoly of timing, attempted to copy with that task. For a long time, for instance, there were, seen within one and the same state, traditional local diversities with regard to the beginning of a year and, thus, to its end. As far as one can see, it was Charles IX, king of France, who, after some discussion, decided in 1563 to impose on French society a uniform date for the beginning of the year, setting it at 1 January. His edict, put into practice in 1566, broke with a more or less official tradition which linked the beginning of the year to the Easter festival. Accordingly, the year 1566, beginning on 14 April and ending on 31 December, had only eight months and seventeen days. Thus the months of September, October, November and December which, in accordance with a Roman tradition of beginning the year in March and with the corresponding meaning of their names, had been the seventh, eight, ninth and tenth months respectively, now became somewhat incongruously the ninth, tenth, eleventh and twelfth months. At the time this change aroused strong opposition. Now one hardly notices the incongruity. Calendars as a social institution have a regulating social function. Now one takes it for granted that 1 January really is the beginning of the year. One does not see clearly that a year has a social function and a social reality related to, but distant from, a natural reality; one is apt to perceive it simply as something established by nature. Again, Pope Gregory XIII decided to revise the Julian calendar because, in the 400 years that had elapsed since it had been established, the spring equinox which determined the Easter festival had slowly receded from 21 March to 11 March. A Papal Bull suppressed ten days of the year 1582 and decreed that the day following 4 October was not 5 but 15 October. The Gregorian reform of Julius Caesar's reform of the old Roman calendar was the last attempt, so far, to provide a calendar system for a social year which, over the centuries, did not diverge too much from the 'natural year', that is, from the time in which the sun—in relation to men as observers and centres of reference—returns to a point in the sky which has been singled out by them as a point of departure.

As an example of developmental continuities persisting in spite of a good many political and other discontinuities—of what has been called before a 'continuum of changes'—the evolution of a timing framework in the form of a calendar is not uninstructive. It can serve as a reminder that what we call 'time' is an often rather complex network of relationships and that timing is essentially a synthesis, an integrating activity. In this case men use initially, as a standard for the relatively fast-moving continuum of social changes, the natural continuum of changes in the sky which is, by comparison, changing so slowly that, in relation to themselves, it does not appear to change at all. By fixing, more or less arbitrarily, a certain position of the sun, perhaps in relation to other stars, as the starting- and finishing-point of a social timing-unit—a year—they are able to establish a frame of reference for the synchronizing of human activities. The slowness with which people succeeded, over the centuries, in working out a calendar time-scale well tailored in relation to the physical continuum and capable of providing an articulated, unified synchronizing standard for human beings integrated in the form of states and, now, beyond these, for a global network of states, shows how difficult this task was.

9. It was, apparently, even more difficult for people to establish an era time-scale for sequence of hundreds or thousands of years which enabled the living generation to determine with accuracy their own position in the sequence of generations. The working out of this type of *non-recurrent* time-scale raises particular problems. An early form is the counting of a sequence of passing years in terms of a sequence of rulers and the sequence of years in each reign. One of the widely used era time-scales of our time is that which counts centuries and years in terms of before and after the birth of Christ. To establish a measuring rod of this type for long non-recurrent time-sequences was possible only when social units such as states or churches had the character of a long-lasting continuum of changes within which living groups—usually ruling groups—found it necessary for the functioning of their institutions to keep alive the memory of the continuity of these constitutions in a precise and articulate manner. In antiquity the longest and best-known era time-scale was that which counted the non-recurrent sequence of years from the reign of a Babylonian ruler Nabonassaros. The time-reckoning in terms of consecutive reigns and their years, established first for purposes of state in the Chaldaic Babylonian tradition, made it possible to put on record, in a purely descriptive manner, the distance between unusual events in the sky, such as eclipses of the moon, in terms of the number of years that lay between them. Later, Ptolemy used this Babylonian era time-scale, the oldest and longest available to him within his knowl-

edge continuum, for the construction of his model of the physical universe. His case illuminates the intertwining of the development of social and physical time-meters. Today it is often taken for granted by philosophers and, perhaps, by physicists that 'time flows in one direction, and the flow of time cannot be reversed', although Einstein's theory, while maintaining the serial order of time, questioned its unidirectional character. It is hard to imagine that physicists could have developed the concept of a unidirectional and irreversible flow of time within their sphere without the slow and difficult emergence of social time-scales, with the help of which one could accurately determine the non-recurrent, continuous sequence of years, centuries and millennia. The emergence of long-lasting and relatively stable state-units, in other words, was a condition of the experience of time as a unidirectional flow.

If one extends, in imagination, the developmental trajectory of timing backwards to the conditions of early agricultural societies, such as that mentioned before, one can see that very clearly and why neither elaborate yearly calendars related to recurrent events nor long-lasting era time-scales (the condition of an experience of 'time' as a continuous, irreversible flow) have at that stage come into existence. Problems which require a precisely subdivided timing framework for social activities divided into time-units such as 'months' or 'years' have not yet arisen or, if they have, are still difficult to solve; and problems concerning dozens or hundreds of years are, at most, dimly perceived in terms of a line of ancestors or entirely beyond one's horizon. A priest, as one saw, determines the 'right time' not yet by relating the movements of the sun to the 'fixed' stars but in relation to some earthly landmarks; and he tries to discover it, not yet by relating the activities of his people to a continuous calendar time-scale extending over a whole year, but only by relating the 'right time' in each instance to a particular event, such as sowing or organizing a feast for the gods.

## Notes

1. I deliberately avoid speaking of a 'level of abstraction'. For from what is the concept of time abstracted?
2. Norbert Elias, *What is Sociology?* (London, 1978), p. 68.
3. It may be helpful to explain why I am using, in this context, the term 'continuum of changes'. The reason is, briefly, that in many processes of change the unity of the process is due, not to any substance which remains unchanged throughout the process, but to the continuity with which one change emerges from another in an unbroken sequence. Take the example of a specific society, of the Netherlands in the fifteenth and twentieth centuries; what links them to each other is not so much any core which remains unchanged but the continuity of changes by which the twentieth-century society has emerged from that of the fifteenth century, reinforced by the fact that it is a remembered continuity. Take a hu-

man being; Hume once confessed that he could not understand in what sense the grown-up person he was now was 'the same' as the little child he used to be. Again, the answer is that the identity is not so much one of substance, but rather of the continuity of changes leading from one stage to another, and, in this case too, it is a remembered continuity. What we call the 'animal kingdom' in the evolutionary sense is a continuum of changes: it is the continuity of a multiplicity of changes linking fish to men. The same can be said of the physical universe. There are many other examples. In all these cases it is the continuity of changes which links a later stage to earlier stages.

4. N. A. A. Azu, *Adangbe History* (Accra, 1929), p. 18.

5. The change from 'winter time' to 'summer time' is an example of the exercise of this monopoly in contemporary state-societies.

# 15

## *Homo Clausus:* The Thinking Statues

1

Discussions on the relation of individual and society are often based explicitly or implicitly on an idea that can be summarized as follows: "What can really be *seen* are individual people. Societies cannot be seen. They cannot be perceived with the senses. One cannot therefore say that they exist or are 'real' in the same sense or to the same degree as one can say it of the individual people forming them. In the end, everything one can say about social formulations is based on observations of individual people and their utterances or products."

In keeping with this fundamental position, many people arrive at the conviction that all statements about social phenomena are really generalizations of observations made of individuals; and one sometimes hears the remark that not only *statements* about such phenomena but the phenomena themselves, societies and all individual social formations, are as such nothing but abstractions. "It is all very well", someone may say, "to present social formations simply as relations between individual people. But as only the latter can be perceived, is not everything that can be said about such relations deduced indirectly from observations of individual people? As relations as such cannot be directly perceived, how is it possible to investigate them? How, to adapt Kant's well-known question, are social sciences possible at all?"

In considering one of the fundamental problems of the social sciences, therefore, one encounters questions which have a certain kinship to problems of classical epistemology. In both cases the starting point of reflection is the idea that all our knowledge is primarily knowledge of individual bodies or at least of physical events that we perceive with the senses. One of the fundamental problems with which this confronts us is the question how we arrive at our knowledge of all relations between individual bodies that are not perceptible with the senses. In one case it is the question of the origin of our knowledge of relationships between in-

From *The Society of Individuals*, pp. 91–106

dividual people, in the other the question of the origin of our knowledge of relations between non-human objects and changes in them, for example, their relationship as cause and effect.

The similarity of the questions is by no means accidental. In both cases it is connected to a peculiar form of self-consciousness and of the image of people. But one is not usually aware of it as such, as a special variant of our consciousness of ourselves and others. It usually presents itself to the person concerned as something natural and universally human, as *the* form of human self-consciousness, the image that people have of themselves at all times.

One may be aware at the same time that there are and have been other ways of experiencing oneself and others. One may know that our own familiar form of self-consciousness, our image of people, emerges late in the history of mankind, at first slowly and for a relatively short period in limited circles of ancient society, and then in the so-called Renaissance in occidental societies. Nevertheless, it usually appears as the normal, healthy way of perceiving ourselves and others, which unlike others needs no explanation. Even today this image still seems so self-evident that it is difficult to detach it from its fixed place in one's own consciousness and to hold it out, as it were, as something new and astonishing.

On the other hand, as long as we are unable to do so we run the risk of encountering insuperable difficulties in solving both practical and theoretical questions, in both action and thought. To be sure, criticism of self-consciousness, the demand for a revision of the basic forms of perceiving oneself and others prevalent in our own society, will meet understandable resistance. The basic structure of the idea we have of ourselves and other people is a fundamental precondition of our ability to deal successfully with other people and, at least within the confines of our own society, to communicate with them. If it is called into question, our own security is threatened. What was certain becomes uncertain. One is like a person suddenly thrown into the sea, with no sight of dry land. Unquestioned assumptions, the basic structures of thought that we take over with the words of our language without further reflection, are among the indispensable means of orientation without which we lose our way, just as we lose the ability to orientate ourselves in space if the familiar signposts that determine what we expect to perceive turn out to be unreliable and deceptive. But without throwing oneself for a time into the sea of uncertainty one cannot escape the contradictions and inadequacies of a deceptive certainty.

It may help to throw the strangeness of our own image of ourselves and of people into sharper relief if we see it retrospectively, in the mirror of the image of self and people that was again and again fundamental to the struggle to solve the problem of knowledge over the centuries.

Let us consider, for example, the man who first posed, in a paradigmatic way, the problem of knowledge and cognition in more or less the form it has kept to our day, Descartes. The dictum associated with his name, "I think, therefore I am", has become a kind of slogan. But this dictum gives only a pale and misleading idea of the image of self and people underlying his meditations. To understand this basic conception we must recall at least the outlines of the process of thought, the period of doubt and uncertainty that he passed through before he found firm ground under his feet in the new certainty that the indubitable fact of one's own reflection also put the existence of one's own self beyond doubt.

He asked himself first whether there was anything of which one was absolutely certain, anything that could not be doubted under any circumstances. In social life, he realized, one had to accept many ideas as if they were the gospel, though they were anything but certain. Descartes therefore decided to set out in search of that which was absolutely certain, and to discard all conceptions on which there could be even the slightest doubt. "Everything I have learned," he said to himself, "everything I know, I have learned through or from sense perceptions. But can one really trust one's senses? Can I be certain that I am sitting here beside my warm stove in my dressing-gown, holding this piece of paper in my hand? Can I be quite certain that these are my hands and my body? Of course, I see my hands; I feel my body. But", said the dissenting voice of doubt, "are there not people who believe they are kings while in reality they are paupers? Are there not people who are convinced that their heads are of stoneware and their bodies of glass? Is it not possible that God has so arranged things that I *believe* I see heaven and earth, and *believe* I have a three-dimensional body, while in reality nothing of the kind exists? Or, if God has not done so, is it not possible that an evil spirit may be deluding me into thinking that I feel, see and hear all these things which in reality do not exist? One cannot", he told himself, "dismiss this possibility." And as he felt compelled in this way to reject one by one all ideas of himself and the world as dubious and unreliable, he finally succumbed, like other people under the unremitting pressure of doubt, to the blackest despair. There was nothing certain in the world, so it seemed to him, nothing that could not be doubted.

"I must therefore", he wrote, "take into account the possibility that heaven and earth, all forms in space, are nothing but illusions and fantasies used by an evil spirit to trap my credulity. I shall conceive that I myself have neither eyes nor hands, neither flesh, blood nor senses, but falsely believe I possess all of them."

Only after he had spent some time wandering in the tunnel of uncertainty and subjecting all his experiences to the trial by fire of his radical doubt did he see a faint gleam of light at the end. However doubt may have gnawed at him and threatened to destroy all certainty, there was, he discovered, one fact that could not be doubted: "Would it be possible", he asked, "for me finally to convince myself that I myself do not exist? No, I myself exist. For I can convince myself that I am able to think something and to doubt it."

Here we reach the core of this peculiar form of self-consciousness: sense perceptions and therefore the knowledge of physical objects including one's own body, all that may be doubtful and deceptive. But one cannot doubt, Descartes concludes, that one doubts. "It is not possible for me to think that I do not think. And that I think is not possible unless I exist."

The conception of the human self that we come across here, and the questions it implies, are far more than the mental games of a particular philosopher. They are highly characteristic of the transition from a conception of human beings and the world with strong religious underpinning to secularized conceptions, a transition which was making itself felt in Descartes's day. This secularization of human thought and action was certainly not the work of an individual or a number of individuals. It was connected to specific changes affecting all relationships of life and power in occidental societies. Descartes's deliberations represent a typical step in this direction in an original version. They indicate in a paradigmatic manner the peculiar problems with which people found themselves confronted in thinking about themselves and the certainty of their image of themselves when the religious picture of self and world became an open target of doubt and lost its self-evident status. This basic picture that dispensed certainty, the notion people had of themselves as part of a divinely created universe, did not thereby disappear, but it lost its central and dominant position in thought. As long as it held this position, that which could be perceived by the senses or confirmed by thought or observation played at most a secondary part in people's questions, thoughts and perceptions. The questions which mattered most to them concerned something that, in principle, could not be discovered by observation with the aid of the sense organs, or by thought supported by that which people ascertained by a methodical use of eyes and ears. They concerned, for example, the destination of the soul or the purpose of men and beasts in the framework of divine creation. To questions of this kind people could only find an answer with the help of recognized authorities of one kind or another, holy writings or favoured men—in short, through direct or indirect revelation. Individual observations were of very little help, individual reflection only helped in so far as it presented itself as an interpretation of one of the sources of revelation. And people accordingly felt themselves to be part of an invisible spiritual realm. They could feel themselves embedded in a hierarchy of beings the lowest rung of which was formed by the plants and animals, the highest by the angels, the pinnacle being God Himself. Or they may have experienced themselves as a kind of microcosm whose destiny was closely bound to that of the macrocosm of creation. Whatever the particular form, it was a basic feature of this picture of man and the world that what could be perceived by the senses took on its meaning from something that could be discovered and confirmed neither by individual reflection nor by individual observations.

One precondition of Descartes's thinking was a certain relaxation, a loss of power by the social institutions which had been the custodians of this intellectual tradition. His thought reflects the growing awareness of his time that people were able to decipher natural phenomena and put them to practical use simply on the basis of their own observation and thought, without invoking ecclesiastical or ancient authorities. Because of the prior work of thinkers of classical antiquity this discovery appeared to the people of the time like a rediscovery. It was a rediscovery of themselves as beings who could attain certainty about events by their own thought and observation, without recourse to authorities. And it moved their own mental activity—reified by the term "reason"—and their own powers of perception into the foreground of their image of themselves.

## 2

Now that all these ideas are taken for granted it is, perhaps, not very easy to put oneself in the position of people living in the time when such experiences were a new development gradually intruding, not without powerful resistance, into human thought processes. But to remember an epoch when what is almost self-evident today still had the lustre and freshness of unfamiliarity throws into sharper relief some features of our own basic conceptions of ourselves and the world, conceptions which, through familiarity, normally remain below the threshold of clear consciousness. It makes us fully aware of the fact that the image which members of the pioneering European and American societies have of themselves today—an image of beings who understand events solely by the application of intelligence, by individual observation and thought—should not be taken for granted as something which exists a priori. It cannot be understood in isolation from the social situation of those who see themselves in this way. It evolved as a symptom of and a factor in a specific transformation which, like all such changes, simultaneously affected all the three basic coordinates of human life: the shaping and the position of the individual within the social structure, the social structure itself, and the relation of social human beings to events in the non-human world. It may be easier to see in retrospect how closely this transition from a predominantly authoritarian mode of thinking to a more autonomous one, at least as regards natural events, was bound up with the more comprehensive advance of individualization in the fifteenth, sixteenth and seventeenth centuries in Europe. It formed a parallel to the transition from a more "external" conscience dependent on authorities to a more autonomous and "individual" one. One can see more clearly in retrospect how closely this new form of self-consciousness was linked to the growing commercialization and the formation of states, to the rise of rich court and urban classes and, not least, to the noticeably increasing power of human beings over non-human natural events.

In the course of these discoveries about natural events people found out new things about themselves. They not only learned increasingly how to gain certainty about natural events by methodical thought and observation; they also became increasingly aware of themselves as beings who were able to gain such certainty by their own individual observation and thought. Their image of the physical universe changed, and their image of themselves also changed. With regard to themselves, they were less inclined to accept the traditional image advanced by authorities. They examined themselves more carefully in the mirror of their consciousness, observed themselves, thought about human beings more consciously and systematically. In short, they climbed to a new level of self-consciousness. Both changes—in their image of the non-human universe and of themselves—were closely linked. And the Cartesian enquiry, the whole "epistemological" enquiry itself, was nothing other than an expression of this new human self-image.

3

That is not to say that the people undergoing these changes were aware of such changes in the same way as we are today, from a distance. From about the "Renaissance" on, the basic form of self-consciousness and the human image prevalent today slowly formed in a number of societies until they were taken for granted. The fact that we can now perceive this is itself an expression of the gradual advance to a further stage of self-consciousness. Another such expression is the fact that the form of self-consciousness that is taken for granted and now seems like a universally valid concept of humans can be perceived as something that has evolved by a certain process, in conjunction with the wider social context.

As compared to their medieval predecessors, the members of European societies from the "Renaissance" on climbed to a new level of self-consciousness. They were increasingly able to see themselves as if from a distance, taking the sun as the centre of the universe instead of naively assuming the earth and thus themselves to be the centre. This "Copernican revolution" was highly characteristic of the new level of self-consciousness which these people slowly attained.

But as compared to that level of self-consciousness, we find ourselves today beginning here and there to climb to the next. We are learning to see our own image simultaneously in the mirror of self-consciousness and in another, larger and more distant mirror. As the rise of the natural sciences was earlier, today their rapid further advance together with the rise of the social and human sciences are both a driving force and a symptom of this change.

It would undoubtedly be preferable if one were able to speak simply of an enlargement of people's knowledge about themselves. But although such a formulation would not be incorrect, it is not enough; it does not quite do justice to the facts. The process of acquiring knowledge, the constant increase in our knowledge of facts, the closer approximation of human ideas and procedures to what can be established as fact by critical observation, the whole change in our mode of experience over the generations—and thus in the course of an individual life—is not in all cases simply an extension in one dimension. We are not concerned only with a growing accumulation of factual knowledge, ideas or methods of thought or research that exist on the same plane like objects on a table.

There are also differences between *levels* of observation—comparable to those between the view one has of people in the street when one is among them, and the different view they offer when seen from the first floor of a house, from the fifth floor or even from an aeroplane. From time to time—for example, at the end of the "Middle Ages", or in our own age since the end of the eighteenth century, or analogously in contemporary African or Asian societies—one can observe, accompanying the steady accumulation of social knowledge and a specific transformation of social life, this broader and higher perspective being attained, a perspective characteristic of a new level of consciousness.

The special difficulty which this state of affairs puts in the way of understanding and description lies in the fact that the new perspective does not simply abolish perspectives from other levels of consciousness. The comparison with the viewpoints of the pedestrian and the aircraft pilot is a lame one. People are made in such a way that, to pursue the metaphor, they can experience themselves and others directly as pedestrians while at the same time watching themselves and others walking up and down the street from an upper floor of a building. And perhaps, at the same time, they can even make out their own figures from the pilot's viewpoint, both as they walk along the street and as they look down from the building.

Simpler societies—and children in all societies—still offer examples of people for whom the ability to see themselves and their companions from a distance, like spectators from the window of a building while at the same time walking along the street, is still quite unattainable. They have, of course, a consciousness of themselves and other people. But they still live and act in direct connection with others. They have no access to a form of experience and a range of ideas which enable people to experience themselves as something apart from and independent of their own group, as a person in a sense standing opposed to their group. They are not "individualized" in the sense in which the word can be used when applied to people of more complex societies. One might be tempted to say that they are conscious without being self-conscious. But although this formulation does touch on something significant in the situation in question, strictly speaking it is not quite adequate. For all the simpler societies still existing seem to have in their vocabularies, besides "we", concepts corresponding to our "I" and "you". One must consider the possibility, at least as a hypothesis, that there have been human groups in which even adults could not perform the act of self-distancing that is needed in order to speak of oneself as "I" and of others as "you". On the other hand, it is quite possible that people of many simple and even quite complex contemporary societies are unable to perform the further act of self-distancing that is needed in order to experience oneself not merely as "I" but as a possible "you" for others who say "I" of themselves.

The simplest examples of the many-layered nature of consciousness at the other end of human development so far are probably to be found in certain areas of literature. One might think of the development of the novel since the second half of the nineteenth century. In the prose writings of earlier centuries—and certainly not only in the *prose* writings— the writer was mainly preoccupied with telling the reader what people did, what happened. Gradually attention became concentrated not only on the narration of events but on how the people experienced them. The authors described a landscape, for example, and at the same time the so-

called "inner landscape" in the narrower or broader sense of the term—
*le paysage intérieur.* They described meetings between people and at the
same time the "stream of consciousness" of the people as they met. But
no matter what slogans were used, the change that found expression in
literature was by no means confined to literature. The writers' special
sensitivity enabled them, as a kind of vanguard of society, to perceive
and express changes that were going on in the broad field of the societies
in which they lived. If this had not been the case they would have found
no readers who understood and appreciated them. These literary forms
are indeed testimonies to the slow rise to a new level of consciousness
that can be observed in a number of societies. And the present discussion
is really nothing other than an attempt to carry forward the description
of this further stage of self-consciousness and of the human image that is
gradually rising above the horizon, in conjunction with further discoveries by people about themselves as individuals, societies and natural
formations.

## 4

One of the difficulties facing one in such an attempt is connected to the
fact that as yet there are hardly any long-term investigations of such
changes in the history of societies or of individuals. Nor are there convincing theoretical models of this development towards a multi-layered
consciousness. Expressions like the "transition to a new level of consciousness" may perhaps have a somewhat Hegelian timbre for those familiar with that philosopher. One can say very generally that the words
currently used when seeking a somewhat adequate expression for what
is slowly coming into view inevitably have all kinds of prior linguistic associations that warp and falsify that view.

One might be inclined, for example, to see the idea of a series of
levels in the changing viewpoint people have of themselves and their
world as the extravagant product of a speculative fantasy. Or one may
suspect it of implying the notion of an automatic, predetermined development, a necessary historical sequence, a self-evident improvement and progress, an unfolding of some supra-individual spirit; or
of harbouring the idea—normally referred to by terms like "relativism"
or "historicism"—that with the opening of a new perspective on consciousness everything that people have previously experienced, thought
and said must become false and insignificant.

Nothing of the kind is true. The idea that what we reifyingly call
"consciousness" is multi-layered is the outcome of an attempt to set up a
new mental framework within which specific observations can be

processed and that can serve as a guide for further observations. It is open to and in need of verification and revision in the light of further empirical research. That it has a Hegelian flavour really only proves that Hegel was in some respects on the track of phenomena that are open to empirical verification, even if he himself wove them into the structure of his speculative system to the point where it is difficult to disentangle what is capable of verification by other people from what is simply his personal metaphysics, as well as a justification of the social order in which he lived. Perhaps this intermingling actually put others off the track he had discovered.

The direction of this track can perhaps be most simply indicated by referring to an elementary feature of human experience: people are in a position to know that they know; they are able to think about their own thinking and to observe themselves observing. Under certain circumstances they can climb further and become aware of themselves as knowing that they are aware of themselves knowing. In other words, they are able to climb the spiral staircase of consciousness from one floor with its specific view to a higher floor with its view and, looking down, to see themselves standing at the same time on other levels of the staircase. Moreover, the perspective characteristic of these other levels is assimilated into their own in one form or another, although its characteristics are not the same for people who take it for granted as for those who are able to view it with a certain detachment from a higher level of consciousness. How far up or down one climbs this staircase depends not only on the talent, personality structure or intelligence of individual people, but on the state of development and the total situation of the society to which they belong. They provide the framework, with its limits and possibilities, while the people either take advantage of the possibilities or let them lie fallow.

## 5

What happened in Descartes's time was a transition to a new level of self-consciousness. The difficulties that he and some of his contemporaries and successors encountered arose to a large extent because people were unable to reconcile the characteristics they observed in themselves on the spiral staircase when viewing themselves as the subjects of knowledge and thought, and the different characteristics they found when they saw themselves simply as the objects of human thought and observation. They took the different views they had of themselves as knowers and known to be different components of themselves.

Thus Descartes's reflections, for example, express the experience of a person who on one hand began to perceive himself as a thinker and observer independent of authorities and reliant only on himself in his thinking, and on the other as part of what he observed, a body among others. But with the means of reflection available to him at that time it was difficult to attain a proper conceptual understanding of this double role as observer and observed, knower and known, subject and object of thought and perception. In one way or another the two roles presented themselves as different modes of being or even as separate entities. Or concepts were used in speech and thought that seemed to refer to different and perhaps quite separate things. And this tendency to speak and think about conceptually distinct, if indissolubly connected, roles and functions as if they were separate entities was typical of a whole age. One might say that a first, theologically and religiously orientated age, the Middle Ages, was followed by a second, metaphysically oriented one, in the thought and speech of which reified functions and feelings played a primordial role. This is one example.

As an observer the individual person confronted the world as a fairly free and detached being; he distanced himself to a certain extent from the world of inanimate things as from that of human beings, and therefore of himself. In his capacity as the observed, the human being perceived himself as part of a natural process and, in keeping with the state reached by thought in Descartes's time, as a part of the world of physical phenomena. This was viewed as a kind of clockwork mechanism or machine which, like other things of the same kind, was perceived through the senses. Accordingly, Descartes in his intellectual experiment posited his own existence in his capacity as a body as something that was just as uncertain, just as exposed to radical doubt, as all the other objects that we know through the mediation of the senses. The only thing he saw as indubitably existing was himself in his capacity as thinker and doubter. He observed and experienced himself on one hand in the way he was perceived by others, as if through their sense organs, or by himself in a mirror; and on the other hand, at the same time, he perceived himself in a manner which, he assumed, did not involve the mediation of the senses, i.e. as thinker and observer, the subject of experience. And like many other people who climbed to this level of self-consciousness, who observed themselves as observers, knew themselves as knowers, thought of and experienced themselves as thinkers and experiencers, he attributed each of the different ways in which he perceived himself to a different and separate plane of existence.

It was this type of dualism, of positing two views of oneself as separate and absolute, which for a long time determined the kinds of questions posed by epistemology—the more so because this same dualism increasingly formed the basic pattern of self-consciousness among the general population in most Western societies. Such a step on the way to a new form of self-consciousness was certainly not unique. The Bible describes a step of the same kind. In paradise the ancestors of mankind were unaware of their nakedness; then they ate the forbidden fruit of knowledge and became aware of their nakedness. We find here a vivid expression of how closely the increase in self-consciousness is bound up with an increase of conscience.

What became perceptible in Descartes's age was a movement in the same direction, on a higher level of the spiral staircase. If people on the preceding level of self-consciousness had perceived themselves, in keeping with their education and mode of life, as members of associations such as family groups or estates embedded in a spiritual realm ruled by God, they now increasingly perceived themselves as individuals, though without entirely losing the old conception. The changed social modes of life imposed a growing restraint on feelings, a greater need to observe and think before one acted, with regard to both physical objects and human beings. This gave greater value and emphasis to consciousness of oneself as an individual detached from all other people and things. The act of detachment in observing others and oneself was consolidated into a permanent attitude and, thus fixed, generated in the observer an idea of himself as a detached being who existed independently of all others. The act of detachment when observing and thinking condensed into the idea of a universal detachment of the individual; and the function of experience, of thinking and observing, which can be perceived from a higher level of self-consciousness as a function of the *whole* human being, first presented itself in reified form as a component of the human being like the heart, stomach or brain, a kind of insubstantial substance *in* the human being, while the act of thinking condensed into the idea of an "intelligence", a "reason" or, in the antiquated term, a "spirit". The two aspects of the double role that people have in relation to themselves and to the world at large—as knowers of themselves and as known by themselves, as experiencing themselves and others and as experienced by themselves and others, as detaching themselves from the world in contemplation and as indissolubly enmeshed in the events of the world—these two aspects were so hypostatized in the habits of thought and speech that they appeared to be different objects, such as "body" and "mind", one of which was housed inside the other like the stone in a plum. Indeed, the tendency to picture functions as substances went so far that the relation between them was conceived in spatial terms. The activity of observing and thinking peculiar to man and the accompanying retardation of action, the growing restraint of emotional impulses and the associated sense of being detached from and opposite to the world, were reified in consciousness as the idea of something that could be located inside human beings, just as they appeared as bodies among bodies in their capacity as observable objects of thought.

## 6

The basic problem of epistemology corresponded to this form of human self-consciousness. It took its starting point from the absolute status conferred on the temporary self-detachment that is a part of the act of cognition at what we call the "scientific" stage of development. It was based on the notion of a knowing subject which stands opposed to the world of knowable objects, from which it is separated by a broad divide. The problem was how the subject was to gain certain knowledge of objects across this divide. The answers varied. But whether they took an empirical, rationalist, sensualist or positivist form, the basic structure of the question remained the same for centuries, up to our own day. It was one of the axiomatic truths of the period. One needs only to select a few examples from the multitude of classical theories of knowledge to see its special nature more clearly, and also the insoluble problems in which people constantly found themselves entangled as a result of this image of man, with its reification of specific human functions.

This was the basic position—always the same one. The self-perception of the person as observer and thinker was reified in speech and thought, giving rise to a notion of an entity within the human being which was cut off from everything going on outside itself by the walls of its bodily container, and which could gain information about outside events only through the windows of the body, the sense organs. How reliable this information was, whether the senses presented a distorted picture of what went on "outside", whether, indeed, there was anything "outside", whether and how far the "thinking thing" inside us, the *res cogitans* as Descartes called it, influenced and changed what came to us through the senses in its own way—all these were questions that had to be discussed over and over again, given the presuppositions that have been described.

A number of philosophers, first and foremost Berkeley, saw no way of convincing themselves that anything could exist independently of one's own perceptions. The statement "there is", Berkeley maintained, really means nothing other than "I perceive something". It does not imply that anything is happening outside myself, only that something is happening in me. My senses are excited, that is all. And it seemed to him that the only guarantee available to the "self" in its container that anything lasting existed outside it and corresponded in some way to its conceptions, was God.

That was certainly an extreme position in the epistemological controversy. But perhaps because it is extreme it shows up the image of man common to all the contending positions particularly clearly. Other philosophers no doubt showed greater confidence in the reliability of our senses. They assumed that eyes and ears give us a fairly faithful picture of the outer world. We receive sense impressions from the things outside us, they thought, and distill from them simple conceptions of certain qualities of things, such as the ideas of colour, form, size and solid mass. That was the position adopted by Locke, for example. But even the exponents of this standpoint came up against certain characteristic difficulties. They might say: "I can perceive something which is green, rectangular, solid and heavy. But how do I know that all these qualities are related to each other as qualities of one and the same thing? Everything the senses convey to me is information on certain qualities. Objects as such cannot be perceived with the senses. The question is therefore how I arrive at the more complex idea of a unified substrate for a collection of sense impressions." And at this point Locke, like many others who attempted to derive their conceptions of things and their relations from their own experience, found himself and his arguments in considerable difficulty. Starting from the basic pattern, accepted as self-evident even by his fiercest opponents, of an image of people comprising an "inside" and an "outside" with sense-impressions as the only bridge between the two, Locke adopted the position that consciousness, reason or whatever else the insubstantial inner thing might be called gradually filled with knowledge derived from sense-impressions like an initially empty vessel. The difficulty was how to explain, from this standpoint, how a person can arrive at a conception of relationships, particularly regular and necessary relationships, between individual sense-impressions or what gave rise to them. Where does one find concepts for relationships such as like and unlike, whole and part, cause and effect?

A number of philosophers following in Plato's footsteps offered an answer to questions of this kind which was simple enough in its approach. Concepts and ideas of this sort, they argued, could not be imprints made inside us by material objects outside us. They were part of the natural equipment of our reason or our soul. Some exponents of this line of argument put more stress on the divine origin of such ideas while others considered them an innate part of human nature. But, of course, it was still open to question how far people could experience things "outside" them through the veil of these preexisting ideas, what they were like independently of the person experiencing them—unless, like Leibniz, one sought a way out of the dilemma by assuming a pre-stabilized harmony between "inside" and "outside". Whatever these pacifying hypotheses might be, on the other side were the sceptics who declared that nothing of the kind could be demonstrated. In many cases it was probably only the pressure of public opinion or the power of church and state that prevented them from saying openly that all these ideas were comforting daydreams in the guise of reason. David Hume, for example, with his incorruptible intellectual integrity, contented himself with noting—very logically in relation to his presuppositions—that he could find no reason for asserting a necessary relation between individual sense impressions. As far as he could see, such ideas were probably based on the repetition of experiences, on habit or habituation. And Kant, who applied the extraordinary acuity and fertility of his mind to an attempt to produce a synthesis of these antinomies, found himself no less deeply embroiled in the labyrinth of insoluble problems generated by the common assumptions underlying this philosophical dispute. He imagined that, in our knowledge of the world, experiences coming to us from outside through the senses merged with forms of relations and ideas present in our consciousness prior to all experience. And even if his contribution represented a considerable refinement of the notion of the innate ideas, the elementary difficulties in which they became caught up were the same. In the end he too found himself confronted by the question of whether one could really know things in themselves, as they were independently of the preexisting forms of consciousness, or whether these primal ideas and forms of relationship which existed a priori and which, he assumed, were the eternal and unalterable appurtenances of human consciousness, condemned human beings for ever to perceive objects as they appear as a result of these appurtenances.

There we have the problem. The protracted argument about knowledge revolved basically around this question: are the signals received by the individual through his senses related together and processed by a kind of innate mechanism called "intelligence" or "reason" according to mental laws which are common to all people, eternal, existing prior to experience? Or do the ideas the individual forms on the basis of these signals simply reflect things and people as they are independent of his ideas? There were intermediate positions, compromises, syntheses, but they all lay somewhere on the continuum between these two poles.

And this common basic schema underlying the questions was closely bound up with another common schema concerning self-consciousness

and the image of man, and with basic ideas about the self and its relation
to the non-self which thinkers accepted without question.


7

The unquestioned image of man underlying this philosophical dispute
was undoubtedly different from the one that played a part in the preceding argument among the great scholastic philosophers. But it was also a
continuation of it. In a more or less secularized form, and conceived now
in relation to and now in isolation from God, it showed its descent from
an ecclesiastical ancestor. The idea of a duality of body and soul had previously provided people with an intellectual framework for understanding themselves and now lived on in a special enclave, in conjunction with
other-worldly questions concerning invisible, unobservable relationships such as the destiny of people and things. It was now changed, in
conjunction with this-worldly questions about the nature of our knowledge of visible, observable objects, into the idea of a duality of body and
mind, reason, consciousness, or whatever it may be called.

"I am a person," this basic schema might run in a simple form, "and I
have a body. My body is made of matter, has spatial extent and therefore
a certain position in space. But my reason, my mind, consciousness or
self is not made of matter nor does it extend in space. Reason and intelligence, mind and consciousness have their seat *in* my body, but are different *from* my body." And it was this strange notion of an un-thinglike
thing which, though not spatial, occupies a very definite position in
space, inside my body, the idea that "I" or "my intelligence", "my consciousness", "my mind" is contained in my body as in a diving suit, that
provided the common basis even to diametrically opposed views in the
epistemological controversy. As the unquestioned framework of self-
perception it underlay the question whether and how far the ideas
"within" corresponded to the objects "outside". That is the core of the
matter. People experienced themselves as closed systems.

Moreover, the "subject of knowledge", called by the most diverse
names in the various theories of knowledge, corresponded to this idea.
The model underlying it was an individual "I" in its container. Everything that was "outside", whether thing or human being, approached it
as if after the event, as something unknown and strange which stood
alone in face of the world, like the philosopher, as an observer and
thinker seeking an answer to a question. Even if the idea of other people
was included in one's arguments, they were seen essentially as a collection of closed systems each of which, exactly as one seemed to do oneself,
looked from "inside" at a world lying "outside". In keeping with the ba-

sic pattern of self-perception they were not seen as something to which one could say "you" or "we", but, so to speak, as a mass of "I's". And this "I" of knowledge, the *homo philosophicus* of classical epistemology, was, on close inspection, a grown-up who had never been a child. The question was how a "rational" person, a person with the mental apparatus of an adult, could gain knowledge of the world. For the purpose of epistemology one abstracted from the observation that every adult was once a child; it was set aside as irrelevant to the problem of how knowledge was acquired. The question was how a rational, adult individual could here and now gain knowledge of things "outside". The concept of development was hardly available, as a means of thinking about society, to the schools of philosophy engaged in the epistemological controversy up to about the beginning of the nineteenth century, or only in a primitive form. It was a concept of relationships that had not yet properly developed.

Hume, who never allowed himself to shrink back from any conclusion to which the logic of his ideas led him, expressed this quite unequivocally in his fundamental position. It is not a little instructive, even for understanding one's own thought, to see him wrestling vainly with a problem which is often answered today without further reflection by using the commonplace concept of development—at least in everyday life. On a more technical level there are still many unsolved problems attached to the concept.

A person, Hume said to himself, was once a child and is now a man. He has changed in every respect, even physically. What, therefore, is the likeness or identity between the child and the man? What do we mean when we say he is the same person? The usual answer is: Whatever the changes he has undergone, his different parts are connected together by a causal relationship. But Hume found this answer highly unsatisfactory. The idea of an identical substrate seemed to him suspect even when applied to inanimate objects. It seemed much more suspect when applied to human beings. As he could never convince himself that words like "cause" and "effect" referred to a relationship subject to regularity or law, as he could not understand why a causal connection was anything other than a relationship that could be frequently observed, the talk of an identity between child and man seemed to him fundamentally fictitious. It is, he wrote, of the same kind as that which we ascribe to plants and animal bodies. Most philosophers seem inclined to assume that personal identity springs from consciousness. But consciousness, as he saw it, is nothing but a collection of ideas and sense perceptions. "I can discover no theory which appears to me fitting and satisfactory on this point." Here too Hume was following his train of thought to its extreme conclusion. Unlike other metaphysicians, who generally found unanswered questions intolerable, he was able to look it straight in the face and say: "I do not know the answer." But the basic structure of the image of people which gave rise to the question was, as we see, always the same. The point can perhaps be more easily grasped with the help of a parable—the parable of the thinking statues. On the bank of a broad river, or perhaps on the steep slope of a high mountain, stands a row of statues. They cannot move their limbs. But they have eyes and can see. Perhaps ears as well, that can hear. And they can think. They have "understanding". We can assume that they do not see each other, even though they well know that others exist. Each stands in isolation. Each statue in isolation perceives that something is happening on the other side of the river, or the valley. Each forms ideas of what is happening, and broods on the question how far these ideas correspond to what is happening. Some think that such ideas simply mirror the happenings on the other side. Others think that much is contributed by their own understanding; in the end one cannot know what is going on over there. Each statue forms its own opinion. Everything it knows comes from its own experience. It has always been as it is now. It does not change. It sees. It observes. Something is happening on the other side. It thinks about it. But whether what it thinks corresponds to what is going on over there remains unresolved. It has no way of convincing itself. It is immobile. And alone. The abyss is too deep. The gap is unbridgeable.


8

The type of human consciousness this parable refers to is certainly not only a thing of the past. The individual's feeling of being ultimately alone which it expresses, the feeling of standing in isolation, opposed to the "outside world" of people and things, and of being "inwardly" something forever separated from what exists "outside", may be even more universally taken for granted in many western societies today than it ever was in the past, even in the age of the classical European philosophers a few centuries ago. It has struck deep roots in the languages which are implanted in young people as tools of understanding in these societies, roots so deep that it is almost impossible, in speaking and thinking about the functioning and behaviour of human beings, to avoid reifying spatial analogies like "inner life" and "outer world", "seat of reason", "contents of consciousness", "his reason ought to tell him that . . .", "he knows inside himself . . .". They usually impose themselves on thought as quite self-evident. We hardly realize that in using such expressions we ascribe to certain human activities spatial qualities, like other functions and activities of human beings, which they do not in reality possess. It makes sense to say that the heart and lungs are situated inside the chest cavity. One can locate the brain inside the cranium and certain brain functions in the brain itself. But it makes no proper sense to say that something takes place *inside* these functions, inside consciousness or thought. One cannot really say that something takes place inside speaking or outside walking. Equally, there is little point in saying that consciousness has its seat in the brain or reason its seat inside the human being. One does not, after all, say that speech has its seat in the throat and mouth, or walking in the legs.

The parable of the thinking statues gives us an indication why the idea that consciousness, feeling, understanding or even the actual "self" is located "inside" the human being, seems so convincing, at least to people in certain social groups. It suggests that we are dealing with the self-perception of people on whose behaviour a relatively high degree of restraint has been imposed by the nature of social life and the corresponding mode of bringing up children. Behaviour control of one sort or another no doubt exists in all human societies. But here, in many western societies, such control has for several centuries been particularly intensive, complex and pervasive; and more than ever before social control is linked to the self-control of the individual. In children instinctual, emotional and mental impulses and the muscular movements, the behaviour towards which they impel the child, are still completely separated. As they feel, so they must act. As they speak, so they think. As they grow up the elementary, spontaneous impulses on one hand and the motorial discharge, the actions and behaviour following from them on the other are separated more and more. Countervailing impulses formed on the basis of individual experiences intervene between them. And as the basic pattern of these experiences differs in different societies, the basic pattern of his self-control and its whole relation to the elementary, spontaneous impulses common to all people differs in different societies. This intervention of contrary impulses betwen the spontaneous, universal human impulses and the discharge in action has, over several centuries in European societies—for reasons we need not go into here—become especially deep, uniform and comprehensive. A finely woven net of controls fairly evenly encompassing not just some but all areas of human existence is, in one form or another, sometimes in contrary forms, instilled like a kind of immunization into young people by the example, the words and actions of the adults. And what was first a social command finally becomes, mainly through the mediation of parents and teachers, second nature to the individual, in accordance with his or her particular experiences. "Don't touch it", "Sit still", "Don't eat with your fingers",

"Where's your handkerchief?", "Don't make yourself dirty", "Stop hitting him", "Do as you would be done by", "Can't you wait?", "Do your sums", "You'll never get anywhere", "Work, work, work", "Think before you act", "Think of your family", "Think about the future", "Think of the Party", "Think of the church", "Think of England", or "Germany, Russia, India, America," "Think on God", "Aren't you ashamed?", "Have you no principles?", "You have no conscience".

The direct discharge of impulses in activity or even movement grows more and more difficult. Diverse and often highly complex detours for such tendencies—away from the discharge they spontaneously seek—become the rule. To react precipitously, without lengthy trial actions, the silent anticipation of future chess-moves that we call "reflection" is hardly possible for adults in such societies. Often enough it is dangerous, punishable or invites ostracism; and for the one who loses control the threat from others is often less strong than the threat from himself—through fear, shame or conscience. The time-lag between the thought, the trial actions rehearsed without any movement, and the actuation of the limbs in the act itself grows longer and longer. Leaving aside a few situations which are socially clearly defined, the socially instilled control-impulses, reified by terms such as "understanding", "reason" or "conscience", usually block the direct access of other, more spontaneous impulses, whether of basic drive, feeling or thought, to motorial discharge in action. The feelings, the self-perception of the individual which present themselves in thought and speech as an encapsulation of his "inside" from the world "outside", from other things and people, are very closely bound up with this growth of individual self-control in the course of a specific social development. What is expressed in it is the deflection of spontaneous tendencies away from direct discharge in action by the interposing of the stricter and more complex control functions of the individual himself.

Where love and hate can be easily and spontaneously discharged in action, the communal life of people, unless secured by powerful social organs of control, is highly volatile. People come easily and frequently into contact with each other and make heavy emotional demands of each other, demands that are satisfied or unsatisfied, that bring joy or sorrow. Where such impulses are only able to express themselves in action in a muted, delayed, indirect manner, with strong habitual self-control, the individual is often overcome by the feeling of being cut off from all other people and the entire world by an invisible barrier. And in keeping with the logic of emotive thought, in which things that are objectively irreconcilable can easily appear reconcilable and identical if they are imbued with the same feeling, this invisible barrier is often felt to merge with the visible body. The body, as it appears to feeling, separates person from person like a wall, even if one is well aware that it is also what unites them. It seems like a container that cuts one off from the "outside" and "contains" one's own person or, as the case may be, "consciousness", "feeling", "reason" and "conscience", like a receptacle.

Transformations of consciousness of this kind are both *historical*, in that whole societies have undergone or are still undergoing them today, and *personal*, in that every child undergoes them in growing up. As they proceed, more and more activities that originally engaged the whole person with all his limbs are concentrated on the eyes, although, of course, excessive restriction of this kind can be compensated by activities such as dance or sport. With the increasing suppression of bodily movements the importance of seeing grows: "You can look at that but don't touch it", "Nice figure", "Not too close, please". Or the same can happen with speech: "You can call someone names, but not hit them", "Sticks and stones may break my bones but names can never hurt me", "Keep your hands off me". Pleasures of the eyes and ears become richer, more intense, subtler and more general. Pleasures of the limbs are hemmed in more and more to a few areas of life. One perceives much and moves little. One thinks and observes without stirring from the spot. The parable of the thinking statues exaggerates, but it achieves the effect it is supposed to. The statues see the world and form conceptions of the world, but they are denied movement of their limbs. They are made of marble. Their eyes see, and they can think about what they see, but they cannot go up to it. Their legs cannot walk, their hands grasp. They look from outside into a world or from inside out into a world—however one chooses to put it—a world which is always separate from them.

The feeling of such a void or, to use the other image, of an invisible wall between person and person, self and world, is expressed very frequently, directly or indirectly, in the recent history of the West. It may be completely authentic, but quite often it hangs like a veil across the idea we have of the relationship between the human being in search of knowledge and the object of his knowledge, giving it, as we have seen, a quality of fantasy. It also gives a misleading twist to our ideas on the relation of person to person, individual to society. And it is by no means the universal human feeling it often appears to be to introspection. It is a symptom of the situation and the particular make-up of people in specific societies. One might suppose that it might be of some value to the practical task of communicating with members of different societies to divest this experience and the images of man associated with it of their self-evident quality. If one were to sum it up in the reifying language we are accustomed to, one might say that it is, above all, a specific form of conscience that is responsible for the feeling of an invisible wall between the "inner" and "outer" worlds, between individual and individual, "self" and "world".

In the metaphysical philosophies of the present, particularly in a number of existentialist writings, the problem of the invisible wall is expressed in the very choice of questions to be discussed. The writers concentrate on problems affecting the individual alone, such as solitude, *Angst*, pain and death. And as the exponents of contemporary metaphysics usually dismiss questions of perception and knowledge from the centre of interest, concentrating instead of problems of human "existence" as such, or of "immediate experience", one can often see more clearly what distinguishes their concerns from those of the classical European philosophers of the seventeenth and eighteenth centuries than what they have in common with them. But the great classical philosophers were certainly not concerned exclusively with questions of "reason", as is often alleged—a reason sometimes characterized rather condescendingly, though with a considerable use of rational argument, as "dry" or "arid". In their way they, like their recent successors, sought an answer to questions concerning the place of human beings in the world, or their relation to other people. And in this respect their approach hardly differed from that of the metaphysical philosophers of the present. With very few exceptions, both were primarily concerned with questions of *the* human being, as if the existence of a plurality of people, the problem of the coexistence of human beings, was something added accidentally and extraneously to the problems of the individual person. Problems such as aloneness or "direct experience", and that of knowledge, in which an isolated "subject" stands opposed to the world of "objects" in his search for certainty, are closely related. The unquestioned image of people and the notion of self-perception underlying it is essentially the same in both cases. The philosopher, if his ideas do not lose themselves in nebulous notions of supra-individual existence, takes up his position "in" the single individual. He looks through his eyes at the world "outside" as if through small windows; or he meditates from the same standpoint on what is happening "within".

# Bibliography

PUBLICATIONS OF NORBERT ELIAS
*In English (including translations from German)*

1950    "Studies in the Genesis of the Naval Profession." *British Journal of Sociology* 1, no. 4: 291–309.

"Inquest on German Jewry." Review article of Eva G. Reichmann, *Hostages of Civilisation: A Study of the Social Causes of Anti-semitism. Association of Jewish Refugees Information*, April, p. 5.

1956    "Problems of Involvement and Detachment." *British Journal of Sociology* 7, no. 3: 226–52.

1964    "The Break with Traditionalism: Report on the Discussion." *Transactions of the Fifth World Congress of Sociology* 3 (1962): 51–53. Leuven: International Sociological Association.

"Professions." In Julius Gould and William L. Kolb, eds., *A Dictionary of the Social Sciences*. New York: Free Press, p. 542.

1965    (with John L. Scotson) *The Established and the Outsiders: A Sociological Enquiry into Community Problems*. London: Frank Cass. (New edition, enlarged, with an introduction originally published in Dutch translation in 1976, [London: Sage Publications, 1994].)

1966    (with Eric Dunning) "Dynamics of Sport Groups with Special Reference to Football." *British Journal of Sociology* 17, no. 4: 388–402. Reprinted in Eric Dunning, ed., *The Sociology of Sport. A Selection of Readings* (London: Frank Cass, 1971), pp. 66–80, and in Elias and Dunning, *Quest for Excitement* (1986), pp. 191–204.

1969    "Sociology and Psychiatry." In S. H. Foulkes and G. Steward Prince, eds., *Psychiatry in a Changing Society*. London: Tavistock, pp. 117–44.

(with Eric Dunning) "The Quest for Excitement in Leisure." *Society and Leisure* 2:30–85. Reprinted in *Quest for Excitement* (1986), pp. 63–90.

1970    Introduction to "African Art from the Collection of Professor Norbert Elias, April 24th–June 14th 1970." Leicester: Leicester Museums.

(with Eric Dunning) "The Quest for Excitement in Unexciting Societies." In Günther Lüschen, ed., *The Cross-Cultural Analysis of Sport and Games*. Champaign: University of Illinois Press, pp. 31–51.

1971   Foreword to Eric Dunning, ed., *The Sociology of Sport: A Selection of Readings*, pp. xi–xiii. London: Frank Cass.
       "The Genesis of Sport as a Sociological Problem." In Dunning 1971, p. 88–115. Reprinted in *Quest for Excitement* (1986), pp. 126–49.
       (with Eric Dunning) "Folk Football in Medieval and Early Modern Britain." In Dunning 1971, pp. 116–32. Reprinted in *Quest for Excitement* (1986), pp. 175–90.
       (with Eric Dunning) "Leisure in the Sparetime Spectrum." In Rolf Albonico and Katherina Pfister-Binz, eds., *Soziologie des Sports. Theoretische und methodische Grundlagen. Referate des 10. Magglinger Symposiums, 7. bis 13. September 1969 in Magglingen (Schweiz)*. Basel: Birkhäuser. Reprinted in *Quest for Excitement* (1986), pp. 91–125.
       "Sociology of Knowledge: New Perspectives." *Sociology* 5, no. 2: 149–68, and no. 3: 355–70.
1972   "Processes of State Formation and Nation Building." *Transactions of the Seventh World Congress of Sociology* 3 (1970): 274–84. Sofia: International Sociological Association.
       "Theory of Science and History of Science: Comments on a Recent Discussion." *Economy and Society* 1, no. 2: 117–33.
1973   "Dynamics of Consciousness within That of Societies." *Transactions of the Seventh World Congress of Sociology* 4 (1970): 375–83. Sofia: International Sociological Association.
1974   "*The Sciences: Towards a Theory.*" In Richard Whitley, ed., *Social Processes of Scientific Development*. London: Routledge & Kegan Paul, pp. 21–42.
       "Towards a Theory of Communities." In Colin Bell and Howard Newby, eds., *The Sociology of Community: A Selection of Readings*. London: Frank Cass, pp. ix–xli.
1978   *The Civilizing Process*, Vol. 1: *The History of Manners*. Trans. Edmund Jephcott. New York: Urizen Books, and Oxford: Blackwell.
       *What Is Sociology?* Trans. Stephen Mennell and Grace Morissey. London: Hutchinson and New York: Columbia University Press. © 1978 by Columbia University Press.
1982   *The Civilizing Process*, Vol. 2. Trans. Edmund Jephcott. Published under two different titles: *Power and Civility*, New York: Pantheon Books; and *State Formation and Civilization*, Oxford: Basil Blackwell [only the latter had Elias's approval].
       "Civilization and Violence: On the State Monopoly of Physical Violence and Its Infringements." Trans. David J. Parent. *Telos* 16: 133–54.
       "Scientific Establishments." In Norbert Elias, Herminio Martins, and Richard Whitley, eds., *Scientific Establishments and Hierarchies: Sociology of the Sciences Yearbook 1982*, pp. 3–70. Dordrecht: Reidel.

(with Richard H. Whitley) Introduction. In id., pp. vii–xi. "What Is the Role of Scientific and Literary Utopias for the Future?" In *Limits to the Future: Prescriptions and Predictions in the Humanities and Social Sciences—Essays on the Occasion of the Second NIAS-Lustrum 1981.* Wassenaar: Netherlands Institute for Advanced Study.

1983 *The Court Society.* Trans. Edmund Jephcott. Oxford: Basil Blackwell, and New York: Pantheon Books.

1984 "On the Sociogenesis of Sociology." *Sociologisch Tijdschrift* 11, no. 1: 14–52.
 "Some Remarks on the Problem of Work." In *Aktief, inaktief; de wederzijdse afhankelijkheid van aktieven en inaktieven in een verzorgingsstaat.* Noordwijkerhout: Centrum St. Bavo, pp. 5–8.

1985 *The Loneliness of the Dying.* Trans. Edmund Jephcott, with a new afterword by the author. Oxford: Basil Blackwell.

1986 (with Eric Dunning) *Quest for Excitement: Sport and Leisure in the Civilizing Process.* Oxford: Basil Blackwell.

1987 "The Retreat of Sociologists into the Present." Trans. Stephen Kalberg and Volker Meja, rev. and enl. by the author. *Theory, Culture and Society* 4, nos. 2–3: 223–49.
 "The Changing Balance of Power between the Sexes—A Process-Sociological Study: The Example of the Ancient Roman State." *Theory, Culture and Society* 4, nos. 2–3: 287–317.
 "On Human Beings and Their Emotions: A Process-Sociological Essay." *Theory, Culture and Society* 4, nos. 2–3: 339–63. Reprinted in Mike Featherstone, Mike Hepworth, and Bryan S. Turner, eds., *The Body: Social Process and Cultural Theory.* London: Sage, 1991, pp. 103–25.
 *Involvement and Detachment.* Oxford: Basil Blackwell.

1988 "Violence and Civilization: The State Monopoly of Physical Violence and Its Infringements." Translation from German, in J. Keane, ed., *Civil Society and the State: New European Perspectives.* London: Verso.

1989 "The Symbol Theory." *Theory, Culture and Society* 6, no. 2: 169–217, no. 3: 339–83, and no. 4: 499–537.

1990 "Fear of Death," in Hans G. Kippenberg, Yme B. Kuiper, and Andy F. Sanders, eds., *Concepts of Person in Religion and Thought,* Berlin: Mouton de Gruyter, pp. 159–71.

1991 *The Symbol Theory.* London: Sage.
 *The Society of Individuals.* Trans. Edmund Jephcott. Oxford: Basil Blackwell.

1992 *Time: An Essay.* Trans. (in part) Edmund Jephcott. Oxford: Basil Blackwell.

1993 *Mozart: Portrait of a Genius.* Trans. Edmund Jephcott. Oxford: Polity Press and Berkely: University of California Press. © 1993 Polity Press.

1994    *The Civilizing Process.* 1 vol. Oxford: Basil Blackwell.
        *Reflections on a Life.* Trans. (in part) Edmund Jephcott. Oxford:
        Polity Press.
1995    "Technization and Civilization." *Theory, Culture and Society* 12, no.
        3: 7–42. Trans. Frank Pollock and Stephen Mennell, ed. and with
        a foreword (pp. 1–5) by Stephen Mennell.
1996    *The Germans: Power Struggles and the Development of Habitus in
        the Nineteenth and Twentieth Centuries.* Trans. Eric Dunning and
        Stephen Mennell. Oxford: Polity Press and New York: Columbia
        University Press. © 1996 by Columbia University Press.

*In German (not including translations from English)*

1921    "Vom Sehen in der Natur." *Blau-Weiß-Blätter: Führerzeitung* 2:133–44.
1924    (published under the name of Dr. Michael Elias) "Anekdoten."
        *Berliner Illustrierte Zeitung* 33, no. 29 (20 July 1924): 811–22.
1929    "Zur Soziologie des deutschen Antisemitismus." *Israelitisches
        Gemeindeblatt* 7, no. 12 (Mannheim, 13 December): 1–6.
1935    "Kitschstil und Kitschzeitalter." *Die Sammlung* 2, no. 5: 252–63.
        "Die Vertreibung der Hugenotten aus Frankreich." *Der Ausweg* 1,
        no. 12: 369–76.
1939    *Über den Prozeß der Zivilisation: Soziogenetische und psychogeneti-
        sche Untersuchungen.* 2 vols. Basel: Haus zum Falken.
1960    "Die öffentliche Meinung in England." In *Vorträge gehalten an-
        läßlich der Hessischen Hochschulwochen für staatswis-
        senschaftliche Fortbildung, 18. bis 25. April 1959 in Bad
        Wildungen.* Bad Homburg: Max Gehlen, pp. 118–31.
1962    "Nationale Eigentümlichkeiten der englischen öffentlichen Mein-
        ung." In *Vorträge gehalten anläßlich der Hessischen Hochschul-
        wochen für staatswissenschaftliche Fortbildung, 2. bis 8. Oktober
        1960 in Bad Wildungen,* pp. 124–47. Bad Homburg: Max Gehlen.
1969    *Die höfische Gesellschaft: Untersuchungen zur Soziologie des
        Königstums und der höfischen Aristokratie, mit einer Einleitung:
        Soziologie und Geschichtswissenschaft.* Neuwied: Luchterhand.
        *Über den Prozeß der Zivilisation.* 2d ed., with new introduction.
        Bern: Falke.
1970    *Was ist Soziologie?* München: Juventa.
1977    "Respekt und Kritik." In Norbert Elias and Wolf Lepenies, *Zwei
        Reden anläßlich der Verleihung des Theodor W. Adorno-Preises,*
        pp. 37–68. Frankfurt: Suhrkamp.
        "Zur Grundlegung einer Theorie sozialer Prozesse." *Zeitschrift für
        Soziologie* 6, no. 2: 127–49.
1978    "Zum Begriff des Alltags." In Kurt Hammerich and Michael Klein,
        eds., *Materialien zur Soziologie des Alltags (Kölner Zeitschrift für
        Soziologie und Sozialpsychologie,* Sonderheft 20), pp. 22–29.
        Köln: Westdeutscher Verlag.

1980     "Die Zivilisierung der Eltern." In Linde Burkhardt, ed., . . . *und wie wohnst du?* pp. 11–28. Berlin: Internationales Design Zentrum.

"Vorwort." In Renate Rubinstein, *Nichts zu verlieren und dennoch Angst: Notizen nach einer Trennung,* pp. 9–11. Frankfurt: Suhrkamp.

"Soziale Prozeßmodelle auf mehreren Ebene." In Werner Schulte, ed., *Soziologie in der Gesellschaft: Referate auf den Veranstaltungen beim 20. Deutschen Soziologentag Bremen 1980,* pp. 764–67. Bremen: Universität Bremen.

1981     "Zivilisation und Gewalt. Über das Staatsmonopol der körperlichen Gewalt und seine Durchbrechungen." In Joachim Matthes, ed., *Lebenswelt und soziale Probleme: Verhandlungen des 20. Deutschen Soziologentages zu Bremen 1980,* pp. 98–122. Frankfurt: Campus.

1982     "Thomas Morus' Staatskritik. Mit Überlegungen zur Bestimmung des Begriffs 'Utopie.'" In Wilhelm Vosskamp, ed., *Utopieforschung: Interdisziplinäre Studien zur neuzeitlichen Utopie,* Vol. 2: 101–50. Stuttgart: Metzlersche Verlagsbuchhandlung.

*Über die Einsamkeit der Sterbenden in unsergen Tagen.* Frankfurt: Suhrkamp.

"Soziologie in Gefahr: Plädoyer für die Neuorientierung einer Wissenschaft." *Süddeutsche Zeitung,* (9 October 1982), p. 107.

1983     "Über den Rückzug der Soziologen auf die Gegenwart." *Kölner Zeitschrift für Soziologie und Sozialpsychologie* 35:29–40.

"L'espace privé—'Privatraum' oder 'privater Raum'?" In *Séminaire "à propos de l'histoire de l'espace privé,"* pp. 31–44. Berlin: Wissenschaftskolleg.

"Der Fußballsport im Prozeß der Zivilisation." In Modellversuch Journalistenweiterbildung an der FU Berlin, ed., *Der Satz "Der Ball ist rund" hat eine gewisse philosophische Tiefe: Sport, Kultur, Zivilisation,* pp. 12–21, Berlin: Freie Universität.

"Zur Diagnose der gegenwärtigen Soziologie." In *Sozialwissenschaften und Berufspraxis,* pp. 6–19, *Vortrag auf dem 2. Kongreß für Angewandte Soziologie, Bochum.*

1984     "Nachwort." In Meike Behrman and Carmine Abate, *Die Germanesi,* pp. 197–202. Frankfurt: Campus.

"Notizen zum Lebenslauf." In Peter Gleichmann, Johan Goudsblom, and Hermann Korte, eds., *Macht und Zivilisation: Materialien zu Norbert Elias' Zivilisationstheorie,* pp. 9–82. Frankfurt: Suhrkamp.

"Vorwort" to Horst-Volker Krumrey, *Entwicklungsstrukturen von Verhaltensstandarden,* pp. 11–15. Frankfurt: Suhrkamp.

1985     "Das Credo eines Metaphysikers: Kommentare zur Poppers *Logik der Forschung."* *Zeitschrift für Soziologie* 14, no. 2: 94–114.

"Gendanken über die Bundesrepublik." *Merkur* 39, nos. 9–10: 733–55.
    Humana Conditio: *Beobachtungen zur Entwicklung der Menschheit
    am 40. Jahrestag eines Kriegsendes (8. Mai 1985).* Frankfurt:
    Suhrkamp.
    "Vorwort" to Michael Schröter, *Wo zwei zusammenkommen in
    rechter Ehe*, pp. vii–xi. Frankfurt: Suhrkamp.
    "Wissenschaft oder Wissenschaften? Beitrag zu einer Diskussion mit
    wirklichkeitsblinden Philosophen." *Zeitschrift für Soziologie* 14,
    no. 4: 268–81.

1986    "'Figuration,' 'Soziale Prozesse' and 'Zivilisation.'" In Bernhard
    Schäfers, ed., *Grundbegriffe der Soziologie*, pp. 88–91, 234–41,
    382–87. Opladen: Leske und Budrich.
    "Über die Natur." *Merkur* 40:469–81.
    "Wandlungen der Machtbalance zwischen den Geschlechtern: Eine
    prozeßsoziologische Untersuchung am Beispiel des antiken
    Römerstaats." *Kölner Zeitschrift für Soziologie und Sozialpsy-
    chologie* 38:425–49.
    "Hat die Hoffnung noch eine Zukunft?" *Die Zeit*, 26 December, p. 29.
    "Conditio Humana: Beobachtungen über die Entwicklung der Men-
    schheit." In Hartmut Krauß, Helmut Skowronek, and Gerhard
    Trott, eds., *Bielefelder Universitätsgespräche* Vol. 2: 4–10. Biele-
    feld: Universität Bielefeld.

1987    *Los der Menschen: Gedichte—Nachdichtungen.* Frankfurt: Suhrkamp.
    *Die Gesellschaft der Individuen.* Frankfurt: Suhrkamp.
    "Thomas Morus und die Utopie." In Hans-Jürg Braun, ed.,
    *Utopien—Die Möglichkeit des Unmöglichen*, pp. 173–84. Zürich:
    Verlag der Fachvereine.
    "Das Schicksal der deutschen Barocklyrik zwischen höfischer und
    bürgerlicher Tradition." *Merkur* 41:451–68.
    "Vorwort" to Bram van Stolk and Cas Wouters, *Frauen im Zwies-
    palt: Beziehungsprobleme im Wohlfahrtsstaat*, pp. 9–16. Frank-
    furt: Suhrkamp.

1988    "Was ich unter Zivilisation verstehe: Antwort auf Hans Peter Duerr."
    *Die Zeit*, 17 June, pp. 37–38.

1989    *Studien über die Deutschen: Machtkämpfe und Habitusentwicklung
    im 19. und 20. Jahrhundert.* Frankfurt: Suhrkamp.
    "Als Assistent Karl Mannheims in der interdisziplinären Diskus-
    sion." In Bertram Schefold, ed., *Wirtschafts- und Sozialwis-
    senschaftler in Frankfurt am Main. Erinnerungen an die
    Wirtschafts- und Sozialwissenschaftliche Fakultät und an die An-
    fänge des Fachbereichs Wirtschaftswissenschaften der Johann
    Wolfgang Goethe-Universität*, pp. 96–99. Marburg: Metropolis.
    "Der charismatische Herrscher." *Der Spiegel*, no. 2, pp. 42–44.
    *Norbert Elias über sich selbst.* Frankfurt: Suhrkamp.

1991    *Mozart: Zur Soziologie eines Genies.* Frankfurt: Suhrkamp.

SELECTED WORKS ON NORBERT ELIAS
AND FIGURATIONAL SOCIOLOGY

Arnason, Johann. "Figurational Sociology as a Counter-Paradigm." *Theory, Culture and Society* 4, nos. 2–3 (1987): 429–56.

Bogner, Artur. "The Structure of Social Processes: A Commentary on the Sociology of Norbert Elias." *Sociology* 20, no. 3 (1986): 387–411.

———. "Elias and the Frankfurt School." *Theory, Culture and Society* 4, nos. 2–3 (1987): 249–85.

Brown, Richard. "Norbert Elias in Leicester: Some Recollections." *Theory, Culture and Society* 4, nos. 2–3 (1987): 533–40.

Burkitt, Ian. *Social Selves.* London: Sage, 1992.

Chartier, Roger. "Social Figurations and Habitus: Reading Elias." In Chartier, *Cultural History: Between Practices and Representations*, pp. 71–94. Oxford: Polity Press, 1988.

Duerr, Hans-Peter. *Nacktheit und Scham: Der Mythos vom Zivilisationsprozeß I*. Frankfurt: Suhrkamp, 1988.

———. *Intimität: Der Mythos vom Zivilisationsprozeß II*. Frankfurt: Suhrkamp, 1994.

———. *Obszönität und Gewalt: Der Mythos vom Zivilisatioinsprozeß III*. Frankfurt: Suhrkamp, 1995.

———. *Die erotische Leib: Der Mythos vom Zivilisationsprozeß IV*. Frankfurt: Suhrkamp, 1997.

Dunning, Eric. "Comments on Elias's 'Scenes from the Life of a Knight.'" *Theory, Culture and Society* 4, nos. 2–3 (1987): 299–307.

Dunning, Eric, and Chris Rojek, eds. *Sport and Leisure in the Civilizing Process: Critique and Counter-Critique.* Basingstoke: Macmillan, 1992.

Eldridge, John. "Sociology in Britain: A Going Concern." In Christopher G. A. Bryant and Henk A. Becker, eds., *What Has Sociology Achieved?* pp. 157–78. London: Macmillan, 1990.

Fletcher, Jonathan. *Violence and Civilization: An Introduction to the Work of Norbert Elias.* Oxford: Polity Press, 1997.

Gleichmann, Peter R., Johan Goudsblom, and Hermann Korte, eds. *Human Figurations: Essays for / Aufsätze für Norbert Elias.* Amsterdam: Amsterdams Sociologisch Tijdschrift, 1977.

———. *Materialien zu Norbert Elias' Zivilisationstheorie.* Frankfurt: Suhrkamp, 1977.

———. *Macht und Zivilisation.* Frankfurt: Suhrkamp, 1984.

Goudsblom, Johan. *Sociology in the Balance.* Oxford: Basil Blackwell, 1977.

———. "Responses to Norbert Elias's Work in England, Germany, the Netherlands and France." In P. R. Gleichmann, J. Goudsblom, and H. Korte, eds., *Human Figurations*, pp. 37–98.

———. *De sociologie van Norbert Elias.* Amsterdam: Meulenhoff, 1987.

———. "Norbert Elias, 1897–1990." *Theory, Culture and Society* 7, no. 4 (1990): 169–74.

———. *Fire and Civilization*. London: Penguin, 1992.

———. "Elias and Cassirer, Sociology and Philosophy." *Theory, Culture and Society* 12, no. 3 (1995): 121–26.

Israëls, Han, Mieke Komen, and Abram de Swaan, eds. *Over Elias: Herinneringen en anekdotes*. Amsterdam: Het Spinhuis, 1993.

Kilminster, Richard. "Evaluating Elias." *Theory, Culture and Society* 8, no. 2 (1991): 1165–76.

———. "Structuration Theory as a World View." In C. G. A. Bryant and D. Jary, eds., *Giddens's Theory of Structuration: A Critical Appreciation*, pp. 25–55. London: Routledge, 1991.

Kilminster, Richard, and Cas Wouters. "From Philosophy to Sociology: A Response to Maso." *Theory, Culture and Society* 12, no. 3 (1995): 81–120.

Korte, Hermann. *Über Norbert Elias: Das Werden eines Menschenwissenschaftlers*. Frankfurt: Suhrkamp, 1988. 2d ed., Opladen: Leske und Budrich, 1997.

Kranendonk, Willem. *Society as Process: A Bibliography of Figurational Sociology in the Netherlands*. Amsterdam: Publikatiereeks Sociologisch Instituut, 1990.

Krieken, Robert van. "Violence, Self-discipline and Morality: Beyond the Civilizing Process." *Sociological Review* 37, no. 2 (1989):193–218.

———. "The Organization of the Soul: Elias and Foucault on Discipline and the Self." *Archives européennes de sociologie* 31, no. 2 (1990):353–71.

———. *Norbert Elias*. London: Routledge, forthcoming 1998.

Kuzmics, Helmut. "Embarrassment and Civilization: On Some Similarities and Differences in the Work of Goffman and Elias." *Theory, Culture and Society* 8, no. 2 (1991): 1–30.

Maso, Benjo. "Elias and the Neo-Kantians: Intellectual Backgrounds of *The Civilizing Process*." *Theory, Culture and Society* 12, no. 3 (1995): 43–79.

———. "The Different Theoretical Layers of *The Civilizing Process*: A Response to Goudsblom and Kilminster & Wouters." *Theory, Culture and Society* 12, no. 3 (1995): 127–45.

Mennell, Stephen. *Norbert Elias: Civilization and the Human Self-Image*. Oxford: Basil Blackwell, 1989. [Rev. ed., *Norbert Elias: An Introduction*, 1992.]

Niestroj, Brigitte H. E. "Norbert Elias: A Milestone in Historical Psycho-Sociology: The Making of the Social Person." *Journal of Historical Sociology* 2, no. 2 (1989): 136–60.

Rehberg, Karl-Siegbert, ed. *Norbert Elias und die Menschenwissenschaften*. Frankfurt: Suhrkamp, 1996.

Russell, Steven. *Jewish Identity and Civilizing Processes*. Basingstoke: Macmillan, 1997.

Scheff, Thomas J. *Bloody Revenge: Emotions, Nationalism and War*. Boulder, CO: Westview Press, 1994.

Sica, Alan, "Sociogenesis versus Psychogenesis: The Unique Sociology of Norbert Elias." *Mid-American Review of Sociology* 9, no. 1 (1984): 49–78.

Smith, Dennis. "Norbert Elias—Established or Outsider?" *Sociological Review* 32, no. 2 (1984): 367–89.

# Index

Please remember that this is a library book, and that it belongs only temporarily to each person who uses it. Be considerate. Do not write in this, or any, library book.

## DATE DUE